ISRAEL IN THE MAKING

ISRAEL IN THE MAKING

Stickers, Stitches, and Other
Critical Practices

Hagar Salamon

Indiana University Press

Bloomington and Indianapolis

This book is a publication of

Indiana University Press
Office of Scholarly Publishing
Herman B Wells Library 350
1320 East 10th Street
Bloomington, Indiana 47405 USA

iupress.indiana.edu

♾ The paper used in this publication meets the minimum
requirements of the American National Standard for Information
Sciences—Permanence of Paper for Printed Library Materials,
ANSI Z39.48–1992.

Manufactured in the United States of America

Cataloging information is available from the Library of Congress.

ISBN 978-0-253-02280-6 (cloth)
ISBN 978-0-253-02308-7 (paperback)
ISBN 978-0-253-02328-5 (ebook)

1 2 3 4 5   22 21 20 19 18 17

Contents

Acknowledgments

THIS BOOK, THE result of nine different research endeavors spanning over more than thirty years, would not have come to fruition without the trust and help I received from numerous people and institutions.

It is impossible even to begin to thank the many scores of Israelis who generously shared their thoughts and feelings with me. This book owes everything it may treasure to what they told me. Whether during a meeting set in advance with people I knew or in a random meeting during which people agreed to share their ideas with a complete stranger; in a single interview or in a series of meetings that spanned many years, it was always with awe-inspiring generosity and contagious excitement, which made me understand the strong emotional dimension of their sheer words.

To be privy to the kind of intimate and sometimes even risky information that many subjects imparted demands the vital presence of mutual empathy. I am greatly indebted to the many individuals and groups, who by the work of ethnography are revealed as the creators and articulators of culture, who lend their empathy and join in the dialogic enterprise.

As my research progressed, I became increasingly aware that the dialogues with them not only helped me gain insight into my research topics but also enriched and refined my own worldview and opened up my heart.

I thank the students at the folklore studies program at the Hebrew University of Jerusalem and especially Sharon Agur, Hila Eisenberg, Simona Tammuz-Cohen, Michal Cohen-Shemesh, Rivka Gavra, Sarina Chen, Michal Nefesh, Dganit Laznow, Mulugete Mahari, and Yael Aizic, who assisted in conducting interviews. I am grateful to colleagues for commenting on different chapters of the book, and especially to the late Dov Noy, Alan Dundes, and Melford Spiro, and to Ibrahim Muhawi, Esther Juhasz, Carmela Abdar, Anbessa Tefera, Lynn Schler, Ruth Ginio, and Louise Bethlehem, as well as to Ruth Dayan, Yair Garbuz, Rama Yam, Jessica Bonn, Fern Seckbach, Doron Modan, Ilana Goldberg, and Jackie Feldman for their special help, and to Jacqueline Laznow for her wholeheartedly and crucial assistance with the figures. To the anonymous reviewers throughout the years and especially to the reviewers of this entire manuscript, I am deeply thankful. Their careful reading, sensitive comments, and enlightening suggestions were immensely valuable. They made me shape and reshape my thoughts and elevated the final version of the book.

Throughout the years my studies have benefited from the generous support of the following research grants. The Folklore Research Center at the Hebrew University, the Shain Center for Research in the Social Sciences of the Hebrew University of Jerusalem, The Harry S. Truman Research Institute for the Advancement of Peace at the Hebrew University, the Memorial Foundation for Jewish Culture, and the Mann Foundation of the Mandel Institute for Jewish Studies at the Hebrew University. My stay at the University of California, sponsored by the Fulbright Foundation, afforded me the distance required to open my eyes to the obvious. I am grateful to all these fine foundations and in particular to the people behind them. Finally, I wish to extend my deepest thanks to the devoted staff of the Harry S. Truman Research Institute for providing me with a professional and supportive work environment.

Two chapters in the book are based on articles written in collaboration. The chapter dealing with Ethiopian women's *iqqub* was composed with Steve Kaplan and Harvey Goldberg, two cherished colleagues. I thank Steve for his wisdom and audacity, as well as for his trustworthy companionship. I am grateful to Harvey, who has accompanied my research path from its very beginning. Our collaborative work has enriched our unique research topics and has been the source of an ongoing dialogue that is both productive and enjoyable. I feel blessed by the close friendship with him, with Judy, and with their wonderful family.

The study of the group of Jerusalemite embroidering women was written in collaboration with Galit Hasan-Rokem. Her presence in my work reached far beyond that, and her contribution to the conception of this book has been greatly significant and profound. Our numerous conversations on the power of folk culture, on its various components, on its characteristic subjectivities, and especially on thinking critically about the distinction between supposedly "high" and "low" culture, echo throughout these pages. The present book focusing on folk creativity is thus one of the happy results of our long-term dialogue and friendship. Grateful for the various interpretation venues that these discussions have opened and for the joy we share in studying folklore, I dedicate it to her with great love and appreciation.

I do not have enough words to express my great love and gratitude for my family, which has accompanied me throughout the years of research. My father, Dov, had gone through the horrors of war in Europe as a child and arrived as an orphan to Israel. My mother, Miriam, and her parents had managed to flee Europe at the last moment and reached Palestine as the war broke out. Both my parents, who viewed the state of Israel as a safe haven and the ultimate and only possible home, have witnessed in the course of their lifetime its many harsh upheavals. I owe them the privilege of growing up, together with my sister, Noa, and my brothers, Yoav and Nadav, in the shelter of the liberal and critically thinking family that they managed to create out of the broken pieces of their own families.

Their gift nurtures everything that I can or cannot write on the reality surrounding me.

My most profound gratitude goes to my daughters, Mika, Noga, Zohar, and Netta, who deeply love Israel with all its restless, fascinating creativity, and to their father, Amos, my closest companion and partner in my voyages everywhere. We all take part in *Israel in the Making*.

ISRAEL IN THE MAKING

Introduction

Studying Israeli Folklore

THIS BOOK WAS born out of research undertaken over a period beginning in 1993–94 and continuing up to the present day. Taken together, it offers the reader views of life in Israel, while illustrating the critical and reflective insights that folk creativity treasures. The subtitle, "Stitches, Stickers, and Other Critical Practices," stressing creativity and critique, alludes to the totality of ethnographic encounters, engaging both social dialogue and private experiences (Markowitz 2013). Through conversations with producers and consumers of folkloric materials, the evolving discourses of a changing society take on new life. I invite you to witness this alchemy with me.

Each of the following chapters represents an ethnographic encounter with a folk cultural artifact and the persons involved with it. In each encounter, the presence of a multivocal space made up of intuitions and understandings "hovering over the waters" is sensed (Hazan and Hertzog 2012, 1–4). Previously unexpressed and unformulated concepts and emotions take shape in the intersubjective ethnographic space and often yield valuable insights into the nature of community, the distribution of power, the richness of culture, and the all-too-human struggle for survival and dignity.

The link between the chapters, in terms of manifest content, is far from being typical or evident. What is the connection between bumper stickers and embroidery, and how are these two linked to the humor of immigrant groups? Each cultural realm, on its own, could have been the basis of a specialized monograph! I therefore begin by relating to the genesis and rationale of this book, which bring together ostensibly unconnected materials and concerns.

Admittedly, in the years during which the studies that comprise the chapters of the present book were conducted, even I was unaware of the link connecting the different topics. Each study was carried out separately and normally represented a digression from my main line of research, which focuses on issues related to the past and present life of Ethiopian Jews. Within each specific subject, the initial study generated several offspring—a series of interrelated articles. I did not see any connection among the ostensibly diverse research topics. No associations arose as I separately analyzed each topic. My assumption was that each theme happened to present itself to me as a result of more or less random circumstances.

As I now look back, I realize the key was there all the time, waiting for me to grasp it. Hints were hidden in my basic attraction to such completely different research opportunities. I invite the reader to join me step-by-step in retracing a research chronology that stretches over more than three decades and reaches into different realms of Israeli culture. Such a chronology reveals the coincidental circumstances of choosing the divergent research topics, while simultaneously providing the basis for deciphering the links connecting them.

In 1993, as a junior PhD candidate working on ethnohistorical research focusing on the Ethiopian Jews, I was asked to coordinate, along with my adviser Galit Hasan-Rokem, a research team that would gather material on Jerusalem's folklore to present it at the annual American Folklife Festival in Washington, DC. Research teams had been created, and rich material representing Jerusalem's folklore was collected. Among the fascinating variety of material brought together to represent Jerusalem's folklore was a group of women embroiderers, led and guided by Megina Shlain, who had been meeting for many years to practice embroidery together. The group members were invited to talk about their practice and describe its significance. While their stories and descriptions were fascinating, what was even more remarkable was the tone of enthusiasm and excitement in which they were told. After the entire festival project had been written off the agenda because of political limitations, the embroidering women's voices continued to echo in our minds.

The combination of the group's excitement, on the one hand, with the calm, at times even Sisyphean, praxis of embroidery, on the other, launched Galit and me on a joint research project focusing on this embroidering group. We had the feeling that the collective force we encountered reached far beyond what was to be expected. The emotional storm we sensed in the embroidering women's group and the engaging discussion that accompanied their years of practicing needlework together diverted our scientific attention away from our other projects and toward what was taking place in the embroidery group. It was the first time either of us had ever dealt with the study of threads and needles.

In retrospect it becomes clear that a similar sense of urgency and excitement, revealed in other folk cultural contexts, is the foundation of each of the studies that together make up the chapters of the present book. We conducted observations and in-depth interviews with the group members and thus gained an understanding of the ways in which needlework is used as a channel for expressing a wide range of emotions and relations, and how ethnic embroidery in particular is employed to examine questions of locality as well as the intricate relations between here and there, there and here. The study, which now appears as a single chapter, was published in a journal dealing with theory and the critical examination of culture in a volume dedicated to the study of folk culture.

A few months later I left for a sabbatical year at the University of California, Berkeley. I worked on a book dedicated to the relations between the Ethiopian Jews and their neighbors in Ethiopia. Here again, however, in a different way altogether, another topic called for my attention. In Berkeley I had the opportunity to meet Professor Ibrahim Muhawi and learn of his study on Arabic metalinguistic jokes. This brought to my mind the corpus of Israeli jokes popularly known in Hebrew as *Bedihot David Levi* jokes connected with the Israeli politician David Levi (one of the first politicians from the generation of immigrants from North Africa to occupy high cabinet positions), which were also largely based on metalinguistic humor. During that year we lived in the UC Berkeley housing project called the Village. Several young Israeli families were living in the same compound in close contact, slowly becoming a kind of substitute family. During one of our shared Shabbat dinners, I asked my Israeli friends if they knew any David Levi jokes. The table erupted. Not without some embarrassment, a surprising number of such jokes were immediately told, and the atmosphere around our table became charged.

Once again, this emotional storm concerning something so seemingly marginal as a series of jokes, some of them embarrassingly simplistic and rude, was precisely what demanded that I put aside what I was doing and listen to what caused all this commotion. That we were all Israelis, all affiliated with a prestigious academic center, and all struggling with academic English, made the issue of metalinguistic jokes especially compelling. In Berkeley, with the help of my Israeli friends and the Israel Folktale Archives (IFA), I expanded the joke corpus and attempted to decipher the essence of the charge that arose as a reaction to this rich and varied humoristic corpus. Yet once I felt I grasped the underlying humorous mechanism of this cycle, I hurried back to my ongoing research. I completed the writing of an article based on the jokes ten years later, to be published in a journal dedicated to the study of humor.

We returned to Israel in the fall of 1995, and I returned to my main research focus. However, on November 4 of that year, Israeli prime minister Yitshak Rabin was assassinated by a right-wing extremist Jew who, in the name of the highest authority, wished to stop the peace process led by Rabin. There is no need for a folklore study to understand the internal upheaval brought about by this murder. The topic was mentioned and discussed in every possible arena, and memorial rituals, some spontaneous, were held in public squares all across the country. As this was taking place, cars sported an unprecedented deluge of bumper stickers that bore the Hebrew words *Shalom, Ḥaver* (good-bye, friend), quoted from Bill Clinton's eulogy for Rabin.

In the following months, I identified more and more new bumper stickers. The windshields and bumpers of cars in Israel filled up with a sticker discourse in which *Shalom, Ḥaver* stood as the starting point. I observed these bumper stickers with an ongoing effort to understand the meaning of the new ones that were appearing on a daily basis. At a certain moment, while sitting in my car looking at an especially richly covered windshield, the enthusiasm and emotion that filled this discourse dawned on me. The force and passionate creativity revealed through these simple stickers did not leave any room for doubt—here was a fundamental folklore discourse coming to life right in front of my eyes. I wished to understand the experience that underlies this discourse and promotes and enables its development, so once again I left my main line of research and turned to the documentation of the stickers and the analysis of their folk interpretation. Once this study was done, it was published in a folklore studies theoretical and methodological journal, and I thought I was done with chasing windshields.

While conducting the bumper sticker research, the women's voices from the Jerusalem embroidery group did not leave my mind. I felt there was still something I had left behind. An important figure was missing: it was Zohar Wilbush, who had been referred to time and again in their discussions, in their singular embroidery praxis, and even in the name they chose for their group: Zohar Larikma (Zohar for Embroidery). They repeatedly mentioned this particular woman, an expert in local Palestinian embroidery, as their founding mother, speaking about her with special emotion, not lacking in ambivalence.

Zohar used to hold weekly meetings, centered on needlework, in her home. Yet, the meetings were not intended for the actual practice of needlework, as the meetings at Megina Shlain's house were, but rather for listening to Zohar speak on needlework. Zohar's character was also riddled by the enigmas surrounding all that she knew about needlework, on the one hand, and all that she perhaps did not know—namely, how to actually embroider with a needle and thread. Her family's local history and her unique personality were at the center of a charged debate. Since she was ninety years old, I was not sure that I would be able to interview her, and I therefore approached her with great caution. Such concerns were quickly revealed as unfounded: Zohar's memory was sharp as a razor, and her tongue was even sharper.

For a few months we held long and fascinating meetings during which she related her life to me and explained the cultural insights that arose from it. The interviews took place in the living room of her modest and charming apartment, with many local traditional embroidered fabrics covering the walls, an old map of the Ottoman Empire at its center. Her talk was a combination of personal stories and sayings, full of pathos, on nativeness and needlework, on here and there, on her and others, on women and men. She constantly posed riddles while telling her stories, and I failed again and again to figure out the right answers. This enabled her to demonstrate authority, based on native knowledge, which made her such a charismatic character. She held the secret of the authentic, foundational

Israeliness. These meetings led me to write an article that was published in a book on women in Israel's early pioneering culture.

Jewish life in Ethiopia regained the focus of my academic attention. Before long, though, Israeli car windshields began to engage in a new discourse. The camera that had been in the car with me since I documented the *Shalom, Ḥaver* cluster began capturing photos of more and more bumper stickers referring to the concept of *Ha'Am* (Hebrew for the people, the nation, and much more). The references were made in extremely creative and emotionally loaded ways, as this rich cluster erupted in a very short time. Once again, I could not help leaving my main line of research and turning my attention toward this new phenomenon. I returned to the research field of Israel's roads. *Ha'Am* presented itself to the eyes of the public within a few months, using the range of meanings that the word *'am* has in Hebrew, explicitly, in folk discourse. The question of the borders of this "nation" and its territorial limits, what belongs to it, and what is excluded from it, as well as its aspirations and wishes, was dynamic and lively in its local expression of driving on Israeli roads and thus symbolically occupying the land. The study on this topic was published in journals dealing with folklore and the Hebrew language.

My next research encounter with bumper stickers took place years later, after I had taken the camera out of my car, thinking that I would not have to risk my life again in the attempt to take photos while driving.

In the next few years I returned to my research on Israelis of Ethiopian origin and to interviews at their apartments. At one of these interviews, held at the home of an Ethiopian-born friend I have been interviewing for many years, a surprise awaited me. My interlocutor immigrated to Israel as a teenager and now juggles work with caring for her six children. At that specific meeting we talked about daily life in Ethiopia as compared with life in Israel, and about the contrast between caring for children in Ethiopia, where they help out with the house economy, and caring for them in Israel, where they seem only to cost more and more money. Suddenly, as if hit by a lightning bolt of enthusiasm, she looked at me with shining eyes and said: "*Iqqub!* Why don't you join us for the *iqqub*? It's really fun! I'll talk with everyone so that you too can join us."

I did not know what this *iqqub* was to which I had been invited, and why it was supposed to be related to the expenses of raising children in Israel. I learned that, like many Ethiopian immigrants to Israel, my friend was a member of a women-only *iqqub*, a traditional collective funding group that holds meetings once a month. As the founder of this particular group, she showed me the "contract" that the members had formulated for themselves and described for me the atmosphere of enthusiasm and humor at the meetings. Though I did not become an *iqqub* member, the excitement around it and the importance of the meetings for its members, as well as its humoristic and ritualistic characteristics, indicated to me that this was an important site for their process of adaptation to life in Israel for Ethiopian immigrants. It helped internally negotiate, within their own community, their Ethiopian-Israeli identity. To carry out this research, I invited two of my close colleagues—Harvey Goldberg and Steve Kaplan—to join me. The results appeared in a journal dedicated to African identities as well as in a book on immigrant women in Israel.

While studying the *iqqub*, I learned that along with the humor concerning relations between women and men that was at the center of the meeting, there were also funny stories concerning the women's first encounters with Israeli reality. Following my request to hear the actual stories, more and more of them began to flow into the space in which the interviews were held. My interlocutors could not stop laughing. The strong appeal and the generative nature of this unique corpus, which brought so much pleasure and enthusiasm both to those who told it and those who listened, reminded me of the David Levi jokes. The analysis of this unique corpus appeared in a journal dealing with folklore studies, as well as in a black studies journal, in a volume dedicated to Ethiopia and the Ethiopian diaspora.

The next study in the research chronology of the present book's chapters brought me back, after many years, to the more personal field of needle and thread, as a consequence of my research into *gobelin* counted cross-stitch embroidery. Unlike the proud excitement that led to our first needlework-related research, the heightened reaction concerning the *gobelin* cross-stitch style had more to do with embarrassment. My mother has been creating art in textile ever since I can remember, and even though she herself does not embroider, pieces of textile that include embroidery fill her world and house. At some stage she began to find embroidered pictures that had not been there before at a local flea market. In Israel the name *gobelin embroidery* is given to the tight stitches on the canvas of a pre-printed picture that women fill with embroidery, place in an elegant frame, and proudly hang on the living room wall. Finding a great number of such embroidery works thrown away in flea markets testified to the changing attitude toward them. Yet I arrived at my research from a different direction: my mother took a large number of pieces and put them back on the wall, this time in a new context—she set them inside larger textile artworks, which distanced them from their traditional context. When I opened my house in Jerusalem for an exhibition of her work, there was no room for doubt that new enthusiasm could be detected. Almost without exception, women reacted strongly, emotionally, and with much embarrassment to the cross-stitch pieces, and thus indicated to me a new direction for my research. An article on these *gobelins* was published in the jubilee book honoring Professor Galit Hasan-Rokem.

In terms of the research chronology, the final chapter in the book is actually the third article in the group of bumper sticker studies. As I have already implied,

I did not imagine that I would ever return to research concerning Israeli roads. Car windshields had stopped producing a stimulating sticker discourse for more than a decade, and although one could spot some interesting new stickers here and there, they did not represent a phenomenon with the type of folk cultural energies I had witnessed in the past. My camera became antiquated and left my glove compartment, and the mission I faced while driving on Israel's roads included only the same survival aspect faced by all other drivers. However, a few years ago, and fifteen years after the study of *Shalom, Ḥaver*, I gradually realized that the road was producing a new sticker discourse.

This was characterized by an entirely different font size from those that preceded it, and by its dogmatic religious content. This was not another discourse on political identities on earth, but rather one directed toward the heavens. Moreover, it did not produce any controversial discourse. The development of such a novel type left me no choice, and I returned to the research field of Israel's roads. One morning, while entering the Harry S. Truman Research Institute for the Advancement of Peace, where I work, I detected a newly hired secretary, a young woman who by her attire clearly was an Orthodox Jew. Her screen saver was a colorful drawing popular among the Breslov Hassidic group that read: "My fire will burn until the coming of the Messiah." I understood that "the field" had just arrived at my doorstep. After welcoming her to the Hebrew University staff, I asked if I could interview her for my study of bumper stickers. She seemed surprised over the topic, but her curiosity and willing disposition won out. I went to my office, returned with my flash drive, and plugged it into her computer. To her astonishment, image after image of cars covered with stickers appeared on her screen. Upon my request, she explained each one with great enthusiasm. Suddenly she looked at me and said, "I knew that everyone here at the university did research, but I never thought you could do research on such things, because these are things we meet 'on the way,' things just rolling on the road—so it seems like there's nothing to them—but look at all I had to say about my family, my faith, Israel, and the whole world!"

Her words definitely struck a chord and were later revealed as foundational. They continued to echo in my mind until I came to understand that even though each of the research topics were investigated at a separate time and in a separate context, they were all related. The various studies in this book reflect my consistent focus on the seemingly marginal, the unremarkable things at "the side of the road" that indeed reveal profound perceptions and deep-rooted emotions.

Moreover, the subjects of the different chapters are probably strangers, and in all likelihood, have not met one another in reality. Ethiopian immigrants who came to Israel and became its citizens during the past thirty years have never met the group of embroidering women from Jerusalem; Zohar Wilbush, the "founding mother" of the embroidering women, who was interested in local needlework, did not even have a car and certainly never put any bumper stickers on it; Megina Shlain and the group she led never shared an *iqqub*, and the humor related to the meeting of Ethiopians with Israeli reality was never heard in any forum outside this community—I doubt if they have ever heard a David Levi joke. Still, suddenly they all stood before me as powerful expressions of a folk creativity connected by a subterranean connection that does not openly declare itself as such.

While continuing to observe the kaleidoscopic field of Israel over the course of more than three decades, and while rereading previously written articles, new patterns became apparent. They revealed connections between phenomena that at first seemed widely disparate. When I felt that the titles of individual articles began to speak to one another, I knew that a different kind of book was emerging. The invisibility of this connection makes it deeper and more meaningful than may be expected. It is precisely this quality that connects between the topics that was the foundation for my choice in them as research topics in the first place. It now combines them into a collage illustrating the "Israel in the making" that is constantly being created in the folkloric sphere. This collage is testimony to the powerful work of the many who turn to look for connection, support, meaning, and perhaps even happiness in accessible folk aesthetics. The present book wishes to inscribe in writing an essence that is inscribable, and is, therefore, in a way, an invitation to discover of what it consists and how it is put together.

The fascination and the tension exuded by the common objects and practices examined derive, to a great extent, from the unique nature of the state of Israel as a dynamic site of tensions and cultural contradictions. The utopian vision that drove the processes of nation building spread a unifying mantle over divergent experiences, whereas the relationship between founding myths and prosaic lives of individuals has always been laden with tension, concealment, and elision. In Israeli folklore, utopian (and even actively Messianic) ideologies confront the entrenched reality of inconsistent cultural engagements (Zerubavel 1995). The attempt to subject everyday realities to a unifying, familial, and heroic myth has created a framework in which openness to difference has been encoded under the constant surveillance of ideology. In this unifying myth, whether encoded as the "Jewish State" or the "State of the Jews," questions of belonging and, consequently, of exclusion, are of central importance (Ben-Amos 1981; Haskell 1994; Goldberg 2001; Schrire and Hasan-Rokem 2012).[1] The chapters of this book travel the tortuous pathways of intergroup relations, with an emphasis on the vagueness and complexity inextricable from questions of identity and belonging (Bar-Itzhak 2005; Kirshenblatt-Gimblett 1978, 1983).

I am aware, even at present, of the coincidental and arbitrary side of finding and picking my research topics. Yet when I focused my attention on the delicate webs that formed between the different studies, I identified a powerful connection among them, which involved the processing of life in Israel and of Israeli identity in an active and engaged manner through the creation of folklore. The force of such folk creativity rests precisely in the lack of awareness of itself and of its potency. Despite the great disunity between them, and far from being evident, the topics analyzed here comprise a single entity that has the capacity to collaboratively process incongruities and sometimes even irony. The making of Israel in folklore is a multifocus, generative framework. The voices involved are highly diverse: voices full of pathos and self-confidence; voices that are humble and unsure of themselves; voices that are angry, loving, hating, compassionate, laughing, and sometimes, to my joy, even funny.

The noisy excitement that led me toward each of the different research fields is based on such a multiplicity of voices. It is this variety of characters that gives authority to the insights that arise from the research.

Folk creativity acts and manifests itself in many unexpected cultural contexts. Surely, many more intense research fields that demonstrate this folk cultural work remain to be discovered. The often competing attempts of individuals and groups to be included in the definitions of peoplehood bring into relief questions of power and authority regarding national and religious boundaries that affect the variety of Israel's Jews.

Folklore is an arena in which binaries such as tradition and innovation, similarity and difference, inclusion and exclusion are constantly expressed and reworked while producing contact zones between them. The sharpness of these contrasts makes them potentially explosive, while their reworking into folk cultural aesthetics enables them to enter daily life in a manner both unobtrusive yet highly revealing. Illuminating these cultural dynamics and their subtleties is the purpose of this book.

Each chapter introduces and gives voice to different participants in Israeli discourse who embody and interpret folk cultural expressions (Bendix and Hasan-Rokem 2012). The research, encountering these folk expressions in diverse settings, is based on in-depth interviewing and related documentation methods, as well as systematic observation and recording of indirect expressions. These reflect and shape the intergroup dialogues in ever-changing forms and contexts. I invite the reader to engage intellectually and emotionally with this ongoing conversation.

Composed of three parts, this book is also organized along another dimension: it analyzes meetings that occur respectively in public spheres, in private spheres, and heterotopic spaces where the public and the private intersect. Each part is devoted to one of these settings and is framed by a brief theoretical preface (invitation) and a postscript (recapitulation) summarizing the main findings and linking the part to the following one.

Part I investigates in detail an ethnographic encounter in the public sphere, which is typically multivocal, explicit, and extroverted. This sphere is represented in the book by the lively discourse of bumper stickers, which has become a dominant feature of Israel's ethno-scape. Since their thundering eruption on the scene two decades ago, the stickers vocalize axes of identity, inclusion, and exclusion in the high-intensity zone of Israel's roads and highways. As this arena is the most public and accessible, it is also the most diverse, inviting all to voice their views. This part comprises three chapters, chapters 1–3, moving from the direct reactions to the murder of Prime Minister Rabin to other national and religious issues.

Part II welcomes the reader into the private sphere, that of an emphatically interior feminine expression: women's embroidery. The reader is invited through three different portals. Chapter 4 looks at embroidery and the discourse that accompanies it among a group of Jerusalem women who met regularly, over the course of many years, to create "folk embroidery." Chapter 5 profiles a "founding mother," an expert on local Palestinian embroidery, whose personal narrative explicitly challenges the notion of "Israeliness." Chapter 6 visits the needlepoint scene, a widespread pastime in former years, which is now looked down on. The studies of embroidery stitch together characteristics of the local and the international and also reveal a complex process of intergenerational transmission.

Part III turns its gaze to folk expressions that are conspicuously the locus of social change and the reworking or even transformation of identities. In what may be seen as a mediating sphere, concepts such as "tradition," "ethnic group," or "absorption" manifest their complexity through the work of folklore by mediating between in- and out-groups, minorities and majorities, diasporic identities and Israeliness. Chapter 7 looks at the humorous stories of Ethiopian Jews who immigrated to Israel from rural Ethiopia and whose life realities are accompanied by the prevailing indecision in the official realm as to their identity and religious status. Chapter 8 leads the readers into the lives of Ethiopian women immigrants, focusing on the empowering local cultural enterprise of credit associations, which inherently tie together tradition and innovation, while it also reveals some of the existential difficulties of these women. Chapter 9 analyzes "David Levi" jokes, a vital and especially fertile humorous cluster focusing on one of Israel's leading politicians. Like trends among bumper stickers, and the "rise and fall" of *gobelin* needlework, this humor cycle was highly popular during a particular period in Israel and then faded out. In all these cultural expressions, an analysis of their appearance and waning is central in unraveling their significance.

The tension between nation, community, and individuals, as well as the intermediate spaces between them, are powerful generators of meaning. The conceptualization of the various folkloric artifacts treated in the book as contact zones is also a methodological device reiterated throughout the variety of spaces dealt with in all the book's chapters. Taken as a whole, the book illuminates folkloric spaces as contact zones, "the space in which peoples geographically and historically separated come into contact with each other" (Pratt 1991a, 6), or "social spaces where cultures meet, clash, and grapple with each other" (Pratt 1991b, 34). The book's analysis of such spaces enables us "to reconsider the models of community that many of us rely on" (ibid.). In the research itinerary that unfolds in the chapters, the concept of experience, both in the sense of experience gained and of gaining an experience, is central.

The book observes and analyzes dynamics of folk creativity that process the complex Israeli experience. Israel's folklore, with its vital creativity and the multifaceted aesthetics that characterize it, evokes strong sentiments of identification and renunciation, acceptance and exclusion, while connecting those who partake in its creation. When taking a new perspective on the various studies, I discovered that they all dealt, in one way or another, with the concepts of home place and the relationship with the "other." I did not initially choose these topics as those that explicitly represent Israeli identity, and certainly not because I originally identified any connection between them. Rather, I simply came across folk cultural expressions that I could not ignore in the Israeli reality. This underlines the importance of the role of these topics in the generation of the elusive quality of Israeliness and helps explain the attraction (and repulsion) they produce in those who participate in the work of processing life in Israel. Such cultural work can explain, if only partially, Israel's surprising place in the Happy Planet Index, despite the widely recognized difficult aspects of its reality.

Note

1. Whereas the present book significantly addresses folkloric creativity in which identity formations do not include the Palestinian citizens of Israel, my research in progress extensively addresses particularly Israeli Palestinian topics, indicating the varying identity groupings existing in parallel and in complex interaction in our country.

PART I

FOLKLORE IN THE ISRAELI PUBLIC ARENA

Part I Invitation

Bumper Stickers as a Podium in Motion

MY DAILY JOURNEY to campus on Mount Scopus in Jerusalem is more than a routine act of commuting. I usually follow a route that crosses the borderline, officially obliterated but socially still very much in existence, between West Jerusalem (which was under Israeli sovereignty prior to the 1967 war) and East Jerusalem (under Jordanian rule until that war). Sometimes the way is blocked as a result of political tension, demonstrations, or visits by foreign dignitaries. Then I take an alternate route, crossing a second dividing line within Jerusalem, between the neighborhoods inhabited by secular or moderately religious Jews, and those inhabited by ultra-Orthodox and often anti-Zionist Jews. In this case, I must avoid being delayed by an ultra-Orthodox demonstration, wedding, or funeral procession.

Even if my journey passes without incident, however, it offers an opportunity to consider the complex and multifaceted nature of Israeli political and religious reality as embodied by these dividing lines. The cars that pass me are plastered with political and religious stickers, creating a rich mosaic of terse slogans engaged in a dynamic and profound discourse. Thus, metallic vehicles of transportation are transformed into vehicles of political and religious sentiments. The cars on the road are emblems of the profound emotions of owners and audience alike. This phenomenon of folk politics and religion expressed in the dynamic and public genre of bumper stickers is not unique to Jerusalem and has become widespread throughout Israel over the past two decades. The personal experience that led me to investigate this field is one shared widely in Israel, where members of the public are involved as willing or unwilling participants in this popular discourse of the roads.[1] The changing nature of the sticker discourse reflects the ebb and flow of a variety of sociopolitical and religious sentiments in Israeli society.

Bumper stickers have become an increasingly common expressive medium throughout the postmodern world. In Israel, the principal themes of the stickers reflect the dominant preoccupations of the ever-changing society: during the peace process, and especially after the assassination of Prime Minister Yitsḥak Rabin in November 1995, the stickers were mainly of a political nature, while ten years later, in the second half of the first decade of the twenty-first century, a large number of religious stickers emerged. At the time of the writing of this book, religion has become the dominant theme of Israeli bumper stickers. This lively, animated, and often highly critical folkloristic political discourse offers an alternative and innovative perspective on major political and social developments, which, in Israel, occur at a dizzying pace.

In recent years, Israel's roads (and highways) have turned into a public, open, and permanent sphere for discursive political and religious dialogues that give voice to strong feelings of identification and conflict. The private car has become a site in which the complex communication of schism and unity plays out, as well as a proselytizing billboard in which individuals proclaim their political and religious identities, often in charged terms that provoke onlookers to invent their own equally charged responses. At the same time, the popular and creative play with traditional and sacred language produces a powerful tension between these concepts and the rapidly shifting events to which the discourse refers.

In Israel, car stickers are concise texts with nearly no graphic images. As a visual expressive medium that must be read by its audience, they seek to convey complex social, political, and religious realities in a condensed, easily readable message. As in other forms of expressive folklore, they manifest a terse poetics that addresses a world of shared images. The audience, in turn, adds its own layers of meaning through attention to rhythm and rhyme, allusion and alliteration, and other properties.

Sticker slogans are formulated in a language that draws on a dense web of images and associations. Here, medium and message, form and content are inseparable. Complex realities are distilled into short slogans, which are then deciphered through equally complex processes, whose meanings are far from uniform or self-understood by participants. Beyond their diversity, however, the stickers artfully express taken-for-granted truths that underlie diverse identity commitments and orientations toward social reality. For example, the salience accorded to written texts in Israeli society is a centripetal force that draws participants to shared understandings and infuses the sticker discourse with vitality.[2]

An analysis of the discourse of stickers may cast light on social, political, and religious processes in Israel, and reflect the level of involvement of specific groups in this discourse and the relationships between them. These aspects are the background for studying bumper stickers as a folkloric phenomenon. In the following three chapters, in which a presentation of the sticker texts is combined with active exegesis gathered in the field, I invite the reader to listen to the many voices of the Israeli road and unravel their discursive nuances. Through this dual approach, we also explore the definition of folklore in the modern world; illustrate the flexible boundaries between folklore, popular culture, and media; and affirm the central place of folklore in plural societies.

All three chapters are based on documentation and photography of stickers and interviews with a variety of Israeli interlocutors. The stickers were photographed and the texts shown to interviewees. As technologies developed, photographs were also shown on computer screens. The photographs and the saturation of the public sphere with the stickers ensured that the message was never divorced from its graphic representation. Thus, the interviews engendered shared reflection on the form and esthetics of the stickers and not merely on their verbal content. The interlocutors often provided political and religious self-classifications as part and parcel of their interpretations. These make an interesting statement on the major fault lines in Israeli society.

The voiced reactions to the stickers were varied, passionate, and often mutually exclusive. Those reactions provide additional voices not always visible on bumper stickers. They are also opportunities for individuals to express anger, solidarity, skepticism, or faith in ways that may be seen as reproductions of everyday discourses. Because the medium of the written word, especially if it invokes sacred texts, rarely leaves Israelis indifferent, the spoken interpretations of the stickers often tell us as much about the individuals and the dynamic nature of their political and religious commitments as they do about collective processes in Israeli society.

The popular nature and accessibility of the medium (stickers, cars) make it a forum for constant innovation and creativity, inviting a wide variety of expressions. Stickers can cut and paste, quote or parody. It is an open game. In placing them on one's car (and arranging them along with other stickers), reading, interpreting, and removing them, stickers blur the distinction between creators and consumers. This mutual activity between performers and audience make them an exemplary folkloric subject.

The three chapters in this part reflect research conducted over more than a decade. We may track the appearance of new clusters of stickers, the disappearance of certain themes, and the references to previous sticker texts. Chapter 1 follows the stickers that appeared immediately following Rabin's death and demonstrate how a particular slogan (*Shalom, Ḥaver*) developed and incurred reactions and counterreactions both in composition of new slogans and in the interpretations provided for them. Chapter 2 focuses on *Ha'Am* (the people), a term whose popularity emerged in a sticker in support of retaining the Golan Heights. Chapter 3 unfolds the religious discourse appearing on cars, which increasingly has taken center stage and continues to proliferate on Israel's roads. These stickers are charged with popular energy, and the interlocutors we spoke with link traditionally sacred expressions with varied and even subversive meanings.

The aforementioned discursive transformations over the course of two decades reflect changing orientations within Israeli society, each building on and echoing previous practices. Whereas in other cultural contexts, stickers serve as an element of popular culture, manifestation of personal identity, what makes Israeli stickers particularly vibrant and powerful is the sanctity and gravity granted to texts in general as well as an intensive, almost obsessive preoccupation with questions of politics and shared identity. Perhaps the latter is a function of the small size and high density of the country and its roads, and a penchant for disputatiousness hard-wired into Israelis' "cultural DNA." The polyphonic discourse encouraged by the stickers may draw on a traditional Talmudic culture of polemics and express the contentiousness of contemporary Israeli life.

As we take to the road, we provide a diachronic view of changes in stickers and reflect on their interrelationships. What understandings of Israeli society are expressed? How do the form and content of the stickers interact? How closely do positions of interlocutors correspond with their self-identified religious and political positions? The mutations of the stickers over time and the salience of their rhetorical strategies shows collective Israeli identity—as it is formulated in the discourse of the stickers—to be a dynamic process, informed by history and filled with passion. On Israel's roads, political and religious views are always close to the surface, always in debate, and, like the vehicles that bear those views, constantly on the move.

Notes

1. On public folklore, see Kodish (2012).
2. This quality of folklore was beautifully phrased by Briggs (1988, xv): "Folklore performances provide common ground between a shared textual tradition and a host of unique human encounters, thus preserving the vitality and dynamism of the past as they endeavor to make sense of the present." On the centrality of texts in everyday life of Jewish communities, see Goldberg (1987, 315–29).

1 Folklore as an Emotional Battleground

Political Bumper Stickers

In the postmodern world, of which Israel and Jerusalem form an idiosyncratic but integral part, bumper stickers are an increasingly common expressive medium.[1] The Israeli variant of this iconic phenomenon illustrates the rapid growth of the medium since the early 1990s, reaching new peaks of folk innovation and creativity in the context of the peace process, and above all following the assassination of Prime Minister Yitsḥak Rabin in November 1995. These stickers are predominantly political in nature.[2] This lively and animated folkloristic political discourse offers an alternative perspective on major political developments, which occur at a dizzying pace in Israel, and an important complement to—and critique of—the hegemonic political discourse that takes place in this country (figure 1.1).[3]

An analysis of the sticker discourse reflects the most pressing social and political issues processed in Israel. The cars on the road become vehicles of political sentiment—emblems of the profound emotions of owners and audience alike. This phenomenon of folk politics has become widespread throughout the country, and often evokes immediate and emotionally charged responses—both orally and in the form of new counter-stickers.

In this chapter, we attempt to unravel the multivocality embodied in this postmodern genre and discuss the relationship between this form of expression and the discursive nuances it embraces. This may further our understanding of such aspects as the definition of *folklore* in the modern world; the fluid boundaries between folklore, popular culture, and media; and the place of folklore in multicultural societies that are the arenas of covert and overt struggles between various groups representing competing political and even cosmological perspectives.[4]

As with other forms of expressive folklore, stickers are phrased with terse poetics that address a world of shared images. In attempting to interpret the message, the audience further expands the exegetical game through attention to aural aspects (such as rhythm and rhyme), multiple meanings, and other actions.[5] The survey aims to document the complexity and sophistication of this unique

Figure 1.1. Top left: *Shalom, Ḥaverim* (Shalom, Friends); above middle: *Ze Lo Shalom, Ḥaver* (This Isn't Shalom, Friend); below middle: *Shalom Balahot* (A Nightmarish Peace).

form of discourse, focusing on the experience of exegesis it inspires. The documentation process included open-ended and semistructured interviews. The enthusiasm with which interviewees tackled the task of interpreting the messages revealed an argumentative and sermonizing rhetoric in which dexterous textual analysis is rife with powerful emotions. Popular discussion of these short and transient messages also reveals a surprising measure of emotion that emerges in all the participating voices.

The present analysis positions folklore as a cultural arena in which the distinctions between addresser (deliverer) and addressee (audience) are constructed and deconstructed through an emotive process. The presence of affective affinities emerges as the central feature of folkloric discourse. Due attention to these affective affinities in theoretical discussion of the nature of folklore and the experience it embodies may help define this field and conceptualize its characteristic dynamics.

Shalom 'Akhshav and Shalom, Ḥaver

The first documented political bumper sticker in Israel is usually considered to be the *Shalom 'Akhshav* (Peace Now) sticker, designed by Israeli artist David Tartakover in 1977 for the left-wing movement Peace Now.[6] Since then political

Figure 1.2. Bottom left: *Shalom 'Akhshav* (Peace Now) in three languages; bottom right: "homemade" sticker *Day LaKibbush!* (End the Occupation!); Top: A "homemade" sticker, *Sheli 'Akhshav* (Mine Now).

stickers have become a common mark on Israeli roads. The present chapter is based on material documented in Israel between November 1995 and May 1999, some twenty years after the first bumper sticker appeared. The material thus testifies to the generative qualities of the first sticker as expressed in the formation of the entire genre in Israel, and specifically the cluster of stickers on which this chapter focuses.

In early November 1995, in the midst of a controversial peace process, Prime Minister Rabin was assassinated in the main public square in Tel Aviv after addressing a well-attended support rally. The public reaction was one of extreme shock, which intensified after it emerged that his assassin was a young Jew, who had acted on the belief that he was obligated by religious law to stop the peace process.[7] This brutal challenge to the foundations, boundaries, and adherents of Zionist nationalism would become a central theme in the public discourse that emerged on Israel's roads. Rabin's funeral was attended by numerous leaders from around the world. President Bill Clinton, a key partner in this peace process and arguably the most influential leader in the world, was among the mourners who made eulogies. He ended his speech dramatically when he repeated the Hebrew

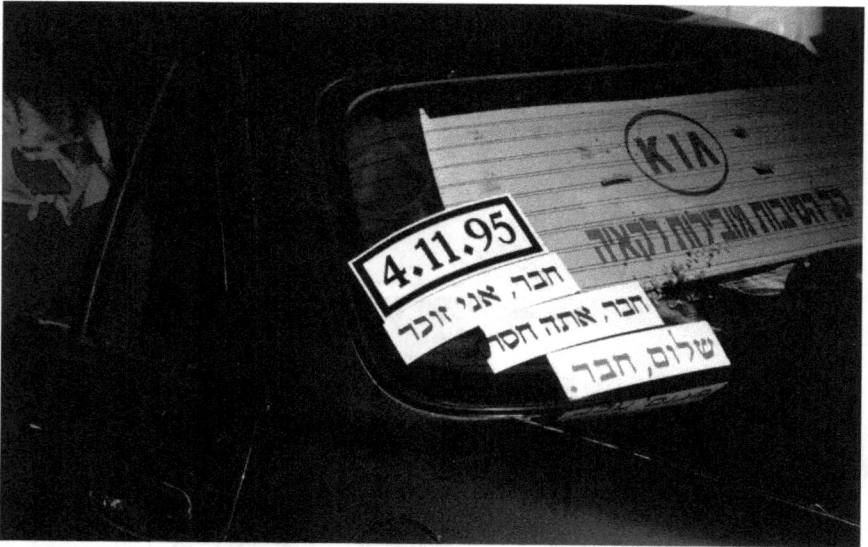

Figure 1.3. Stickers from bottom: *Shalom, Ḥaver* (Good-Bye, Friend); *Ḥaver, 'Ata Ḥaser* (Friend, We Miss You); *Ḥaver, 'Ani Zokher* (Friend, I Remember); the date of Rabin's assassination.

phrase from his response to the assassination just days earlier in Washington: moving the crowd in a sincere display of grief, he called out toward Rabin's coffin, "*Shalom, Ḥaver!*"[8]

Almost immediately this phrase appeared as a bumper sticker. More than one million copies were distributed around Israel (whose population at the time was around five and a half million).[9] The *Shalom, Ḥaver* stickers, blue print on white, with the identical Biblical-style font used on the *Shalom 'Akhshav* sticker of twenty years earlier, were observed on a very high percentage of cars in Israel.[10] This became a personal expression of mourning and separation on the part of the car owners, as well as a unifying ritual in the face of the divisions highlighted by the assassination.[11] At the same time, stickers expressing opposition to Rabin's government and policies were quickly and quietly removed from many cars.[12] However, it was not long before stickers began to appear that challenged the perceived messages of *Shalom, Ḥaver*; stickers deriving from *Shalom, Ḥaver* emerged, alongside other generative clusters (see figures 1.3, 1.4 and 1.5).

The research included long-term documentation of the *Shalom, Ḥaver* cluster, which continued to expand and change. In addition, we asked drivers to comment on the stickers that appeared on their vehicles, and we presented the repertoire

Figure 1.4. From top left, clockwise: *Shalom Balahot* (A Nightmarish Peace); *Shalom, 'Ata Ḥaser* (Friend, We Miss You); *Shalom, Ḥaver* (Good-Bye, Friend); *Shalom, Ḥaverim* (Shalom, Friends); *Shalom, Beyneynu* (Shalom—among Us); *Shalom, Boged* (Good-Bye, Traitor).

of stickers to some one hundred interviewees—men and women, young and old, some previously known and others randomly approached. Interviewees identified themselves with a wide range of political and religious positions within Israeli society. They were asked to discuss each sticker as well as the phenomenon of the discourse of stickers in general.

After a brief explanation, the interviewer pointed to each slogan, without reading it aloud, and the interviewees were asked for their comments. It was important not to verbally pronounce the slogan because standard modern Hebrew, based on an essentially consonantal alphabet, allows room for ambiguities and multiple readings. The interviewees, thus, were not directed to any particular reading of the text. The interviews concentrated on readings of the stickers associated with *Shalom, Ḥaver* and with the unique popular experience expressed and indeed created by this folkloric discourse in an effort to develop a phenomenological theoretical perspective based in this folkloristic experience.

The interviews expressed the wealth and virtuosity of interpretations and the divergent and often contradictory directions taken by the interviewees. In

Figure 1.5. From top left, clockwise: *Ḥavera 'At Ḥasera* (Friend [fem.], We Miss You); *Ḥaver, Bo Nedabber* (Friend, Let's Talk); *Ḥaver, Lo Nishkaḥ VeLo Nislaḥ* (Friend, We Won't Forget and We Won't Forgive); *Hakol Biglalkha, Ḥaver* (It's All Because of You, Friend); *Hazman 'Over Ve'ata Ḥaser, Ḥaver* (Time Passes and We Miss You, Friend); *Ḥaver, Ani Zokher* (Friend, I Remember).

consonance with the anonymity of the stickers for the audience, with the exception of the generative sticker in the cluster, "authored" by the US president, the present study is not concerned with the actual origin of each sticker—even assuming that such a creative moment can be traced.[13]

During the research process, more than thirty different stickers were documented on the roads, all part of the popular political discourse that *Shalom, Ḥaver* generated. The stickers were presented to the interviewees in a manner that created an internal research chronology that, while attempting to reflect the actual chronology on the roads, inevitably differs from the chronology of each individual's encounter with the stickers in the ethnographic field. Accordingly, the interviewees were asked to recall the interpretative experience they underwent in the original encounter, as distinct from the research context.[14]

From the outset it was evident that the generative capacity of the apparently simple phrase *Shalom, Ḥaver* is due not only to the powerful emotional context in which it entered public discourse but also to the inherent ambiguity of the two words.[15] Above all, the complexities of the Hebrew word *Shalom* must be appreciated. *Shalom* may carry the meanings of the English words *peace, hello, goodbye,* and *farewell*; it is also a male first name and a family name. *Ḥaver* is the masculine form of the word *friend*. The word may be used to refer to a specific personal friend, but it is also widely used in colloquial Hebrew as a generic and amicable term of approach to an unknown (male) stranger in the street. *Ḥaver* may also mean "boyfriend," and in a specifically Israeli context it may refer to the member of various social and political institutions, in particular those closely identified with the Labor Party (Rabin's party) on the left wing of the Israeli political spectrum, such as kibbutzim, the General Health Fund, and the Histadrut (Israeli trade unions). In the specific and original context of the sticker, as known to everyone in Israel, *Ḥaver* naturally refers to the late prime minister, by implicit reference to Clinton's address. The ambiguity and multiple meanings of this short text are central to the generative function of this sticker.

The list of thirty-two examples in table 1.1, included in the cluster of stickers generated by *Shalom, Ḥaver* and presented to the interviewees, illustrates the vitality and diversity of this phenomenon. The English translation adopts the most probable interpretation.

The clarity with which the cluster of stickers generated by *Shalom, Ḥaver* reveals itself as a cohesive group is reflected in the fact that all include at least one of the two words in the original slogan, and that all the stickers, without exception, use the same typography for the word *Shalom*—a typography that, as noted above, dates back to *Shalom 'Akhshav* and is reminiscent of the style used by scribes in preparing parchment copies of the sacred Jewish texts.[16] In most cases, the text appears in varying shades of blue on a white background; these are the colors of the Israeli flag, and they are hence associated with Zionism, nationalism, and patriotism. In addition to the graphic design of the sticker—an important factor in unraveling the message—the discourse of stickers makes its interconnected nature evident in the use of common grammatical forms and syntactical rhythms. Thus, the slogans announce their belonging to a single family, however fraught the internal relationships may be. This will be of central importance in interpreting content and in the process of popular exegesis.

After discussing various aspects of the sticker medium as a folkloristic genre, I progress to a concrete illustration of the interpretative discourse relating to the cluster of stickers examined in this chapter. The reader will best appreciate the interrelationships between the stickers by reviewing the entire cluster presented below.[17] This illustration in turn leads to a concluding discussion relating to the discursive and emotional aspects of this contemporary folkloric discourse, and the manner in which these are embodied in the connection between medium and message in new genres.

Table 1.1

Hebrew	Translation*
Shalom, Ḥaver	Shalom, Friend
Shalom, Ḥaverim	Shalom, Friends
Shalom Balahot	A Nightmarish Peace
Ze Lo Shalom, Ḥaver	This Isn't Shalom, Friend
Ze Lo Shalom, Moshe	This Isn't Shalom, Moshe
Shalom, Lea	Shalom, Leah
Ḥaver, 'Ani Zokher	Friend, I Remember
Ḥaver, 'Ata Zokher?	Friend, Do You Remember?
Ḥaver, Lo Nishkaḥ VeLo Nislaḥ	Friend, We Won't Forget and We Won't Forgive
Ḥaver, 'Ata Ḥaser	Friend, We Miss You
Shalom, 'Ata Ḥaser	Shalom, We Miss You
Shalom, 'Ata	Hey, You
Ḥaver, 'Ata Ḥaser Yoter VeYoter	Friend, We Miss You More and More
Hazman 'Over Ve'Ata Ḥaser, Ḥaver	Time Passes and We Miss You, Friend
Ḥevron, 'Ata Ḥaser	Hebron, We Miss You
Ḥaver Mevi Ḥaver Ve'El Ha'emuna Nitḥaber	One Friend Brings Another and We Join the Faith
Ḥaver, 'Ani Gomer	Friend, I'm Finishing
Ḥaver, 'Ani Mokher	Friend, I'm Selling
Bye-Bye, Ḥaver	Bye-Bye, Friend
Bibi, Tagid Shalom	Bibi, Say "Shalom"
Shalom, Shalom	Shalom, Shalom
Kim'at VeShakhaḥti Shalom	I Almost Forgot Shalom
Shabbat Shalom, Ḥaver	Good Sabbath, Friend
Shabbat Shalom, Tel Aviv	Good Sabbath, Tel Aviv
Shana Tova, Ḥaver	Happy New Year, Friend
Ḥaver, 'Ani Zokher 'et HaShabbat	Friend, I Remember the Sabbath
Ḥaver, 'Ani Zokher!! 'Et HaShabbat!!	Friend, I Remember!! The Sabbath!!
Shalom, Beyneynu	Shalom—among Us
Shalom Beyneynu Leveyn HaKaba	Shalom between Us and God
Shalom, Yadid	Shalom, Buddy
Hayita Ḥaver, Shalom	You Were a Friend, Shalom
Sticker, 'Ata Ḥaser	Sticker, We Miss You

*As discussed elsewhere, this is purely a working translation, offering one of the more probable interpretations of the Hebrew text.

Characteristics of the Genre

The Car and the Road

Since Israeli cars are often encountered traveling bumper-to-bumper, the bumper sticker is in most cases raised to the rear windshield.[18] The selection of the car as the forum for folk politics requires specific attention. In terms of the specific political discourse, the road and car—as path and vehicle leading from one place to another—mirror the "process," while the concept of movement, with its associations of political movement, adds to the explicitly political organizing spectrum of meaning.[19] The experience of the rapid encounter between messenger and audience—sometimes for a fleeting moment and sometimes during a prolonged period of staring—constitutes a significant component in the intertextual encounter.

Participation in the encounter exemplifies a grassroots struggle articulated through myriad voices and a particularly vital process of generativity. Yet the very arena for this struggle includes a unifying potential, articulated by the single, shared road along which all travelers pass, as well as the fact that within this discordant and divergent cluster of stickers not one dared deviate from the identical biblical graphic design of the word *Shalom*.

One of the respondents relates the following:

> I sometimes play a kind of game with myself, a sort of quiz. While I am still quite a long way behind another car, and can't yet see exactly what stickers they have, I try to guess their political orientation. For example, I go by the type of car, how many people are sitting in it, or whether there are a lot of children. Sometimes—and I can really get mad at myself about this—I even go according to how they are driving: if they're driving badly, I tell myself that they must have a particular political leaning. I know all these generalizations are really dangerous, but unfortunately in most cases it turns out to be true. . . . All this happens at once. Sometimes I get a chance to see the face of the driver and the stickers, and check whether I was right—I mean, whether the face matches the stereotypes.

Similar comments, with numerous variations, were made throughout the interviews. They must be understood in the unique Israeli context, where the orientation of an individual as left-winger or right-winger, and their oft-related identification as secular or religious, may in many cases be inferred from aspects of physical appearance.[20] On one level, such comments reflect a need to identify and categorize in an exegetical structure centered on the political dialectics of Left-Right and secular-religious. On another level, however, the combination of the diachronic axis of time and distance, and the competitive nature of driving in Israel—almost to the point of a struggle for survival—with the synchronic axis that seeks to cope simultaneously with information from differing and opposing directions, constitute a constantly changing popular arena for political debate.[21]

Mixed Messages

In the interviews, the respondents described the dynamic and complex experience of the discourse of stickers, repeatedly testifying that they interpreted the message in the context of several factors: the car, the driver's appearance, all the stickers on the car, and the way the different stickers were positioned. This last element became particularly important in the case of numerous documented cases of stickers that were cut and repasted or organized to create different and sometimes unique meanings. The following is a two typical example:

> If you're asking about specific stickers, then there are some cases where it is obvious to me what they mean, while in other cases I have to see all the other stickers on the car in order to work out the meaning. In 99% of cases, all the stickers on a car are in the same [political] direction. It's interesting, though: I've noticed that sometimes people put apparently contradictory stickers next to each other, such as *Ḥevron Me'Az ULe'Olam* [Hebron—Now and Forever] next to *Shalom, Ḥaver* or, worse, *Shalom 'Akhshav* [Peace Now].[22] Maybe the idea is to "confuse the enemy," or maybe it's as if they are saying, "Don't put me in a box!"

Another interviewee comments: "I feel uncomfortable about all these stickers we see all the time. I drive along and in front of me there is a car full of stickers. From a distance, it's sometimes hard to see if they are right-wing or left-wing stickers. The colors look the same, and sometimes you can only tell when you get very close. You must have seen those recent stickers that turn the original message on its head, but look just like the original from a distance."[23]

A Removable Medium

The sticker, a small piece of paper usually displaying a concise slogan, is a popular artifact, readily available to all while the praxis connected with it has quasi-ritualistic elements of adhesion, removal, and addition. The relative ease with which stickers may be removed enables a dynamic approach; thus the temporary nature of this medium contrasts with the totality of the political message, which is often perceived as an emblem of affiliation in Israel.

When asked about the stickers seen on their cars, some respondents gave replies such as "It was like that when we bought it" or "Someone stuck it on," denying their own responsibility—despite the evident ease with which the stickers might be removed. This dynamic also operated in the reverse direction: in many cases the audience members, as active players in the drama, engaged in the removal of stickers they opposed in an act identifying the discourse of stickers as the arena for a literal public struggle. This act becomes the focus of an additional duplication of meaning that may be seen as a semiotic moment subordinated to the total discourse, as people rationalize that they do not put stickers on the car because they are afraid that their cars will be damaged. Indeed, one interviewee confessed: "I'll tell you the truth. I'm not proud of this, but I'm afraid to put a sticker supporting peace on my car, because I'm worried about my car. I even remember that I once put a *Shalom 'Akhshav* sticker on my car, and then just before I took the car into the garage, I removed it, because . . . well, you know."[24] Another interviewee, with right-wing sympathies, commented: "Most of the stickers you see are right-wing. I think this is because left-wingers are afraid that their car will be damaged by right-wingers. I'm very sorry about that. This is a fear that doesn't exist the other way round."

The temporary nature of the sticker is reflected not only in conscious removal but also in gradual fading and disintegration. For example, many stickers were documented in which the slogan *Shalom 'Akhshav* had disintegrated, leaving only *Shalom* or *'Akhshav*.

A further avenue of reflexivity concerns the question of the popular nature of stickers. The respondents' comments on this medium presented a class hierarchy between those who put stickers on their cars and those who do not. The assumption is that the widespread availability of stickers—distributed free of charge at intersections, in newspapers, and on streets and squares—detracts from their worth, and potentially projects on the drivers, as well. One respondent explained: "You don't see so many stickers on Volvos or Mercedes, because putting stickers on a car makes it more 'popular' and less stylish."[25] Another commented: "I've got a new car, so I won't put stickers on it because I don't want it to get damaged." And a third stated: "I think that cars with lots of stickers are unaesthetic. They're usually old cars."

Rhetoric and Popular Exegesis

In this section of the chapter, I present interpretations of the cluster of stickers generated by *Shalom, Ḥaver*, and thereby indirectly related to *Shalom 'Akhshav*. As noted, one may identify a number of clusters of political stickers in contemporary Israel that maintain an extensive system of communication through imagination and imagery. To convey this complex and multilayered reality in written form, there was a need to sequence the material in a manner that created internal textual cohesion. Thus, although the diverse and even contradictory interpretations of the stickers clearly reflect a large number of possible structures perceived by the audience, the order in which the slogans appear in this chapter is the product of the structure I formulated during research. This structure attempts to reproduce development along a diachronic axis. Naturally, such an approach contradicts the blurring of time and the simultaneous presence of messages as perceived in folkloric time.

Shalom, Ḥaver

"When Clinton said *Shalom, Ḥaver,* I was very moved by these words. Clinton became a member of our family with that slogan. I felt a kind of pride, tinged with sadness, that the president of the United States had become so close to us." Another interviewee noted: "Whenever I see the sticker, it immediately reminds me of Rabin's funeral. [He was a] *Ḥaver* because you could rely on him. All kinds of people put that on their car: Arabs, Jews, people from all sections of society. The whole people was behind it."

The narrowing of power discrepancies and the dismantling of the hierarchy between the US president and the prime minister of Israel expressed in the words *Shalom, Ḥaver* became a focus of significance in dismantling social hierarchies. The words are simple and mundane, words of greeting without any specific political intent. The popular and routine nature of this greeting enables it to contain both a personal farewell as well as an expression of pain, protest, and personal shock at the assassination. Although the general phraseology of the slogan could allow different political interpretations—such as farewell in sorrow or farewell in joy—all those who were asked were completely unequivocal that it related to the assassination of Rabin; the vast majority agreed that it expressed sadness at his death. This sticker appeared mainly alongside others identified with the left wing, although it also appeared alongside right-wing stickers in some cases. This fact, and the fact that in many cases this was the only sticker on a car, relates it to a sense of national unity and common fate. The unifying basis lies in the shared understanding that this ostensibly mundane daily greeting actually relates to a shared and known friend, who is being greeted not on arrival but on departure, after his assassination. However, many interviewees are aware that subsequent developments have transformed the sticker from one belonging to the "whole people" to one identified in political terms mainly with the left wing.

Shalom, Ḥaverim (Shalom, Friends)

"You see this on cars of people who want peace between all the different groups. They want compromise among everyone, among friends." Another interviewee took a very different view: "It's a right-wing slogan. Very cynical. It's saying that there are others in the ranks who will find the same fate [as Rabin]. It's real incitement. Whenever I see that sticker I expect to see religious Jews in the car."

This sticker was one of the first to appear following the widespread circulation of *Shalom, Ḥaver.* The appearance of this sticker immediately after *Shalom,*

Ḥaver, and the daring act of changing the slogan from a single known person to the plural form, channeled the respondents' interpretations of this slogan toward the world of the complex political divisions and discourse of Israeli society. The seemingly neutral character of the slogan in linguistic and syntactical terms led many respondents to hesitate as to its message, allowing the simultaneous existence of contradictory interpretations. Thus, while some claimed that it was a play on words with no political overtones, intended merely as an aesthetically pleasing variant of the generative slogan, many others argued that it had a clearly political thrust. One person noted: "When you come to [meet, or greet] a group of acquaintances you say, '*Shalom, Ḥaverim*' ["Hey, guys!"]. It's Jewish solidarity, a way for one driver to greet another." Those who identified this slogan with the right wing claimed that it expressed a desire to extend the circle of "friends" on the left to whom they would like to say "shalom" (in the sense of good-bye). Similarly, another respondent said: "This slogan identifies *Shalom, Ḥaver* with the kibbutzniks of the previous generation—the generation that founded the state of Israel, the members of the Labor Party and the left, and says shalom to all of them." There were those who interpreted the sticker in the context of the 1996 Knesset elections, implying that all those from Rabin's party would not stay in power.

Some respondents, however, identified the sticker with the period of Palestinian terrorist attacks several months after the assassination of Rabin. "The sticker bids farewell to those murdered by terrorists during this period, and says that they were also friends and they were also murdered—not just Rabin." Another interpretation: "It means that we still don't have peace, friends."

This sticker also highlights the Israeli-American connection underlying the entire cluster. *Shalom, Ḥaverim* are the opening words of a Hebrew song that was popular in the United States in the 1950s, and it is still sung by many in the American Jewish community. Although it is completely unknown in Israel, for a small number of respondents with American ties these words aroused associations with American Jewish culture.

Shalom Balahot *(Nightmarish Shalom)*

This sticker first appeared after the Oslo Accords and before the Rabin assassination; all the respondents identified it with the right-wing opponents of the Oslo Accords. This sticker related to *Shalom 'Akhshav* in graphical and semantic terms before the appearance of the powerful and generative *Shalom, Ḥaver*. Those respondents who presented a chronology of events as the basis of their attempt to interpret the message dated the appearance of this sticker as the period of large-scale terrorist attacks that followed the Oslo Accords—some of which occurred before Rabin's assassination and some after.

The word *Shalom* in this sticker, which first appeared before the assassination, uses the same typeface and color as the generative *Shalom 'Akhshav* sticker, while the word *Balahot* appears in red, as if dripping blood, a color that would later appear repeatedly in slogans expressing opposition to the peace process. Many respondents claimed that the red signified danger and warning and alluded to the bloody price that the peace process would exact. At the same time, red is identified in Israel, as elsewhere, as the color of the left wing.

The phrase *Shalom Balahot* alludes to the compound Hebrew word for "nightmare" (*Halom Balahot*), implying "something we must awake from as soon as possible, before it is too late," as explained by one respondent who had this sticker on his car.[26] It also plays on the rhyme between *Halom* (dream) and *Shalom* (peace), and thus may be translated as "peacemare." While all interviewees associated the explicit message with the fear that "the peace process will prove to cause more harm than good," some emphasized the internal rifts. "It represents people for whom I feel the absolute opposite of closeness and joint destiny. Those who are doing all they can to destroy peace." Another interviewee added: "I see this sticker as part of the incitement that led to Rabin's assassination. It went along with the sticker *Rabin Boged* [Rabin Is a Traitor] that was very common—and that, the day after the assassination, as if by magic, was suddenly removed from all the cars."[27]

Indeed, many interviewees found that the most convenient way to explain the *Shalom Balahot* sticker was simply to note which other stickers they would expect to find alongside it: "This sticker goes with others: *Hevron Me'Az ULeTamid* [Hebron: Then and Always]. You know, those national-religious ones." Many saw this sticker as part of the wave of opposition and incitement that preceded the assassination of Rabin. The slogan *Shalom Balahot*, which had often appeared with *Rabin Boged* before the assassination, was taken as a single, continuous sequence: *Shalom Balahot—Rabin Boged* and then condensed and reappropriated by the Left as *Shalom, Haver*. In this act of replacement, the facetious *Shalom* as a rhyme for the *halom* component of the compound word for nightmare was thus reconverted into a noncynical usage of *Shalom* as "peace" and "good-bye," while Rabin was transformed from *Boged* (traitor) into *Haver* (friend).[28] The rhetoric employed by interviewees commenting on this sticker was particularly emotive, containing explicit expressions of fear, anger, frustration, and even hatred.

Ze Lo Shalom, Haver *(This Isn't Shalom, Friend)*

"This is a sticker of the opponents of the peace process. The *Haver* 'friend' is whoever happens to be reading the slogan." The interviewee added: "The slogan refers to the hopes raised by the possibility of peace, but states that what has actually occurred is nothing like that. It's a good play on words, drawing on cultural forms. They took an existing form and turned it into something else, altering its meaning. *Shalom* here means a particular political reality, while *Ḥaver* is no longer Rabin, but rather whoever sees the sticker. I like these word plays—they reflect a kind of human imagination that I can enjoy, even if it doesn't match my own political beliefs."

One interpretation sees the words *Ze Lo* (this isn't) as implying that *Shalom* here means "peace," rather than "good-bye." *Ḥaver* in this sticker was interpreted in two ways: as the same specific "friend" who signed the peace accords, and who is addressed here posthumously, or as a generic and nonspecific friend—an individual approach to each participant in this folkloric discourse. In this sticker, the first three words (including the word *Shalom*) appear in a font reminiscent of Hebrew handwriting, while *Ḥaver* appears in the same form as in the generative sticker (both in terms of typeface and its position in the slogan). Most of the respondents identified this sticker with the right-wing opponents of the peace accords and as referring to the bloody events that followed. Surprisingly, one respondent suggested a different interpretation: "It's as if they are saying to Rabin, 'We're not saying good-bye to you or to the path you took.'" This interpretation requires borrowing from English idiomatic usage to translate the slogan, as in "This is not good-bye, friend."

Ze Lo Shalom, Moshe *(This Isn't Shalom, Moshe)*

"Moshe is meant to be anybody—a kind of generic name, since it is very common. Using Moshe to refer to a Jew is like using Muhammad to refer to an Arab." This sticker constitutes a satirical play on the previous one, using the same typeface and colors. Here, *Shalom* is interpreted neither as "peace" nor "good-bye," but rather as a male first name, placed next to another common male first name, Moshe.[29] This slogan blurs the possible interpretations, yet still leaves open the political interpretation of *Ze Lo Shalom* as "this isn't Shalom." One respondent complained: "I don't know what this is meant to be. Who's Moshe?" And another: "Well, I really don't know what this is meant to be. It doesn't mean anything . . . Moshe is just a name. I guess postmodernists would put this one on their car—they don't have any God!"

Shalom, Lea *(Shalom, Leah)*

"This relates to Leah Rabin and the terrible suffering she has undergone." While none of the respondents doubted that the reference is indeed to Leah Rabin, the widow of the slain prime minister, most disagreed with the charitable interpretation offered above. "This is a hateful sticker directed against Leah Rabin, telling her to watch it." Similarly, "It's not a pleasant sticker. As if they want to kill her, too. A right-winger would post this sticker."

This sticker was not widely distributed, perhaps because of its explicit message, which led one interviewee to describe it as "a very cynical statement and a blow beneath the belt," and perhaps because of its personal and nonpolitical character. It was also explained in various directions. Some associated it with a period after the assassination when Leah Rabin frequently expressed her opinion on political issues; the sticker is interpreted as criticizing this behavior. One interviewee explained: "Leah Rabin's image does not win people over. Women are associated with warmth and the family, but she expressed political positions and took them to the extreme, so she was no longer seen as a woman to be pitied because she lost her husband."

Some respondents, who placed great importance on the diachronic axis in their interpretations, claimed that this sticker appeared in response to Leah Rabin's comment that she intended to leave Israel after Binyamin Netanyahu's victory in the 1996 elections: "It made me think of all those jokes about Leah Rabin. . . . It may also be connected to the comments about leaving Israel. . . . It's a spiteful concoction, just like the jokes about Sara Netanyahu [Netanyahu's wife]."

Ḥaver, 'Ani Zokher *(Friend, I Remember)*

"It says that people remember Rabin, and don't forget him even though time passes." Similarly, "It's a left-wing sticker. We won't forget that a prime minister was murdered here. We'll support your heritage, and make sure it doesn't happen again. It's a sticker as part of the war against Alzheimer's."

All the respondents interpreted this sticker as referring to Rabin, as in the generative sticker. "I remember" was interpreted as a personal statement on the part of the car owner relating to his memory of the association—a kind of "renewal of the covenant" with the late Rabin and the memory of this event.[30] Once again, the chronological approach was evident: many respondents noted that this sticker appeared on the first anniversary of Rabin's assassination. All of them identified the sticker with the left wing, although some said it might also be used by right-wingers who wanted to emphasize that, despite the stereotype of right-wingers as supporting the assassination, they also remember and condemn it. Although many respondents expressed this "renewal of the covenant" in positive terms as close in meaning to the original sticker, some described it less positively. "It kind of irritates me. They're stretching out a good gimmick beyond its natural life span. It's all starting to seem a bit pathetic."

Right-wing respondents stated that this "renewal of the covenant" is immediately associated with the political accusations leveled against the right by left-wingers: "This sticker really annoys me. They bear a grudge against a particular group, against the national-religious sector. It's as if they're saying 'I remember what you did, and I won't forget.'" Thus many respondents, both left-wingers and right-wingers, associated this sticker with the related slogan *Ḥaver, Lo Nishkaḥ*

VeLo Nislaḥ (Friend, We Won't Forget and We Won't Forgive), although the second part is implicit in this case. In this interpretation, the message becomes overtly political, directed at those identified with the assassination in political terms.

Ḥaver, 'Ata Zokher? *(Friend, Do You Remember?)*

"It's as if one driver turns to another and implies that they have forgotten him [Rabin]. It feels pretty gross." Another respondent said: "They're trying to be smart; I don't know what it really means. It's kind of neutral." One comment, implying indignation at the apparent reproofs of righteous left-wingers, was: "What's the idea here? They're turning to me and reminding me not to forget?"

All the respondents noted that *Ḥaver* in this slogan relates to a living, though generic, "friend"—that is, the person driving the car alongside them. Many respondents claimed that the message was ambiguous but noted that it made them feel vaguely uneasy, as if the assassination were being belittled. The explicit demand for an answer in the slogan may have created this sense of unease. Another possibility was also raised: "This is an internal sticker among left-wingers—do you remember that we were on the path to peace? *Ḥaver* here means their own friends, fellow left-wingers." Or: "It's exactly the same as *Ḥaver, 'Ani Zokher* [Friend, I Remember], just phrased from a different standpoint. The first one declares that he is among those who cherish the memory of Rabin, while the second demands that others remember the assassination." This comment reflects an organizational axis arranging stickers from inclusive to exclusive.

Ḥaver, Lo Nishkaḥ VeLo Nislaḥ *(Friend, We Won't Forget and We Won't Forgive)*

"This is addressing him [Rabin], promising him that they won't forget or forgive the perpetrator—just as it states." Although the word *Ḥaver* here could be interpreted either as referring to the original *Ḥaver* (Rabin) or to the "friend" reading the slogan, all the respondents adopted the former interpretation, seeing the slogan as a declaration of loyalty to the memory of the assassination. As in the case of *Ḥaver, 'Ani Zokher* (Friend, I Remember), many respondents stated that the phrase "we won't forget and we won't forgive" implies that an entire section of the population is being blamed for Rabin's assassination. One example: "These are real die-hard Rabin supporters. It's a kind of thirst for revenge. A desire to take it out on the other side." Several respondents associated the turn of phrase "won't forget and won't forgive" with the Holocaust. For example, "It's a reference to the Holocaust, to a profound trauma. . . . Seeing this sticker makes me again blame the person who murdered [him] and those who provided support. It rekindles feelings of anger against these people." From another angle: "I strongly identify with the sticker. I identify with the meaning, and with the sense of vengeance against those who portrayed Rabin in SS uniform and pushed him around at Wingate.[31] It tires me out just to remember all that."

Ḥaver, 'Ata Ḥaser *(Friend, We Miss You)*

"This sticker expressed mourning at the assassination of Rabin, and longing for him. I see this as a legitimate sticker." Similarly, "This sticker says that Israel misses Rabin a lot, as a leader and as a general."

All the respondents explained that this one refers to Rabin, expressing personal and national longing for the leader and the path he took—and thus implying direct political criticism against the present leadership.[32] The slogan addresses Rabin directly, as if he were hearing the comment. One respondent stated: "[It represented the voice of] all those who loved Rabin, from all sectors. Even from the Likud.[33] Everyone loved Rabin; maybe they didn't agree with his way, but they loved him." Another interviewee explained: "This is the sticker I most identify with, all the time. It expresses a very great sense of loss. Personally, I was always very much in favor of Rabin, even when it wasn't fashionable . . . I really miss him, on a personal level."

Given the clarity of this message, the following subversive association is particularly fascinating. In one of the interviews, a respondent, asked to relate to this sticker said that he would tell a joke instead: "You can change the meaning of one of the stickers just by adding a word. Which one?" When the interviewer replied that she did not know, he continued: "But I have to tell you that I'm only kidding; it isn't as if I really mean it. We have enough tension in this country; you've got to have a laugh sometimes. Well, anyway, what is the word you have to add? *'Erekh!* So that it reads: *Ḥaver, 'Ata Chasar 'Erekh* [Friend, You Are Worthless]!"[34]

Shalom, 'Ata Ḥaser *(Shalom, We Miss You)*

"It articulates a kind of despair at the state of the peace process in the Middle East. It's dead. It's all over. Nothing will come of it. This sticker appears on the cars of people who think that Bibi killed the peace process." Another interviewee claimed: "It refers to the way the present government is fudging the peace issue." Although the message is ostensibly "neutral" in political terms, reflecting a general longing for peace that has always been part of the official Israeli ethos, the immediate association with *Shalom, Ḥaver* and *Ḥaver, 'Ata Ḥaser* led most respondents to identify this sticker as criticizing the Likud-led government for its equivocal attitude to the peace process. Some respondents interpreted this message on the basis of the replacement of the word *Ḥaver* with *Shalom*, implying that the individual is not missed, but rather peace.

Interestingly, this sticker was sometimes also found alongside clearly right-wing stickers. Thus, although the responses to direct questions showed that it was identified with the Left, it reflected a sentiment that the longing for peace is not the monopoly of one side of the political divide. Thus, right-wing use of this sticker implies rejection of the alleged expropriation of the desire for peace by the other side. As one respondent explained: "I put this sticker alongside *Ḥevron Me'Az ULe'Olam* [Hebron: Then and Forever], because I was sure that it was a right-wing sticker.[35] Then my wife told me that she thought it was a leftist sticker. But I left it on my car, because we also long for peace. It's just that giving up Hebron and other parts of the land of Israel won't bring peace for the Jewish people."

Shalom, 'Ata *(Shalom, You)*

"I think it's really nice. Warm and welcoming. 'Hey, how're you doing?' Kind of easygoing, smiling, and simple. I don't know who you are, but hey there."

This sticker was observed several times, though it was never distributed in this form. Some claimed that it reflected a desire for peace: "You, he, and I will make peace. Vote for the party of peace. You are the person who will make peace." Others, however, claimed that the change in the slogan removed its overtly political content. The subversive nature of the slogan was perceived as coming from the use of an existing sticker, deleting the word *Ḥaser*; for some, the cropping of the slogan was interpreted as a sophisticated reference to the interruption of the peace process. This response relates directly to the fact that this sticker was created by cutting the last word off the sticker *Shalom, 'Ata Ḥaser*, thereby blurring the original interpretation of *Shalom* as peace. The result is a slogan that is overtly vague, in which *Shalom* seems to be more readily interpreted as the regular daily greeting ("hi" or "hey"). One respondent commented: "This is another of those alienated postmodernist jokes. I'm not sure what it's making fun of. I don't think it means anything apart from just cutting off the end of the slogan." Another interviewee added: "The whole point is that people won't understand it. Maybe the idea is that I should put my brain to work trying to think what's happening to peace? I don't really know." Another respondent offered a particularly creative interpretation: "It's a play on words—*Shalom, 'Ata* in the sense of 'peace, now.'[36] This is a sticker for the settlers: they're trying to say that there is no way to peace. It's a cynical comment on *Shalom 'Akhshav* [Peace Now]. 'Peace, you' implies that the peace is not for us, only for you."

Ḥaver, 'Ata Ḥaser Yoter Veyoter *(Friend, We Miss You More and More) and* Hazman 'Over Ve'Ata Ḥaser, Ḥaver *(Time Passes and We Miss You, Friend)*

"These are very emotional stickers, in my opinion. They convey a sense of desperation—longing and intense desperation." Another respondent added: "These always seem exaggerated to me. Even when Rabin was around they weren't satisfied. But it's true that as time passes the situation gets more screwed up and the past starts to look better, even if it wasn't really so wonderful." Another more overtly political interpretation: "Left-wing. It tries to inspire longing and sympathy in us." Yet another respondent explained: "You find this on the cars of Rabin admirers who are frustrated with the deteriorating peace process, and with the fact that Israeli society is becoming less concerned with Rabin's assassination. It's a statement of a political position." Another respondent was more forthright: "Crybabies! Right, maybe we should all pack our bags and fly away from here? Crybabies, for heaven's sake!"

All the respondents interpreted both these stickers as relating explicitly to the original *Ḥaver*, Rabin. Both were interpreted as critical of the Likud-led government that came to power after the assassination, expressing personal and national longing for the slain leader. These stickers were never found alongside overtly right-wing slogans.

Ḥevron, 'Ata Ḥaser (Hebron, We Miss You)

"Those people who think that we mustn't give back Hebron. It's a right-wing sticker." This sticker is a rare, individual cut-and-paste creation, though documented more than once. The majority of respondents interpreted it as an expression of right-wing regrets over Israel's withdrawal from much of the city of Hebron.[37] Some respondents, however, interpreted *Ḥevron* (Hebron) as a diminutive and possibly derogative form of the word *Ḥaver* (friend). One pointed out that this sticker is grammatically incorrect: the words *'Ata* and *Ḥaser* are both marked as masculine in Hebrew; a grammatically correct version of the sticker would read *Ḥevron, At Ḥasera*. She added that she associates such an evident grammatical mistake with right-wing extremists of American origin who are unfamiliar with the details of Hebrew grammar. This interpretative comment thus addresses content and intent, as well as grammar.

The sticker is also associated with *Ḥevron Me'Az ULe'Olam* (Hebron: Then and Forever)—thus, it forms part of a separate cluster of stickers. The two slogans reflect the emotive interpretation of changing political circumstances, with the self-confident and stable message of *Me'Az Ule'Olam* (then and always, or since forever and for eternity) giving way to the somber and uncertain *Ata Ḥaser* (we miss you, or you are absent).

Ḥaver Mevi Ḥaver, Ve'El Ha'Emuna Nitḥaber
(One Friend Brings Another, and We Join the Faith)

"Shas and the like.[38] The rhyme is weak. It's about bringing people 'back to the faith'—each religious person will bring someone else along, and then we'll all be 'born again.'" Most respondents stated that the sticker is clearly identified with a religious political party that aims to bring the message of religion to as wide a public as possible. "Religious" stickers are becoming increasingly widespread, including many that derive from *Shalom, Ḥaver*. On the semantic level, this slogan relates both to *Shalom, Ḥaver* and to the humorous use of a commercial slogan—*Ḥaver Mevi Ḥaver* (One Friend Brings Another).[39] These cultural contexts are thus used as vehicles for the central message of this political party. One respondent noted: "This is a religious one. People should 'return to the faith.' If you bring someone else into the fold, you get a discount from God—you are forgiven for a few of your sins."

Another commented: "Religious preachers are using the *Ḥaver* from the advertisement of the health fund. As if there's a 'special offer'—bring a friend into the faith, and you'll get special privileges. Even God will give you some bonus points if you bring a friend along to the next 'revivalist' meeting."

Ḥaver, 'Ani Gomer *(Friend, I'm Finishing)*

"It makes fun of all the stickers—all those people who get an orgasm out of messing around with all these slogans. It's saying that for these people, the sticker has become the main thing."

This sticker has an overtly subversive message, based on the rhyme between *Ḥaver* (friend) and *Gomer* (finishing). Some respondents reported that this slogan was connected with the sexual reputation of Bill Clinton. The impact of the slogan is based on the various possible meanings of the Hebrew word *gomer*: in standard Hebrew, it simply means "finishing" or "ending"; some respondents followed this line, suggesting that the sticker refers to the end of Rabin's life. Most respondents, however, discussed the more common use of this word in modern Hebrew slang, identical with the English "to come"—to reach orgasm.[40] Moreover, both the people referred to in the slogan—the *Ḥaver* and the "I" who is "coming"—are masculine; apart from anything else, this is required to maintain the rhyme. Accordingly, the slogan raises homosexual associations. One respondent commented: "It's just a joke. If someone is 'coming,' that's his own business. It's a gay thing really, isn't it? Otherwise the sticker would have to be *Ḥavera, 'Ani Gomer* or *Ḥaver, 'Ani Gomeret*."[41]

A woman pointing directly and rather boldly at the subversive nature of this sticker said:

> You know what sticker I'd put on my car if I could find it—only I can't? This is the only sticker I'd put on my car: the one that says *Ḥaver, 'Ani Gomer*. You get the meaning? . . . Because all they've done until now is screw our minds with *Bibi-Shmibi, Ḥaver 'Ata Ḥaser, Ḥaver 'Ani Zokher*—do remember or don't remember, one lot say day and the others say night. So now all we can say is *Ḥaver, 'Ani Gomer*. I mean, they're screwing with us so much that we're coming. That's the message of it. We're sick of being screwed about by this lot and that

lot [i.e., by the Left and the Right]. When someone screws you, you come. . . . Of course it's a political sticker. It's saying that they're all the same—all they do is screw us.

Ḥaver, 'Ani Mokher *(Friend, I'm Selling)*

"It's cute. This is a nice sticker, kind of personal." Another respondent noted: "This sticker leaves all the lofty issues and comes down to daily life, to selling and buying cars."

This slogan is a prototypical personal creation inspired by the political stickers. Here, too, it is interesting to note that the sticker strictly follows the typeface and structure of the general cluster. The sticker met with a mixed response among the interviewees. While many shared the above apolitical perspective, others remained within the general political direction of the cluster: "It relates to the claim that Rabin was 'selling off' the land of Israel. I imagine it's someone from the right-wing, but it depends which stickers appear next to it." One respondent was inspired to make a broader comment on the cluster as whole: "The things they've done with that *Ḥaver* business . . . I'm telling you, Clinton's provided employment for the whole country."

Bye-Bye, Ḥaver *(Bye-Bye, Friend)*

"It's just like *Shalom, Ḥaver,* but it expresses contempt. It's as if they're saying farewell, but actually they are happy about it, in a kind of light mood." Another added: "This is a terrible sticker. Simply vindictive."

In this sticker, the Hebrew word *Shalom* is replaced by the English *Bye-Bye* (written in Hebrew letters—this greeting is well known and widely used in Israel).[42] The fact that the sticker uses *Bye-Bye* raises another association, interpreted as a message to Clinton. In other words, just as he used a Hebrew word in addressing Rabin, now an English word is being used to address him, with the implicit hope that he will go home. For example, "The sticker was distributed immediately after the Monica Lewinsky affair erupted into the headlines." Yet another explanation relies on the similarity between *Bye-Bye* and *Bibi*, raising the possibility that Netanyahu is the friend who is being wished bye-bye. (Indeed, stickers bearing the legend *Bye-Bye Bibi* were seen around the time of the 1999 elections in Israel.) This line of interpretation was also followed by some respondents in addressing the next sticker in the cluster.

Bibi, Tagid Shalom *(Bibi, Say "Shalom")*

"This is a sarcastic one. A contemptuous comment to the prime minister." This sticker is one of the most sophisticated examples in the cluster, containing numerous covert meanings. One interpretation is that the slogan addresses

Netanyahu, in place of the original *Ḥaver*, and orders him to say *Shalom*, in the sense of "bye-bye." The clever play on words between "Bibi" and "Bye-Bye" was certainly appreciated by the audience. However, the slogan was also interpreted as telling Netanyahu to say *Shalom* in the sense of "hello" or in the sense of "peace." Moreover, the overall structure of the slogan in Hebrew is reminiscent of a common form of address to very small children who are learning the basic rules of behavior: "Little boy, say 'Shalom.'" Some respondents combined this apolitical social context with a specific political argument relating to Benjamin Netanyahu's refusal (during a certain period) to shake hands with Palestinian leader Yasser Arafat, the implication being that he could not bring himself to follow a basic rule of courtesy learned in childhood.

Shalom, Shalom *(Shalom, Shalom)*

"It reminds me of 'Peace, peace—but there is no peace' [Jeremiah 6:14; 8:11]." Another respondent commented: "There won't be peace this way. The first *Shalom* is saying 'good-bye,' the second means 'peace.' This sticker appears on the cars of left-wingers who are worried that peace isn't coming." Similarly, an interviewee stated: "This is a short and concise expression of the feeling that the longed-for peace is slipping away."

All these interpretations see the sticker as protesting the lack of progress in the peace process, saying that Israelis could say *Shalom* "good-bye" to *Shalom* "peace." Another, more optimistic explanation was offered: "It's nice; I like this one. Let there be peace. I'd be glad to see this everywhere. It's fun. Someone who puts this on his car wants peace between everyone, not just between Jews and Arabs. It's a really nice slogan that makes me feel good."

In addition to these two opposing interpretations, many others were also offered. For example, one respondent explained: "There's something a bit old-fashioned about it. I imagine that today a left-wing religious person might put it on his car, because of the association with Isaiah: 'Peace, peace, to those far and near, said the Lord' [Isaiah 57:19]. It's a sticker for *Meimad* or *Netivot Shalom*.[43] It belongs to my father's generation—they used to say 'Shalom, shalom' as a greeting, using the word twice."

Kim'at VeShakhaḥti Shalom *(I Almost Forgot Shalom)*

"It's saying that peace has been forgotten, removed from the national agenda and become a matter of history."

The word *Shalom* appears in the same typeface as in all the others that relate to the generative sticker. However, this is one of the few cases that does not rely on a rhyming allusion to the generative *Shalom, Ḥaver*. This seems in keeping with the verbal message, which relates to something cardinal that has been marginalized and forgotten. The interviewees saw this sticker as a counterpoint to Ḥaver, 'Ani Zokher (Friend, I Remember): "Peace has been forgotten. . . . Sometimes they remember it and say the word just to pay lip service, right before leaving."

One printed version of this sticker makes a direct reference to a children's television program watched by an entire generation of Israelis, in which a puppet character always ended the show by saying *Kim'at VeShakhaḥti—Shalom*, in the sense of "I almost forgot to say good-bye."[44] This sticker uses a somewhat childish font, with two figures on either side: the puppet from the old television series and Benjamin Netanyahu.

Shabbat Shalom, Ḥaver (Good Sabbath, Friend)

"Religious people. When I see it, I think how nice it is that religion has this desire to welcome people without any personal interest." Another respondent noted: "This is a friendly sticker, because it is saying *Shabbat Shalom* to everyone, whatever their political opinions. It's trying to bring everyone closer. It isn't necessarily a religious sticker—it could reach out to anyone. You can't interpret it negatively, only in a good way."

This sticker was observed with increasing frequency toward the end of the research. Its force comes from the fact that by adding just one word to the generative sticker, a tremendous change in meaning is achieved. This sticker represents a different kind of subversion, associated with the religious group of stickers. It is based on the traditional greeting *Shabbat Shalom*.[45] The greeting maintains the meaning of *Shalom* as "peace," but the peace alluded to is no longer a political one, between Israel and her neighbors, but rather peace in the personal, family, and national Jewish sense. Despite the ostensibly mundane nature of the greeting *Shabbat Shalom*, it's attachment to the word Ḥaver constitutes a subversive statement that seeks to shift the balance of gravity to a new point, focused on the Jewish faith—in which the Sabbath is a cardinal element.[46] In the context of this sticker, it is worth noting a traditional Jewish legend that is often quoted in debates on Sabbath observance in Israel. The legend states that if all the Jews would keep the Sabbath just once (in the sense of observing the religious commandments related with the Sabbath), full redemption would come to the people of Israel; naturally, such redemption would also include peace.

Shabbat Shalom, Tel Aviv (Good Sabbath, Tel Aviv)

"This addresses residents of Tel Aviv, who are mostly secular. It's a call from religious people who are tolerant of the secular." Another respondent offered a similar view: "[It's] someone religious who wants to gently remind the residents of Tel Aviv that Shabbat exists, and it would be nice if they observed it a little." A third perspective returned to the political tensions between religious and secular: "Maybe it's religious or traditional people who want to emphasize that they observe the Sabbath even in secular and depraved Tel Aviv. But you could also see it on a restaurant that opens on the Sabbath."

This sticker relates to *Shabbat Shalom, Ḥaver,* but here the reference is specifically to Tel Aviv, Israel's most "secular" city, promoted under the slogan "The City That Never Stops." Interestingly, this slogan appeared not only on car stickers. It also appeared on Friday afternoons just before the approach of the Sabbath. The enlarged version, posted on giant billboards at the entrance to Tel Aviv, apparently by a religious group, was an appropriate medium for a slogan that addresses an entire city.

Shana Tova, Ḥaver *(Happy New Year, Friend)*

"This is a really cynical sticker. I can't stand it. I bet they produced it on the first anniversary of his murder.[47] It's a right-wing slogan, telling the 'friend' that they had a good year since he died." Another respondent offered several possible interpretations: "It's turning to Rabin up there. Greeting him in a very uncynical way. Or it could be addressing any individual in the street. But it might also be an ironic comment about how bad this year has been—that is, that since the assassination it's been a bad year."

This slogan appeared on the front page of one of Israel's leading daily newspapers in the issue published immediately before the Jewish New Year. In our fieldwork, we documented cases where it was cut out of the newspaper and stuck on the windshield of cars. Since the greeting *Shana Tova* relates specifically to the Jewish New Year, all the respondents focused on this point as symbolizing the end or the beginning of periods. One respondent noted: "This is another cynical sticker, but it depends on timing. If it appeared immediately after the assassination, then it's bitter and angry, because clearly this was a bad year. . . . But if it appeared a long time after the assassination, it's saying that we still remember you."

Ḥaver, 'Ani Zokher 'et HaShabbat *(Friend, I Remember the Sabbath), and a Close Variant, Ḥaver, 'Ani Zokher!! 'Et HaShabbat!! (Friend, I Remember!! The Sabbath!!)*

"This is a disgusting sticker. First of all, it's saying that the memory of Rabin and his assassination is completely unimportant. All that matters is the Sabbath. Now since we also know that the person who murdered Rabin was a religious Jew, who certainly kept the Sabbath, and even more importantly, that the assassination was encouraged by a group of rabbis who justified it in terms of religious law, then it really annoys me and repulses me and God knows what. All this preaching is just unbearable as far as I'm concerned." Another interviewee offers a quite different view: "It's saying that we should remember the Sabbath. Jews should remember and keep the Sabbath. It's a kind of playful comment on *Ḥaver, 'Ani Zokher* [Friend, I Remember]—'Friend, I remember the Sabbath.' I like it."

Shalom, Beyneynu *(Shalom, between Us)*

"Before we make peace with our neighbors, we must make peace at home, among the Jews." Or, similarly, "The stickers all talk about yes to peace or no to peace, and everyone argues with each other. So before we make peace with our enemies, we must first make peace among ourselves."

In the context of the central discourse discussed here, this sticker relates to the previous one, but without the specifically religious and cosmological orientation. Thus the slogan becomes a call for internal peace. When asked to discuss the meaning of this sticker, there was universal agreement: This sticker seems to relate directly to *Shalom, Ḥaver*, from a particularistic perspective cloaked in a mantle of unity and inclusiveness. One respondent approved this approach: "It's an excellent sticker! In order to stand up to someone from outside the family, the family must be united." Another reacted quite differently: "This is the sticker that most annoys me. Phony harmony. It's an anesthetic in the war that's going on here."[48]

Shalom Beyneynu LeVeyn HaKaba *(Shalom between Us and God)*

"It's a message from the religious, who say that there must be peace between the Jewish people and God because so many people here do not believe." This sticker is another "religious" member of the generative family. This time, the message is conveyed explicitly through the image of peace between Jews and God: "This is one from the 'God squad' who think they know best what people should do, and try to claim that all our problems from A to Z would be solved if we all became religious like them."[49]

Shalom, Yadid *(Shalom, Buddy)*

"It could be anyone. Who could be a 'buddy' instead of the 'friend'? Maybe Bibi?" Another respondent suggested: "I think it's when they said farewell to Hussein. It's saying that Israelis mourned his death."

This slogan appeared as the top headline in a leading Israeli daily reporting on the funeral of Jordan's King Hussein in the winter of 1999. It reflects the close relationship between folklore and the media.[50] The word *Ḥaver* used to address Rabin is replaced by the word *Yadid*, another Hebrew word for "friend," but one that is less intimate. Among its uses, *Yadid* is also associated with the adjective used in the media for countries that are "friendly" to Israel. The slogan conveys the strong sense of loss and mourning in Israel over the death of Hussein, who was profoundly admired and even loved by Israelis, particularly in recent years.

The remarkable creativity of the interpretative process was also evident in the case of this sticker. One respondent, for example, drew an analogy between its textual and contextual character and the generative *Shalom, Ḥaver*: "When Hussein died, it was important to recall that he had made peace alongside Rabin, so they bade him farewell in a similar manner. But I think they should have produced a sticker in Arabic. It's a pity no one thought of that."

Hayita Ḥaver, Shalom *(You Were a Friend, Shalom)*

"It's a fine address to Hussein, who passed away. They want to tell him that just as all Israelis mourned for Rabin, so they mourn for him. He was very widely loved in Israel." Another respondent recalled: "Hussein came to Israel to visit the bereaved families of young girls murdered by a Jordanian soldier. Although he was a king, he came and knelt down before them and asked for forgiveness. The Israelis appreciate this and remember that he acted like a true friend."

This slogan also appeared in the press following King Hussein's death from cancer. It was understood as a direct address to the late monarch, based on the inversion of *Shalom, Ḥaver* (Shalom, Friend) to *Ḥaver, Shalom* (Friend, Shalom), as well as the addition *Hayita* (You Were), emphasizing the past activities of the king and the nature of the slogan as a eulogy for the late king.[51] One interpretation maintained the reference to King Hussein but perceived the sticker as expressing fears about the future of peace due to the change of rule in Jordan. "It's saying that peace was our friend, and now we're worried what will happen under the new ruler in Jordan."

Sticker, 'Ata Ḥaser *(Sticker, We Miss You)*

"This summarizes a comment about all the stickers. After all these variations and slogans, the end result is that what's missed now is not the *Ḥaver* 'friend' but rather the sticker itself."[52] Another respondent was angered by the sticker: "It's contemptible! After all, a sticker is just a sticker. It's not important. Here they talk about it as if we miss a sticker like we miss a person, and I think that's a contemptible comparison. I'd never put a sticker like that on my car. It's really annoying." A third explained: "They're making fun, as if what matters to everyone here is just to find some slogan to follow."

This one is evidently satirical, overturning the intense political weight attached to the stickers. It first appeared in a satirical column in a leading newspaper. However, we also saw it on cars, enlarged using a photocopier and taped on the rear windshield. Within the overall discourse discussed here, the respondents related to this sticker in various ways. One explained: "The message is that we need to find a sticker that will unite us all—religious and secular, left-wing and right-wing. We really need a sticker like that."

Discussion

In recent years, Israel has witnessed a cultural phenomenon of lively and public folk politics, embodied in the iconic genre of bumper stickers. Documentation and analysis of this genre create theoretical potentialities, extending our understanding of the nature and limits of folklore in the pluralistic postmodern era and confronting traditional definitions of the field with new cultural phenomena. In focusing on a dominant cluster of stickers in the Israeli ethnographic field, we sought to learn about the popular experience and unique interpretation that is expressed, and indeed created, in this folkloric discourse. The ability to respond to challenges posed by expressive genres that are not conveyed through interpersonal interaction, together with the deconstructivist tendencies currently evident among folklore researchers, are at the center of the field's debates.[53] It is in this context that Briggs and Shuman note the need to dismantle the dichotomy between traditional and modern and to replace it with a discussion of traditionalizing as a central cultural dynamic.[54] The rich interpretations comprising the Israeli road discourse, with their deep historical and cultural roots, reveal a folkloric, multivocal dialogue conducted through a contemporary medium. This dialogue offers a unique empirical contribution to understanding the dynamics of traditionalizing.

The scope of creativity and virtuosity revealed to us reflects the local characteristics of the genre that, as part of the process of the globalization of culture, has moved overseas from one ethnographic field to another and has assumed unequivocally folkloric form.

As is evident from an analysis of the reactions and intracultural interpretations, this phenomenon shows a particularly high level of folk political debate and embodies an exegetical and persuasive aesthetics. This folk politics is organized in argumentative spirals, creating a broad structure of discourse and meaning, the different parts of which replicate and are subservient to each other. The argumentation is embodied in the diversity of versions in the cluster; in that all the versions relate to a single sacred text, albeit in differing manners and degrees; and in the intricate and sometimes abstruse nature of popular interpretation, which is reminiscent of traditional Jewish exegesis. An analysis of the range of interpretations offered reveals a number of organizing axes around which interpretative rhetoric is structured. In some cases a single axis may be followed, while in others the interpretation vacillates between different axes and combines them in the act of exegesis:

a. A diachronic axis, according to which the interpretation is based on a chronological sequence of political events. This axis is expressed in rhetoric such as "This sticker bids farewell to the victims of terror during that period"; "The sticker was produced on the first anniversary of Rabin's assassination"; "It's connected with the Oslo Accords"; "It depends on the timing: if it came out immediately after the assassination, then I think it's very cynical. . . . If it was a long time after, then it means 'We still remember you.'"

b. A synchronic axis relating to the simultaneous presence of a range of stickers and to the encounter between these stickers. This axis draws its interpretative legitimacy from the broad context underlying the different stickers. For example, "This one goes along with 'Hebron Then and Always'"; "[My interpretation] depends on which stickers appear together with it—whether they are right-wing or left-wing."

c. A sectarian axis that establishes meaning through factional categorizations. This approach is characterized by rhetoric such as "This is a sticker of the settlers"; "a left-wing sticker"; "religious Americans, you know what I mean?"; and so on. This axis emphasizes the dialectics of inclusivity-exclusivity, reflected both in the slogan on the sticker and in the varied associations of solidarity and alienation: "It's saying that we all want peace"; "they're blaming a whole section of the people for Rabin's assassination."

d. An axis bridging copywriter or creator and audience, and offering explanations relating to the creation and "invention" of the sticker. This approach focuses on an imaginary copywriter, often entails value judgments as to his or her level of sophistication and aesthetic creativity, and blurs the dialectics between copywriter and audience. For example, "They came with a reference to the Holocaust. It's clear that they're trying to link the assassination to an enormous trauma"; "plays on the association of Rabin and peace"; "a nice invention, a very cute idea." The attempts by many respondents to offer their own slogans for stickers may be included in this axis.

e. A private axis, transferring discussion of the various stickers to the personal level of aesthetics and emotion. Typical comments reflecting the private axis include "I didn't like that one," or "it doesn't really move me either way." These comments are always accompanied by others relating to different axes, and employ a characteristically capricious rhetoric; arguments are drawn mainly from the emotive sphere and the level of cognitive processing is minimal.

These axes emerged repeatedly in the respondents' interpretative comments, blending public, private, emotional, and reflexive levels. In some cases this resulted in exegetical corroboration, in which the different axes contributed to an interpretive totality. In other cases incompatibility along the axes made for incoherent dissonance, which may result in an unnerving lack of exegetical clarity.

An increasingly important characteristic in illustrating the nature and borders of folklore seems to lie in the distinction between folklore and popular culture.[55]

Hasan-Rokem defines the difference as relating to the level of mutual activity between creator and consumer, and to the ability to distinguish between the two.[56] In contrast to popular culture, folklore is created through a mutual action involving the talent and cognizance of singers and audience alike, of storytellers and listeners, in a manner that blurs the distinction between them. These mutual relations raise the folkloric experience to the level of *jouissance*—a feature that would seem to be absent from popular culture. Folkloric creativity, therefore, is characterized by the simultaneous presence of artist and audience, by the constant dismantling of the partition between the two, and by the principled dialogues they embody, at the levels of both consciousness and emotion. For Hasan-Rokem, the attempt to reveal all these while continuing to acknowledge the creativity of the individual is the act of acrobatics practiced by researchers of folklore.

In the dialogue of stickers discussed here, the creation was expropriated from the "creative individual," commuting the acrobatic act of research from the individual to the collective domain. This process was surely acknowledged by the creative individuals themselves; for their part, they appear to have cooperated with the processes by which the identities of copywriter and audience were blurred. The public in Israel was involved as both copywriter and audience in the discourse of stickers derived from *Shalom, Ḥaver* on various levels, from the level of diverse and creative interpretation, through criticism and the creation of imaginary slogans, rituals of placing and removing stickers, and overcoming technological barriers to create "homemade" stickers (figures 1.2 and 1.6). Thus, discussion of the discourse of stickers as folklore focuses attention on the mutual affinities connecting and differentiating popular culture and folklore, and the mechanisms involved in their creation. As we have seen in the chapter, the discourse of stickers of such impressive popular force generated by *Shalom, Ḥaver* associates itself with the mythological *Shalom ʿAkhshav* (Peace Now). Yet this latter sticker, for all its many years of existence, has not developed into a full-fledged folkloric entity. While this may be due in part to the explicitly sectarian political identity of *Shalom ʿAkhshav*, the main reason probably lies in the other sticker, that is, *Shalom, Ḥaver*, which generated an emotionally charged folkloric discourse, dismantling barriers between copywriter and audience. The founding moment of this discourse, and the traumatic juncture at which the words *Shalom, Ḥaver* were spoken, in an American accent, by the president of the United States, was one of emotional force and the transcendence of hierarchies. Thus, this slogan possessed a founding potential to create a folkloric discourse that also invited blurring, such as that of the distinctions between copywriter and audience; both are fed by and flood emotions.[57] This discourse blends aesthetics and humor along with profound emotions of fear, frustration, anger, sadness, identification, joy, and the pleasures of gloating.

Figure 1.6. An example of a "homemade" sticker. Left, the "homemade" sticker *Ken LaMashiah* (Yes to the Messiah); right, the original sticker *Ken LaShalom, Lo La'Alimut* (Yes to Peace, No to Violence).

The discourse discussed here draws its interpretative authority from processes that create diverse, and even contradictory, readings, reflecting the emotional dimensions of the political folkloric arena. These dimensions are characterized by an argumentative aesthetics that hints, through form, content, associations, and connections, at various levels of explicitness, to the common and the divisive underpinnings of this entire discourse.[58] Forms of transmission, the relations between form and content, messenger and audience, tradition and innovation, original and dissemination, and, above all, the relations among folklore, emotions, and power, continually generate new forms of folkloric discourse. The bumper sticker discourse, as a focal point for these dialectics, challenges and widens traditional limits of the folkloric scope.

Postscript

In the years following the research that this chapter is based on, the cluster of stickers branching out from *Shalom, Ḥaver* continued to grow. Around the 1999 general elections in Israel, the stickers *4.11.95, Boḥer, 'Ata Zokher?* and (with a more explicit message as to the political ramifications of memory) *Ḥaver 'Ani Zokher, Barak 'Ani Boḥer* appeared.[59] *Salaam, Ḥaver*, substituting the Arabic *salaam* for *shalom*, is a more recent variation. Another cluster was initiated by the wordplay, *Ḥaver, Hashalom Ḥozer*, which in turn generated *Ḥaver, 'Ani Ḥozer (Bitshuva).*[60] This last development marks a transition from the earthly politics to transcendent religious commitments, from the voting booth and the protest march to the synagogue and the study hall (*Beit Midrash*). This latter tendency picked up force in later years, as we will see in chapter 3. The continuing evolution of these stickers is further evidence of the vitality of folkloric discourse and its ability to contain and produce new voices, and to react creatively to a dynamic and changing reality.

Notes

This chapter is based on an article originally published as "Political Bumper Stickers in Contemporary Israel: Folklore as an Emotional Battleground," *Journal of American Folklore* 114, no. 453 (2001): 277–308. © 2001 by the American Folklore Society. Used with permission.

1. In the United States bumper stickers are an extremely widespread phenomenon and are usually considered part of a related group of genres including other car signs, buttons, and T-shirts (Smith 1988; Case 1992). Articles on this subject have addressed the medium from either the historical and historical-parricide perspective (Smith 1988, 141–43) or the functional standpoint (Case 1992, 107).

2. The pioneering literature on this genre has hitherto concentrated on the ethnographic field of the United States. Theoretical works have assumed without question that stickers are a genre of popular culture in which political themes play only a secondary role. Research in this field has concentrated on classifying the phenomenon according to predetermined criteria and on using the external exegesis of researchers to order the messages according to clearly delineated categories. See, for example, Smith (1988); Aguirre (1990); Case (1992); Endersby and Towle (1996).

3. The popular engagement in this form of creativity emerged clearly both in the existing material I collected and in the slogans people spontaneously offered when I mentioned the subject of my research.

4. For a discussion of the phenomenon as a "plague," see Levinson and Ze'evi (1995). On the connections between folklore, politics, and nationalism, see Dow (1991).

5. As seen in chapters 2 and 3, the manner in which the sticker text is framed invites a specific reaction, an audience interaction, which has much in common with other petite folk expressions, especially slogans, sayings, and proverbs.

6. The transcription follows the Hebrew Language Academy recommendations for "simple transcription" from Hebrew into Latin letters, with the addition of the distinction between letters *'Alef* and *'Ayin*. See Rashumot Ha'Akademya LaLashon Ha'Ivrit, Yalkut Pirsumim 5764, January 17, 2008, 1428–31. I thank Doron Modan for the Hebrew transliteration throughout the book. *Shalom, Ḥaver* was documented both with a comma between the two words and without punctuation; for the sake of convenience, the comma has been used universally. On

"Peace Now," see Bar-On (1985). On the connection between this movement and the sticker, see Levinson and Ze'evi (1995).

7. For a discussion of the conflict that the assassination brought to the fore, in which new political forces challenged some of the most deeply ingrained paradoxes of the vision of the modern Israeli nation state, see Hazan (1998).

8. See below for discussion of the various meanings of this expression. Since the ambiguities, nuances, and sounds of the Hebrew slogans discussed in this volume must be understood to appreciate the generative process presented here, all slogans will be given in transliterated Hebrew, with a basic translation in parentheses. On the language of Israeli bumper stickers, see also, Shlezinger and Livnat (2001). It should be noted that although President Clinton first used the phrase *Shalom, Haver* shortly after learning of Rabin's assassination, most respondents in this study associated the expression with his funeral oration in Jerusalem.

9. The sticker, seen in figure 1.3, was produced and distributed on a voluntary basis by the employees of an advertising firm and a printing house. A further five hundred thousand copies of the same sticker were printed and distributed by a leading Israeli daily newspaper. The paper's main rival countered with its own sticker expressing the sense of shock at the assassination and bearing the words *Day La'Alimut* (Enough Violence); this slogan belongs to a parallel cluster of stickers in Israel.

10. Though the level of dispersion is not central to this chapter, a random examination of several parking lots during this period showed that three out of every ten cars bore political stickers; in some parking lots, the figure was four out of ten.

11. For discussion of other manifestations of "mourning rituals" following Rabin's assassination, see Hazan (1998).

12. Removed, most likely, by the car owners, perhaps owing to the recognition of the potential destructive impact of anti-Rabin rhetoric, or perhaps to avoid being identified with the accused camp. In some cases, vengeful mourners removed stickers without consent of the owners.

13. In this context, for example, Smith notes that this genre is a form of folk poetry with iconic characteristics, adding, "Their analysis requires the reader-viewer to reread and review formal content in several explicit and implicit contexts in order to decode them" (1988, 141).

14. Naturally, alternative categorizations of the stickers could have been followed. One approach is to order the stickers according to political orientation (in the Israeli context, this would require attention both to the Left-Right and the religious-secular axes). This was inappropriate in the present study, however, since our central goal was to examine the respondents' categorizations and interpretations. Moreover, and as is clear from the discussion below, we were surprised to see that respondents offered diametrically opposed interpretations even of stickers that seemed to us to present an unequivocal political perspective.

15. This explains the complexity encountered in attempting to translate the stickers from Hebrew to English. As mentioned in note 4 of this chapter, the solution we have adopted is to introduce each sticker in its Hebrew form, in transliteration.

16. The only exception to using one of the two words of the original slogan is that which maintains the pattern "X, We Miss You," but replaces the word *friend* with the word *sticker*.

17. Some readers may prefer to simply review the list of stickers that appears here and proceed directly to the summarizing discussion, using the detailed illustrations only for reference.

18. The research also identified cases where stickers were displayed in homes—particularly, and I believe significantly, on entrance doors. Other locations included bags, T-shirts, and diaries. The common denominator is that these locations are particularly exposed to audiences likely to read the stickers, and they also constitute border markers of personal identity.

19. In this context, see Aguirre (1990, 92), who reflects on the manner in which people communicate on highways and the function of stickers in this discourse. He claims that the road is a significant element, insofar as it relates to the concrete and symbolic question as to where one is "coming from" and where one is "going to."

20. A beard and/or skullcap (for a man), or a head covering and long sleeves (for a woman) will be stereotypically interpreted as implying a level of orthodoxy in religion and a right-wing political orientation; a man with an uncovered head, shaven, and with a certain type of round eyeglasses will be seen as a left-wing secular intellectual.

21. Israeli driving is notoriously aggressive, exacerbated by poor infrastructure and an exponential increase in the rate of car ownership.

22. A sticker opposing any Israeli withdrawal from Hebron—a position that would not usually be expected to go along with the message of the other stickers quoted by the respondent.

23. For example, *Ken LaShalom, Lo La'Alimut* (Yes to Peace, No to Violence) was turned into *Ken LaShalom, Lo Le'Oslo* (Yes to Peace, No to Oslo), and in a personal version into *Ken La-Mashiah* (Yes to the Messiah); see, for example, figure 1.6. It should be explained that "Oslo" in Israeli political discourse means the peace process with the Palestinians, started through clandestine discussions in the Norwegian capital. The second syllable of the name *Oslo* is the same as the Hebrew word *no*, a coincidence that has been exploited by slogan makers. The very personally prepared version *Ken LaMashiah* transferred the whole debate to the religious sphere.

24. The interviewee was reflecting on the situation in Israel, in which blue-collar workers are identified with a hawkish political position.

25. Volvo and Mercedes are two brand names that serve as a code for prestigious cars.

26. The sticker *Shalom Balahot* appears in figure 1.1.

27. See note 11 of this chapter.

28. Other stickers similarly capitalize on reversal and contrast, such as *Hevron Hevron Me'az ULeTamid* (Hebron: Then and Always), seen also in figure 1.1, which is a politically opposing variant on *Shalom 'Akhshav* (Peace Now).

29. In modern Hebrew, this entails a shift in the stress of the word: while *Shalom* is usually pronounced with the emphasis on the second syllable, when used as a first name the stress colloquially shifts to the first syllable.

30. Figure 1.3 demonstrates this kind of proximity, with a group of three stickers, recalling Rabin's assassination.

31. The interviewee noted two of the incidents during the period immediately before the assassination. In the first, montage photographs of Rabin in SS garb were displayed and disseminated at a right-wing demonstration. In the second, Rabin was accosted in public by citizens who opposed his policies.

32. This refers to the Netanyahu government, which came to power six months after the assassination and ruled during the research and writing of this chapter (prior to the May 1999 elections).

33. The mainstream right-wing party opposed to Rabin's policies (who, under Netanyahu's leadership, subsequently won the 1996 elections).

34. The joke is based on taking the word *Haser* (missing or lacking), and transforming the affective word meaning "missing," in the sense of longing, to the word that signifies straightforward absence of something, then adding the word *erekh* (value or worth). Strict Hebrew grammar requires a slight change in pronunciation (from *Haser* to *Hasar*), but this would not always be evident in colloquial speech, and in any case there is no change in the written form of the word.

35. *Hevron Me'Az Lle'Olam* is clearly a right-wing message expressing opposition to the transfer of Hebron to Palestinian control, as agreed in the Oslo Accords.

36. In addition to the word *'Akhshav* (Now) as in the classic *Shalom 'Akhshav* sticker, there is another, more literary word for *now*: *'A ta*, which most Israelis pronounce the same as *'Ata* (you), though the spelling is different.

37. Hebron has a special status for Jews as a historic-religious place, and the withdrawal thus created particularly strong emotions.

38. Shas is an ultraorthodox party that has gained increasing strength in Israel over the past decade, building its political base largely on its image as a religious antithesis to secular Zionism.

39. The slogan was used by a health insurance company, where existing members received various benefits if they persuaded new members to join.

40. This use of the verb has become so ubiquitous that many Israelis now avoid using the form *gomer* to mean finish or end, using a different verb instead (a process akin to the narrowing of meaning of the English word *intercourse*).

41. The respondent offered two other versions of this phrase; both also translate into English as "Friend, I'm Coming," but the first presupposes a male speaker talking to a female friend, while the second presupposes a female speaker talking to a male friend.

42. The disparaging aspect comes from the semantic field of "bye-bye" in Hebrew—and perhaps in English, too. Wishing "bye-bye" to Rabin might be compared with a sticker in Britain saying "Ciao, Diana."

43. The respondent mentioned two political movements representing the minority of Orthodox Jews in Israel who support dovish and left-leaning policies in terms of the peace process.

44. Some respondents interviewed after the decision to hold early elections in 1999 developed this line of association, claiming that the slogan was implying that Netanyahu had almost reached the end of his "program" and it was time for him to say good-bye.

45. Literally "A Sabbath of Peace," although the usual equivalent greeting among English-speaking Jews is "Good Sabbath!"

46. This combination of innocence and subversion is also evident in another successful sticker of indirect relevance to this cluster: *Shabbat Shalom 'Akhshav* (*Shabbat Shalom* Now), which performs precisely the same operation on the original sticker (*Shalom 'Akhshav*) as the present sticker does on the generative *Shalom, Haver*.

47. The respondent meant the murder of Rabin and assumed there was no need to state this explicitly.

48. In context, the "war" to which the respondent alluded was clearly that between religious and secular Jews in Israel.

49. The respondent used the modern Hebrew slang *dos* to relate to religious people; depending on context, *dos* can vary in tone from humorous to contemptuous.

50. See, for example, Degh (1994).

51. The fact that the interviews took place shortly after Hussein's death meant that most interviewees immediately associated these stickers with this event.

52. Interestingly, this interpretative perspective relates to Haim Hazan's (1998, 743) discussion of the absence of commitment to identity inherent in practices of commemoration.

53. Kirshenblatt-Gimblett (1998, 319–21). Examples of these genres include e-mail folklore or the folklore of the office photocopier. On urban office folklore, see in particular Dundes and Pagter (1978) and Dundes (1987, 1991); in this context, see also, for example, Abrahams (1993) and Dorst (1983, 1990). For various developments of this discussion, see, for example, Georges (1991); Kirshenblatt-Gimblett (1988, 1996, 1998); Ben-Amos (1971, 1998); Bendix (1998).

54. See Briggs and Shuman (1993).

55. The concepts of popular culture and folklore are often used interchangeably. For a discussion of the similarities and differences between these two concepts, see, for example, Bauman (1992); L. Levine (1992); Hanson (1993).

56. Hasan-Rokem (1997, 12), in the preface to the special volume of *Theory and Criticism*, which she edited. In the context of this distinction, Richard Bauman notes that the definitions of these two phenomena sometimes overlap and are sometimes counterpoised (Bauman 1992, 17).

57. For a discussion of the connection between emotions and discourses, see Gumperz (1982) and particularly Abu-Lughod and Lutz (1990, 1–23), in the preface to their book on the language and politics of emotions.

58. On the basis of this understanding, one might propose that "text" and "context," as two distinct concepts, may be transferred in theoretical and methodological terms into the "moment of semiosis" at which several discourses meet and intertextual relations occur in the spaces between the discourses. For a discussion of the term *moment of semiosis*, see Mechling (1993). A central concept in this new understanding is that of intertextuality as coined by Kristeva (1967). Such concepts as structure, form, function, or even meaning are no longer imminent components of the discourse, but rather the products of an ongoing process of production and reception of discourse. In the current context, this process is located at the junction or point of encounter of a number of directions of discourse.

59. That is, *November 4, 1995, Voter, Do You Remember?*, drawing on yet another rhyme, between *boher* (voter) and *zokher* (remember). November 4, 1995, is immediately recognized by most Israelis as the day of Rabin's assassination. *Friend I Remember, Barak I Vote*—using the same underlying rhyme as the previous slogan, though *boher* is here a verb rather than a noun.

60. The first slogan here is *Friend, Peace Is Returning*, while the second is *Friend, I Return (In Repentance)* This syntax, awkward in English, is a literal translation of the Hebrew phrase *to return in repentance*, used to describe a process of drawing close to God through taking on the commandments. The presence of parentheses around (In Repentance) allows for interpretations that employ a nonidiomatic usage for the verb *to return*.

2 "We the People"

Ha'Am in the Turbulent Sphere of Israeli Roads

THIS CHAPTER IS concerned with expressions of identity and boundaries of the word *Ha'Am* (the people, or the nation), which is articulated in the popular discourse of bumper stickers on Israeli roads.

Chapter 1 explicated the unique experience of a popular hermeneutics produced within the discourse of bumper stickers. This was found to represent a folkloric voice, which addresses itself to the "big" political events taking place in Israel and to the hegemonic discourse surrounding them. The Israeli public was found to be involved, either as producer or consumer, at various levels of the discourse. This involvement included diverse and creative interpretation of stickers, critique as well as creation of verbal formulations, rituals of sticking on and peeling off, and even the domestic fabrication of stickers.

Sticker slogans are formulated in a condensed poetics that refers to a common world of images and associations.[1]

In Israel this turbulent popular political discourse is shaped through an aesthetic of disputation. This aesthetic is embodied in "disputational clusters" whose various parts relate to each other and even intermesh. The bumper sticker discourse contains midrashic elements, giving participants the sense of joining a *hevruta* (exegetical study session) on Israel's highways. One of the richest and most complex "disputational clusters" involves the term *'am*, which can be seen as a battle over metaphors of nationhood (figure 2.1).[2] The increasing expansion and ramification of this cluster testifies to the vitality of this road discourse, which responds, in its own fashion, to the social and political chronology. The concept *'am* receives a detailed and multifaceted articulation in the road discourse, either directly or through related concepts and diverse semantic associations. Aside from the specific content associated with the concept *Ha'Am*, the very fact of its prominence within this discourse serves to reinforce the "folk voice," which is a characteristic of the discourse as a whole. However, *Ha'Am* is not a unitary voice that confronts the voice of government. *Ha'Am* is composed of many voices. The unique semantic field that encompasses the concept *Ha'Am*, as the stickers indicate, is implicated in a dynamic of splintering, which may, upon inquiry, point to

Figure 2.1. Top: *Nishbar MeHapolitikaim* (Fed Up with the Politicians); below: "homemade" sticker: *Tnu La'Am Ledabber* (Let the *'Am* Talk).

new directions for understanding the multiple meanings of Jewish and Israeli identity.[3] Questions of identity and identification are both critical and loaded issues in Israel, marked as it is by dual definition as a Jewish and democratic state. The inherent complexity of this dual definition is echoed in a variety of cultural forms, giving expression to different aspects of the debate.

The concept *Ha'Am* occurs in Hebrew language and culture within a wide range of images and contexts. Many of these occur in the Hebrew Bible, which constitutes a rich reservoir of images and associated meanings for the term. The most central related concepts are *'uma* (national community), *le'om* (nation), and *goy* (ethnos, people), as well as terms indicating the multitude's subjection to rule: *hamon* (crowd, horde), *tsibbur* (public), *kahal* (assembly, gathering), and *'asafsuf* (crowd, rabble). This range of meanings poses a challenge in translation: any selection of one term, while unavoidable, limits the appreciation of the full resonance and connotations of the other meanings associated with *Ha'Am*.

Stickers observed on Israeli roads included, among others, explicit mention of the following terms: *Ha'Am*; *yisrael*; *'am yisrael*; *'ahdut yisrael* (Israel's unity); *'am ehad* (one *'am*); *harov* (the majority); *anahnu* (we); *'am hazak* (a strong *'am*); *shney 'ammim* (two nations); *yehudi* (Jew); *beyneynu* (between us); *mahane* (camp); *kulam* (everyone; written in the sticker with exaggerated length); *lanu* (for us); *yahad* (together); *'ahim* (brothers, brethren). These expressions occur in the typically brief stickers, as though in conversation with one another, sometimes agreeing and sometimes resisting, for the sake of provocation and debate,

Figure 2.2. Among others: *Barak 'Oker Lanu 'et HaLev!* (Barak Is Tearing Out Our Heart!); *'Akirat Yishuvim kora'at 'et Ha'Am* (Tearing Out Settlements Rips Apart the *'Am*); *Shalom Balahot* (A Nightmarish Peace); *'Akirat Yishuvim—Milhemet Ahim* (Uprooting Settlements— Civil War); *Hevron Me'Az ULetamid* (Hebron . . . Ever Since Then and Forever).

the way the very same term is used elsewhere. The present chapter focuses on the popular expressions of the discourse about identity, the boundaries of *Ha'Am*, and the issues of identity and identification which it raises. The use of expressions of identity such as *'am yisrael, yisrael, mahanenu* (our camp), *'ahdut yisrael* (the unity of Israel), and other expressions, underscores and exemplifies the unique connections between the mythical and hallowed and the contemporary and popular.[4]

The associations surrounding these Jewish terms of identity gain a particular edge when represented in such a popular and temporary medium—cheap and easily available stickers—thereby eliciting quite polarized reactions. Exposure to these terms appears to be quite fluid, displaying shifting characteristics, constructive and deconstructive.

In his book *Cultural Intimacy*, Michael Herzfeld (1997) closely examines the culturally specific ways in which nationalism is shaped, thus endowing nationality with meaning in various cultural contexts. Herzfeld coins the term *cultural intimacy*, which designates the close involvement between citizens and the nation-state.

The construction of cultural intimacy repeatedly invokes metaphors and expressions of closeness, which are shared by the "state" and the "nation," and which testify to their existence as parts of a common reality of cultural involvement. The concept of cultural intimacy allows Herzfeld to recognize those aspects of cultural identity that provide members of that culture security in their "togetherness": concepts of familiarity and collective security as well as a measure of subversiveness and resistance to their culture—even when these concepts are in themselves a cause for a sense of embarrassment for the participants. Thus, expressions of embarrassment, and sometimes even sorrow, in relation to cultural intimacy function as key signs.

Armed with this perspective, Herzfeld expands Benedict Anderson's field of inquiry. Anderson's description of "imagined communities" employed a top-down approach, by focusing on the inseparable nature of the "top-down" and "bottom-up" relationship. In relation to "cultural intimacy," the terms *top* and *bottom* lose their distinction.[5]

In the present discussion, I treat Israel's highways as such an intimate cultural sphere. When tracking the stickers' messages, it is easy to recognize the saliency of expressions of identity and nationalism that occur in a variety of political contexts to which the stickers allude. The alternatives to terms of identity and the nation suggested within this particular discourse serve as demonstrations of plurality versus unity and "recycling," whether by reproducing, dismantling, or reconstructing, the homogeneity prescribed by the national ideology. This discourse, with its conspicuous use and play with terms of identity and nationhood, displays the great creativity of the participants. It illustrates the power of the folkloric sphere as an intimate cultural one, and underscores the exegetical power of the subtleties of the ethnographic endeavor. The elucidation of the unique terms that make up the foundation of the multiplicity leads us into the core of the popular discourse, represented by the voices of the interviewees.

This chapter is based on research that included the documentation of bumper stickers over a period of six years, between November 1995 and October 2001, and more than fifty open and semiopen interviews, which were conducted from October 2000 until April 2002. Our desire to understand the popular experience occasioned by the stickers' use of the terminology of identity led us to interview a diverse cross section of Israel's Jewish population.[6] In the open interviews, people were asked to comment on photographs of cars with bumper stickers, and in the semiopen interviews they were asked their opinions of a confined set of stickers. Among hundreds of stickers documented on Israel's highways, only those containing references to the concept of *Ha'Am* or related expressions of identity were chosen, a total of fifty-two.

The selected group of stickers was presented to the interviewees, who were then asked to respond however they saw fit. At the end of the interview we asked them to say a few words about their identities, a request interpreted in reference to the stickers. This led, as we discovered, to self-identification by means of politico-religious labels: "radical Left," "left-wing," "centrist," "sane center," "right-wing," "extreme Right," "secular," "religious-Meimad," "national-religious," "non-Zionist ultraorthodox," "Shas ultraorthodox (*haredi*)," "traditional," "apolitical," and even, as one interviewee described herself, "between the extreme Right and radical Left."

The multiplicity of interpretations elicited point not only to the dialectics played out between the Left and Right, or between the secular and religiously identified, but first and foremost to a popular, polemical, emotional, and dynamic relationship to the complexities of the social and political debate taking place within Israeli society. The participants' enthusiasm for the interviews was immense. In the process of interviewing, it was clear that people strove to put into words the sentiments evoked by reading the stickers and to describe their response with precision and profundity. Themes of identity, boundaries, and politics were presented as mutually reinforcing, and their interpretations were elaborated in a manner that bolstered their fundamental views. In this manner, the interviewees projected their views onto the stickers and enlisted them in different ways to their political position. The interviewees attached importance to the opportunity they were given to interpret the stickers, sometimes betraying in their words an awareness of competing interpretive possibilities. It is therefore possible to attribute an ideological intention to their willingness to participate in the research. In analyzing the corpus of interviews collected, we identified diverse, volatile, and even mutually exclusive interpretations. Yet beyond this rich diversity, the stickers exposed deep rhetorical strategies that point to the collective taken-for-granted truths at the base of these expressions of identity. The more the stickers revolved around distinct themes of identity, the more the interviewees tended to identify and even to reinforce these thematic rhetorical strategies. The salience of these deep rhetorical strategies shows collective Israeli identity—as it is formulated in the dynamic popular discourse of the stickers—to be organized around several axes of meaning. This chapter is structured around these axes of meaning, which organize the variety of voices as they relate to the various stickers.

The examples presented in the following pages constitute a representative selection of stickers, which were documented over the research period. Following each sticker we bring several examples of responses to it. These responses, some quite blunt or even jarring in tone, testify to the level of emotion the stickers provoke and the willingness of the interviewees to give vent to these sentiments. The representative examples brought here were selected with reference to several criteria—political identification, gender, and rhetorical type—to allow the reader to encounter a variety of interpretational voices attached to each sticker.

Selections from twenty-one interviewees are presented below. Each interviewee is identified by a first name and political identification that they themselves volunteered, to help the reader identify a person whose words appear, on occasion, more than once throughout the chapter.[7] The participants in this discourse are Miriam ("apolitical"); Boʻaz ("left-wing secular"); Yaʻel ("centrist left"); Tsippora ("right-wing, ultraorthodox"); Elʻad ("secular, very right-wing"); Yoʻav ("left-wing, Meimad"); Yaron ("left-wing, very secular"); Tamar ("secular, centrist"); Mikhal ("right-wing, traditional"); Batya ("national-religious, right-wing"); Gila ("traditional, centrist"); Shmuʻel ("national-religious, right-wing"); Yossi (ultraorthodox [*ḥaredi*], non-Zionist"); Sara ("ultraorthodox, non-Zionist"); Daniel ("secular-centrist"); Naomi (between extreme right-wing and radical Left"); Geʻula ("ultraorthodox, Shas, *baʻalat teshuva* [newly religious]"); Rivka ("extreme right-wing, religious"); Talya ("secular, left-wing"); Shulamit ("secular, left-wing"); ʼAmnon ("extremely secular, radical left").[8]

An examination of the relevant stickers suggests the following classification of rhetorical categories: somatic rhetoric, family rhetoric, historical rhetoric, rhetoric of loyalty and betrayal, rhetoric of inclusion and exclusion, and even rhetoric of the God-people (*HaʻAm*) relationship. These categories, conspicuous both within the rhetoric of the stickers and in the interviewees' interpretations, are axes around which the sources of legitimization and delegitimization pertaining to the identity of the collective involved in the discourse and its boundaries, are organized.

Somatic Rhetoric

> Jewish blood is spilled as a result of concessions
> Israel wake up! Our blood is forsaken.
> Jerusalem—the heart of Israel[9]
> Barak is tearing our heart out.
> Tearing out settlements rips apart the ʻam.

The construction of cultural intimacy repeatedly addresses terms and metaphors of relatedness that typically contain images of the body, the family, and kinship. Abstract concepts of identity, belonging, and sacrifice are often channeled into the building blocks of private experience.[10] Indeed, the use of these concepts stood out within the rhetoric of the sticker and in the interviewees' interpretations. The first group of stickers presented is characterized by expressions of identity, identification, and nationalism that include somatic images, specifically images of the circulatory system.[11] Words referring to the circulatory system often appear in red, next to words in other colors, usually in blue or black.

These images are related to a sense of the functional and ideological unity of the whole body. The most conspicuous somatic images are associated with the heart and the circulatory system it controls. Jerusalem, as a heart, fulfills a function for the benefit of a duplicate body: the territorial body *erets-yisrael*, along with the human body (*'am yisrael*:Israel:Jew:myself). Interestingly, detraction from the wholeness of the body—the kind that causes bleeding—led each side of the political spectrum to interpretations that warn against disintegration.[12]

Israel Wake up! Our Blood Is Forsaken

Ya'el, centrist, left-wing, interpreted as follows:

> The intended meaning is *'am yisrael*, but the word *'am* is missing: *"'am-yisrael*, wake up, our blood is forsaken," as if we are asleep and need to be woken up. It's odd that it says "wake up" in singular and not in plural, because it is an address to a collectivity, but perhaps on the contrary, they are trying to emphasize that we are one, and united, or we need to be united as one body. This is an appeal for action. The sticker appeals to Judaism, to Israel, to our roots, to our tradition, so from that point of view it seems to me that these are right-wing groups.

Shulamit, secular, left-wing:

> You will find this sticker on many of the roads leading to the settlements, on the "by-pass" roads. They are trying to wake up those who don't exactly travel along these roads and to tell them that they are forsaking the [settler's] lives by not caring about what's going on in the settlements. It makes me think immediately how they are constantly manipulating us emotionally and how much their messianic desire for the "whole land of Israel" is costing us.

Miriam, apolitical, responded passionately:

> This is an appeal to the people, big time. "Israel wake up!" is a kind of outcry. The people are asleep—it's time to wake up! It's like "a voice calls in the wilderness," something . . . a real tempest . . . "Israel wake up," in a very dramatic way. All sorts of allusions to times when the Jews were in exile and their blood was forfeited, and everyone could abuse them as they please, and so if we are an *'am* in its own land, then if our "blood is forsaken," this is antithetical to the fact that we have a state of our own. Every word here pierces, this is a very dramatic sticker.

Tearing Out Settlements Rips Apart the 'Am

Mikhal, traditional, right-wing:

> It's like pulling a tooth, pulling out at the roots; we have things in common, so it's not exactly pulling a tooth, it's like tearing the heart out of the *'am*. Without the heart you would not be able to live! There are a few things that are very important in order to exist as an *'am*: it's their symbols, their settlements . . . without these it cannot go on existing.

Yaron, secular, left-wing, accompanied his interpretation with a suggestion for his own sticker:

"Tearing out" [literally "uprooting"] is like pulling a tooth. From their point of view it is painful; I would phrase it: "Evacuating settlements unites the 'am, so everyone will come to Tel-Aviv, we'll be united, it will be fun, we'll work it out. They are personifying the land of Israel . . . uprooting settlements tears the 'am apart. I disagree with this concept of "uprooting." Uprooting a tooth is painful, but to tell you the truth, I kept on living afterward; it didn't tear apart the whole 'am. It tore a few small blood vessels, and you go on living.

Yo'av, left, Meimad, responded polemically:

Aha . . . here we have word-play that uses a similar root: Uprooting ('akira) and tearing (keri'a). Keri'a (tearing) associatively evokes terms connected to mourning customs, tearing of one's garment. So when you are tearing out settlements it connects to mourning. And uprooting, here the association is with the evacuation of Yamit, at which time it was still small scale, yet the evacuees made a big ruckus over it, and the insinuation is, that this will bring about a civil war. "Tear's the 'am apart": a tear, a rift, a war between brothers.[13]

Jerusalem—Israel's Heart

Miriam, apolitical:

This is a sticker that relies on you to come to your own conclusions, it's a more intelligent, and less blunt sticker in its wording. Suppose that it appeared as a song for Independence Day, a song of praise, "'Jerusalem, Israel's heart"—how beautiful, [So] you say: "Trivial, Jerusalem—of course!" So they say to you, "Aha! We caught you, so you agree?" "I agree." "So what is the meaning of this? Is it possible to be without a heart? Pay attention!" It's a right-wing sticker, a subtle one, sophisticated, that relies on the consensus and the general understanding. It pretends innocence, and is simply phrased, with this childlike innocence, but within it there is sophistication.

Gila, traditional, centrist:

There is a group of stickers, whose purpose is to give a good feeling, to bring the 'am closer together, to create a bit of unity, to warm the heart a bit. Maybe they are looking at it in context because Jerusalem was put on the negotiating table, maybe this is a political statement: Jerusalem is the heart of Israel and therefore it is forbidden to give up even one centimeter of it.

El'ad, secular, very right-wing, granted this sticker a special status:

This is a sticker that I definitely identify with; I definitely think that Jerusalem is the heart of Israel, and not only of Israel, but of the entire world. This is a right-wing sticker, extreme, religious. It is forbidden to divide this capital ever till the end of time! It is even forbidden to utter it on our lips or think such a thought. Jerusalem is a problem unto itself, a very unique and important problem. Because it is a separate problem, this sticker is set apart, and has a unique significance.

Familial Rhetoric

> Brothers should not be forsaken
> Barak, brothers should not be forsaken
> Uprooting settlements—civil war (lit. brothers' war).
> I don't have a brother who is a settler

This category may be viewed as a continuation and expansion of the somatic category, though it clearly includes a nonsomatic aspect which relates it more closely to categories pertaining to the social or to categories pertaining to relationships (such as that of ʿam—God).

The familial rhetoric of the stickers is a rhetoric of sibling relationships: ambivalent relationships of intimacy and rivalry, based on blood ties, and common descent, but also on jealousy and competition. The sibling relationship appears in the stickers, as it properly does in the Hebrew Bible, in a male context only, where the potentialities of the relationship are expressed explicitly as two polarized options: "all of Israel are brethren" as against *milhemet ahim* (a brothers' war = civil war). A related rhetoric, which upholds the sibling relationship, and even reinforces it, is characteristic of another group of stickers that deal with a common divine "father" and his "children," who appeal to him. I explore this rhetoric later, under the heading "Between ʿAm and Its God."

Brothers Should Not Be Forsaken

Yaron, very secular, left-wing:

> This belongs to the beginning of the last Intifada of October 2000 with the fiasco of Joseph's tomb . . . because they abandoned the soldier from the border police there.[14] Ah! By the way, this could be the same at present, with the road wars—that brothers should not be forsaken—you can't leave the settlers there to be shot at like sitting ducks.

Gila, traditional, centrist:

> This could be from the beginning of the riots, with Joseph's tomb. I think it was that, when they left the soldier behind in the October riots, until he died. It could be that it's not political but social—referring to the unemployed or to the development towns, a lot of people who did not feel good, let's say before the election . . . to bring their issues to the surface. Or it's about the settlers, who don't receive enough money for armoring [cars] or whom they want to bring back despite their efforts. So then the settlers or the Yesha Council are the ones who put it out . . . about themselves.[15]

Mikhal, traditional, right-wing:

Brothers is the rest of your *'am*, all the Jews are one people, you don't forsake a member of your family.

Miriam, apolitical:

It's from those [people] with the myths and with the pathos who will give you the feeling that you are a traitor . . . and you aren't fulfilling the values that are expected of you . . . with a kind of force, because everyone actually would agree with the statement that one does not forsake brothers. So now they are saying to you, "You agree that brothers should not be forsaken?" "Yes." So, "What about us?" It's as though they're telling you: "Have you noticed?" You are being called to order in the name of all the values and social norms. I expect that it is the settlers who made the sticker, or right-wing people who feel, especially lately, as though there are others who say that their blood is less valuable.

Tsippora, *haredi*, right-wing:

It seems to me that it's referring to the settlers, which, according to the leftist approach, was until not long ago a situation where the settlers were the ones who chose to live there, so let them look after themselves, and even after they asked for more security, they really didn't care, until it [i.e., the violence] reached the kibbutzim and all sorts of places like that. With this sticker they are trying to arouse a soft spot within the leftists, coming from the place where "we are all brothers," [because] apparently the other ways didn't really work. I don't think the settlers themselves put it out, but rather people who identify with them.

Uprooting Settlements—War between Brothers (Civil War)[16]

Ya'el, centrist, left-wing:

Okay, this is a right-wing sticker that refers to the settlements in the territories. Maybe it is also a threat directed at the left who are those who might bring about the situation where a Jew raises his hand against a Jew. There is actually a huge question among the settlers, whether, if they are evacuated, they should fight the IDF soldiers. It's an extremely sensitive issue. I suppose that this is some kind of threat, because there is support here for the sweeping claim that uprooting of settlements justifies a war of brother against Jewish brother. It is as though they are warning them in advance that if they evacuate them then there will be a war.

Miriam, apolitical:

This is a sticker that can sort of be read in two ways. The first way is that this is like a fact: "pay attention, pay attention, uprooting settlements is an action that is acceptable only to part of the population and therefore the inescapable result is a war, or disagreement, or controversy. So you should be aware that it will cause a rift." Another possibility is that it is a threat—the threat is that "you are the cause of the war. You, who decide on, or support, uprooting of settlements, you think you are only uprooting a house, but you should know you are bringing about a war." This is a militant sticker.

Tsippora, *haredi*, right-wing, illustrated with her interpretation the dialogical potential of the stickers:

Uprooting settlements—whoever is capable of uprooting settlements, which are mostly leftists who support the Arabs. Brother's war means that uprooting settlements creates a war between Meretz and Mafdal, who are actually brothers. There is something here that on the one hand is supposed to join [people] together, and on the other hand accomplishes the complete opposite. It's not something like "brothers should not be forsaken," which connects to your positive side. Here you relate to both sides, and both are very strong, and this creates a situation that can actually be quite provocative and could actually bring about a greater commitment to the uprooting of settlements. As a left-winger I would actually want to uproot settlements: "You took it away from the Arab and therefore from my point of view it's not a war. On the contrary, you are my brother. I will bring you into my city. I will find a place for you; the fact that you have chosen to call it a war is your problem." But if I were a left-winger it wouldn't make the least bit of impression on me. As a leftist it would confirm in me the opinion I have of the screwed-up settlers who take everything and turn it into a war. They have this thing, where they take everything to the extreme, in order to serve their interests. So as a leftist I would classify it as the same thing.

El'ad, secular, very right-wing:

This sticker is meant to warn Barak and the left wing that if they uproot settlements, it's not us who will have started the war—the Yesha people and all, but it might lead to civil war. As if to say, "You should know that this could happen even though we don't want it to happen!"

I Have No Settler Brother

This personal and direct formulation, which militates against the familial notion of an internally Jewish sibling relationship, drew passionate responses from the interviewees, regardless of their political orientation.

Yaron, very secular, left-wing:

It's sad. This is an indifferent, alienated sticker. It seems like a *tsfoni* [northern] sticker, from north Tel Aviv. It seems to be a leftist sticker, alienated, uncaring. It's arrogant: "You are settlers; you deal with it." It's not me.

Tamar, secular centrist:

This sticker really bothers me, because there is a social statement here. It's a response to the statement "brothers should not be forsaken." There are two levels here, the superficial level is the disparaging level: "There's no brother in my family who is a settler." This negates the claim on the other side, and simply erases it, ignores it. At a higher level, it [derives] from a social attitude, that I don't have brotherly feelings toward the settlers; they are not my brothers. I don't identify with them. I don't feel any obligation toward them. It's kind of like a saying that there is no solidarity with the settler; I don't belong to them. It's a very harsh statement and it really bothers me.

Miriam, apolitical:

This could be sticker that says, like someone that says: "Your sister is a slut," so he says: "I don't have a sister." That is to say, it could be that he simply is alienating himself from the whole situation—"I don't have a settler brother." That is, this is a completely enigmatic text, and that's why I say it is taken out of a literature quiz. You could understand all sorts of thing from it. You might even interpret it sarcastically, as being pro-settler: like, how unfortunate I am that I don't have a settler brother. You understand, if I saw this sticker I would stand in front of it confounded, and would not be able to figure out who invented it, and if there is an intention underlying it, then there are multiple intentions. This is a very, very successful sticker, sticker-wise. You confront a riddle.

El'ad, secular, very right-wing:

This is a left-wing sticker, again, a nasty one, you can see that the right wing are constantly desiring unity, talking about unity, talking about closing ranks, and all that, and what does the left do? "No, I don't have a settler brother," doesn't even recognize these people. "Who are these settlers? They aren't my brothers at all! For all I care let them die there!" Here, this shows how low they are. For me, any Jew whoever he might be is a brother, even though I might talk about him a lot and attack him quite a bit. Look how far they are ready to go for their offensive peace with their Arab brother. They are willing to have the Arab and not a settler for a brother; it doesn't matter if his views are similar or if he is an extremist. They prefer the Arab to him.

Historical Rhetoric

Hebron . . . Ever Since Then and Forever
Hebron, for our forefathers and for us
Hebron, our Patriarchs' city for generations to come[17]
Peace Now or Forever[18]

This rhetoric draws different kinds of ties among the past, present, and future. In several of the textual variations, the present functions as antithetical to the traditional and eternal, while in others, continuity is underscored. In many examples this historical rhetoric follows from the family rhetoric, because it employs the metaphor "forefathers of the nations" as the basis of a historical claim. The past, and the future derived from it, are grounded in religious and traditional sentiments, whose central concepts (some of which are connected to the family dimension, through the kinship terminology) are "our forefathers," "generations," "generations to come," "then and forever," while the present is expressed in the terms "for us," "always," "now."

Hebron . . . Ever Since Then and Forever

Bo'az, secular, left-wing, used diminutive language:

> This is a very unambiguous, totalizing sticker. And I have a problem with to-talizing in this world, because life has a dynamic of its own, and even if the Bibeleh [Bo'az's diminutive appellation for the Bible] says that it's not true and it's not written anywhere. Even the Bibeleh has changes in it, but that's another issue. That's about the totalizing of the Bibeleh, of course, I don't forget the fact that immediately there are five hundred commentators who explain it.

Ya'el, centrist, left-wing:

> This is talking about "since then"—since when is Hebron ours? Is it from the time of the Patriarch Abraham? Or is it from the time of the conquest of Joshua? In any event, I don't think it's legitimate to say, "since then and for-ever," because it wasn't always ours, but this is a kind of statement that negates the peace process. It's talking about "ever since then," without it even coming up as a question.

Miriam, apolitical:

> There are the expressions "from now and forever" [*me'akhsav uletamid*] or "since ever and ever" [*me'az ume'olam*]. So he says "since then and forever." They created a conflation here that draws your attention because you're not used to hearing this combination "since then and forever" [*me'az uletamid*]. On the one hand, it has a kind of music, because it sounds familiar, because it's constructed from two familiar expression, its short and pithy. It seems like a very good sticker for right-wing groups.

Tsippora, *haredi*, right-wing:

> This reminds me of a song by Avraham Fried, or Mordechai Ben-David. It con-nects me to a place of belonging that the Jewish people possess in Hebron. If you ask me why [the phrase on the sticker] "Jerusalem—without you I'm half a person" achieves more, since that's a song, too, well there it's something much stronger; there it's talking about what you love the most. I personally hold Hebron in great esteem, with the Tomb of Abraham, this is something very

dear to me, since Abraham purchased the Cave of Machpela, for always, for eternity.

Hebron . . . for Our Forefathers and for Us

Ya'el, centrist, left-wing:

> Today people don't even know what this whole deal with the forefathers is, from their perspective these are people who lived a few thousand years ago, it has nothing to do with us today, it's not something I'd send my children to get killed for. On the other hand, someone religious will view it as a will and testament—something that belonged to the forefathers is a will and testament that I am obliged to fulfill. "Hebron . . . since then and forever," "Hebron . . . for our forefathers and for us," and especially since they put in the three dots . . . the bottom line is that it is "since then and forever" and that is that.

Miriam, apolitical:

> "This is what stood by our ancestors and for us"—so it builds on the fact that everyone reads the Passover Haggadah at least once a year, and the sounds "our ancestors and us" ring very familiar. It is as though to say that we are no different from our heritage and we are one people, as if one piece, and what was good for them is good for us, and what is good for us is good for them, and this produces a feeling of heritage and a historical outlook and then when you say it about Hebron, it is as though they took, they pieced together something that is agreed upon: "You should know that Hebron is in this category."

El'ad, secular, very right-wing:

> This is a religious sticker. Hebron for our forefathers and for us—as if it was bestowed from above both to our forefathers and to us, and it will remain ours. This is an improved version of "Hebron . . . since then and forever," it is addressed mainly to the religious public and it is a kind of "memo sticker" that reminds you what was given and to whom it was given.

Rhetoric of Loyalty and Betrayal

This group of stickers, dominant in figure 2.2, accords centrality to the concepts of loyalty and betrayal, and designates who is to be included among the "loyal" and the "traitors." This rhetorical axis relates to the family axis, and therefore also to the somatic and historical axes, via the associations of blood, and the ideas of blood vengeance and the bloodletting of those who betray the family and its hallowed truths. Similarly, this axis is closely tied to the rhetoric of inclusion and exclusion, central to the entire "identity" cluster, through the manner in which it erects intragroup boundaries by use of terms of treason: traitor, trespasser, informer.

A Jew Does Not Betray Jerusalem

Accursed is he who trespasses Israel's Holies
They are handing over (*mosrim*) the Jordan Valley too.

Batya, national-religious, right-wing:

A real Jew would not give up Jerusalem, because he knows why we are here. And if he won't fight for Jerusalem, it is as if he were not a Jew.

Bo'az, secular, left-wing:

It's like what is written in Psalms: "if I forget thee Jerusalem may my right hand wither." This is the inspiration for it . . . "treason": if you are willing to hand over East Jerusalem and the Temple Mount to the "cousin," you are betraying Jerusalem.

Yaron, very secular, left-wing:

This is classic, it harks back to olden days—treason, Jews, Jerusalem. Those were times when they would hang someone with a dissenting opinion in the town square. It's clear that whoever put this out is from the extreme right wing, like Yigal Amir [the assassin of Prime Minister Rabin, whose politics were in fact right-wing] . . . this is not a vicious sticker, it communicates a painful message. People are really sad, it hurts them that [others] want to give Jerusalem up, and they stress that the most shocking thing is the pain—Jews betraying Jerusalem is the worst thing of all. Jews who want to sell Jerusalem, it's like a mother hurting her child.

Tsippora, *haredi*, right-wing:

The juxtaposition of "Jew" and "treason" is effective, because a Jew is the opposite of treason: a Jew is something that you want to be part of, and treason is something that you move away from, and so placing these two words together with Jerusalem has a huge impact on people.

Shmu'el, national-religious, right-wing:

Profile: Kahanists:[19] Orthodox Americans who came to Israel—typical extremists . . . a "Jew" is someone who is Jewish according to Halakha, and this insinuates that if he betrays Jerusalem, then he is not a Jew. It's similar to one of those phrases: "This is a Jew, this?" "You consider yourself a Jew, you?" These are very common phrases. It's putting someone beyond the pale in the social and cultural sense. The attempt to connect it with the Jewish laws pertaining to *rodef* don't appear to me to be relevant.[20] When it is said explicitly—all right. But you have to be really careful because here there is something so . . . "a Jew doesn't do this sort of thing."

Accursed Is He Who Trespasses the Holies of Israel

Yaron, very secular, left-wing, felt personally attacked:

> What is this? First of all, someone is cursing me. I am a trespasser of the Holies of Israel: I drive on Shabbat, there are lots of ways in which I am a "trespasser of the Holies of Israel," in his words. I suppose it's more about the rage and the political issue. It's political because of the rage and because of "accursed." The Holies of Israel—Jerusalem, Hebron, Shabbat, the Jewish Festivals, and so on.

Yaʻel, centrist, left-wing:

> Okay, "the Holies of Israel," that's probably the holy places, and the holy ideas. Accursed . . . that's a curse. Haman, I think, was accursed. Curse, not in the sense of a swearword people direct at you in the street, but rather in the sense that something has to be done about him, because he is accursed, and therefore he has to be killed or harmed, it's a call for action. It's probably right wing against the left, and actually directed against any government that might consider handing over sites that are holy for Israel, or the holy places. It's a religious sticker in the sense that it's originating from a religious place [sentiment], the reason these places should not be abandoned is not that it is dangerous security-wise, or something like that, but because it is holy, and we are prohibited, and therefore this is religious. But its meaning is political. It also belongs to all the violent, extreme stickers; it's frightening.

Miriam, apolitical:

> All right. This is really . . . it's really . . . from the category of curses, defamations, denunciations. "Accursed" and all that. It's also, like, a sort of biblical language. That is, first of all it's very religious, very nationalist. It's really something terrible. You, a curse will lay over you, and an imprecation will come upon your head, because you are trespassing Israel's Holies! That is to say, you know what the Holies of Israel are, and you agree that these are the Holies of Israel, and then with a steeled nerve, you trespass them, and therefore you will be cursed! This is really an outrage at any level you wish to describe it.

Tsippora, *haredi*, right:

> The word *accursed* is inflammatory whenever it's written; it doesn't matter about what. I think that the Holies of Israel are something different for every person. There are a lot of people that swear in the street, and there's no need to pay attention to it. Approximately: "you will go to hell."

Rhetoric of Inclusion and Exclusion

The centrality of issues related to inclusion and exclusion is what makes this cluster the most explicit and diverse. The uneasy tension it conveys between the private identity of the person whose car bears the sticker and the identity that extends beyond it turns the axis of inclusion and exclusion—with its own particular rhetorical characteristics and its various social, political, and even religious and cosmological associations—into a particularly generative one. The uses of terms of identity of generalizing semantic range, which appear in shifting spheres, including personal spheres (for me, me, mine) and broader ones (us, them, to them, together, our camp, Israel, Jew, everyone), are typical for this axis:

> Ha'Am with the Golan; Ha'Am with the peace; Ha'Am with the Torah; I am with the Golan; Don't call me 'am; Ha'Am with Aryeh Der'i; unity of Israel; peace among us; and our camp will be pure; one 'am one draft; Ha'Am is strong, together we will stand firmly for the Land of Israel; Netanyahu is good for the Jews; the Messiah is good for everyone; one 'am—many colors; Why did you give them guns?; They are handing over (mosrim) the Jordan Valley, too; one draft for A-l-l; exemption for all; more than they kept the Sabbath, we kept watch at the camp gate; together in the tank—together at the bank; This land is mine, too.[21]

Ha'Am with the Golan[22]

Mikhal, traditional, right-wing:

> The first time that I saw this it moved me terribly, I got the feeling that here was something general . . . a common, uniform opinion, we are united, but after that you think about it and the idea of a herd comes up. Whoever wrote this sticker is trying to expose everyone to his opinion . . . it's an attempt to dictate a position to people, if you are not with the Golan, you are not part of this people . . . the reference is to the Jewish people, the people of Israel, the Israeli Jews . . . the Arabs don't care about anything, they only want the state to belong to them, for us to be in the sea.

Sara, *haredi*, non-Zionist:

> Ha'Am, that's the entire people of Israel, secular, *haredi*, everyone, without Arabs but also without the left-wingers. The left wing is a "mixed multitude"; they aren't really Jews. Even according to Jewish law you don't have to sit shivah over them; they aren't our brethren at all. In my opinion, they are Jew-haters, haters of religion, with no relation at all to Judaism.

Daniel, secular, centrist:

> [This carries] a biblical aroma.[23] Ha'Am, that's a biblical word. There's something less frightening about it. That is, this sticker is about something more pleasant, of identification, something more empathic. It doesn't reek of ugly politics. Part of the charm of this slogan is the feeling that it enfolds everyone under the same umbrella.

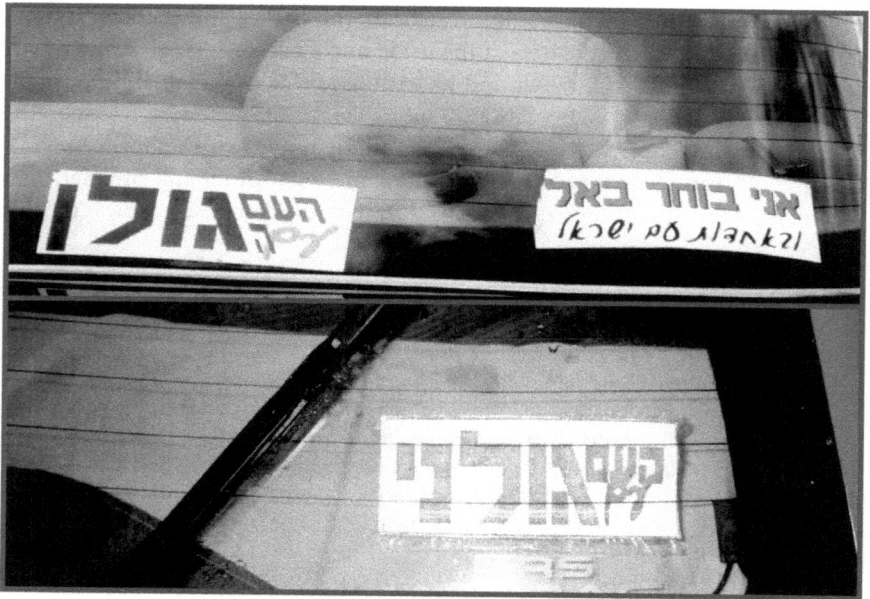

Figure 2.3. Top (left to right): *Ha'Am 'im HaGolan* (*Ha'Am* with the Golan) next to *'Ani Boher ba'El uve'Aḥdut Yisrael* (I Choose God and the Unity of Israel); bottom: *Ha'Am 'im Golani* (*Ha'Am* with Golani).

Talya, secular, left-wing, transposed the sticker from its textual moorings to an oral performance, by spontaneously joining the vocalization of the word "with" with a sweeping horizontal gesture of her hand, indicating a removal or relinquishing of the *'am* along with the Golan. Interestingly, just as other stickers elicited various interpretations, this visual gag was also given competing interpretations. Alongside the sarcastic interpretation of the gesture as getting rid of the *'am* with the Golan, other interviewees, upon hearing from us a repetition of Talya's statement, responded that her implication was certainly tragic: the loss of the *'am* that would ensue after handing over the Golan.

Ha'Am with the Torah

This sticker (figure 2.2), which belongs to the sub-cluster of slogans beginning with the phrase "*Ha'Am* with," considers identity and the connection between the individuals who comprise the *'am* to be founded on the common religion and a relationship with God. It is thus related to another category of stickers pertaining to the larger sphere of identity and identification, such as "I Choose God and

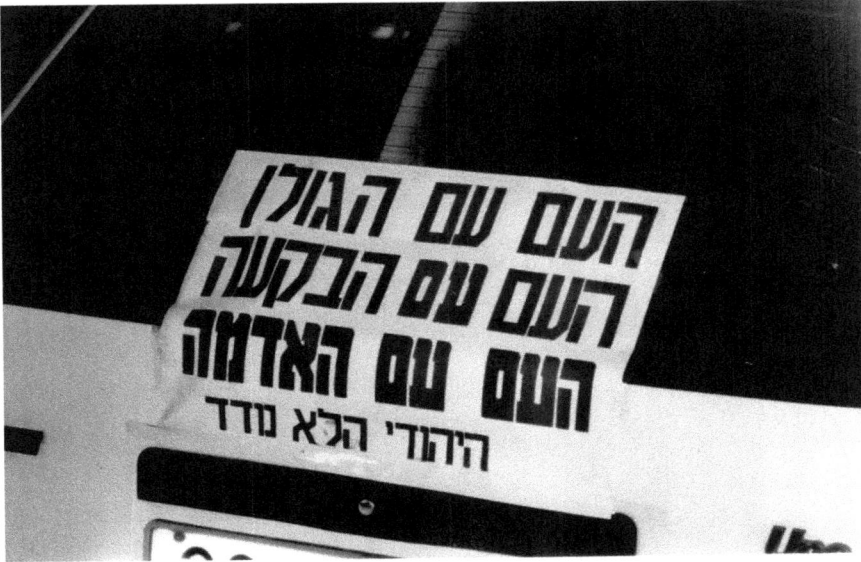

Figure 2.4. *Ha'Am im HaGolan, Ha'Am im HaBik'a, Ha'Am im Ha'Adama, HaYehudi HaLo Noded* (*Ha'Am* with the Golan, *Ha'Am* with the Jordan Valley, *Ha'Am* with the Land, the Jew That Does Not Wander).

the Unity of Israel" and "Only God Will Guard Jerusalem," or stickers that include a direct address to God, such as "We Love/Choose You," "We Make You King."[24]

Tsippora, *haredi*, right-wing:

This is also an imitation of *"Ha'Am* Is with the Golan" because *"Ha'Am* Is with the Golan" was a captivating sticker that had a positive impact. This sticker [*"Ha'Am* Is with the Torah"] expresses a wish, and not something that exists on ground. It's the wish of the *haredi* public, and they are trying to introduce the concept of Torah to the rest of the population so that it will begin to have an impact on them . . . the secular public doesn't relate to this sticker, and it even invites some resistance. It's an annoying and alienating sticker rather than a uniting one.

Batya, national-religious, right-wing:

It's as though—first of all to believe in the Torah. It's something that everyone should believe in; it's not just a book or a sticker, *lehavdil* [for the sake of contrast].

Figure 2.5. *'Am 'Eḥad Harbe Tsva'im* (One *'Am*—Many Colors).

Daniel, secular, centrist, read the letters of *'am*, which in Hebrew without punctuation may be read differently (*Ha'Am 'am hatorah*), instead of the usual reading as a preposition (*'im*), a change that locates the sticker in the religious category:

> This sticker doesn't work for me as a political sticker; it's more of a religious sticker. Maybe a politico-religious one if you insist. It seems to me that who-ever put out this sticker are people who are concerned about the state becom-ing increasingly secular. *'am='am segula* (the chosen people), *'am torah. Ha'Am* is the *'am* of Torah. The Jewish people alone, even the Jews overseas, every Jew by virtue of his being a Jew.

'Amnon, extremely secular, radical left-wing:

> This is an allusion to the sticker "*Ha'Am* Is with the Golan." The Golan is national pride—it's a high place. It's a *kippah*, but what motivates him is the Torah: "more than Children of Israel kept the Torah, the Torah kept the Children of Israel."

I Am with the Golan

'Amnon, extremely secular, radical left-wing:

> This is someone who feels uncomfortable about saying "*Ha'Am* is with," because "I" am not the *'am*, I am an individualist, I have a bit more education, I don't

follow the herd, but I really am with the Golan, because I believe from a rational point of view that it is true, that it is forbidden to evacuate the Golan. "I" might be a student, a very young person. Someone who is at a phase of self-determination, and who is very aware of this fact. "I go to acid parties. I have sex with a same-sex partner, and I am with the Golan. But it's me; it's not the *'am*. This is a young person, who is deep into himself and on a personal identity quest.

Yaron, left-wing, very secular:

Fine, be my guest. You are with the Golan? Terrific. Much more acceptable to me than: "*Ha'Am* Is with the Golan." "I am with the Golan," terrific. Take two daily. I'll put on a sticker "I am with Tel Aviv" [*smiles*]. This is a kind of pareve sticker, neither meat nor milk. To be truthful, fine, without knowing the person, at least he isn't coming and trying to speak in my name.

Batya, national-religious, right-wing:

I feel better with the sticker "*Ha'Am* Is with the Golan," because I feel like part of a collective. I think that when it comes to all of the national issues, the consideration should not be personal, but rather public. For the good of the whole *'am*.

Shmu'el, national-religious, right-wing:

"I Am with the Golan" is a fact that really gets me down; it's related to processes that people have truly identified . . . because they have figured that whatever is conveyed by the wording *'am*—the general, the national, the popular, has lost its significance as a center of gravity . . . the accumulation of individuals qua individuals is what will produce public pressure, while the statement "*Ha'Am* Is with the Golan" has a much more old-fashioned air to it, or even archaic, in the sense that at one time it was possible to speak for the *'am*, to direct the will of the *'am*, now, unfortunately, this is no longer relevant.

Don't Call Me 'Am

The explicit subversiveness of this sticker is reflected in the emotional, sharp, and polarized reactions it elicited.

Yaron, very secular, left-wing:

I don't know what to say about this. I would never put up such a sticker; this was put up by someone who is paranoid [*laughs*]. There was once a musical in Israel: "Don't Call Me Black." What does this mean, "Don't Call Me *'Am*"? This is a totally disproportionate response; the person got carried away.

Miriam, apolitical:

This is based on something: "Don't Call me Black." I don't remember; it's based on something familiar. This is an incredibly stupid sticker, because I am trying to understand who would say something like this, whose mind is behind something like this? Maybe it's a person who is talking to a person who is "Ha'Am is with the Golan," so he answers him by saying: "Don't call me 'Am," as if, don't include me—don't involve me in this—but it has to come side by side. It's as though someone is resisting being included, and he wants to say that he is singular and unique, detests the collective, doesn't want to identify, doesn't want to belong to an ideological group of any kind, so he exempts himself be saying that he doesn't belong.

Batya, national-religious, right-wing:

Don't call me 'Am? Who wrote it? I can't even think about it. Maybe it's actually the Palestinians who don't see themselves as an 'am within the state? Maybe. Because one might also think of them, after all, 'Am Yisrael Ḥay VeKayyam ['am yisrael is alive and well = lit. "alive and abiding"], and they will have to come to terms with this even if they don't want to and they are trying to fight it.

Rivka, religious, extreme right-wing:

This shocks me. Simply shocking. I don't see any purpose in my personal life and that of my family without the collective of the 'am. We were chosen not as individuals but as an 'am. And our moral imperatives all revolve around this concept of the 'am, the collective, even though each individual is nourished by their own personal [domain]. Even history teaches us that to disengage from being an 'am, to become individuals, did not succeed; it didn't work, and each individual Jew went to the incinerator.

Ge'ula, ḥaredi, Shas, ba'alat teshuva (newly religious):

This is a shocking slogan. It is proof of something worse than dissolution . . . so what is left? May God have mercy on us. People who say something like this, they don't have Torah. Because in truth "our nation is not a nation without its Torah."

Batya, national-religious, right-wing:

The secular can talk as though they are disengaging themselves from the state. They don't care if *eretz yisrael* will be only for 'am yisrael or whether there will be a mixture. Like a government that is not only 'am yisrael's, but a government that doesn't have an 'am, that merely survives and that's it. They don't want to be called 'am. If we don't call ourselves an 'am, what shall we call ourselves? In my opinion, whoever cannot appreciate wholeheartedly what the state of Israel is, doesn't belong to the 'am. It wasn't easy to establish the state.

Naomi, who defined herself as "between the extreme right-wing and the radical left-wing":

Nice, very nice. Wonderful, lovely. I don't know. It has some kind of passion to it; it sounds a bit like "Don't Call Me Black." Something with socialist-communist roots, they don't want any people, neither this one nor that one. No nationalities, workers of the world, without national boundaries.

'Amnon, extremely secular, radical left-wing:

Counter-contrariwise: "I am such an individualist, I live here, but I don't live here. I don't really want to live here." What bugs me is that they speak in the name of the *'am*. I am not an *'am*—I am myself. *Ha'Am*—a mob speaking from instinct. "I am not from the herd. I am an individual." This is the thinking of a copywriter, to take a line out of a song . . . very north–Tel-Avivi. Secular, Meretz voters, aware of themselves, living here, but not living here. Living in dissonance from their environment.

Rivka, religious, extreme right-wing:

This you must have found in Tel Aviv, not in Jerusalem. The first word that comes to my mind is Sheinkin; this one, don't bother him with slogans, everything is rotten to the core, there is no ideology; to each his own, everyone leads their own life, it doesn't matter whether it's here or overseas, it's treating Sheinkin as a stigma, but it could just as well be Florentine . . . more than any other sticker it is addressed to all the individuals in this *'am*, so many people who want to break the rules, not to play at the game anymore.[25]

Shmu'el, national-religious, right-wing:

This is a handful of bleeding-hearts [sarcastically]. We're talking more or less about my friends; this implies educated people, even very educated. Mostly from the academic fields, the arts, and philosophy-related education, with very self-conscious postmodern influences, or being artistic and individualistic is very important. And the same marginal groups I mentioned before who are related to this, who are threatened by the word *'am*, because it's a very coercive term and marginal groups don't want to be included in it, there is a need here to affront or to deride. I automatically connect this to young people, unless it is artists.

Shulamit, secular, left-wing:

To me this is someone who says, whether I am for or against, I refuse to have my position presented in name of the *'am*, to be included in the slogans.

To Be a Free 'Am in Our Land

This is usually translated: "To be a free people in our land," from the final line of Israel's national anthem, "HaTikva."

Gila, traditional, centrist:

Every time I hear this, I get excited. It relates to our history. Maybe it's related to "free"—as from enslavement in Egypt, or perhaps "free" from the Holocaust. But it's ambivalent, I understand that this can be disturbing to part of the population, like the Arabs. It's a message of the memory of our past; now we are free in our land. And I like it because it relates to our national anthem, to our memory.

Sara, *haredi*, non-Zionist:

This is a very, very secular sticker. They want to shrug off all responsibility in *eretz yisrael*. This saying: "live and let live" is not right, because all of Israel are bound to one another. When they transgress, we pay dearly for it. Not only are they punished; all of *'am yisrael* is punished. And they, the secular, don't understand this, they just want to shrug off their obligations and they don't understand how much we and they will pay for this in the future. We are all brothers, and we are all one body.

Yossi, *haredi*, non-Zionist:

"HaTikva" is an anthem that is derived from a *haredi* liturgical poem of entreaties, and they distorted it, and used the words to their own ends. "A free *'am*"—they mean free from the burden of the Torah's commandments. But the Rabbinic sages preempted them and said, "*Ba-metim hofshi*" [free among the dead]. As soon as a man dies, he is free from the Torah's commandments, but how can he be alive and free? The sages said that if they were without the Torah's commandments during their lifetime, they are called "dead." A person who did not fulfill his destiny in the world is as good as dead.

'Amnon, extremely secular, radical left-wing:

The Meretz party campaign slogan for the 1984 elections was "*Medinat Halakha—Halkha HaMedina*," which was quite brilliant.[26] To take lofty ideas about the country, the state, the *'am*, the anthem, in the sense of the Jewish *'am*, making the point that is it really possible for a secular Judaism to exist. It's interesting that "free" [*hofshi*] is religious terminology, rather than secular, and relevant to the connection to the land "in our land."

And Our Camp Will Be Pure

Bo'az, left-wing secular, viewed the sticker with disgust:[27]

Aha . . . this belongs to the *dosim* [pejorative term for religious] with a large crocheted *kippah*. It's the feeling of people who think they are chosen. Because all the others are not pure. This is about marriage, about Jewish family law. All the laws. The others are impure and you, your camp must preserve its purity.

Yosef, *haredi*, Shas:

This seems more *haredi* to me. Something from the "modesty patrol."[28] Maybe the final lines of a broadside. They post broadsides against immodesty and this might be the final lines of such a posting. "Our camp" is a limited section. Their camp. The concept of purity comes from the Torah and it relates to matters of immodesty, and therefore it seems to me to come from them.[29]

Daniel, secular, centrist, responded with an amused air:

This has something to do with the Bible. It has biblical associations—Moses, Aaron, who walked ahead of the camp, and their camp was holy. A very religious sticker . . . "our camp" equals the Jewish religious [camp]. We have here an attempt to exclude people, whoever is not in the camp is not pure, and therefore is cast out. Only whoever is with us is pure. First of all it excludes, and after you have been excluded, and you then want to secure a pure identity, come to us, live by our terms. This is not an outright racist sticker; it's a religious sticker, and every religion has something egocentric or racist [about it]. Maybe it carries the connotation of Germany, the purity of the race, so maybe it is somewhat racist.

'Amnon, extremely secular, radical left-wing:

One of the more "nerdy" stickers around. It belongs to Bney-'Akiva.[30] To be pure of evil thoughts, this is a desire for homogeneity, that we walk the right path, the path of Torah. Pure of the perturbations of the corrupt modern age. Let us go back to the old order we once knew: let's die for the motherland, let's stand still for the minute of silence, let's wear white shirts on Memorial Day. Let's return to the original values of Zionism . . . wolves in a sheepskin.

Rhetoric of God-*'Am* Relationship

This rhetoric, which emphasizes the close and special relationship with the God who dwells in heaven, relates to cosmological notions by means of an intimate and folkloric language. This group of stickers includes stickers with identical dimensions to the typical stickers, alongside a group of exceptionally large stickers of unusual dimensions, (about twenty by fifty centimeters as seen in figure 2.6) written in blue letters against a white of yellow background, which the interviewees viewed as being of the same cast.[31]

Among the slogans:

The Holy one Blessed He, we choose you
The Holy one Blessed He, we love you
The Holy one Blessed He, we are your children
The Holy one Blessed He, we make you our King

Figure 2.6. Top: *Ha'Am im HaTora* (*Ha'Am* with the Torah); bottom right: *HaKadosh Barukh Hu 'Anaḥnu Boḥarim Bekha* (The Holy One Blessed Be He, We Choose You); bottom left: *HaKadosh Barukh Hu 'Anaḥnu 'Ohavim 'Otkha* (The Holy One Blessed He, We Love You).

Ya'el, center, left-wing:

Yes, I am familiar with this entire "series"; I associate it also with cars that have stickers of "Der'i."[32] From an analytical point of view this comes from a need for protection: when things are tough, we need to feel that there is something above us, who is our father, and who will look after us. We love you, therefore you love us back. We make you our King, therefore you look after us because you are our king. It's an appeal for help and it is born of lack of security, the need for something. And we choose you, that could come from people who are anti-Zionist, who don't participate in the elections and who even oppose the government. "We don't vote for an Israeli-Zionist government. We choose the Holy One Blessed be He, whatever he tells us, we will do." I also connect it with Shas, because Shas are more out-reaching concerning their religion. You would never see a sticker like that about God on my car or my friend's car, as if this were not the place for [the expression of] religious faith, to express my support and faith in the Holy One Blessed be He.

Miriam, apolitical:

To speak this way to God as though he were some kind of pen pal. "We love you, your children, your darlings" . . . it's an American way of thinking, sort of like in the movie *Clueless*. It's something low, pathetic. What is this—the Holy One Blessed He, we love you? Does God need you to tell him that you love him? You love him in order that others will know that you love him? What is this? This is true of this entire group of stickers. We are making you king; now this turns it into a whole horde of *ḥozrim biteshuva* [newly religious]. It's a kind of wheeling and dealing, a kind of cheap candy made of religious faith, awful!

Tsippora, *ḥaredi*, right-wing:

I know this song. The original is "The Holy One Blessed He We Love You." I don't know who composed it, but the *ḥaredi* community knows who composed it. I remember that Rabbi Aryeh Der'i sang it a bit. Now, Rabbi 'Amnon-Yitsḥak turned it into a real song with verses, and a refrain and he is the one who created the [variations] "we love," "we choose," "we make you king," I don't know . . . now, let's take Rabbi Mendelson, he talked about it at a lecture: What is this about our loving the Holy One Blessed be He? This is something that, according to his outlook, lowers or simplifies things, and he is against taking God and singing songs to him at this level. Because this is a low level, which is undignified. And there are a lot of these types of proselytizers, who, on the contrary, they view it as something that actually creates a bond between man and God, and he feels our love for God. You know, I remember that at Simchat Torah they sang this song, and then someone said: "Hush, hush, hush, I have a message from the heavenly entourage, everyone be quiet one moment: *'am yisrael*, I love you'" [*singing enthusiastically*], so that it is also really good.

El'ad, secular, very right-wing:

These are all religious stickers. Stickers belonging to Shas people, which I have noticed the public identifies with, either the simple religious person, or the *ḥozer biteshuva* [newly] religious person. It isn't a sticker that is out to offend any particular public. It's a sticker that truly tries to show the positive side of the Holy One Blessed be He, it's purpose is to strengthen, to unite, to bind people together, all of them, to Him . . . these aren't harmful stickers, they are simple [aimed] at a particular population.

Discussion

The interviewees' sense of participation and of taking a position, whether through identification, debate, or conflict, testifies to the folkloric experience, which lies at the basis of this study, and which it sets out to illustrate. This was demonstrated time and again, most notably when one of the interviewees, Mikhal ("traditional, right-wing"), offered a comment about a sticker she had never seen before: "Where is this from? I haven't seen such things. Someone gets up in the morning, let's say, my husband, Menash, has often decided to invent [stickers], but never had them printed . . . and you are occupying yourself with this? So to sit with all sorts of ideas that some guy has . . . and to conduct research on it? Come on."

The canvas revealed by the sticker discourse carries potential for broad and flexible interpretation, though it has neither one addressee nor one author. From this point of view, one can view the rhetorical axes drawn across the field as a tool for classification and also as a store of patterns, from which, time and again, the building blocks of identity are consolidated anew.[33] Any attempt to interpretatively summarize the field or distill the message will deprive it of its generative power.

The stickers presented, as well as their interpretation, base their political statements on foundational concepts of Jewish identity, while producing a popular discourse relating to the political agenda. However, while doing so, they also produce a "discourse of depth," which is no less foundational and passionate, concerning collective identity and Jewish and Israeli nationality. The nature of this identity, its boundaries, and its sources in the past, present, and future—including both overt and covert aspects—are woven into the consciousness of the participants in the popular discourse, at different levels of explicitness or even awareness. Seen from this perspective, the kinetic sticker discourse spans the multivocality of positions and the axes of collective identity, extending between that which binds together and that which pulls apart.

The rhetoric of the discourse is saturated with expressions of unity and schism, and with key terms of Jewish and Israeli identity. This rhetoric branches out into five major organizing axes: somatic rhetoric; familial rhetoric; historical rhetoric; rhetoric of loyalty and betrayal; rhetoric of inclusion and exclusion. To these one can add a cluster of rhetoric emphasizing the ongoing relationship between the *'am* and God.

These axes stood out as explicit organizing axes concerning the sources of legitimacy and delegitimacy in relation to identity and the boundaries of the collective engaged in the discourse. An additional axis, which glimmers through the interview material occasionally, relates to the connection between territory and identity. This issue came up, not unexpectedly, in concrete statements concerning the deeply contested territorial politics of Israel (the future of the Golan Heights, the possibility of a future division of sovereignty in Jerusalem, territorial compromise in Judea, Samaria and Gaza [*Yesha'*], and more). Just as in the past, the construction and paving of roads served as a highly charged Zionist metaphor, signifying the process of conquest of the land through development, technological progress, and resettlement. It appears as though the very act of driving on Israel's roads is a political act, which is not devoid of the import of significations woven into the discourse. Thus, an additional axis-binding medium to message was presented to me as I listened again to the interviews and found that interviewees anchored their interpretations in geographic and political space, such as "You found that in Tel Aviv," "This is a sticker you will find on lots of roads leading to the settlements, on the bypass roads." Because stickers are glued to cars, terms of identity circulate on the roads. Consequently, the images of roads, in all their variations, become a clear political signifier. The connection between a concrete space and identity presents itself in a very real way through the cars that conquer the roads.[34]

The central role occupied by the variants of the concept *'am* emphasizes (and focuses) the popular voice that the sticker discourse aims to represent. At the same time, the use of concepts of identity, which are perceived as traditional and hallowed, in such a contemporary and ephemeral discourse produces a fascinating tension between these concepts and the political and social conflicts to which the discourse refers.

The choice of the car for the popular negotiation of the boundaries of identity, as well as social and political issues, is essential to our argument and acts simultaneously as both a cause and effect. The highways, with their rapid flow of traffic, and the traffic jams during which drivers sit and stare at the car ahead, is an everyday representation of life's multivocal hubbub. The sticker discourse allows a flexible and creative reworking of critical and reflexive processes, by those who participate in it—the objects of identity themselves. It can be viewed as an expression of a basic ambivalence pertaining to identity. On the one hand, it is private, marking and publicly declaring the car owner as bearer of a particular identity vis-à-vis the other drivers in the adjacent lanes. On the other, it is an identity that tends to subordinate the individuals' marks of identity to ever-expanding categories (such as *Ha'Am*, Israel, everyone, etc.).

The sticker's physical format becomes itself a "sticky trap" for additional meanings. We thus observe an ongoing tension between the messages of identity and belonging versus the ephemerality of the medium.[35] The acceleration of the closely enmeshed social and political processes imposes a constant need for change and innovation within the conceptual and sentimental realm of identity. This tension appeared when time and again interviewees expressed disappointment that important issues are discussed in Israel in such a temporary, ephemeral, and "nonserious" medium.[36]

When *'am* slogans began to incorporate references to God, some stickers of a larger size began to appear. This shift highlighted tensions within the discourse and was often made explicit by interviewees. In chapter 3, reflecting a continuing stage in the evolution of Israeli bumper stickers, we witness the flowering of religious dimensions within them.

Notes

This chapter is based on an article originally published as "*Ha'Am* in the Turbulent Discursive Sphere of Israeli Bumper Stickers," *Hebrew Studies* 47, no. 1 (2005): 197–234.

1. In this context it is interesting to mention Dotan's treatment of the "sterilization" of the wall of graffiti—a folkloric medium akin to that of the stickers—that sprung up spontaneously at the site of Yitshak Rabin's assassination. Dotan (2000, 27–34) sees this as a single surface where a diversity of opinions and voices in Israel mingles almost indistinguishably, and without even the possibility of reading their mingling.

2. See Lakoff and Johnson (2003).

3. For a critical discussion of the "impossibility" of Israeli identity, its contradictions, and its conflicts, and of the "Israeli-ness fabrication" in the terms of the Frankfurt school, see Zuckerman (2001, 192–202).

4. This tension is underscored even more, when many stickers, or combinations of words, "choose" to use the "Koren" typeface, as seen in chapter 1, marked by its use in a popular printed edition of the Hebrew Bible.

5. See Anderson (1983); Herzfeld (1997, 10–11).

6. In a future study we intend to examine how individuals from different groups, especially Palestinians and Israeli Arabs, relate to the same stickers.

7. The names are all fictitious, preserving only the gender of the speaker.

8. Meimad is a political movement, founded in 1988, that aims to represent a largely religious constituency, while presenting a left-wing or centrist alternative to right-wing, religious Zionism.

9. Examples of similar stickers, which relate the centrality of Jerusalem to somatic metaphors of individual bodies, are "Jerusalem, without You I Am Half a Person" and "If I Forget Thee Jerusalem, May My Right Hand Wither."

10. See Herzfeld (1997, 10–11).

11. For the connection between nationalism and somatic metaphors see Herzfeld (1997, 5, 20). For the uses of adages that form a link between the body and the nation in Nazi rhetoric see, Mieder (1997, 9–38).

12. On blood as a key symbol marking intergroup boundaries, see Salamon (1993, 117–34). The use of blood as a conspicuous element in the rhetoric of the temple adherents, Jewish groups who place the reestablishment of the Jewish temple at the center of their messianic vision, has been pointed out in the excellent work of Chen (2001, 40–44).

13. Yamit, a settlement in the northern Sinai desert, was evacuated because it had been built on territory that was returned to Egypt. It has become a symbol of evacuation within the framework of the Middle East peace process.

14. The first two interviewees saw a connection with the abandonment of Yousouf Madhat, a Druze IDF soldier, during the battle over Joseph's tomb in Nablus, during the early days of the Al-Aksa Intifada.

15. *Yesha* is an acronym for *Yehuda, Shomron, ʿAza* (Judea, Samaria, and Gaza), the territories occupied by Israel in 1967. The Hebrew word *Yeshaʿ* means "salvation"; thus, the acronym expresses the messianic worldview of many of the settlers.

16. The Hebrew term *Milḥemet aḥim*, which appears in this sticker, means "civil war," in the meaning of war within the Jewish groups' population.

17. The phrase *for generations to come* simulates the graphic format of the *Dor Shalom* (Generation of Peace) sticker, a pro-peace volunteer movement that was founded following the assassination of Prime Minister Rabin.

18. *Now* in red and the other words in black.

19. Kahanists are followers of Rabbi Meir Kahane, who founded an extremist political movement that was outlawed in Israel because of its racist platform.

20. *Din rodef* refers to a status defined in Jewish law, which permits shedding the blood of someone considered a traitor.

21. For "One ʿAm—Many Colors," see figure 2.5. This slogan also appeared in relation to the Ethiopian Jews, as a group whose identity caused a discourse to surface concerning the connection between race and religion in Judaism. For a discussion, see Salamon (2001). For "Why Did You Give Them Guns?" as well as many other stickers discussed here see figure 2.2.

22. This popular sticker is documented in figure 2.3. This figure also documents a private domestically fabricated version that says *"Ha'Am* with Golani" (Golani, an infantry unit of the IDF). Another private sticker, which responds to this one, is the huge poster on a car window in Tel-Aviv bearing the following slogans, each written on a separate row, as shown in figure 2.4: *"Ha'Am* with the Golan, *Ha'Am* with the Jordan Valley; *Ha'Am* with the Land, the Jew That Does Not Wander."

23. Note the use of sensory rhetoric, and specifically the sense of smell, as a hermeneutic tool. Mention of the "smell" of a sticker was not a singular occurrence and recurred in the speech of many other interviewees. For the reference of icons of taste and smell and their connection to a national "gastronomy" see, among others, Appadurai (1988).

24. See a version similar to "I Choose God and the Unity of Israel" in figure 2.3.

25. Sheinkin is a shop-lined street in the center of Tel-Aviv, in the residential area between the Carmel Market place and the wealthy Rothschild Boulevard. Most of the businesses and restaurants, fashion clothing and jewelry stores, art and design shops, music and video rentals, new-age haunts, and so on, cater to a young, bohemian, and cosmopolitan clientele. Sheinkin is often spoken of as a local attempt to imitate fashionable urban areas like Greenwich Village or Soho, and since the 1980s Israelis have imagined it is the strongest emblem of the hedonistic turn in Israeli culture and dissociation from national ideologies. Florentine, a poor neighborhood in southern Tel-Aviv, close to Jaffa, has undergone partial gentrification, with an influx of young urban dwellers since the 1990s, opening cafés, bars, restaurants, and design studios; it has on the whole a more downscale, grungy, and politically radical character, somewhat like New York's East Village.

26. Play on words meaning, roughly, "a state based on Jewish law—you can kiss the state good-bye."

27. This sticker evoked strong emotional responses from most of the interviewees and was interpreted by most in a religious or politico-religious context. Despite the fact that this was not mentioned in any of the interviews, it clearly resonates with the biblical verse "let your camp be holy" (Deuteronomy 23:15).

28. "Modesty patrols" are vigilante groups in the Haredi community that use threats and violence to enforce norms of modesty in the community and to bar damaging outside influences.

29. The concepts of purity (*tohara*) and impurity (*tum'a*), and their deep cultural and social associations, evoked the strong response in relation to these stickers.

30. Bney-'Akiva is a religious youth organization, affiliated with the religious Zionist parties, broadly identified with right-wing pro-settlement politics.

31. See figure 2.6. Many of the interviewees related to the size of the stickers. Size is an indicator of importance and seriousness; large stickers were considered to be "above all small disputes," as tied to larger cosmological truths. Other interviewees belittled the message on the large stickers and viewed their size as proof of their falseness ("maybe they need to be large, so that God, who is so far away, will be able to see them").

32. Aryeh Der'i, among the charismatic founders of the Shas movement, enjoyed a meteoric rise to power in the late 1980s and was appointed minister of the interior in 1998 before he turned thirty. During the 1990s Der'i was investigated and later indicted on charges of bribery. He was sentenced in 1999 to a four-year prison sentence. The Der'i case became a rallying point for ethnic political struggles in Israel, with his supporters charging the Israeli judicial establishment of persecuting him because of he represented a threat to Ashkenazi political hegemony.

33. Thus, for example, as this chapter was being written, a new sticker slogan was documented: "The Holy Land for the Holy People."

34. Although beyond the scope of this volume, it is important to note in this context the sticker slogans: "*Yesha*ʻ is Here," "My Home Is in Kedumim, Ariel, Karnei Shomron," and so on. A privately produced sticker, relevant to this connection, appears in figure 2.4. For the spatial aspects of Israeli identity, see, for example, Ben Ari and Bilu (1997). For the practical and symbolic aspects of the struggle between Gush Emunim and Shalom Akhshav in shaping Israeli space, see Feige (2002).

35. In this context it is interesting to think of the "ritual" aspect of sticking on and peeling off as part of broader Israeli culture, similar to the phenomenon documented and analyzed by Tamar Katriel (1988) among schoolchildren who busy themselves with "sharing" and "exchanging" of various collections (including stickers) as a folkloric expression of communication in negotiations. The removal of a sticker, even if stuck to one's own car, was perceived as magically potent, when interviewees spoke about "bad luck" that befell them after removing a sticker with a religious message.

36. The belittling of the stickers' importance both within academic research and in the media is also noted by Bloch (2000a, 49).

3   Kinetic Cosmologies

Sovereign and Sovereignty

As we have seen in chapters 1 and 2, Israeli stickers create an unstable medium that expresses deeply rooted shared assumptions about the world, while enabling individuals to proclaim their political and religious identities. These often appear in terms that challenge onlookers to formulate their own views and counterarguments. At the end of chapter 2, we noted the appearance of religious stickers that linked political discussions to scriptural or divine authority.[1] Yet several years after the assassination of Yitshak Rabin, it seemed as if the curtain had descended on sticker discourse. Even if some new stickers occasionally emerged during this latent period, the previous sticker discourse, with its highly charged voices, impulses, and creativity, entered a period of hibernation.

But this silence turned out to be a stage of incubation. The demise of the stickers dealing with current events made way for the germination and flourishing of a flower of faith, turned toward an atemporal mythic past. As the polemical political stickers grew rarer, new expressions appeared, filled with popular energy that now linked traditional sacred passages with a wide variety of contemporary interpretations, some of them subversive.

Alongside the torn and faded remnants of the turbulent political discussions of previous years, we now witness a new corpus, dominated by values derived from the world of religious faith.[2]

The Visions of the Chariot

In the documentation carried out between August 2010 and August 2011, we photographed hundreds of cars bearing faith-based stickers and clearly witnessed the spread of this phenomenon.[3] While in the past faith-based stickers were but one variation in the cluster of popular political discourse, over the years they blossomed into a new and separate corpus distinguished in various ways. By extricating themselves from the existing sociopolitical discourse, they sought to mark out a superior position. Whereas the stickers of the previous clusters typically bore a uniform and unremarkable format, the appearance of the faith-based stickers on Israeli vehicles was also marked by a change in aesthetics. The previous stickers were small in size and uniform in format; now we witness very large stickers, including verses spread over the entire rear windows or sides of cars.

Among the most "devout," an entire car was consecrated as a *mikdash me'at* (minor sanctuary) (see figure 3.1).[4] In this sense, the faith stickers testify to the continued search for channels of material expression of religious faith; in present-day Israel, verses from Jewish sources are fashioned, printed, stuck on cars, and transmitted.[5] They become ingrained in the materiality of the vehicle, and the verses speed their way over the space of the road.

Throughout the generations, Judaism invested spiritual and material resources to preserve its religious culture through texts written by hand or printed in books, objects that become sacred for the faithful. Their material sanctity and the commandment to preserve them are exemplified when they, like any scrap of writing that contains sacred names, requires *geniza*—preservation and/or burial—and may not be torn, erased, or thrown away.[6]

The praxis of the transfer of sacred verses from holy books to the metallic bodies of cars creates a new experience, arousing a broad range of sentiments among a wide variety of Hebrew-reading publics. This praxis transforms the vehicle—an earthly, mobile, global, mass-produced, and essentially not-Jewish medium, though one of significant monetary and symbolic value for its owners—into a sacred object. This startling innovation in the worship of God arouses tempestuous feelings of acceptance and rejection, transgressing the enigmatic space dividing the traditional from the contemporary, the private from the public, the sacred from the profane. These feelings of approval and strong opposition reflect the boundaries of the permissible and the prohibited, and they refer to a set of constantly challenged relationships between the materiality of religious articles and religious texts from the past, on the one hand, and new technologies and conceptions of the world, on the other. Thus, the stickers are a battleground between competing cosmologies.

The insights in this chapter are based on the documentation of sticker-bearing vehicles and on interviewees' reactions to photographs of those stickers. The interviewees were Hebrew readers, who are the target group of these stickers.[7]

The corpus of faith-based stickers focuses on several themes. This chapter examines the corpus and the interpretative reading of them, through a number of key stickers that presented themselves as essential for the understanding of the current discourse. In the hermeneutic understanding of the subjects of our research, these stickers proved to be the textual-ideological core, generating additional stickers, just as *Shalom, Ḥaver* generated a wide variety of new stickers in response.

After briefly presenting the corpus of stickers and discussing their aesthetic and thematic significance for various interlocutors (including their authors, distributors, and readers), we focus on two especially large and widely distributed stickers. These stickers summarized the prominent themes of the discourse in a

Figure 3.1. All religious stickers. Among others: *Na Naḥ Naḥma Naḥman MiUman* (Na Nah Nahma Nahman from Uman); *Ten Ḥiyukh—Hakol LeTova* (Give a Smile—All Is for the Best); *'Ani 'Ohev Kol Yehudi* (I Love Every Jew); *Shabbat, Shalom* (Sabbath Peace); *'Ein Lanu 'Al Mi Lismokh, 'Ela 'Al 'Avinu SheBaShamaim* (There's No One We Can Rely On, Only Our Father in Heaven). Courtesy of Carmella Abdar.

particularly effective manner. Prior to the analytic moves that are at the core of this chapter, I invite the readers to sample some of the "temple cars" and some reports of the emotions aroused by them.

Ḥagit, newly religious, whose windshield bore the sticker "Smile, You're the Son of a King," explained that her previous cars were full of faith-based stickers:

> People of our generation have nothing to live for. People feel this, they know there is a creator of the world. This leads them to a certain view, that they have no one to rely on any more. No politics, nothing. There is only one entity that can bring them unlimited good. In the past, they spoke of politics and searched for someone to lean on, someone who could save them in their distress. Some prime minster or another. So people distributed stickers all the time, [saying] "come support this one or that one." But the final conclusion is the conclusion of faith. Do research and you'll see that we're really at the end. People collapsed;

things fell. So they won't put their trust in them anymore, so they distribute the true stickers. It's not on the level of political stickers. It's not something they invent. It's something that exists! It's real! They took it from an age-old book and it's still right. It's true. 'Cause I really see that there's no one (else) to lean on.

Shalom, a Breslov Ḥasid (a Hasidic group that attracts many newly religious Jews), whose car was covered with stickers (figure 3.1), explained:

I've gone through a number of cars. One of them I spray-painted and put loads of stickers on it. . . . Now you show some guy (the stickers) "everything is for the best," "no despair," "be happy"—it's exactly the opposite of what's in the world. It's a protest! . . . Stickers—no one doesn't like them; no one opposes them. No one will say: "I've got them already." Everyone just says, "Bring more." There are some people who really beg for them. People who are ready to turn my car upside down to find a sticker that they once saw, and it does them good and they want it.

David, a former *haredi*, said of this photo:

I know those people. . . . They're stuck, they really want to push what they think. I'm telling you—these are people who want to push their views. Proselytizers. . . . I hate talking to them. They don't listen to others; they just want to impose themselves. Look, the ones who cover their cars with stickers want to say something. They want to fix the people of Israel. If it's one sticker, I figure, maybe he just put it there, just so. But if there are a lot of stickers—that's someone who's preoccupied with the idea of bringing the people of Israel back to religion. Those are the kinds of people who think that the secular are really miserable, and that "we" need to show them the light and tell them—"look, that's how it should be!"

Michaela, religious, reacted toward that same car:

Anger. I exclude myself or them from the people that I want to talk to. Actually, there are many things here: "repentance through love"—Judaism in decline—that's one thing. Now—"Moshiach now" and all that, that's childishness, a lack of willingness to take responsibility; they don't want to deal with anything! "Return to our father in heaven" is the same thing: we have a merciful father, who loves us without conditions, and us alone. It's warm and pleasant and familial, and we don't have to prove anything, we don't have to deal with anything, because all is given to us because "thou hast chosen us," in the sense of—we are essentially already the chosen ones, we don't need to deal with anything, to prove anything. There are also different periods reflected on this car—those of the "Moshiach" have vitality, strong energy. We also love babies, we love Jews, we love Jews' babies, that's it, really!

Sticking with God, Sticking with Jews

On an explicit level, many of the stickers in the corpus deal with relations between God and his people. Here, too, we should note that the common basis for the entire discourse is that the people (*Ha'Am*) referred to in the faith-based stickers is the entire Jewish people. Thus, the corpus creates and emphasizes communality, which is first and foremost a call to faith and, consequently, the fulfillment of the system of obligations that derive from this faith.

In general, and as illustrated through the four reactions presented above, the viewers read the corpus as a single unit and make no effort to discern the specific affiliation of a particular sticker. Nevertheless, some of the interviewees undertook a kind of detective work that also contained a mild polemic. They focused their inquisitive gaze, among other things, on the ways of addressing God, on the precision in quotation of the sources of the sticker verses, and on images related to the sources of the text, as well as other hints related to the origins of the sticker. For example, the form of address toward God and the relation with the people of Israel implied in it were the object of criticism and derision, which took the form of arguments within the larger group of the faith-based public, who distinguished among various smaller groups. Thus, the main options created a variety that hints at the faith affiliation of the sticker and the sticker creator's familiarity with the rules prevailing among religious publics. For example, we find the name of God on the stickers in a variety of forms: *'elohim* (Lord), *'eloheynu* (our Lord), *'elokeynu* (our Lord), *ha'el* (the Lord), *YHVH* (the tetragrammaton), *hashem* (the Name—indicating that the tetragrammaton cannot be uttered), *H'* (the letter H'—*heh*, either the first letter of hashem, or a synecdoche of YHVH), *D'* (the letter D'—*dalet-*, the fourth letter of the Hebrew alphabet, is a popular reference to the four letters of YHVH), *ha-KB"H* (the Holy One, Blessed Be He), *'avinu shebashamayim* (our father in heaven), *'abba* (father), *ribbono shel 'olam* (sovereign of the universe), and even *milvado* (none other than him).[8] As we found in the interviews we conducted, the specific title used to refer to God is significant in the reading of the sticker and in its interpretation, both on the normative and the emotional levels. Thus, we witness a discourse presented to outsiders as monolithic and unifying, while preserving nuances of debate and disagreement for insiders. The initiators, producers, and distributors were particularly aware of this duality. They declared that they sought to transmit a unanimous unity of opinion toward the outside, while poking gentle barbs at the cognoscenti.

In documenting the corpus of faith-based stickers, several key topics were salient. Thus, through the stickers, popular discourse, which reflects the voice of the people, draws coordinates of the map of its relationship with God, and marks the boundaries of this conversation. Most prominent were the stickers dealing with revival and "return" to religious faith (for example, "Precious Jew! Don't Wait for Tomorrow Lest It Be Too Late. Return to Our Father in Heaven"; "Why Do You Slumber? Rise Up and Call to Your Lord, for Only He Can Save You"; "Come Let Us Bow Down . . . before the God Who Created Us"; "Precious Jew, Remember the Sabbath Day to Keep It Holy"; "Precious Jew, Remember the Day of Atonement to Keep It Holy"); messianic redemption (for example, "The Time of Redemption Is Very Near"; "One More Second, and He'll Be Here"; "Moshiach Now"); joy, love, thanks (for example, "Give a Smile—All Is for the Best"; "The Creator of the World Loves Everyone"; "It Is a Great Commandment to Be Happy Always"; "Love Your Neighbor as Yourself"; "Love of Israel"; "I Love Every Jew"; "The Order of the Day—Gratuitous Love"; "Thanks Very Much to God"; "Thanks for Everything, Lord of All"; and many more); female modesty (for example, "Modest Girls Prevent Disaster"; "The Beauty of a Woman Is in Her Modesty"; "The Glory of the Princess Is on the Inside"; "Daughter of Israel, Your Honor Is in Your Modesty"; "An Entire Country Says Thanks! To the Modest Woman"); praise of rabbis (for example, "How Fortunate We Are and How Good Is Our Portion That We Had the Privilege of Coming Near to Our Rabbi"; "If Not for Our Rabbi, We Would Be 'Gone,'"; and, of course, the widespread sticker of a group among the Breslov Ḥasidim—"Na Naḥ Naḥma Naḥman from Uman").[9]

The special relationship between God and the people of Israel is depicted in connection with several themes, each of which has a wide variety of expressions: the relations between fathers and sons with its many implications (as expressed through stickers like "Smile, You're the Son of a King"; "Father, Have Mercy"; "The Holy One, Blessed Be He, We Are Your Children"; "We Have No One to Lean On but Our Father in Heaven"; "Whom Can We Lean On? On Our Father in Heaven"; "You Are Children to the Lord Your God, Your Father in Heaven"; and more).[10] Unconditional love between God and the Jewish people, and by extension, among members of the Jewish people, is an increasingly found theme. For example, "God Loves Every Jew"; "The Holy One Blessed Be He, Loves You"; "The Holy One, Blessed Be He, We Love You"; "I Love Every Jew"; "God Loves You"; "Whoever You Are, Whatever You Are, the Holy One Blessed Be He Truly Loves You"; and even "God [with a depiction of a heart] you."[11]

Another central and powerful theme in the faith-based sticker discourse deals with the relations between the sovereign and his subjects and is related to expressions of domination and power in the world, as well as to fundamental monotheistic proclamations. For example, "God Is the Sovereign"; "God Is King"; "Hear O Israel, the Lord Our God, the Lord Is One"; "There Is None Other Than He"; and even "There Is No Ruler (*shalit*) in the Land" (see figures 3.2, 3.3, and 3.4).

Figure 3.2. A collection of religious stickers, most prominent of which is *'Ein 'Od Milvado* (There Is None Other Than Him).

And the People Saw the Voices (Exodus 20:14)

As mentioned earlier, we took photographs of stickers on cars, which were later presented to interviewees who were asked to relate to the photo in any way they chose.[12] The photos included a broad corpus of faith-based stickers, and the relations expressed toward them provide the basis for analysis of tendencies toward unity or fragmentation. Given the nature of the discourse, the composition of the group of interviewees is of great importance; hence, interviewees identified with a wide range of groups in Israel were included. Their attitudes toward the stickers generate a multivocal field of interpretations. The interviewees' reactions were related to their self-identification on a "faith-based" axis; their self-positioning on this scale confirmed standard popular categories—secular, traditional, national-religious, *ḥaredi*—frequently accompanied by personal fine-tuning attributes. They understood their own positioning as essential for their understanding of the present discourse.[13]

The reflexive mechanism the stickers seek to provoke is graphically illustrated through the words of Shalom, a young man who had become newly religious

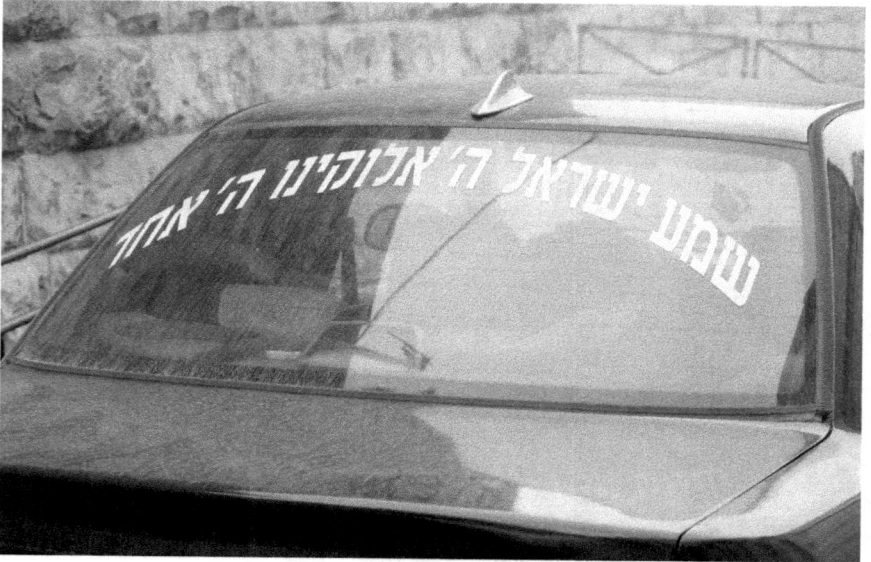

Figure 3.3. *Shema' Yisrael 'Adonay 'Elokeynu 'Adonay 'Eḥad* (Hear O Israel, the Lord Our God, the Lord Is One).

several years previously and who was an active distributor of stickers. He responded to a general question on the stickers he distributed:

> If you decide to transmit a message, better do so in two words. . . . Stickers are good, you give someone a sentence, and he'll arrive at other things on his own. That's a sticker! What's a sticker? A sticker is to give someone two words for him to go with, to arouse questions: What is this? What does it mean? So that he be interested, and if a person is interested in something, the answer will come to him on its own.

His response gets at the heart of the matter. The invitation to reflexive thinking is concentrated in the two central stickers (and their offshoots) that were chosen for detailed analysis in this chapter, each in its own way (see figures 3.2 and 3.3). Both of these increasingly proliferous stickers are derived from founding verses and constitute a voice consciously effacing the plurality of possibilities: the canonical status of the verses is not open to discussion; their message is beyond debate, as it relates to the singularity of God and his name. In addition, their appearance in giant letters intensifies the message of uniqueness that they convey.

Figure 3.4. *'Ein Shalit Ba'Arets* (There Is No Ruler [*shalit*] in the Land).

"Hear O Israel" and "There Is None Other Than Him"

These stickers are fundamental verses or verse fragments, both from the Bible (Deuteronomy). The verse "Hear O Israel, the Lord our God, the Lord is one" (6:4) became the common exhortation of faith in tradition, the most basic credo of Judaism. The accepted view is that many Jews died sanctifying the name of God, with this verse on their lips. This verse is included in the morning and evening prayers; it also completes the fast of the Day of Atonement, following the closing (*ne'ila*) prayer, in a loud call to recognize God as the one and only sovereign deity. In addition, the verse is part of the chapters written on parchment and placed in the phylacteries and *mezuzot*. The recital of this prayer, the *Shema'*, is seen as the most personal call identified with Jewish faith. Among believing Jews, parents are commanded to teach it to their children as soon as they learn how to speak.[14]

The words *there is none other than Him*, at the end of the verse "It has been clearly demonstrated to you that the Lord alone is God; there is none other than Him" (Deuteronomy 4:35), are a fundamental declaration of monotheism. On most stickers, they appear mainly in the form of the concluding words, often followed by three dots (see figure 3.2).

As texts on cars, these two verses appear mostly in large letters covering the entire back window, and sometimes the sides, as well. Let us now listen to the various readings—both of initiators and of addressees—evoked by these stickers. They relate to the texts themselves, the relationship among various texts, and the unique aesthetic appearance of the two stickers.

Michal, "religious, borderline *haredi*":

> If only, if only we could all feel strongly this verse, the entire people of Israel and call to him together! . . . It's in big letters—that means that one must turn in that direction, to pray to the Holy One Blessed Be He—who in turn, turns and summons Israel! Perhaps he [the car owner] sees this as a mission. It's not that he got a sticker on the road or in the mail. It's really important for him to transmit a message. Yes, the size is important—it is a stronger statement. More people will see it; it's written right in the middle of the car!

Abraham, "national-religious," got out of a car bearing two stickers, "God Is King" and, right underneath it, almost disintegrated, "Hear O Israel, the Lord Our God, the Lord Is One." In response to the question as to why he placed the stickers on his car, he answered concisely, "In order to disseminate the name of God. So that as many people as possible see it!"

Malka, borderline national-religious/*haredi*, emerged from a car full of stickers and was asked about the sticker "Hear O Israel":

> For some people, this is the first time they encounter these verses, so even through the mere act of their reading this, they have sanctified the name of God. Perhaps through this, something will be aroused in them; this is the exaltation of the name of the unity of God, and I see this as a very good thing!

'Eran, secular, but not against religion:

> From a religious point of view, it's not certain that this is okay. It's just crazy; it doesn't seem right to place a prayer [there]. It's not like a slogan. Look, man, birds shit on it . . . it bothers me that they place a prayer there.

Mimi, secular:

> You know, this reminds me of the cars from East Jerusalem with the "mashalla." It's the same thing; it's a kind of amulet. Not an amulet but a way of fulfilling one's obligation. To stick the Baba Sali there and let him do the work.[15] "Hear O Israel" has, of course, a more accessible meaning because it's mine, too. Here, too, we have "the L-rd" (*'elokeynu*), and the hyphen upsets me. In my head, it gives me the feeling that [if I were the initiator or owner of the car bearing the sticker] if "Lord" (*'eloheynu*) isn't good enough for me, I must be more devout, I must be better than those who say "*'eloheynu*" (Lord). A kind of holier-than-thou hypocrisy.

Nira, traditional, religious:

Every day when I pray I say this. The fact that "Israel should hear that God is the one"! There's nothing wrong with having it on the car.

Shira, secular, but not against tradition:

It's outrageous that they have to put it this way! In my opinion, it makes the whole thing somewhat cheap! Really, it insults me. This is not the place for it!

Adam, very secular:

A synagogue, I don't know. It doesn't bother me to see it on a car. An act of defiance. But I tend to attribute this to the private realm of the car owner. There is, on the one hand, a turning to the public, but it is not really a call to someone specific. I have no opposition to people that believe that the Lord is our Lord.

Yaron, national-religious:

It's in Blessing of the Moon letters.[16] It's read in Blessing of the Moon letters. It has to . . . it's something that everyone should see! . . . Immediately, I think—no good! It's the name of God and it's not good that they throw it on cars. It's a verse that people say in situations, like, in situations . . . they say it in happy situations and on the threshold of death . . . the spreading of some sort of idea . . . it is just an expression of identity: there's something like that, pay attention, that it not leave your head! This is not good: you place it in the holy ark, in the prayer book, you say it in prayer, but it's not something you throw on cars. That should be, like, published; it's not something that you stick on somewhere. According to Jewish law, it's not good.

Ya'akov, former *haredi* Ḥasid:

I tell myself that whoever put this there is a religious person, a sort of semi-'arsawat, 'arsim, the ones with those white skullcaps, the ones that, like, want to be "with it."[17]
  There's also the story I heard about this when I was still in the yeshiva: The head of the yeshiva in Bnei Brak bought himself a Mercedes-S600 and the Arab who worked in the building went and snatched the car keys and stole it. He drove with the car to the army blockade [at the entrance to the occupied territories], but the soldier at the blockade saw the "Hear O Israel" sticker, 'cause some yeshiva student stuck one on the bottom of his car, and so he was caught with the "Hear O Israel" sticker and they found out that the car was stolen. So thanks to the sticker, the car was returned to its owner. I heard this from the head of the yeshiva himself.

Yitshak, former Lithuanian Ḥasid:

This, in general, is even more aggressive. Whether you want to or not, we'll shove God up your A-S-S [*laughs*]. And with pleasure! That's what comes into my mind when I see this.

'Avidov, religious:

> This is a classic declaration of faith, and I don't understand what it's doing on a car. In this sentence, I see a profanation. . . . When it's a direct quote, "I await your salvation, O Lord," "there is none other than Him," "they shall build me a sanctuary," all this seems somewhat disrespectful, cheap.

In reaction to the torn sticker of "Hear O Israel," which he was subsequently shown, he added:

> It's like the street address "Rabbi Kook" on a garbage can in the street. Here it cries out . . . it's disrespectful. People went to their deaths with "Hear O Israel"— and so big, what for?"

Avraham, Sephardic *haredi*, standing by his car, which bore this sticker, explained:

> So that whoever is behind me remembers that there is none but the king, king of kings! He should remember who rules this world. That's it!

Yaffa's, secular, car bore a large sticker with the words *'en 'od milvado* (None other than him). She said:

> This was put there by my son, who is newly religious. One day he took the car and returned it to me like this. I told him, but I drive this car on the Sabbath— that's OK? So he answered: "With God's help, maybe the car won't drive on the Sabbath anymore."

Michal, religious, borderline *haredi*:

> For me, that's automatically the Holy One Blessed Be He—there's none be-sides the Holy One Blessed Be He. . . . That means—there's no reality in the world other than what God has determined. Now—what does he want to say? I wouldn't put this on the car—even though I very much believe in it. Because it's something, it's such an elevated and supreme value, so if you want to transmit it to the surrounding world, a message to the world, then you have to live it through your life and thus transmit it onward. Apparently his way to tell others is to tell people, "Guys, wake up. All this is from God; wake up!" He took the effort to write this, it's not a mistake. It's to tell people to wake up.

Rami, secular:

> Good, OK, again the monotheistic belief in one God. On the other hand, there may be all sorts of idols in the modern world, all kinds of technologies, cars, blindly following fashions, and so on—so he says, man, leave all this nonsense, 'cause there's none other than him. Everything, everything, a defiance of modernity.

Yaron, national-religious:

This is also something designed to express the unity of God. It's also something strange. OK, it's a bit better than "Hear O Israel," but I think that whoever disseminates these things is not conscious. I think he's not conscious of the depth of the message that it should express; otherwise, he wouldn't advertise it just so. These are not things that should be put in such places. . . . He [the owner of the car] addresses everyone. The entire Jewish people: "Be aware! Be aware that there is, there is an idea like this in reality. Know—this exists!" From a halakhic point of view, it's better than "Hear O Israel"—aside from the fact that it meets the mark better. From an advertising point of view, it's more direct—a very short phrase that does the job. From the point of view of the message, it seems to work better.

Shalom, newly religious (and active in the manufacture and distribution of stickers):

Look, if I now put on a sticker that reads "God Is the King" or "There Is None Other Than Him" or "There Is a God (*HaShem*)." Things like that, people may feel threatened by them. So I do stuff that's for everyone . . . I don't know who will see it. I don't know; I have to do something that will not offend him. So this *Na Nah Nahma Nahman* can't offend him, because he has no idea what it is. . . . Maybe it makes some people laugh. It looks strange, but it isn't threatening. Maybe they'll say he's crazy . . . I won't make a large advertisement now, something huge "There Is None Other Than Him." I'll make a small sticker, not something huge.

Nira, religious-traditional:

It's strange to see this in motion, but it doesn't bother me. I actually see this quite a bit on cars. First of all, I know that the man, the driver, believes in God. He's a religious person. A secular person who finds this on a car he bought . . . would scrape it off. It also says that we, too, should understand that there is none other than him, not just me [who already knows it]. You, too, should know!

Michaela, religious:

To transfer the entire world of actions, struggle, and responsibility to God. Childish behavior. Simply a people that hasn't grown up. To praise his name— he is high and exalted; we are small. And if we are small, we don't need to do anything. He will do it, for he alone has the ability.[18] This gives a stamp of approval to the owner of the car; [it says] that he is an honest person. The aura of a moral person . . . maybe it's a plumber who wants to promote himself; this broadcasts that he won't cheat.

Adam, very secular:

Letters on the windshield—a bit more interesting than the stickers of normal size. A more blatant announcement. The reference is to God of course—there is none other than him, or as currently relevant, maybe the story about the rabbis who only recognize the sovereignty of the rabbis and do not recognize democratic rule. There is nothing beyond divine sovereignty!

Limor, religious-traditional:

First of all, the letters are biblical letters.[19] What is this? He is the one God? What, are there pagans around here? It's strange. You can understand it, that you should trust only in God, as if there is no one else upon whom you can lean or trust in but him.

Ḥaim, conservative:

This is from the verse "It has been clearly demonstrated to you that the Lord alone is God; there is none other than Him." It reminds me immediately of Simchat Torah, when the verse is repeated on the eve of the festival and throughout the day, when the holy ark is opened, before the procession around the podium and the dancing with the Torah scrolls.

First the Text, Then the Translation

As the voices of the interviewees indicate, the uniqueness or the unity of the divine power is at the core of these two stickers. Interviewees were in agreement as to the message embodied in the stickers, whether they identified with them or disagreed. These two stickers, however, are not found in isolation, and their particular influence derives from the aura granted them, which cast light on other stickers in the corpus. Moreover, in the research we conducted, they appeared to be an enthymeme on themes of sovereignty and power.[20]

A rhetorical path links the two biblical stickers and other faith-based stickers with political ones. This path is traversed by those proclaiming, "I have a Lord, God Is Sovereign," "God Is the King," and "There Is No Ruler (*shalit*) in the Land." These lead from the faith message, seemingly devoid of political debates, to political messages. This process is deciphered as religio-political in the readings of interviewees, who related to the stickers "I Have a God"; "God Is Sovereign"; "God Is King"; and "There Is No Ruler (*shalit*) in the Land."

Michal, religious, borderline *haredi*:

I identify with this completely; there is no other sovereign. He is the sovereign! I experience this myself in everyday life—that he is the only place I can turn to in *everything*! God is king, like, I can't think of anything else.

'Eran, secular, but not against religion:

It's ingenious that the letter is the thing, and that it has, the letter, a crown.[21] "Li" [to me], something egocentric, sad, as if God needs me. I assume that most of them are newly orthodox, although, of course, the newly orthodox influence Jewish culture. There is a sadly intense dependency. All the time they say, "*abba*" [daddy] . . . "Daddy, you're a saint." This gives positive reinforcement to your dad, who helped you out.

Mimi, secular:

[*laughs*] There are stickers I've never seen before! Did you photograph this in Jerusalem? This is so weird that is just made me laugh. . . . I have respect for the person who decided to post this. But that God is sovereign is such a deep denial of democracy that I can only laugh, and automatically not relate to the deeper meaning of it. In fact, I prefer not to deal with the deeper meaning of it, because it's very dangerous. It is a very dangerous statement. If I would see this [sticker] in the street, I would simply laugh and say it's weird and continue on my way.

Rami, secular:

This was done in a way that reminds us of an agenda—pages torn out of an agenda, on which is written that Thursday: God is sovereign. That's my association, in any case. A declaration of faith—not demanding, provoking, requesting—just someone declaring their faith.

Yaron, national-religious:

First of all, this is a newly orthodox person, it's someone who just started out today. Otherwise, it would not be so urgent for him to announce it to the world. It's someone who's influenced and says—pay attention! . . . So he wants to transmit this onward. He has a message to tell to the world: "I've gotten into this business and I see who's in charge here, who's running the business." . . . Now: "I've got a Lord; God is sovereign," as if he's telling me a story: If some guy just blurts this out, that means that a few minutes ago, he didn't think that way, that God was sovereign—apparently, as far as he was concerned, somebody else was running the business. . . . He wants to transmit this onward, "now I know who's in charge."

Michaela, religious:

This is very non-Jewish, this thing. Jewish tradition is, on the contrary, not in heaven—since we received the Torah on Mount Sinai, commentary and practice places the keys in the hands of mankind. He is *definitely not* the sovereign. What does the verse "my children, you have defeated me" mean?[22] It says, that he is not the sovereign; people are the sovereign. So this is a very distorted Judaism.

Oded, secular:

Both in the size and shape of the letter *he* of God's name (*HaShem*). In the middle they made it look like on a ballot slip. This says that the vote you cast in the election booth is worthless and you have to choose God.

Shira, secular:

What is certain is that it's against the state of Israel and against the law. They want religious legislation. I really don't like this. It's scary!

Nira, traditional-religious:

This is to call to people, that they should know, that God is the king, and that there is no one other than him. There is no other king—that's clear!

'Eran, secular:

A clear opposition to the rule of flesh and blood. There is no other authority, no other source of power: sovereign, king, father.

Rami, secular:

Every believing Christian or Moslem would approve of this, that God is the king. A sort of generic profession of faith. This is an intense simple profession of faith.

Shalom, newly religious:

Those who printed "God Is the King," it's like the Breslov Ḥasidim who make a big fuss over Rabbi Naḥman, so they say that God is the king.

Adam, secular:

I only hope that it won't happen. People who live in a parallel society, who are not quite part of the broader society, of the consensus. They're separate; there's some sort of boundary. I saw something similar in the settlements in the territories, stickers that read "The Heart Burns for the King."

Yitsḥak—former Lithuanian *ḥaredi*:

This is ridiculous aggressiveness. God is the king. No one seriously thinks that God is the king. I think that even the person who stuck this on his car doesn't think that God is a replacement for the state, right? After all, on the inside, everyone knows that the state is the state and God is something else. Besides, it seems that he doesn't know what it is to be a *ḥaredi*.

Ḥaim, traditional secular:

Interesting. Maybe these are groups opposed to Chabad, and emphasize that God is the king and not the [Lubavitcher] Rebbe who is called the king, the Messiah?

'Anat, religious-traditional:

What's this? This is for Gil'ad Shalit or something, I guess.[23] I suppose that because they didn't bring back Gil'ad Shalit, so whoever rules (*shalit*) is not really the ruler.

'Eran, secular:

They combine criticism of the government and a call to return Gil'ad Shalit. The BS"D ["*BeSi'ata DiShmaya*" (with the assistance of heaven) at the top of the sticker] provides a religious authority. There is no ruler (*shalit*) in the land, says that there is a ruler in heaven. There are several oppositions here: Gil'ad Shalit is not here, the ruler does not rule, and there is a ruler in heaven.

'Avidov, religious:

Wow! This is nice! No *shalit* in the land—gotta think. Is *shalit* Gil'ad Shalit, who's not in the country, and then the BS"D on the top is somewhat misleading. This is not a religious proclamation, or that it says that there is no ruler on earth, but only in heaven, or that it says that our government does not rule: if you wish, this is an expression of support of Gil'ad Shalit, and if you wish, it is a call of defiance against the government.

Rami, secular:

This transmits the sense of chaos—that there is no judge and no justice, and these days [the interview took place during the riots leading to the deposition of Mubarak in Egypt] you think immediately of a mob without a ruler, that tends toward violence and so on. I also imagine that this is what happened to the soldier "shalit," to Gil'ad Shalit—that there is no *shalit*, it has two meanings. This was done by the religious, there is a BS"D on the side. Definitely ambiguous.

Mimi, secular:

Near 'Aza Road [next to the protest tent of the Shalit family] there are all sorts of slogans: "There's No Leader Ruling (*shalit*)" and stuff like that. This BS"D is interesting . . . this sticker mainly speaks to me of disappointment with the rulers, lack of faith in the rulers.

Michal, religious, borderline *ḥaredi*:

This horrifies me; it's sad for me to see this, I find this terrible. One of the most important commandments in Judaism is the redemption of prisoners, and no one is ready to do this. I find it difficult, the thing that they say that if they liberate him, there will be lots of terrorists; so I don't know. That's a thing that's difficult for me. . . . Whoever stuck this on is a Jew who really cares, who cares about Gil'ad Shalit. It's also clear that he is also frustrated with the leadership here in Israel; this makes it clear, and it's part of it.

Adam, secular:

On the one hand, like, that of Gil'ad Shalit, I guess that's what he intended. Here, too, there's a struggle. On the one hand, like everyone else here, I would be happy if Gil'ad Shalit would return, but whoever tries to bring him back through the BS"D that we see here, these are circles I don't identify with, and this creates a feeling of temporary repulsion. BS"D—that's also those who want to make him religious in the end. In any case, that there is no *shalit*, no ruler—that I agree to.

Yariv, secular, previously religious:

Look, good, BS"D is a religious person. This is interesting—it's a religious person who is disappointed with the right here, who have taken his land. It is ambiguous—this shitty government doesn't care to bring back Shalit. Not that I'm for him, but you don't do a thing, either.

Discussion

The faith-based discourse of stickers draws on sacred texts and daily practices to mobilize faith communities. This rich blend—or perhaps pastiche—of holy scripture and contemporary slang, of peeling stickers that produce generations of new stickers, illustrates the process of constant change in the worship of God in contemporary Israel. The phenomenon challenges any study of Judaism relying solely on venerable texts, while offering new insights into an Israeli society that, as "the state of the Jewish people," is shaped by this discourse—often more than it will admit.[24] While we will not speculate on the future of the stickers—or of Israeli society—we conclude with several observations on the directions that this discourse points to.

The kinetic arenas of Israel of 2010–11 provide the viewer with "converted" cars or perhaps cars "on the road to religion"; the private car becomes a religious article—it is transformed from vehicle to mystical chariot. Thus, through the verses that adorn it, the car becomes an intensification of the axis mundi, which passes through permanent sacred spaces such as the synagogue, or temporary ones like the sukka.[25] At the same time, the sticker is a popular artifact, readily available to all, a constantly changing phenomenon, in which new partners are invited to take part in an ongoing ritual arena, by constantly sticking on, peeling off, and adding new messages.[26] This combination creates a constant tension between the sacredness of the text and the transient nature of the medium, a tension frequently manifested in interviewees' responses.[27]

The sticker discourse in Israel of 2010–11 may be viewed as a Traveler's Prayer.[28] Like the prayer, it reveals an existential fear, linking universal aspects of the welfare of the traveler with collective faith, including a high degree of dependency embodied in them. In contrast with the turbulent political discourse of stickers that filled the roads in previous years, which still echoes in the realms of consciousness related to the road, current discourse transfers authority and responsibility to God. These stickers deny terrestrial authority with its multiple voices, and transfer it—in a public, exhibitionistic move—to a higher authority, to that of the "creator of the universe." Through this act, God is brought from heaven down to earth to fulfill the function of the national tranquilizer—an amulet that ensures the collective voyage, a project of nationalizing what the Traveler's Prayer is supposed to do for the individual—to prevent accidents and catastrophes. At the same time, it also powerfully transmits the anguish of the always possible, or even steadily approaching, cataclysm, which requires nothing less than divine intervention.

While on the overt level, the text renders all power to God and usurps the sovereignty of people and terrestrial authorities, it also mobilizes God for our side with all the might attributed to him, and makes him the personal and national insurance agent.[29] This multidirectional transformation employs the names of God in ways akin to the magical uses of the names on other occasions. If we employ the fundamental distinctions formulated by Roman Jakobson, we might say that the catchy messages, which serve also as jingles or as advertising slogans, embody the conative function, that of convincing the addressee to become religious. This function is intimately linked to the emotive function of the stickers— to express the feelings of the transmitter, to convince the addressee through emotional persuasion.[30] Many of the stickers in this cluster are typified by a rhetoric that is seemingly beyond dispute; this derives from their grounding in verses of sacred scripture, their unique graphic form, which links traditional and contemporary aesthetics, and their enormous size.[31] Thus, following Jakobson, their text and form activate the referential function, which combines in a unique way with the emotive and conative functions. The stickers' function may further be illuminated by the insights of speech act theory, with regard to the belief in their concrete effect.

The investigation of the corpus shows the faith-based stickers to be an ostensibly naïve objectification, devoid of all pretense, of the views and world order which they promote.[32] The faith-based stickers apparently look neither left nor right, fixing their gaze on the axis between heaven and earth, seemingly irrespective of the political views held by the car owners. In this way, the disappearance of the multivocal and argumentative political discourse from the Jewish space left a silence which made space for other authorities. The authority expressed through these stickers fashions a direct path between the individual and his or her creator and even between the entire Jewish people and the God who "chose" them. In this dynamic, the accessible, sticky, and temporary medium conveys "eternal" statements, beyond the ravages of time. Thus, the multivocal argument gives way to the authoritative declaration. But, as we have seen, many of the partners in this space were not responsive to this unifying message, and even among the receptive ones, many were upset with the means of its transmission. Thus, the present research turns out to dismantle the unity the stickers propose or impose on the interlocutors. This dismantling has yet to be expressed through the sticker discourse itself, which remains "frozen" and has not given rise to a deconstructing discourse, like that found in the political issues that arose at previous stages.

The choice of cars as the means of transmission of a faith-based worldview is not self-evident, though undoubtedly it results from the lively political sticker discourse that preceded it. The sticker discourse, which was fundamentally polemic in previous stages, has made way for a discourse that, so far, has generated no visible opposition on the roads.[33] Those opposing the faith message that arises are reluctant to react and exploit the arena of the road to present their opinions. The use of traditional and sacred texts in a contemporary and impermanent discourse does not arouse explicit arguments. This, in turn, results in a blurring of the multiple voices of the faith-based discourse. It seems that there is an agreement not to play with the fundamental verses. Thus, even if we find arguments in the current sticker discourse, they will be restricted and will not engage those verses.[34] Consequently, the interviewees' voices, many very opinionated, were found here only in the research field, rather than in the realm of public discourse. We might say that in deliberately avoiding argument, the "kosher" car, with the sticker discourse it helps sustain, becomes a stage for presenting sermons and facilitating the links with God—a kind of synagogue or temple, a movable medium of what presents itself as beyond all debate. Thus, the sticker discourse, whose multivocality was at the base of its popular force, asks all to join in a single Jewish voice, directed toward a messianic paradise, heralded by the cars on Israel's roads.

To a great extent, this is a discourse of verses and pseudoverses, which has a long tradition in Jewish folk speech, especially in the application of verses from various canonical texts as proverbs.[35] At the same time, the fundamental verses at the forefront of the kinetic stage facilitate, through semantic-ideological links, the infiltration of broader political (cosmological) as well as concrete contexts. As seen through the specific examples, the fundamental verses proclaiming the unity of God gave rise, whether on an overt or implied level, to political connections, which in turn arise from their hard-wired faith cosmology.

Yet, unifying rhetoric notwithstanding, additional circles of interpretation exist, in which these stickers exhibit implicit but significant arguments. Here, too, as in the previous clusters of stickers, we find argumentation over religious language, leadership, and understandings of faith.

The rhetoric and themes of the faith-based stickers focus on common sentiments and conceptions, which are expressed in the texts and in the links among the stickers when juxtaposed on a single car. The interpretations of the interview-

אֵין עוֹד מִלְבַדָּה....

Figure 3.5. *'Ein 'Od Milvada* . . . (There Is None Other Than Her . . .).

ees focused on the legitimacy of placing such messages on cars, on the specific religious identities of the car owners, and on the intentions revealed by these connections. Reactions included the "authenticity" of the verse quoted in the sticker, the question as to whether the verses (and especially the explicit mention of God's name) on cars is a desecration of the holy, what term is most appropriate in addressing God, and a variety of interpretations of the car owners' intentions. These speculations concerned the dissemination of faith, the use of the sticker as an amulet, the lack of confidence of those uncertain of the existence of God, infantile dependency, lack of responsibility (even to the extent of abandonment), faith in the power of the sticker to "revive" and strengthen faith, haughty and exclusionary expressions, strengthening of messianic promises, and even manipulative intentions designed to mark the driver as an honest person. The interviewees, whether sympathetic or hostile, fearful or apathetic, projected their generalizing interpretations on the stickers, seeing them as an expression of subversion or denial of any authority other than the divine.

The sovereignty of God was expressed by interviewees, expressly or implicitly, as one that overrides all human debate. From a conversation between holders of different opinions, the current interlocutors become children of the creator, who alone bears power and authority. The prominence of the reading of the stickers as a denial of terrestrial authority arises from the rhetorical power of the enthymeme. The discourse of faith-based stickers shapes a cosmology in which earthly arguments are of no importance; hence, action and social and political discourse become insignificant. Will the fundamental arguments witnessed in the interviews find their way onto cars on Israel's roads in the future?

Notes

1. See C. Noy (2011). Another political expression linked to cars in Israel is that of attaching ribbons in one of three colors. These ribbons accompanied the popular discourse on the evacuation of Jewish settlements from the Gaza Strip in 1995. The various colors represented differing attitudes toward the evacuation issue: orange for opposition, blue for agreement, and green for the Greens and aspects of environmentalism. For a comparative analysis of stickers on cars as expressions of identity, see, for example, Case (1992); Dasenbrock (1993); Endersby and Towle (1996).

2. In the previous phase of research, dealing with *Ha'Am* (see chapter 2), we mentioned several faith-based stickers that surfaced toward the end of the research period in 2003. This group of stickers included direct addresses by the Jewish people to God, including: "The Holy One Blessed Be He, We Love You"; "We Enthrone You"; "We Choose You"; and "We Are Your Children."

3. The complex network of ties between popular culture and religion has been the subject of scholarly research in various disciplines in recent years, among them art, religious studies, anthropology, folklore studies, and psychology. Special issues have been dedicated to the topic (such as, *material religion*, which serves as a platform for interdisciplinary research on the material expressions of faith and religious praxis). As for Judaism, the studies of Kravel and Bilu (2008); Bilu (2009); and Stolow (2006, 2007, 2010) are particularly relevant. For a comparative view, see Morgan (1998, 2005, 2010).

4. For a similar manifestation consider the Chabad-Lubavitch Hassidic group "Mitzva tanks"—vehicles utilized to reach out to nonobservant Jews and function as an "education center" or a "moving synagogue," widespread in the many countries, including Israel, where Chabad is present. For a study of the politic of Hassidic folklore in present present-day Israel as well as "return to the faith" folklore, see Yassif (1999, 371–459).

5. As with the verse from Ezekiel 1, which is known in Hebrew as *ma'ase merkava* (the Vision of the Chariot).

6. According to Jewish law, any written matter that contains one of the names of God, such as prayer books, Bibles, phylacteries, *mezuzot*, and other sacred writings may not be destroyed or erased. Such objects must be stored in a special repository—a *geniza*—or buried in consecrated ground. For a detailed study of traditional aesthetics of displaying the sacred name in Jewish *Shiviti-Menora* pictorial-texts, see Juhasz (2004).

7. An interesting expansion of the field, which is beyond the purview of this chapter, is the reading of the stickers by non-Jewish readers of Hebrew. A sticker like "There Is None Other Than Him" is in dialogue with the Moslem "credo," including the *fatiha*, the first part of the Quranic verse *Laa ilaha illa Allah* ("There is no God but Allah, and Muhammad is his messenger"), often placed on cars in Islamic spaces.

8. All these are substitutes for the name of God (bypassing the explicit expression in speech or in writing of God's holy name). They take different forms: substitute words or substitute sounds or letters and abbreviated forms. As seen, there are even substitutes for substitutes, as well as a variety of explanations regarding the evolution of the various forms.

9. The sticker "If Not for Our Rabbi, We Would Be 'Gone'" exceptionally uses the Arabic word *raht* (gone, doomed). This makes the sticker somewhat enigmatic, while at the same time linking it with Mizrahi in-group discourse. The "mantra" *Na Nah Nahma Nahman MiUman* (see figure 3.1) is linked to a subgroup among the Breslov Hasidism, colloquially known as Na Nachs, basing the mantra on the Hebrew letters of Rebbe Nahman's name. According to their tradition, the mantra was not used by Rebbe Nahman himself but was taught in the twentieth century by Rabbi Yisrael Ber Odesser. It has been widely diffused in graffiti and stickers throughout the country.

10. On the relations between God and the people of Israel as father-son relations, see Goshen-Gottstein (1987). The familial rhetoric is prominent in previous sticker clusters, as well. For example, in the *Ha'Am* cluster (see chapter 2), we find a rhetoric of brotherhood and ambiguous relations of closeness and competition, reflecting common blood and origin, as well as jealousy and strife. The familial rhetoric of relations between brothers among groups within the *'am* interacts with the relations of fathers and children; each familial relation places particular emotions in the foreground. This relation of fathers and sons aroused highly emotional reactions among interlocutors. These emotions, which were expressed in clear and often explicit words, covered a range between confidence and gratefulness, on the one hand, and repeated expressions of pain at the "childishness of the nation," on the other. The latter were expressed through derision and contempt—"weird," "irrelevant," "I could not care less," and so on. See, for example, Michaela's reaction in this chapter.

11. With respect to this group of stickers, there were some who spoke of the will not to frighten others, to create amiable relations. Thus, Shalom (a Breslov Hasid, newly religious) explained that his aim in the many stickers he placed on his car and also distributed was to foster an inclusive discourse that did not threaten or create relations with God based on threats. On the other hand, many interviewees opposed the very fact of the conversation between man and God, or messages in God's name: "What, is he our friend?" Some went so far as to criticize the missionizing message, and discerned racist or chauvinist implications in the sticker's addressing Jews alone or in its use of masculine forms.

12. Some of the interviews took place in front of a computer screen, in which I displayed the pictures of the stickers in various orders, while other interviewees were shown printed figures of those cars. In addition, I sometimes had the fortune to interview the owners of sticker-bearing cars alongside their automobiles. All interviews took place face-to-face, and I transcribed their reactions to each figure word by word.

13. This is in contrast to the interviews dealing with the clusters of political stickers, in which the interlocutors generally did not identify themselves politically and their political identity was revealed to me only after I asked, if at all.

14. On the history of the *Shema'*—the Jewish daily declaration of faith—see, for example, Elbogen (1993); Scheindlin (2001); Reif (2006, 107–25); Fleischer (2012, 763–97).

15. The "Baba Sali," (Praying Father) Rabbi Yisrael Abuhatsera (1890–1984), was a leading Moroccan rabbi and kabbalist. The interviewee refers here especially to his alleged ability to work miracles through his prayers.

16. Unlike most public prayers, which take place in the synagogue, the Blessing of the Moon is recited outside the synagogue, where the moon can be seen. The prayers are often printed on signs attached to the synagogue walls in huge letters.

17. *'Ars*—pimp, a derogatory Hebrew slang term for the Israeli stereotype of a low-class young man.

18. An interesting, explicit reference to driving responsibility and the sticker "There Is None Other Than Him," was found in an internet article that appeared on ynet, entitled "Driver, on the Road There's No One Other Than You," following a deadly accident on the way back from the annual Lag Ba'omer *hilula* in Meron: "The observance of traffic laws is a privilege of those who keep the Torah and its commandments! When, on the road, I see a car that has committed a severe moving violation and on the back window there's a sticker "no one other than Him," or "there's no one we can rely on." I think of the driver, since on the road there's really no one other than him, and with driving like that one can only rely on our Father in heaven, and I am possessed by great fear and despair" (Rabbi Shaul Wider, ynet *Yahadut*, www.ynet.co.il/home/0,7340,L-4403,00.html).

19. A font usually used for Torah scrolls or other sacred texts.

20. The enthymeme is a kind of incomplete argument, which includes premises that are assumed but not made explicit. It is based on a relation between a rhetorical link and an associative link. The enthymeme is usually employed in speeches or debates and is an argument with the rhetorical purpose of convincing the listener (Zoran 2002).

21. The crown is the ornamental flourish at the top of the Hebrew letter *lamed* in the sticker. In the reader's interpretation, the *lamed* also signifies *li*, for me. This form of *lamed* appeared in several contemporary political symbols.

22. "Not in Heaven" is commonly used as a justification for people's authority to interpret the Torah, an idea dealt with in the Talmud in the story of the Oven of Akhnai (Babylonian Talmud, Baba Metzia 59b). See also, for example, Walzer et al. (2000, 269).

23. Gil'ad Shalit is an IDF soldier held captive by Hamas in Gaza for more than five years. He was released in a prisoner exchange deal (*'Iskat Shalit*) in October 2011. When this sticker was documented, he was still held captive.

24. For a relevant discussion on the complex relations between competing worldviews secular and religious within the democratic, pluralistic society of a neutral state, and the need for a "translation proviso," see Habermas (2011). For more of his ideas on religion and the modern state, see especially his key writings on religious belief (2002, 2008).

25. For an analysis of the sukka as a temporal and mobile space of cosmological meanings, see Hasan-Rokem (2012).

26. It is interesting to think of the "ritual" activity of sticking on and peeling off as part of broader Israeli culture, akin to the phenomenon that Katriel (1999) analyzed as *shitufim* (partnership) and *hahlafot* (exchanges) of collections (including stickers) among Israeli schoolchildren as a popular expression of communication through trade.

27. The removal of stickers, even by the owner of the car, was seen as a magical expression, as interviewees spoke of the "bad luck" that stuck to them or their cars after removing religious stickers. For the denigration of the importance of stickers both in academic research as well as in the press, see Bloch (2000a, 49).

28. *Tefillat HaDerekh*, the Jewish Traveler's Prayer, says: "May it be Your will, Lord, my God, that You lead me toward peace, direct my footsteps toward peace and uphold me in peace. May You rescue me from the hand of every foe and ambush along the way. May You send blessing in my every handiwork, and grant me grace, kindness and mercy in Your eyes and in the eyes of all who see me. Blessed are You, Lord, Who hears prayer" (B. Berakhot 29b, as translated in Weil 1988, 38).

29. This was seen as dangerous on a personal level, as we see from the article cited in note 18 of this chapter.

30. See Jakobson (1970, 1990). On speech act theory see Austin (1962); Searle (1969, 1975, 1991). For the use of the concept in Jewish magical traditions, see, for example, Harari (1997, 2010).

31. In this context, and especially in the combination between the material and the textual, between the abstract and the material, it would be interesting to compare the faith-based stickers to the *shiviti* candelabra, as examined in the extensive study of Juhasz (2004). A detailed comparison of the two is beyond the purview of this chapter.

32. For a relevant discussion of issues connected to relations of religion and state, see, for example, Zuckerman (2001, 192–202).

33. Several oppositional stickers which relate to common faith-based stickers may be found, not on the road, but on private internet sites, and those of the Hofshi Association, which declares itself as arising to promote "freedom from religious coercion." Although stickers of the organization may be ordered through the website, these were almost never to be seen on the roads in Israel.

34. Thus, for example, we found a rare sticker that responded to "We Have No One to Rely On but Our Father in Heaven": "We Have No One to Rely On but Our Father in the Reserves." According to the interpretation of interviewees, this sticker simultaneously countered the worldview in the faith-based sticker and the practice of granting religious exemption from military service. Another sticker, which apparently echoed the common "There Is None Other Than Him," was "There's No One Like Mom," which was sighted only once. Another example of a feminist car sticker read, "There Is None Other Than Her," relating, as the owner testified, to the fact that God may as well be a woman (see figure 3.5).

35. See Hasan-Rokem (1982, 54–69). Such quotes are also employed in the discourse of advertisements.

Part I Recapitulation

Public Interaction on the Move

Israel's roads and highways have turned into a public, open, and permanent sphere for discursive political and religious dialogues that give rise to strong feelings of identification and conflict. The private car has become a site in which the complex communication of schism and unity play out. Far more than an idiosyncratic advertisement of personal tastes and opinions, sticker slogans are formulated in a condensed poetics that refers to a common world of images and associations. Complex social, political, and religious realities are recapped as pithy slogans and, more recently, citations from sacred texts; the attribution of meanings to these texts are far from uniform and express deep engagement.

Through the stickers and the reactions to them, Israel's highways have become a place that illustrates the close imbrications of citizens, and the nation-state. Metaphors of closeness are shared by the "state" and the "nation," which testify to their existence as part of a common reality of cultural involvement. Part of that cultural intimacy involves a shared aesthetic of disputation, popularly summed up under the slogan "Two Jews, Three Opinions." Beyond their diversity, the rhetorical strategies of the stickers point to taken-for-granted truths at the base of expressions of identity and are articulated in key terms of Israeli and Jewish identity. These shared terms may index current events, such as Rabin's assassination or the peace process, and imbue them with the gravity of iconic expression rooted in deeper shared commitments ("the people," "blood," "brothers," "a Jew"). Alternatively, they may turn their gaze away from the vagaries of earthly politics, imploring a transcendent father in heaven for salvation.

By using the Hebrew language and references that have settled into "common knowledge," the stickers mark out the boundaries of the collective engaged in the discourse. Thus, the wording used evokes subjects of public debate, makes puns or double entendres, indexes traditional Jewish texts, or refers back to previous or competing sticker slogans. Such references perpetuate communities and traditional loyalties and attempt to forge them through their language of inclusion, exclusion, and empowerment.

Chapters 1, 2, and 3 provide evidence of the enduring preoccupation of Israeli society with questions of competing cosmologies, as expressed through politics and identity, and the amazing capacity of stickers to give voice to the complexities that are linked with them.

The stickers generated by *Shalom, Ḥaver* following Rabin's assassination demonstrate how the folkloric voice addresses itself to the "big" political events taking place in Israel and to the hegemonic discourse surrounding them. The kinetic sticker discourse thus spans the multivocality of positions and the axes of collective identity, extending that which binds together and that which pulls apart. Because they are glued to cars, terms of identity circulate on the roads, and driving on Israel's roads becomes a political act.

Documenting the stickers as a contemporary folkloric genre suggests intricate links between form and content, medium and message. In the case of the political stickers, we demonstrated this through the *Shalom 'Akhshav* sticker, which became the graphic template for *Shalom, Ḥaver*" and all its spin-offs and rebuttals, as well as the lettering of *Ha'Am 'im*, which serve in similar ways for the cycle of stickers documented in chapter 2. The shift from political to religious messages adds an additional dimension: the sanctity of God's name and the biblical text intensify the tension between the intended eternity of the messages of identity and belonging and the ephemerality of the medium. Some see the spread of religious messages to car windows and bumpers as proud public testimony to religious truths. Other interlocutors see the inscription of sacred verses on bumper stickers as a profanation of the word and an indication of the ignorance or superficiality of the car owner's religious commitment. In the words of one of the interviewees: "Come on—birds shit on it."

If the political stickers identify the left-right orientation of the driver or his or her position on the territories, the religious stickers, often much larger and more colorful, transform the car into a "minor sanctuary," a vehicle for transcendent messages; the placement of stickers on the car becomes an act of public worship. Insofar as the car is placed under divine protection, the sticker may serve as an amulet, an apotropaic defense of the passengers from all harm. Thus, the removal of a sticker is seen by some as bringing bad luck, exposing its driver to possible catastrophe. This invites comparisons with the changing forms of material religion on public vehicles and among increasingly mobile believers throughout the world, as well as the proliferation of new sacred sites in nonplaces, the airports, roads, and billboards of the contemporary world.

The sticker is not merely a proclamation but a call for solidarity. Thus, the appeals to "the nation" are a rallying call for broad consensus around a contested position (e.g., retaining Israeli sovereignty over the Golan Heights). But they are no less an act of border marking and exclusion. *Ha'Am* entails an implicit argument as to the exclusion of non-Jews from the "nation." The reminders of God's fatherly providence and his sovereignty over his people are calls to render the contested "natural." Yet what is seen by some as an extension of the blessings provided by their faith to the entire people of Israel is resented by others as religious coercion, a patronizing intrusion into their public space.

The interviews with viewers of the stickers are often surprising in the multiplicity of interpretations and responses elicited from people who (self-) identify with the same political or religious communities. This variety reflects the multivocality of some of the slogans, but also the personal choices and tastes of many, beyond the camp with which they identify. This is particularly salient in the discussions of religious stickers, where people from the (seemingly) same camp provide widely differing views. Some expressed their superior religious capital by deprecating others as superficial, ignorant, and even sacrilegious. Still others differed as to their acceptance or rejection of the public display of commitments that, in their view, should remain in the private sphere. While some of the interviews may merely amplify voices present among viewers, others may provoke them by insisting that the stickers become the object of (self-) reflection and interpretation. Thus, in the religious stickers in particular, the interviews elicited oppositional voices that have not (yet?) found their way to new stickers. In any case, the studies show how the sticker becomes a "sticky trap" for additional meanings.

Finally, the shift from bumper stickers with political messages to those with religious ones over the past years reflects profound changes in Israeli society. The message of God's sovereignty is linked to an understanding of those stickers as a denial of terrestrial agency. The rule of the Lord trumps all human argument. Thus, from opinionated persons engaged in debate and dispute, all become children of the creator, who is the sole possessor of power and authority. The discourse of the religious stickers thus shapes a cosmology in which humankind's arguments and deeds are of negligible value. The multivocality and popular nature of the sticker discourse is reduced to a single voice, directed toward a messianic paradise, a paradise whose trail is blazed by the car on Israel's highways.

Several words on the metacritical level: I have chosen the "ethnographic encounter" as the master category for grouping the folkloric expressions in this book.[1] Consequently, this project also seeks to reproduce that encounter through the meetings between my interviewees and myself. These encounters are the venue of intersecting gazes of participants, including the interviewees in my project, who often observed the research procedure and sometimes questioned its cultural value. Their questions also enriched the research project with new materials. Thus, the focus on stickers, which all considered a popular quotidian expression, evoked reactions ranging from derision to appreciation. As mentioned earlier, one person wondered how stuff that her husband invented upon waking up in the morning—and sometimes didn't even bother placing on a sticker—could become the subject of serious research. Another interviewee, commenting on the religious stickers, clapped her hands together in amazement and said, "I never thought of what complex things can be found on stickers that always seem nothing special. You know, 'on the way (*'al haderekh*).'" In the phrase *'al haderekh* she captured three diverse fields of meaning: (i) on the literal space of the roadway; (ii) in slang, as a supplement, some added value; (iii) and, finally, in the sense of a deep discussion of the road, the journey, the path we share. In an increasingly mobile world, the wayside may point out the clearest way to the center of things.

Note

1. On meta-folklore and related understandings, see Dundes (1966); Ben-Amos (1969); Bauman (1975); Limón (1983); Bauman and Briggs (1990).

PART II

Expressions in the Intimate Arena of Embroidery

Part II Invitation

Embroidering Identity—Needlework and Needle-Talk

W E NOW SHIFT to folk expressions of a very different nature. If the first part dealt with the public sphere, the second part of the book invites the reader into the private sphere. It focuses on an eminently interior feminine expression: women's embroidery. The venue shifts from the cacophony of the road to the intimacy of living rooms and households, where women meet to embroider, study, and place the fruits of their labors on their walls or in their closets. Embroidery is most closely identified with intensive, solitary, domestic women's work. The embroiderer was understood as focusing her glance inward and, for generations, was seen in the West as an exemplar of the ideal girl or woman. Through their acts of embroidery, the stories they embroider around the edges of their activity, and the words they employ to describe their meticulous, often painstaking practice, women embroider their own lives. Yet the analysis demonstrates the broader resonance of embroidering and embroidered pieces. They create family and kinship ties, encourage reflexivity, exemplify relations with men, and comment on broader cultural contexts. The analysis also demonstrates that despite their apparent differences, embroidery and bumper stickers have relevant commonalities. Embroidery and bumper stickers can be interpreted as auto-ethnographic and as means to define group boundaries, commenting on intra- and intergroup relations. Analysis reveals how these genres involve coding and become contested sites; it also exposes the manner in which practitioners are able to employ these forms of expression to address issues of the prohibited and the permitted, the intersection of traditional and contemporary, traditional and sacred, cultural intimacies, and aesthetics, and the relationship of these issues to the performance of cultural identities. At the same time, these genres are connected to the question of what is visible and invisible in everyday interactions. In each realm practitioners are shown to use systems of signals to communicate messages in contexts where not all audience members are able to decode them. In chapters 4, 5, and 6, I show that although the coding exercised by the embroiderers is much more delicate than that exercised by the users of bumper stickers, it is equally present.[1]

As in the research on bumper stickers, many reacted to this product of folk creativity with haughty dismissal. While I was less surprised by the attitude of men to "women's work," I found that many women also looked down on embroidery works of other genres and their makers. This was highly noticeable when dealing with certain forms of embroidery that were marked as nonheritage.[2] When I expressed interest in *gobelins*, many, men and women alike, reacted with a raised eyebrow and said things like, "They're just bored housewives who sought some way of passing the time." It's a waste of your time—why deal with this?"

The humble objects of embroidery are anything but insignificant. They are a silent, Sisyphean travail. The embroidered threads communicate from the cloth, entwining women's lives and their relationships with other family members, with men, and, especially, with their fellow women. Thus, they are integrally woven into women's discourse. From their place in the quiet interior of their household, women embroider dreams of larger worlds of luxury and fantasy. The analysis explores how the project of embroidery expresses the gap between the quotidian and imagined places, as well as the power of the desire to transcend it.

Guided as in previous chapters by the voices of my interlocutors, I now open three portals to the intimate realm of embroidery, successively following the practice, the character, and then the product. In chapter 4, initially written in cooperation with Galit Hasan-Rokem, we follow the practice of acquiring knowledge and creating community and a finding of a deeper sense of womanhood through performance. It also shows how the embroidering women relate to other women, ranging from needlework peers to scholars. Chapter 5 follows the character. It shows how embroidery becomes the substance of a woman's exemplary life story of independence and action, but also of Orientalism and affirmation of traditional female role models. Through her genealogy as offspring of a prominent pioneering family, through her authoritative voicing of cultural expertise, through the details of her life narrative, she presents a particular local model of emplaced selfhood. In so doing, she stakes out an enigmatic and liminal position as a woman speaking in a male voice—an authority on embroidery who does not embroider herself. In chapter 6, we follow the object, the embroidered *gobelin* itself. Its physical trajectory from one site to another mirrors broader processes of intergenerational transmission and rupture, modernization, Westernization, and changes in the aesthetics and values associated with womanhood in Israeli society.

This approach combines emic, that is, internal, and etic, that is, analytical, perspectives, the synchronic view of women's embroidery with a historical contextualization of the practices and products. Thus, the analysis of embroidery demonstrates not only the transformative potential of seemingly banal objects but also the ways in which the reactions to the choice of those objects for research reflect gender, social status, ethnicity, and attitudes to tradition.

Notes

1. See Lanser and Radner (1987).
2. On cultural heritage and the complex politics involved, see Bendix, Eggert, and Peselmann (2012). On the need to expend the discourse based on ethnography, see De Cesari (2012). Hierarchies of heritage-ness attached to different forms of embroidery demonstrate its relevance to the study of cultural heritage, which the coming chapters only hint at.

4   Embroidering Their Selves

*Femininity and Embroidery
in a Jerusalem Women's Group*

Once a week, for more than fifteen years, a group of ten to twelve women has been meeting in one of Jerusalem's relatively well-to-do neighborhoods to embroider together. Each woman works on her own piece of embroidery, but the group as a whole operates as a single working unit, engaging in "folk embroidery," "ethnic embroidery," or "world embroidery" (*rikmat 'ammim*), as the partners to this enterprise call it.[1] "Folk embroidery" refers to the samples of traditional embroidery by ethnic groups from all over the world. Among them are pieces from neighboring cultural and geographical regions, ranging from the local Palestinians, to distant cultural regions, such as South America, the Far East, and others. These traditional embroidery samples are deciphered by the group members through a collective interpretive process and are then "re-embroidered" individually (see figures 4.5, 4.6, and 4.7).

Most of the participants are Jewish, native Israelis. One is Arab. And the youngest was fifty years old at the time we conducted our research. The group includes women who describe themselves as "religious," "secular," "right-wing," "left-wing," and as belonging to diverse ethnic groups of origin. Our acquaintance with the embroiderers began in the context of a research project that we were hired to coordinate locally for the annual Folklife Festival organized by the Smithsonian Institute in Washington, DC, which in 1994 was to include an exhibition of the folklore of Jerusalem (Hasan-Rokem 2007). The group of embroiderers came up as one of the potential representatives of contemporary Jerusalem folklore. Consequently, the members of the group were asked, as part of the research project, to describe the group and its activity. The self-description project involved a series of interviews in which each member responded to an open-ended, personal questionnaire. It became evident that the members deployed a shared idiomatic and symbolic articulation, which presented their embroidery as a group experience and as a feminine discourse. These descriptions brought to the foreground an element of verbally expressed reflexivity that the narrators wove into a structured narrative in a mode that enabled them to be viewed as comprising a kind of auto-ethnographic discourse (Pratt 1991a, 34). The narrative that thus emerged evolved alongside the activity of embroidery, with its own characteristic ritual features. The imbrication of these varied forms of expression inspired a further ethnographic and theoretical exploration of the group.

To shed interpretive light on the activity of this group of Jerusalem embroiderers, the following investigates the interlaced expressivity of materials (embroidery) and of language (women's discourse) constructed as distinctive elements of a broad holistic system of cultural formulation and reworking, revising many elements of a male-dominated tradition (Ginsburg and Tsing 1992; Babcock 1993a). An integrative approach to the diverse expressive elements interconnected in one ritual performance allowed the decoding of the cognitive and emotive semiotics informing the group's activity and the revelation of the expressive system that characterized it. This chapter focuses on processes of symbolic transformation between collective forms of expressivity and the specific construction of femininity and female identity by means of folklore in contemporary Israeli society. The genre of thick description is employed, integrating emic and etic points of view (Geertz 1973), seeking to avoid an artificial separation of such viewpoints, and to present a description that grows out of feminine negotiations between the researchers and the embroiderers, as well as between ourselves.

Folklore is in traditional communities often gender-specifically created, transmitted, and preserved. In most cultures, some genres are exclusively associated with one gender. A genre associated with men in one culture may in another be associated with women (Farrer 1986, 14). Embroidery, perhaps more than many other modes of expression, is seen as characteristic of gender specificity: "The art of embroidery has been the means of educating women into the feminine ideal, and of proving that they have attained it. . . . To know the history of embroidery is to know the history of women" (Parker 1984, ix; see also Schneider and Weiner 1989, 20–21). Views regarding the existence of a fit between traits required for embroidery and allegedly feminine traits are common and recognizable in everyday discourse as well as in a variety of folkloric expressions.

At the outset of the research, the assumption was that the group's choice of its particular activity—that is, embroidery—related to issues of cross-gender discourse. This led to the expectation that both the *emic* (inner group) and *etic* (research) discussion would focus on relationships between women and men, between femininity and masculinity. Indeed, such articulations are not absent from the embroiderers' discourse, but they are not the most salient aspect of it. In fact, from the initial reading of the questionnaires it became clear that embroidery was, for the members of the group, a privileged arena for investigating feminine identity, which, while certainly implicated in cross-gender negotiations, even more significantly engaged a discourse among women. The cross-gender dialogues are constructed integrally from within a feminine discourse, so that the women's own negotiations do indeed occupy a much more prominent portion of the overall discourse. Relations between women and men, as well as issues of womanhood, fertility, child rearing, and family, are examined and reworked through the embroidery.

The group of women and the embroidery that knits them together embody a structural intergender relationship founded on opposition, while this relationship is perceived symbolically as one of mutual transformation. This view of intergender transformability, which reveals itself both on the symbolic and the idiomatic level, has no comparable expression in the everyday lives of these women. Its embodiment by means of folk embroidery seems to us to be its chief articulation.

In the course of the research, it became clear that these Jerusalem women's embroidery appropriates masculine cultural resources, such as interpretive study, knowledge, and scholarship, which in their case do not transfer to other areas such as political or economic power, or to the deployment of power in other public domains (Bruner 1993, 330–31). Their discourse engages with various types of embroidery and with women embroiderers; it reveals a thematic preoccupation with various understandings of femininity and the relationship between such understandings, while applying value judgments to address focal points of ambiguity, both on the level of practice and at the symbolic level. The narrative elements that comprised the reflexive narrative about the group's activity (as manifest in the detailed interviews with its members, in the questionnaires, and in the video *Embroiderers' Talk*, which they themselves produced) was composed of descriptions of major women protagonists and of a projection of a linear narrative trajectory on the group's own activity. The idiomatic interaction between the embroidery and the narrative constituted, therefore, the weaving of a story into the woof and warp of a verbal narrative.

The complex relationships between dominant and subordinate discourse are central to the theoretical consideration of alternative models for understanding reality and coping with it, within adjacent cultural spaces. The construction and expression of such relationships by means of distinct cultural expressions extends the discussion to broader questions concerning the relations between genre and gender.

The relationship between genre and gender has often been considered—whether explicitly or implicitly—chiefly in relation to the male-female dichotomy, because gendered systems of hierarchy, meaning, and symbolism are generally formulated within this binary scheme. Characterization of this cross-gender polarity in terms of genre suggests that feminine models are generally embodied in vehicles of expression that are "non-verbal, inarticulate or veiled, while the discourse of men is more verbal and explicit" (Gal 1991, 189). This approach entails implicit assumptions regarding the relationships between specific genres and gender, as embodied within and beyond any particular culture, such that "women's genres can best be read as commentary that shows a range of responses—acceptance, resistance, subversion and opposition to dominant, often male discourse" (ibid., 192–93).

The point of departure for the current discussion is more open-ended, and refrains from accepting the terms *gender, performance, tradition*, and *text* as taken-for-granted terminological signifiers. This discussion regards these terms rather as concepts at the center of a theoretical negotiation, in which, as Arjun Appadurai, Frank Korom, and Margaret Mills (1991, 5) have appositely noted, the study of folklore functions as the host who takes the role of chief discussant in orienting this debate toward the field of critical theory, media research, and cultural studies.

The reciprocal action involved in the ongoing process of constructing culture vis-à-vis a distinct and recognizable praxis is bidirectional. Culture constructs praxis and praxis constructs culture (Bourdieu 1977).The interpretation of this system is refracted, on the one hand, by means of praxis as performed by the individual, and on the other hand, by means of distinct expressive forms, which correspond to diverse forms of gender consciousness. In this manner, distinctive forms of expression are treated as discursive constructions at the level of the individual and the group (Ginsburg and Tsing 1992; Kondo 1990; J. Butler 1993; Allison 1994; Babcock 1986, 1993b).

The embroiderers meet once a week, in the afternoon, for a two-hour session at the home of Megina Shlain, the group's founder and facilitator. Upon entry to Megina's pleasant home, it is impossible not to be struck by the walls, which are heavily decorated with colorful pieces of embroidery, collected from locations around the world, and hung snugly together alongside her own handiwork. The women arrive at the session with plastic shopping bags in hand, which contain the pieces of embroidery on which they are currently working. The meeting takes place next to the kitchen, around the family dining table that Megina has arranged in advance by extending its extra leaves to accommodate the large group (figure 4.1). Each woman finds her regular seat around the table, while their host circles around to inspect and review each participant's work. The table is set with books displaying traditional embroidery from all over the world, old pieces of stitchery, as well as photocopies of embroidery patterns and samples. The question of which themes and particular patterns to be grappled with and embroidered in the coming months, as well as the cultural regions of provenance to be chosen are debated in a patently collective decision-making process. The collectively made decisions rely on the perusal of photographs of embroidery in the books or the examination of the exemplars on the table, which are perceived as vestigial artifacts of traditional embroidery (figures 4.2 and 4.3). Once every few months, a new theme is selected by the group members, whereupon Megina draws the relevant pattern and distributes it among the participants.[2] The decision is unencumbered by considerations of cost-efficiency in terms of time or labor and is based purely on considerations of interest and enthusiasm. After a joint decision is reached, the women hold a detailed discussion during which the pattern, the materials, and the specific embroidery technique of the source model are deciphered, and a strategy for what they call "re-embroidering" it is chosen. The discussion moves from the piece of embroidery itself to the broader cultural context of the original embroidery; its pattern, stitches, and colors are deciphered at both the functional and symbolic level. At the end of the discussion, the women help themselves to coffee and cake contributed by one of the participants, and they finalize the plans for the subsequent meeting. During the week, each woman spends longs hours of individual work on her own piece, until the next group session convenes. In addition to the weekly meetings, the group's activity includes exhibitions and presentations of their work to the public at large, events concerning which the participants harbor mixed feelings and responses.

Embroidery, Women and Men

The women's articulations concerning the embroidery and the group reveal a preoccupation with the dialectic between doing and knowing, between practice and cognizance. The following is from one of the interviews: "Since I work full time as a nurse, I was searching for something outside work hours, for the heart, but also for the head. And I must say, that it's been ten years already and there has not even been one day where I have had second thoughts about what I'm doing, [not] a day when I have come here and not learned something. Sometimes something minute and sometimes bigger." And in a different interview:

> There's an issue of culture here. Our activity is not only concerned with printed needlework tapestry (*gobelin*), or with killing time by sliding our hands around a needle . . . for us this is research about a country, its culture, the materials used in the country, and the techniques.[3] For example, if I know that in Pakistan silk threads are used for embroidery and yet it is a very poor country, so [I learn that] they have found a technique to avoid squandering the silk threads, stitching the embroidery only on the obverse and not on the reverse. So there is magic in *researching* phenomena belonging to other countries and cultures, comparing stitches, and rediscovering each time . . . and this is *intellectually exciting*. This is not merely manual work. . . . This is a culture of doing, and this is what we love to meet for. It isn't just for passing the time, because we don't have time to pass. We are extremely busy [women], and I wouldn't even put aside two hours to sit at a café and chat, because I don't have the time. But *this is knowledge that arises from doing* . . . and this is not a technical craft, but it is [a product] of profound research, [consulting] yet another book or pamphlet for explanations, and another tattered piece of fabric, which, quote-unquote, contains a gorgeous world.

At the symbolic level, the process of embroidery expresses the binary opposition of feminine/masculine through its use of thread and fabric (feminine) and a needle (masculine), although the needle's form, including a piercing end and an opening for the thread at the other end, definitely opens it up to androgynous interpretation. However, the piercing—"male"—aspect seems to prevail in the discourse that we have encountered. By taking the needle into feminine hands, a symbolism is enacted that alludes to the wielding of masculine elements by feminine power and by means of an array of signs that are uniquely feminine. This universal act of appropriation of masculine power by women is in this particular case anchored in a concretely Jewish context of tension between *practice* and *study*. In the context studied here, this tension is also cloaked with an intercultural curiosity enhanced by modernity and informed by the ambivalence generally characterizing the attitude toward femininity in Israeli society.[4]

Practice and study are perceived by the group's members as diachronically and processually linked, so that in order to embroider, one must first understand and know. Such a link does not exist, according to their own assumptions, in the experience of other women or in that of women who produced the source models for their embroidery, who presumably do not keep the same kind of interpretation and understanding that they consider themselves to hold. To embroider they must learn how to execute the stitches particular to each type, a learning acquired in the process of superadded learning of the source's cultural context. This learning endows the entire enterprise with a special modern significance, with each stretch of group time dedicated to the study of another culture (figure 4.4). Whereas the original embroideries that the women study and re-embroider were learned within a tradition in which knowledge is orally transmitted by its carriers, the body of knowledge to which the Jerusalem group is oriented is intercultural. Thus, it engages cultural models that characterize learning as mediated by literature, global communications, and modern tourism. Within a traditional gendered pattern in which the woman "turns inward" and the man "turns outward" (Bourdieu 1979, 133–53; Csikszentmihalyi and Rochberg-Halton 1981, 121–45; Alexander and Hasan-Rokem 1989), this orientation toward learning through travel represents an essentially male one.

In the process of deciphering, interpreting, and analyzing the traditional embroidery, the sample fabrics are collectively studied as texts, as the women engage in *hevruta* (the traditional Jewish mode of Talmudic study in—male—pairs) next to the kitchen, which in turn is symbolically transformed into a *yeshiva* (a traditional rabbinical higher institution of learning). In our interviews, the embroiderers referred to their work with the following: "This embroidery, you can read it like an open book," projecting a textual terminology tied to the male tradition onto the world of embroidery. Thereby a powerful tool of interpretation is transposed from the dominant universe of discourse to an alternative, less

Figure 4.1. Embroidering meeting, Megina's kitchen.

Figure 4.2. Meeting of the group, deciphering embroidered pieces.

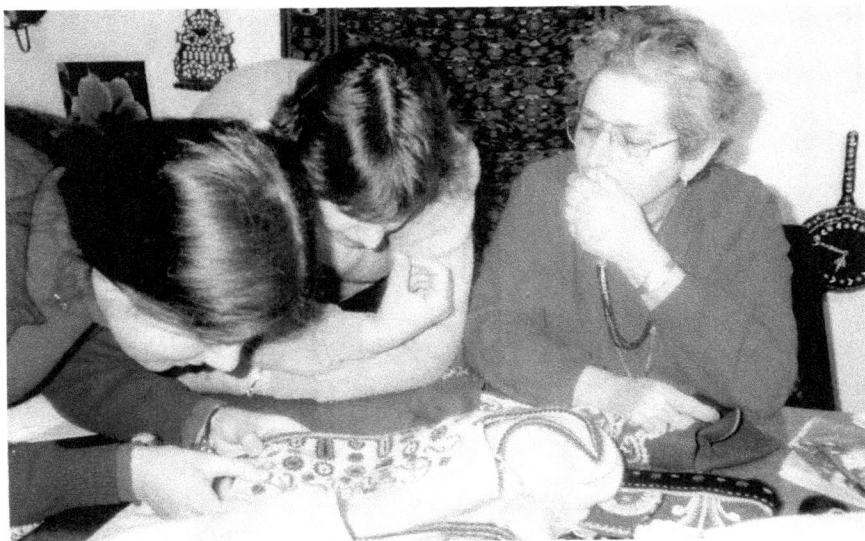

Figure 4.3. Meeting of the group, deciphering embroidered pieces.

privileged one (Freeman 1987, 58). Another participant recounted: "Someone brings a piece of fabric . . . so we begin to decipher and see the beauty hidden in it. Then we consider whether we want to do this or not . . . we begin to look [closely] with or without a magnifying glass, [looking] left and right to see how it is really made."

This description is somewhat reminiscent of textual exegesis, especially of the Talmudic kind—but with fabric and thread—a model that was invoked repeatedly in many other descriptive accounts during the course of our fieldwork, whenever arguments and collective processes of decision making came to mind. In this manner, the masculine textual model reproduced itself within the women's group, and yet was not presented by the group members as a contrary model to that embodied in women's handicraft.[5]

Embroidery, Family, and Fertility

The concept of gender is key in the self-definition of the group under discussion, and this concept is similarly central to this interpretive research. As a key ideological and emotional principle of the group's discourse, gender is conveyed through symbols and feminine metaphorical expressions that circulate through the work and the group alike. In terms of continuity, the embroidery of the Jerusalem women is the product of a coupling of masculine and feminine characteristics—study and practice—as well as of group processes described as processes of *fertilization* taking place within the framework of the group.

Figure 4.4. Megina Shlain in front of her embroidery library.

The idiomatic language of the embroiderer's discourse reveals repeated references to life and fertility, in articulations such as, "We give life to the embroidery" or the following: "When I saw the embroidery for the first time, I saw something that I have been searching for my whole life. It is something that is alive. The embroidery is alive, it breathes, speaks. Everything speaks, the textiles, the colors, the shapes, and that's what is moving about it. And then there is the group: when we talk and a piece of embroidery arrives, we begin to discuss and decipher the stitches. As for the group itself—if I fail to attend even once, I feel I have missed something. The group is fertilizing."

In another interview with Megina, she said, "We fertilize one another. In order to succeed, one traces and deciphers the stitches, and when we begin to work together, one helps the other." Articulations revolving around fertility and childbirth recur in a variety of forms in the women's discourse as well as in rituals directly associated with embroidery. The process of embroidery is described as giving birth, as the endowing of life, whereas the group as a whole is characterized, symbolically in terms of an alternative family comprising male and female elements. The embroiderers exhibit a maternal relationship to their handiwork. No one sells the embroidery pieces, or makes gifts of them, apart from the narrow circle of family. The embroidery is used for wall hangings, pillows, and tablecloths, but more often than not, it is folded and kept in the closet.

In several of the interviews, women articulated embroidery in terms of the granting of life: "We take a piece of old embroidery, whose stitches and colors are no longer in use, and we take it and give it new life. And when you give it new life, then, so as to preserve the spirit of the work . . . I preserve the hues because the hues have a great deal of meaning, and I want to preserve the spirit of the embroidery."

The perception of embroidery as the offspring of the embroiderer is paralleled in Messick's study (1987) of women weavers in Morocco. By the very imbrication of technique and ritual, this weaving articulates feminine meanings and especially mother-son relations. Among the Jerusalem embroiderers, the articulation of the imagined relations between the embroiderer and her handiwork is not specific to male progeny, as in the Moroccan case. But here, too, technique and ritual—including that of choosing the themes to be embroidered—combine to endow the relationship between maker and product with meanings associated with mother-child relations, as inflected by expressions of intimacy, unconditional giving, devotion, and loyalty, all of which are closely analogous to the traits required for the long and tedious process of embroidery. The nature of these relationships serves as a barrier to alienation or separation from the objects of embroidery (Weiner 1992, 1994).

The completed pieces of embroidery are carefully documented in color photographs, then arranged and displayed in ways reminiscent of family photo albums,

Figure 4.5. Traditional embroidered piece (right), next to the "reembroidered" one.

and referred to in language that evokes the intimate speech reserved for children. Thus, for example, when discussing the possibility of exhibiting the embroidery in a group exhibition and exposing it to a viewing public, one of the women protested: "How can you let them go [i.e., the pieces of embroidery] for two full months?"

The issue of loyalty to the original embroidery is associated with the perception of embroidery as progeny, explicitly invoked as such in the group's discourse. One of the embroiders confessed: "I, for example, feel disloyal about making this pillow, whose authentic coloring is shades of brown; when I finished embroidering, I said, now I shall use the colors I like, and I made these colors. And I feel a sense of betrayal. I have betrayed the original authentic embroidery."

The powerful invocation of mother-daughter relations in reference to the embroidery piece came up following an accident caused by a fire that broke out one summer around Jerusalem. Megina lost all the pieces that had been exhibited in a wooden stall at a kibbutz. When describing the accident, Megina couched her speech in the rhetoric of mourning, normally reserved for family. To convey the enormity of the disaster, she even compared her personal loss to the calamity of a family she knew, who had lost a son in a car accident. The very act of comparison underscored that the closest analogy that could possibly convey her sense of emotional intimacy with the embroidery was a relationship of childbearing.

Figure 4.6. Traditional embroidered piece (right), next to the "reembroidered" one.

In addition to the explicit idioms of fertility, birth, and progeny, the embroiderers' verbal narrative is characterized by powerful metaphors of life and vitality, such as, "When I started out I felt as though I was setting a field of thorns on fire." Or elsewhere: "This embroidery is like a wellspring that increases its flow, like a flowing water stream."[6]

Embroidery on the Feminine Front

Feminine identity is subject to negotiation within both the male and female worlds. The material and verbal discourses of this group of embroiderers can be characterized by the particular way in which it constructs feminine identity through outspoken comparisons between different women. The various articulations that form the basis of our analysis reveal an attitude toward the feminine world, which is thoroughly caught up with embroidery in one way or another. Several specifically designated groups of women were repeatedly mentioned in the interviews. The women had encountered some of these groups in person on a continuous basis, while their contact with others was maintained only by means of their embroidery craft.

The four categories of women that are thematically bound up in the embroiderers' discourse are the following:

Figure 4.7. Megina with both the traditional embroidered piece (right), and the "reembroidered" one. Courtesy of Ephraim Shlain.

    a. Zohar Wilbush, the founding mother
    b. Anonymous traditional folk embroiderers
    c. The group of "free embroiderers"
    d. The "museum women" and the "researchers"

The above division, as well as the ordering of this list, is not necessarily a reflection of the embroiderers' own reflexivity: the discourse on other groups of women is interlaced into the personal and group narratives in explicit descriptions of their encounters, or in their characteristic rhetoric of comparisons.

Zohar Wilbush, the Founding Mother

Zohar Wilbush was the central, charismatic figure at the center of the embroiderers' discourse who will become the main character of chapter 5 (figure 4.8). A former curator at the Department of Ethnography at the Israel Museum and at least a generation older than most of the embroiderers, her name was mentioned in almost every interview or conversation and in almost all written material produced by the group. The group's attitude toward Zohar is emotionally and symbolically complex. During her long years of employment at the museum's ethnography department, she developed a particular interest in embroidery, and

Figure 4.8. Zohar Wilbush, the "founding mother."

especially in the local Palestinian and regional Middle Eastern traditions. According to the interviews, her retirement from the museum had left a vacuum that would later be filled by women who were neither comparably knowledgeable about embroidery nor capable of appreciating it as Zohar was.

For many years, and even up until the research that led to this chapter, some years before her passing, the circle of women would meet once a week on Sunday evening at the home of the "founding mother," who resided in Jerusalem. This gathering took place parallel to the meetings at Megina's home and was attended by embroiderers from that group, as well as by Megina herself, who joined Zohar's group after the session at her home had ended. The scheduling of the two gatherings on the same day of the week should be understood as expressing the fact that one of the gatherings was viewed as having engendered, or given birth, to the second.

The birth of the group of embroiderers as an organized and self-conscious body, with a discrete identity, is linked, both on the level of praxis and on the symbolic-cosmological level, with the figure of Zohar Wilbush. This link is expressed both in the embroidered textile and in the narrative text, which articulate the complexity of the founding mother's figure as a system of oppositions between embroidery and narrative. During a meeting at Zohar's home, which Galit Hasan-Rokem and I also attended, the group's creation narrative was told to us in a polyphonic unison of voices:

> Do you know how many years we are together? At least fifteen . . . Megina and I attended a class by the Society for the Protection of Nature on traditional crafts and markets. We listened to the lectures like good girls. All the talks were attended by a tall, impressive, bejeweled lady who behaved disruptively at every lecture. She interrupted all the presenters. Every time the speaker inserted a Latinate (non-Hebrew) word into her speech, she was immediately corrected in a thundering voice and offered an equivalent, Hebrew term. Later, that same woman presented a lecture about Arab dresses. I sat there with my eyes rolling around, and truly, altogether, because of this course and her personality . . . and then we began to push Zohar to teach at home.

Zohar was aware of her special standing within the group of embroiders, as her following statement reveals. "Yes, I know, they've made me queen . . . they say that the embroiderers' group is because of me."

When the group met at her home, Zohar lectured about embroidery and various crafts, illustrating her presentation with examples from her personal collection, which was composed mostly of local and regional embroidery and jewelry. The room in which she hosted the group was simply but pleasantly furnished, allowing all the women—usually a group of around ten—to be seated comfortably. The walls and the seats were covered with traditional textiles. An old map of the Ottoman Empire hung above the desk in front of which Zohar was seated, providing a backdrop for one of Zohar's repeated statements. "I was born in the Ottoman Empire, one year before the Sultan was ousted." Nonetheless, her age was a topic of much discussion and speculation. In two different interviews, when Zohar's name came up, our informants said, "She knows a great deal . . . she "embellishes" . . . her age is Baroque, an age of ornamentation . . . she could be eighty-seven or perhaps eighty-nine years old." And elsewhere: "She possessed tremendous knowledge, but she did not know how to put it into writing. Her lectures are always fascinating, even though she is now ninety-six years old." Zohar's personal embroidery collection also assumes mythical dimensions interlaced with sibling rivalry—an issue that came up now and again in respect to her inheritance.

From the maternal viewpoint, Zohar was seen as a feminine mother figure, a founder a dynasty whose lines of descent are groups of embroidering women. The enigmatic references to her age are tied to the maternal familial discourse in which the relationship with her so-called loyalists is couched. Her acts of giving, whether she was sharing knowledge or lending pieces of embroidery from her personal collection for copying, were perceived as a nursing relationship that provided constant nourishment. It is no wonder, then, that the group of women learners who gathered at her home designated itself "Zohar's daughters." Megina also belonged to this small circle, and her disciples therefore viewed themselves— especially the younger ones—as "Zohar's granddaughters." In Jerusalem, in Tiv'on, and even in Tel Aviv, yet other groups exist, which view themselves as her genealogical descendants. Megina reiterated more than once that she designated the groups of embroiderers that meet at her home by the name "Zohar [translates as Splendor] for Embroidery," out of respect and loyalty to their progenitor. This designation appears in a number of texts that are used for presenting the embroiderers to external audiences; it is perceived as a sign of Megina's gratitude and modesty. She herself noted: "I also insist on calling the group 'Zohar for Embroidery' because she gave us the embroidery." Furthermore, the three books on embroidery that Megina Shlain published in the years following Galit Hasan-Rokem's and my original Hebrew paper, were printed under "Zohar Larikma" (Zohar for Embroidery Press) (2003, 2007, 2009).

Alongside the question of Zohar's age, the embroiderers were preoccupied with the question of whether Zohar herself actively embroidered, with her own hands. The very fact that this question even came up, in light of Zohar's tremendous knowledge *about* embroidery, indicates that her figure was perceived as exhibiting certain male characteristics, and that in her role as a mythical founding mother she blurred gender boundaries. Although bedecked with jewels and embroidery, Zohar's striking appearance was devoid of gender-specific traits, while the ornamentation was clearly associated with her sphere of knowledge and not as an index of gender.

Zohar's life story, too, was clouded in obscurity, as far as the group members were concerned: "It's a real mystery, no one was able to tell me any facts or dates concerning her . . . she will tell you that she rode horses, that she is the niece of Manya Shohat [founder of the first Kibbutz] . . . she claims her mother was a handicraft teacher, and that all her concepts and early collections are from her mother. It is said of her that she was always unforgettable. She was very beautiful and apparently was also always dressed uniquely."

Legends associated her with the heroic past of struggle for political independence in the pre-state period. Her genealogy was related to well-known mythological figures from the past of the Yishuv, the Jewish population residing in pre-state Palestine.

The mutual relations between the group and the founding mother figure were symbolized, therefore, both in maternal terms and in intergender terms. Thus, the embroiderers designated themselves in respect to Zohar as the "loyal ones" and as "daughters" and "grandchildren," and described rituals such as communal eating and caring for her needs. The women's complex attitude toward Zohar reflects ambivalence with respect to femininity in contemporary Israeli society, a society caught in conflict between the myth of gender egalitarianism and a reality of traditional quasi-hierarchical gender relations (for similar close relations between food, handicraft, and femininity, see Freeman 1987, 60; Sered 1987).

Anonymous Traditional Folk Embroiderers

The pieces of embroidery that the Jerusalem women reworked are conceptualized as traditional both in the synchronic sense (deriving from contemporary "traditional" societies) and in the diachronic sense (products of historical societies or family traditions). They thus refer to specific traditional cultural frameworks that may be investigated in terms of identification as well as classification. The pieces of embroidery were made for family use and included dresses, towels, drapes, bedclothes, and so on. Alternately, they may have been made for communal use in houses of prayer or for public ceremonies. Although in some locations men embroidered—as mentioned above—the practice in general was perceived by the members of the group (and not only by them) as a women's craft. The women who engaged with these traditional embroideries were perceived as "whole" women, representing a kind of authentic traditional clarity, through which a static and uniform world is given expression. In these worlds, women labored hard for the family's welfare, and embroidery was part of the rhythms of everyday life. These women were never faced with a choice of whether or not to embroider. In their personal narratives, nearly all the Jerusalem embroiderers suggested that their connection with embroidery began within the family, in an intergenerational mode, as in this illustrative quotation: "I had the privilege to encounter family embroidery as part of the stable surroundings. There were always pieces of family embroidery that passed down through the generations . . . there were certain patterns that recurred over and over again, such as the phylactery bag embroidered with botanic motifs."

Nonetheless, despite the narrative emplotment that underscored continuity, the attitude toward the traditional embroiderers explicitly stressed the differences between the two groups of women: "I say that at one time this was folk embroidery. In the past, the dowry was made for the whole family, and it's amazing that you can identify the embroidery of a certain town, because that is how they embroidered there. . . . For them it was part of life, the same way they made stuffed grape leaves and cooked things that were time-consuming, investing a whole lot, and then they come and eat it up in no time at all." And elsewhere: "A needle and thread, I expressly believe that this is a feminine creation with (its own) feminine tradition and feminine attitude . . . although I myself did not like the embroidery on the clothes. That disappeared. Because it's a shame (to waste time on?) the embroidery, because then the object is thrown away, or fashion changes, or the embroidery is left with no role to fulfill . . . and yet we still hang it up for decoration, or keep it in the closet."

The embroiderers' discourse is informed by a notion of a metacultural system of women's collaborative work. And yet the products of this work are transformed when they are kept in the closet and remain "unconsumed"—transposed from "necessity" to "choice," and from "native" to "touristic," an object of "research" or even a "conquest": "People are incapable of understanding how a normal human being can occupy so many hours with this. People cannot understand it. We conquer another country, and yet another country, and a piece of embroidery from here and from there; each piece of embroidery is its own world, and they are not similar to one another."

Thus, the transformative relationship between men and women is inherently projected on traditional women's relations to the Jerusalem group and vice versa. The set of oppositions the embroiderers invoke to explain the differences between themselves and the traditionalists is cast in a different light when applied to the relationship between the Jerusalem group and Zohar Wilbush. When the group was invited to exhibit at a kibbutz in the Jerusalem area, Zohar was asked to deliver the opening remarks. On this occasion, she reiterated how important it was that the women were returning to the traditional feminine crafts, using celebratory expressions such as "May the hands that embroider be blessed and may the group of women dedicated to restoring feminine craft be blessed." She concluded by expressing the hope that women would go back to embroidering clothes for their children "instead of wearing the prepared synthetic things." She further intoned, "May the hands that still occupy themselves with embroidery be blessed." In sum, in this discourse one can see a binary scheme that pits knowledge and modernity against making and tradition. While Zohar posits this scheme as distinguishing between her and the women's embroidery group, the latter reproduce this very same scheme, roles reversed, in shaping their own attitude toward the "traditional women."

The Group of "Free Embroiderers"

Another category of embroiderers that engages the discourse of the Jerusalem women is a group that calls itself the "free embroiderers." This designation refers to several venues in which women embroider freely and design their own patterns, adopting them as a vehicle for self-expression. These women regard their embroidery as art, and themselves as acknowledged artists; they have also been granted opportunities to exhibit their work at a variety of exhibition spaces and even at the Israel Museum.

When comparing themselves with the free embroiderers, the Jerusalem group enlisted images and metaphors from the natural world. For example, one of the women said, "There it is called free embroidery, and then you come and you see everyone making the same stream surrounded by trees and flowers. While we, who work with a pattern, each one of us produces something different." While their own embroidery is linked to tradition and scholarly knowledge, and is described in terms of renewal and fertility, such as "an abundant spring" or a "flowing stream," in contrast, each exemplar of the "stream" embroidered by the free embroiderers had the same appearance and lacks vitality or continuity. The natural imagery, both at the narrative level and in the embroidery works, draws attention to different ways in which the links between nature, naturalness, and femininity can be formulated. The paradox wryly alluded to in the designation "the free embroiderers"—implying innovation and renewal as opposed to derivative nature of the work—was more bluntly declared elsewhere:

> As for the free embroiderers—I do not view that as creativity. Because if you are making a picture—why use a needle and thread? You enter their homes and you can see what they do, that they all immediately hang it in their home. It's their first picture, and they already have it hanging on the wall. And it will hang there for a lifetime, because who would change it? I see no creativity in that, because they all make the same stream, so they all took it and copied it from the same place. . . . I don't pretend to creativity or to being artistic.

The free embroiderers, whose embroidery is regarded as innovative—both by themselves and by the museum establishment—evoke a strong sense of aversion and are presented as an utter antithesis of the Jerusalem group. Both groups viewed the medium of embroidery and feminine identity through a polarized lens. The Jerusalem group drew its vitality from tradition and regarded its embroidery as a wellspring of renewal and innovation, while free embroidery, which was supposed to express individual creativity, was repetitive, pretentious, disrespectful, and disloyal. These negative attributes were associated with modern feminism, viewed as opposed to the kind of femininity that flourished within the group and is akin to traditional femininity.

The "Museum Women" and the "Researchers"

Another category of women that carries significant meanings in the discourse of the embroiderers is that of women from the Department of Ethnography at the Israel Museum and researchers from the academy. This composite group represents institutionalized, judgmental, and hegemonic knowledge, a kind of knowledge that when wielded in respect to the embroiderers may be perceived as powerful and potent. The women's discourse revealed that the "museum women" or the "girls from the museum," as they were sometimes called, were not interested in their work. As the embroiderers saw it, the museum women valued either the traditional women's embroidery or that of the free embroiderers, but regarded the embroidery of the Jerusalem group as unworthy of the museum's attention. Consequently, Galit Hasan-Rokem's and my choice as academic researchers to devote attention to the group, document their discourse, photograph their work and their meetings, speak with them, and, most significantly, to put their words into print, endorsed their occupation as "worthwhile" and added a dimension of meaning to their identity.

The embroiderers' discourse plots the fourth feminine category between two poles that are perceived as engaged in a struggle. This conflict is constructed through descriptions of actual encounters, in personal stories, and in narratives about well-known figures from both institutions. Symbolically viewed, the group's narrative articulates a male struggle transposing focal points of male political power into the opposite gender. "The museum women" represent institutionalized and authoritative norms with respect to art and creativity, while the embroiderers' dialogue with women researchers embodies the complex negotiations surrounding feminine identity. On the one hand, our advances toward the group might have been interpreted by them as an invasive incursion, possibly also male in character. The forms of knowledge that Galit Hasan-Rokem and I represented, and by which we are granted legitimacy by institutionalized sources of authority, constitute another aspect that marks us as potential "men." On the other hand, our interest in this particular group of women placed us at the direct opposite pole of the other agents, chiefly the museum women. Our dialectical position, as the ones who collected their words and engaged ourselves with their knowledge, was perceived as empowering. It was not surprising, therefore, that the research process was received with great interest, leading to group members' participation at a scientific conference, where we presented the work, and reflected in Megina's request to obtain a draft of the lecture.

Discussion

The reworking of femininity and feminine identity in the genre of embroidery embodies a complex gender identity fraught with tension, as the semiotics of embroidery carries a broad gamut of understandings, oppositions, and reflexivity. In this study, the relations, the idioms, the metaphors, and the symbols that comprise the cultural expressions of women who embroider themselves and their selves have been examined in the context of a hermeneutic process simultaneously unraveling these expressions and re-embroidering them.

The reflexivity of the Jerusalem group, as well as their interpretive perspective on the embroidery, both studied and created in the group setting, led us to posit the notion of "embroidering themselves/their selves." These women embroidered their selves while engaging a complex feminine consciousness, which was expressed and reworked through the medium of fabric, colored threads, needle, the ritual interactions involved in the group's activity, and the accompanying verbal discourse. In this sense, it can be said that the categories of "gender" and "genre" are not taxonomically differentiated, to the extent that one might even say that "genders are genres" (Ramanujan 1991, 53). The embroiderer-storyteller becomes a focal point for constructing experience in the sense of *Bildung*, that is, a development into full consciousness, which an individual attains through the acquisition of specific knowledge and cultural understanding. Thus, the group of women pays exquisite attention to the sources of its own expertise and investigates the special technical and symbolic aspects of each culture, while conducting a detailed comparison with other cultures.

The discourse of the embroiderers is embodied in various modes of expression: material, ritual, and verbal. By engaging these modes, the embroiderers dynamically negotiated issues of the group members' identity, negotiations that require conceptual and emotional semiosis. The embodiment of this identity in a variety of rituals, drawing on a diversity of discursive worlds, validates and underscores the tensions inherent in it. The references and correspondences of such expressions are not necessarily consistent. And yet the narrative construction of the story that the group tells *about* itself and *to* itself attains a high degree of consistency and invests it with integrative meanings and organizing themes.

The organizing themes of the group's discourse revolve around the categories of men and women; women, family, and fertility; and most conspicuously the "women's front." These meanings reoccur in a variety of texts: written knowledge versus orally transmitted knowledge, tradition versus innovations, local versus universal or "other" internally versus externally oriented creativity, and so on.

One such organizing theme is "time," which in this study threads its way through the level of the text and the level of the context and syntax. It is with this dimension that we wish to conclude the discussion. Embroidery and time intertwine through their very nature, as described by Bakhtin (1981, 84) in the concept of *chronotope*—an expression of nonseparation between time and place, a kind of permanent conflation of the concepts of time and space. Embroidery corresponds clearly and directly to *feminine* time: "the time of embroidery" is long and patient, progressing stitch by stitch. Since "time" is a human supragender and supracultural parameter, the discourse of the embroiderers focuses on time as an expression of feminine identity vis-à-vis the masculine world, insofar as time refers to various types of continuity in face of competing models of femininity. The process of embroidery does not heed the time constraints of the embroiderer, and even if this process is circumscribed by the life span of the embroiderer, since it passes down through generations, it transcends the lifetime of the individual. The very focus on an object, on a piece of embroidery, indexes a yearning to touch a dimension of atemporal, everlasting existence. The group of embroiderers seeks to deliver old, traditional embroideries from extinction to perpetuity, from traditional everyday uses to preservation in a closet or on a wall hanging, to reproduction as photographs or in an academic article. The transition from a perishable to a preserved state, from the temporal to the everlasting, is symbolically associated—in the embroiderers' discourse—with the adoption of male patterns/paradigms.

Finally, the interpretation of the relationship between genre and gender has suggested a transcendence of the dominant scholarly paradigm of a male/female dichotomy, assumed as generated by gendered systems of hierarchy, meaning, and symbolism. We have pointed out especially the ways in which the discourse of the embroidering women of the Jerusalem group straightforwardly appropriates traditionally male modes of creativity such as textual interpretation—either literally or metaphorically by interpreting patterns. Moreover, on the symbolical level the symbolical conceptualization of penetration, mostly associated with male sexuality has by them transformed into the penetration of textile by needle. Thus we believe to have countered the claim that feminine models are generally embodied in vehicles of expression that are "non-verbal, inarticulate or veiled, while the discourse of men is more verbal and explicit" (Gal 1991, 189). However we agree that "women's genres can best be read as commentary that shows a range of responses—acceptance, resistance, subversion and opposition to dominant, often male discourse" (ibid., 192–93).

Notes

This chapter is adapted from Hagar Salamon and Galit Hasan-Rokem (1997, 55–68).

1. The use probably consciously emulates terminology extant in discourse on music.

2. The images in figures 4.5, 4.6, and 4.7 illustrate the passage from the original embroidery (on the right side of the figure) and the "re-embroidered" piece (on the left side). Shiloah and Cohen (1982) present a typology of transformational trends in Mizraḥi (Oriental) music in

Israel. From a similar perspective of analysis of folk culture, one can say that the Jerusalem women's embroidery, in their own definition, is "neo-traditional" (ibid., 17).

3. *Gobelin* is a genre of needlework deriving its name from a family of Parisian tapestry manufacturers who produced such artisanship from the fifteenth century onward. See chapter 6 in this book for a study of the *gobelin* genre in Israel.

4. On gender gaps, see Swirski and Safir (1991); Raday (1991); Azmon and Izraeli (1993). On the ambivalence regarding gender equality in institutions such as the army and the kibbutz, see Agassi (1977); Blumberg (1976); Izraeli (1981); Spiro (1979); and Palgi et al. (1983).

5. See Messick (1987, 216–17), who writes about two contradictory outlooks in the Moroccan world, writing versus weaving and masculine versus feminine; see also Tedlock and Tedlock (1985) and March (1983).

6. In traditional Jewish texts, fire and water (especially in the form of spring water) frequently symbolize the study of Torah as well as the studied texts. See, in a contemporary folkloristic context, Hasan-Rokem (1978, 204).

5 Life Story as a Foundation Legend of Local Identity

A PARTICIPANT IN a Jerusalem women's embroidery group emotionally described her meeting with Zohar Wilbush, whom the embroiderers consider the "founding mother" of a female dynasty organized into embroidery groups in various places in Israel (see chapter 4). The centrality of the figure of Zohar Wilbush, the conundrum of her age, and the mythological characteristics relating to her past stood out starkly in the embroidery group's discourse. The women in the embroidery group drew a connection between her and the heroic past and struggle for independence in the pre-state period. This stemmed from her family tree bearing famous figures from the history of the Yishuv, along with Zohar's rhetorical demonstration of her knowledge, which made her, in these women's eyes, an actual, visual representation of feminine knowledge binding identity and history, the object of attraction, and a threat, all at the same time.

This chapter is based on Zohar Wilbush's own life story, as told in her Jerusalem home to two women, one in her twenties, the other in her thirties, during long evenings in winter 1997.[1] Zohar Wilbush, born in 1908, defined herself at the outset of her narrative as a "nontypical" woman. The story of her life spans more than ninety years and moves in Eretz Israel between Ḥadera, Haifa, Deganya Bet, and Jerusalem, and in the Middle East region and Europe to Damascus, Alexandria, Constantinople, Athens, Saint Petersburg, Paris, and Germany.

Her overflowing story is characterized by authoritative, declaredly antifeminist rhetoric within which pulses Orientalism. Authoritativeness suffuses both the plot-content dimension and the formal-rhetorical dimension that integrates questions of knowledge the listeners are supposed to answer, the use of concepts and sayings in every language of the region, and ethnographic "explanatory snippets" from Eretz Israel society. Knowing the Oriental other, a definite component of Orientalism, dominates her biography both in content and rhetoric. Thus, when she collected traditional local embroideries and conducted groups for the study of folk embroidery, she again explained, "One must know the embroidery of nations. One must understand what they are thinking. Because when you want to know the country's climate and the nation's way of thinking, you only get to know this through material."

The rhetoric of her story is an unchallengeable rhetoric of knowledge. There is no question to which Zohar did not respond, and her answers showed no hint of hesitation. The Oriental axis, with its decidedly colonial characteristics, relies on the special place of the narrator within the Eretz Israel *halutsiyyut* (pioneering)—as the daughter of a local family of industrialists with a prestigious family tree (related on her maternal side to Avshalom Feinberg, on her paternal side to Manya Shohat). She linked her childhood with village life, to closeness to the earth, to animals, and to Arab villagers in the area. She presented her life wisdom as flowing from her location on the seam *between* the cultures and *between* the genders.[2]

For Zohar this special position was the source of cultural and political insights that reveal multidirectional characteristics of the concept "culture," as Pierre Bourdieu proposes in his theory of practice.[3] Culture, according to his approach, is rooted in *experience* in the sense of the merging between the axis that stresses the understanding that culture constructs practice (as in Geertz's conception) and the complementary axis, the one that stresses a reverse, parallel process in which practice constructs culture. This dynamic, circular direction that Bourdieu embodies in the idea of the "habitus," passes like a scarlet thread through the unique Orientalist experience of the narrator.[4] In her life story, Zohar looks backward to the past and the present, through decoding and processing by means of a system of opposites shaped by body and practice.[5] The design of this system focuses on thematic nodes considered definitely feminine, prominent among which are embroidery and cooking. These differentiate between contrasting pairs of femininity and masculinity, emotion and logic, East and West, and are duplicated by additional, definitely asymmetrical contrasts that are presented all through Zohar's life story in varying relationships not subject, as it were, to a uniform organizing authority. By that, Zohar's private voice strives to become a multivocal, gender-transcending text that merges opposites into a local, Eretz Israel culture to which the title "feminine Orientalism" attempts to allude.

Edward Said's highly influential book *Orientalism* examines the districts of Western discourse that presents the Orient and Islam as an object for research and domination, imagination and romanticization.[6] The book examines a wide-ranging textual world characterized in rhetoric and images that constructs imaginary geographical borders between West and East. These borders serve as the West's set of coordinates for representation and knowledge of the Orient and the Oriental. Thus, Orientalism is the dynamic discourse by means of which the other is fashioned as an object—and specifically, through which the Orient is shaped by the West. On the overt level the Orientalist discourse is linked to the cultural and political, and is the means by which the West turns the East into "Oriental" and Eastern. The East became a cultural fact in the view of the West by means of "knowledge," that which was obvious in the Orientalism produced by the West itself and was common knowledge among nineteenth-century Europeans. This "knowledge" constructed, on its own, the very object that it wanted to know, and with its help the borders of the East and of the West alike were indicated.

E. Said's Orientalist mold raised theoretical and political issues that became central in various disciplines. Analysis of the Orientalist discourse became a focal point for dealing with—to mention just some of the topics—the representation of sexual and cultural differences, overt and covert dimensions of the discourse on otherness, discursive construction of other and self, and the expressions of this construction in the links between culture, knowledge, and power as illuminated by Foucault.[7]

The arena of the discussion, nurtured by Said's analysis in such varied ways, includes the opening of the systematic, closed model that he presented toward the development of complex models of mutuality, or deconstruction, or such as the one that developed within the framework of Lacanian thinking (which leads the discussion in which Bhabha took part) that attempts to decode racial discourse, the systems of connections between representation of self and other in psychoanalytical terms.[8]

It is possible to conceptualize the Orientalist discourse from yet another angle, the representation of Western identity to itself by means of the Oriental other. In such an analysis, emphasis is placed not only on the construction of otherness but a no less pivotal construct—that of the Western subject as having hegemonic status, knowing, discerning, and investigating the object of study.

In this sense its mechanism of action is similar to other fields of identity clarification, which are related to the construction of hierarchical relations of knowledge and control. Such a link is the one between culture and sexuality and between cultural identity and gender identity. The connection between the Western cultural representation as masculine and the Eastern representation as feminine had been raised by Said but developed in detail only recently by Yeğenoğlu.[9] She focuses on the veil through which she attempts a feminist reading of Orientalist and colonialist discourse. The discussion in her book buttresses the concept that cultural representations and gender differences reinforce one another and that the discursive structuring of otherness is achieved simultaneously by marking cultural and gender differences.

The narrated life of Zohar Wilbush moves between masculine and feminine identities and between varied Occidental and Oriental cultures, whose definition is based on detailed ethnographic knowledge that she attributes to her unique life experience. This chapter examines the way in which she interweaves the contrasts and the national historical events along with routine daily endeavors. Characteristics of a mixture of areas, and the creation of new structures, in the course of

Figure 5.1. The living room in Zohar's apartment in Jerusalem.

her life story, repeatedly break down categories and unite them.[10] Her life story deals time and again with actual cultural representations in which food and handicrafts are prominent—areas also chosen by the "Oriental Others" to represent themselves and their culture in different contexts.[11] The analysis in this chapter presents a theoretical model that integrates Orientalist discourse and Bourdieu's approach to practice, which attempts to decipher the connections between the routine and the ideological. This analysis is a kind of dialogue, just like the life story told to us, between the narrator's viewpoint and rhetoric and that of the writer of this chapter, who discerned this model and gave it prominence over other possible models.[12]

Zohar Wilbush is a woman of striking presence even at her advanced age (figure 4.8). From her embroidery-adorned clothing and her ethnic jewelry radiate the detailed attention she gives to her fields of interest and knowledge and combine a gender declaration with an ethnic-colonialist declaration. She told her life story in the living room of her modest apartment. The room was furnished in pleasant simplicity and decorated with ethnic crafts, particularly local traditional textiles (figure 5.1). Above a large desk hung a map of the Ottoman Empire, which was mentioned earlier and will be discussed below. In her life story, the narrator did not follow a general chronological framework; this is a recruited, conscripted text, in which personal life experience is fashioned into an authoritative, didactic text, during the course of which the narrator moved among different events in her life unbound by rules of time.

Despite the lack of the chronological dimension in the life story unfurled, our accepted cultural discourse requires a chronological construct. We glean from her story biographical details. Zohar was born in Jaffa in 1908 with the name Sarah Zohara Wilbushewitz, which she later changed to Zohar Wilbush. Her early memories are connected to the *moshava* Ḥadera, where her grandfather and grandmother lived, parents of her mother, Shoshana, and her uncle Avshalom Feinberg. She was raised as an only child (figures 5.2 and 5.3) until she was ten years old, when her younger brother Yoel was born. Her father, Nahum Wilbushewitz, the brother of Manya Shoḥat, was a far-seeing engineer and industrialist who traveled widely throughout the Middle East and Europe, each time for a number of months. In her childhood Zohar spent time in many countries and was raised by private nannies. Her mother, to whom Zohar's attitude is overtly ambivalent, was a teacher who taught her pupils to sew delicate European embroidery (figure 5.4). Zohar describes her as a pretty woman, always dressed in the highest European fashion, delicate, fragile, and "spoiled." For high school Zohar studied at Reali school in Haifa, and for a time was the "leader of the [female] scouts" there. After her studies she moved to Deganya Bet, and later on traveled to Germany, about the time of the Nazi accession to power, to pursue academic studies that she never completed.

In 1946 Zohar moved to Jerusalem, working first as an arts and crafts teacher and then for Tahal (Water Planning for Israel) for many years (figures 5.5 and 5.6). From the age of sixty, for some twenty years, Zohar worked in the Israel Museum Ethnography Department; she specialized in the textile crafts and material culture of the Middle East. For many years Zohar held, in her home, women's groups for learning embroidery and its origins as well as ethnography of the area. Her students describe these meetings as a source of tradition for many groups of embroidering women throughout the country. Zohar was married, but she never mentioned her husband's name during the telling of her story; she divorced after a few years of marriage, during which she gave birth to a son, to whom she only alludes in her story.

"Even at Six or Seven You Can Ride a Horse"

In an authoritative tone, basing herself on examples taken from local folklore, Zohar sketched a hierarchical cultural system, suffused with emotions. The Arab inhabitants of the country represented for her a "natural," authentic culture whose customs and "way of thinking" were actually known by only a few of the country's Jews.[13] As a native of the land whose earliest recollections go back to life in the moshava, Zohar considered herself an authority of cultural knowledge and understanding. She recollected, "We used to go hiking everywhere. And for each

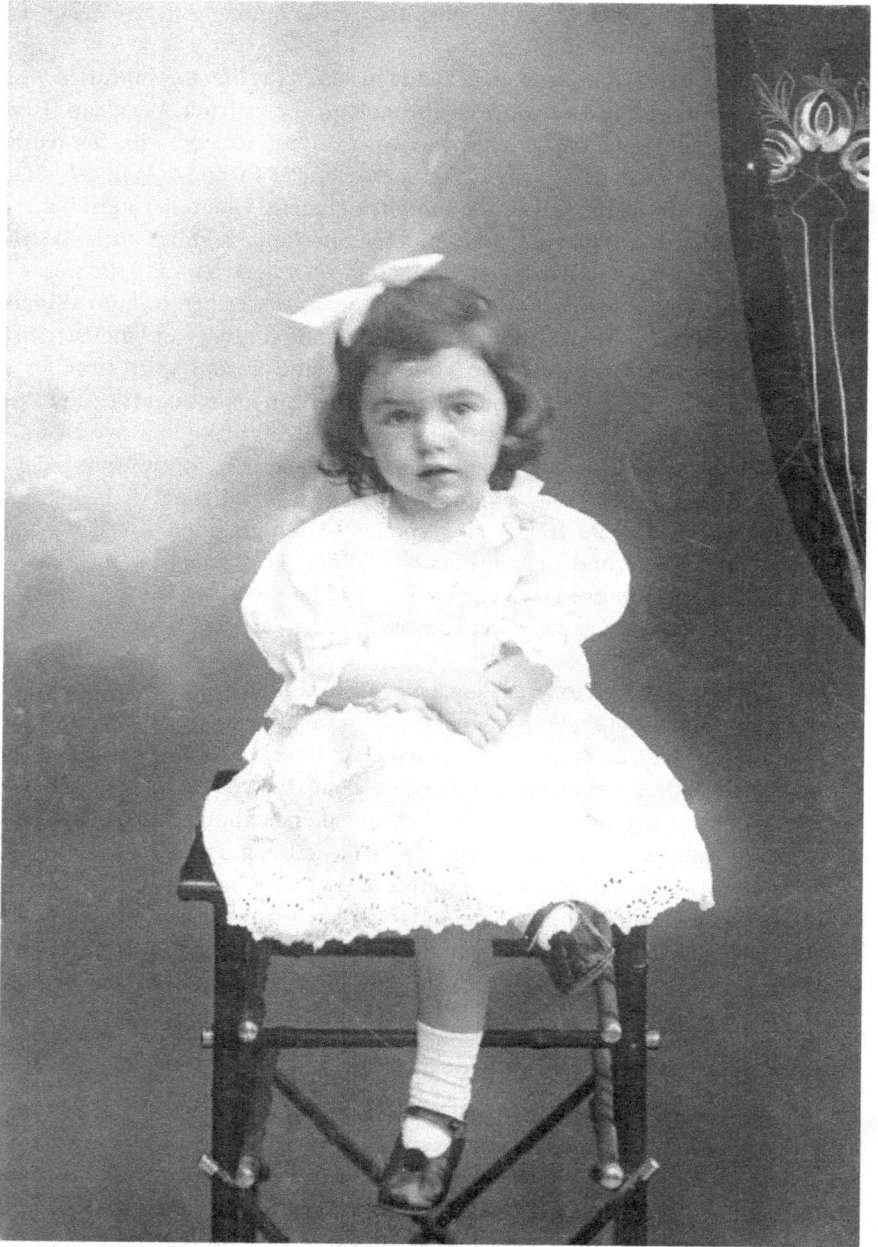

Figure 5.2. Zohar at the age of two.

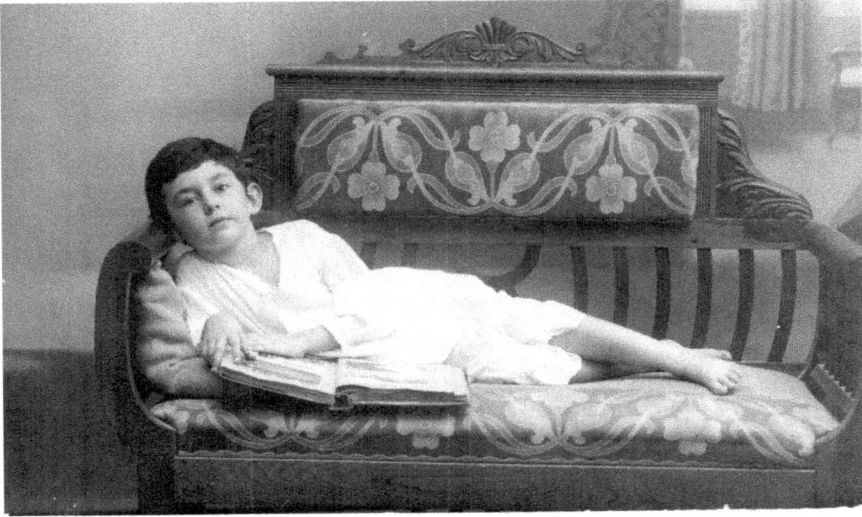

Figure 5.3. Zohar at the age of five.

trip we had an excuse. So the excuse might be to pick a certain species flowers, or to see a certain type of Arab tribe, since there are different kinds of Arabs in each place." Museological Orientalism—a concept I wish to propose from the current reading—that creates such a crude parallelism between species of flowers and types of Arab tribes accompanies Zohar's life story and is well known from other colonialist ethnographic contexts. She saw herself as someone who received European education combined with primary, "natural" familiarity with the local Arabs:

> When I was at Grandmother's, what would we do? Grandmother would sit me on the big donkey. There was Hmār, and there was Jakhsh, that was the little Arab donkey. Hmār, this was the big one that came from Lubnan [Lebanon], he was not local and he had saddle bags, khurj, so Grandmother would sit me down on Friday morning or Thursday afternoon and say, "Go to Buzaburah" and go to this or that fisherman.... How many kilometers is it from Hadera to the sea? ... so I would go to him, "Tefadli, tefadli" ... and he would wrap the fish for me, put them in the khurj, in the saddlebags, and I would go back. I was not at all afraid. Then, not everyone would send a child alone. I said I was not afraid.[14]

In many other places over the course of her life story Zohar emphasized her lack of fear of local nature, which includes, as she saw it, the local residents, too. So, for example, she claimed that she was never afraid of animals, that dogs would

Figure 5.4. Zohar's mother, Shoshana Feinberg-Wilbush.

sniff her from afar and "identify" through the smell of her body that she was part of the authentic local experience. As she told it:

In Grandmother's yard there were dogs. In the house there was a small dog, but in the yard was a boxer, a real boxer, if you know. Well, now dogs are decoration. Instead of giving love to a child, they give it to a dog. But a boxer, I don't suggest you meet a terrifying boxer, because he won't do anything to you; he won't bark. He'll only take a piece of shnitzel from your body. But I was not afraid. I was a girl of six, five, six, seven. I was not afraid of him or of horses. I said to my uncle Avshalom—"I want to ride, too. Everyone's riding, and I'm not." Then he said to me, "But you can't sit here on the saddle, and the horse's head is here." Then I said, "Put me on it." So Avshalom taught me that you can sit on the horse's neck, but hold very, very tight to his mane, not only to the reins. So I would get up [there], and if you give a light tap, he runs. You don't need any saddle with all its stuff, so I rode. Then, you see, even at six-seven you can ride a horse.

Horseback riding—featured prominently among the elite women of the Yishuv in those days—is a subject Zohar returned to again and again in her life story. Riding among the Yishuv aristocracy is characterized by a decidedly English charm, while Zohar described it as a different type of riding than that associated with the life of the moshava:

It was the fashion then to ride horses. But not all women rode. For example, the mother of Ezerke [using the diminutive to refer to the president of Israel, Ezer Weizmann, when she told her story]. So Ezerke's mother and three other women would get together in Haifa. In Haifa there are horses. In Tel Aviv, they apparently drove the horses out. I remember that as little girls we always used to look at them, how they were riding. Because then there was Krichevsky, one of them was Hadassa Samuel. For then the English high commissioner was Herbert Samuel who was a Jew, and his son Edwin married Hadassa Grasovski, Goor. He was once Grasovski, now Goor. So Hadassa Grasovski and Ezerke's mother and two three others of this type used to go out in Haifa to ride horses.

They weren't moshava ladies, and the British set the tone like this. In England people ride horses. I don't know what you watch on television, but if you turn on a British station you always see horses. Always . . . in the city there was British influence. In the moshava there was no English influence, in the moshava it was simple since you can't wait, once or twice a day there is a [transportation] connection, and if you need something urgently,

Figure 5.5. Zohar as a young woman.

than you get on a horse or a good donkey. Because there was Jakhsh—a little donkey—and there is Hmār—a big donkey. You didn't grow up like that. But horses as one of the social things; this came from the British.

"Smell If This Is *Khamrā* or *Samrā*"

Like her riding on horses, described as an authentic contrast to the fashionable British riding, Zohar also explained her authenticity by means of her familiarity with the village animals and with the different smells of the soil she grew up with from an early age. She turned to us and asked:

I was in the moshava, so I knew about chickens. Chickens now begin the season of the eggs, and you eat eggs all year round, right? But what color are the chickens, *nu* [come on], answer me? ["White?" I try, and Zohar smiles in victory] . . . It was never white. If you've been in the Arab village and seen the speckled chickens and the handsome rooster with the brown and green and black tail, then you know the rooster and the hen. After all, this land was not commercial agriculturally. Remember I told you that when we were children the game was "*Nu*, tell me what's this smell; is it *khamrā* or *samrā*?" We grew up differently. I know that your children will not grow up like that. Your grandchildren won't even know the word *khamrā*, they won't know that red soil is called *khamrā* and that black soil is called *samrā*, 'cause that's Arabic, and Arabic is disgusting, to know the Arabic language. God forbid. See, even those who study Arabic in high school, they learn literary Arabic. Who needs it?

Figure 5.6. Zohar as a mature woman, balcony of her apartment, Jerusalem.

Recognizing the different smells of the soil is linked in a single continuum to the names of the types of earth in Arabic and to the Arabic language. She successfully tested her knowledge of Arabic and the use of a specific dialect that indicated she was from the Shomron, or a "Samaritanite," as she attested of herself; this was affirmed by an Arab she spoke with at a chance meeting in Jerusalem. Zohar said:

> Look what happened to me a few days ago. I happened to be in some Arab store, I opened my mouth, so then there was a young fellow there, so he says to me: "*Anti mish min al-quds*" [you're not from Jerusalem]. I said to him: "Right, I'm not from Jerusalem." Then he says to me: "Where are you from, Netanaya?" I say: "No." He thinks and thinks, then says: "Min Samarin." From the Arabic, the Arab has an ear. He could tell from the accent from where. The Jew, talk to him Yiddish as much as you want, but he can't tell from their Yiddish from what country they come. The Arab has an ear. He knows how they talk in each village.

"An Arab Woman Doesn't Sit Like Me"

Heightened senses, which Zohar attributed in her story to local Arabs, were linked for her to a whole world of colonialist hierarchical concepts. Her specializing in textiles, and mainly in local embroidery, gave her a unique position of knowledge and exposed a romantic perception of the other, as close to nature and embodying "natural" traditionalism, of a time-bound nature: "First of all, an Arab woman doesn't sit like me. She sits on the ground. And then she needs to make a line. Then she threads a needle and stretches and embroiders. They wove the textiles by themselves. I have all the types of textiles. But what they didn't know was proper dyeing. So how to decorate it so that the textile won't be one color? You have to also put a few green lines, you see the Arab women: here a green line, here a white or black or red line."

In Arab culture, as embodied in the women's weaving and embroidery, thoroughness is missing ("she doesn't know proper dyeing"). It is a decorative, colorful culture. In many places in her story, expression is given to hierarchy and relations of dominance and suppression between knowledge and lack of knowledge, between logic and emotion, between masculinity and femininity, a hierarchy that inverts itself intersects at many nodes.

The meeting between the local, "authentic" Arab and Westerners was described by Zohar as destructive, when she told of the meeting between the Arab women embroiderers and the English women:

> The English ruled here for thirty years. That's not a day, that's not two days, thirty years. And then all the self-righteous English women appeared. And they made from this not only propaganda, but also benefited from this because they gave Arab women textiles and threads from England, and already then, the embroidery slowly turned into non-natural embroidery. When all the English

women who helped the Arab women showed up, Arab embroidery stopped being Arab embroidery . . . because when they bring you the threads from abroad instead of you sitting and making the thread, because when they teach you that there is canvas, instead of you embroidering according to the thread, then all the value of the folk work evaporates.

"Natural" embroidery, and here especially the local Arab embroidery, is set vis-à-vis the precise, fine European work, of the kind that Zohar's mother taught. The local embroidery is described as ancient, static, and "natural," while European embroidery ruins it through an encounter based on exploitation.[15] Zohar dealt in her narrative, in combination, with two types of meetings between the European and the Oriental: the one portrayed by the self-righteous English women, by her mother, who embroiders the delicate European embroidery, or even by leaders—including women—is an arrogant and "destructive" encounter, positioned in her narrative opposite another choice, an "integrative" meeting characterized by romantic images of similarity and affinity to the Arab-village culture. Yet the haughty, destructive meeting, dominated by male images, is precisely the one linked repeatedly in the life story with female figures. Another contrast that Zohar's narrative revolved around was the one between female and male embroidery. The way this contrast was fashioned gave rise to complicated interrelations with the contrast between Oriental and Occidental embroidery:

If, when you were younger, you would have seen saddles, you would have seen that the Arabs usually embroidered something on the sides. Do you think that women embroidered that? There is a difference between the embroidery by women and by men, since the women's finger is softer. So she embroiders soft items. On leather a woman does not embroider, embroidery on leather is [a type of] work that a woman does not embroider, there is also a difference in the stitches. A woman likes everything to be delicate. I think that a man always takes everything in a rougher way. This means, if [it is] a thicker metal thread—a man will work better; if it is a thicker woolen yarn—a man will work better. A woman, naturally, has delicacy. See, there are decorations made with nails. There are wonderful things decorated this way. A man has to do it. A woman will never work this way with a hammer. Because of her senses, she needs to feel; everything she does she has to feel. Look! This is unpleasant. It's as choppy as from a grater [*Zohar points to embroidery on a leather belt she owns*]. When a women wants to embroider, it must be delicate, pleasant.

And more:

If you've noticed, the men always work in straight lines, a woman makes everything curved. That's the way it always comes out for her . . . and a flower and everything, when a man embroiders a house the room comes out like this for him [*she demonstrates with her hand a triangle with straight lines*], when a woman embroiders it comes out like this [*again, she demonstrates a curved line*].

"You Won't Find a Scent Like This in Any Bottle"

When Zohar talked about body care, she pointed out the creativity she customarily applied to everything related to makeup or perfume.

> Makeup is a wonderful thing. Because as early as the period of the Pentateuch, the Mishna, and the Talmud, they already knew that it was necessary to anoint with oil, that skin dries, already then they knew that it is necessary to put in a certain [kind of] flower. If it was makeup, then I always put in what was fitting for hot days, in winter you don't have to, in summer you go out in the sun more. I used to go out on a lot of trips, so I used a lot of all kinds of lotions, and then, finally you get burned, then you need powder, so I had French powder of a certain kind that was supposed to help, but what I really always used was talc for the feet, 'cause if you don't apply it [your] toes stick, and talc is the simplest thing. I didn't deal in this stuff. I had many more things to deal with, I didn't have time for this. What I did do, I would smear my hands with any cream so they would not be dry. Because [when] hands are dry, then later the skin cracks. That's so. ["And perfume?" I added.] Perfume, no! Why? I would also try to take a flower with a scent, now you can take [it], you see the scent it gives? [I said, "The narcissus?"] Did you see? You can go out to see. You won't find a scent like this in any bottle. If you go outside now here, you can smell the narcissus, and see that the Jerusalem narcissus is all scent [and here we go out to her apartment's balcony to smell the narcissus in a flower pot]. This is the real scent, but in the swamp, the narcissuses are much more beautiful, the petal is thick and white. But they do not have such a scent like these, the scent is very strong, and if you can put it just like it is into a handkerchief.

In the "habitus" she wove in her life story, traditional femininity—embodied in the daily physical realities of clothing and jewelry, embroidery and cooking—conducts an open dialogue with masculinity generally embodied in building, politics, and "grand history"; this method repeatedly set up and broke down contrasts between categories. So, for example, the centrality of handicrafts in the shaping of identity and gender relations stands out in her descriptions of courtship customs common when she was in high school, and from them we learn about the attitude to feminine and masculine hands, and to the handicrafts of "the boys" and "the girls" alike. Zohar related:

> Drying flowers was the main thing. What do you dry? You dry the tiny flower "Forget-Me-Not," to dry flowers you have to know how. There was a sponge. And everybody had a sponge on their desk; there was a blotter. And drying flowers in a sponge is totally different from drying flowers in paper; then the flower still stands out a bit. So you dried the flower in a special way. Then you gave this to the young man who was with you. You tried to arrange them in a pretty shape, writing something, let's say, "forget-me-not," or "remember the trip," "remember the sunrise," "remember the sunset," what do you think, it was so easy? [*laughs*] See, the boys have hands [good for] a pliers, for tongs. How

does your name start? *H* and your family name, *S*, right? So he would sit down and cut it out for you. So it won't be from silver, it will be from some kind of tin or a piece of copper. He will cut, and work it, and make triangles that you can stick on anything. And so, that is something a girl can't do. She cannot do it! Because to cut out the metal and work the metal she can't do it, a girl. That he does. But a girl can take many beads and embroider his name. Yes. So she can embroider the letters of his name, and make a ribbon bookmark.

"Tehina and Mayonnaise Are Things Women Can Invent"

Again and again Zohar linked women and embroidery, embroidery and cooking:

Look, women love embroidery because the woman deals with minor aesthetics. A man, see, no women ever made a camel saddle. Now take the girls [referring to the women's embroidery group that met in her house once a week], they were in Transjordan, they brought camel saddles with wonderful woodwork, and there were leather saddles, gorgeous, you've certainly seen [them] in all kinds of museums. No woman made a saddle, it's not for her. But for "Baby Dearest" when she brings him to the circumcision [ceremony], she wants him decorated. When "Baby Dearest" starts to walk—she wants him decorated. So, then she pays attention to the little things, like a chef, the king of chefs, makes very tasty dishes, [so, too,] a woman makes a small decoration surrounding the fish. A woman for some cooked dish will make tiny decorations all around it for you. [I asked, "And do you like to make tiny decorations?"] Me, no, but if I do something, then I will take something that will give me the decorations all at once. So then I take thick green pepper and cut it and plunk it down all around, not a tiny piece for each one.

I will return to her self-perception, on the seam between the genders and the seam between the Orient and the Occident, that she exemplifies through embroidery and cooking of "little things," and through "large" cultural and historical characterizations.

The perception of male embroidery as aggressive and "sharp" in contrast to the perception of feminine deeds as emotional and "round" was transferred also to another traditional female field—cooking. It was described by using diminutives— cooking in "small quantities," dealing with decorations:

A woman, as I said before, with her delicacy can only deal with details. Yes. When it is an issue of details, the woman [can do it]. But when [at hand] is quantity, it's the man. He takes the entire calf, takes all the good meat out of the calf, and does everything. She does not have the power to carry this out. The woman is afraid of quantities. The woman is born for fine things . . . the chefs who cook quantities are only men. All their inventions always lean toward quantities. They never invented something for four people, they always invent for thirty, fifty people. They are not capable of inventing of four people. I heard that a woman invented mayonnaise. So it seems to me. Anyway, the problem of tehina and mayonnaise are things women can invent. Whether they did invent it or not I don't know.

The miniaturization of feminine endeavor down to limited quantities and tiny, delicate decorations stands out regarding both embroidery and cooking. The idea of sauces fits in with this construction, which presents the man naturally as firm logic, as a base, and the woman as feeling, as a liquid sauce. The relations between basic food and sauce are presented in an asymmetrical manner, through the hierarchical perception of emotional female thinking and logical male thinking—a concept completely congruent with the declaration by Zohar herself that she "is not a feminist." But Zohar described herself as someone "who has learned how to go into depth." She brought together feminine embroidery and the other handicrafts, which she deciphered and taught her students, with male logic that developed within her, as she saw it, owing to her studies in the West—and particularly in the German tradition. Thus, in contrast to other women who "see pictures" (as she stated elsewhere), she herself delved deep, and her proof of that was in taking the picture apart in an attempt to understand the system, the logic, and the order that stands behind it. Zohar explained:

That I delve deeply is my father's fault, because he claimed that "only in Germany," "in Germany they plow everything with a sharp blade." I had teachers who forced me to go into things seriously. Ask your [female] embroiderers whether the thread twists to the left or to the right; they won't know. The Mishna states that "one thread is spun, two-three woven." Now, if it is woven to the right or to the left makes a tremendous difference! Most of the [female] embroiderers can't tell you!

And in another place:

See, I must always know more details. From where, how, and what. One has to go in depth. No young woman raises questions like these. . . . The problem is that they see a picture and that's nice. But you have to know the foundation and that's the problem. A man is more thorough. Logical, thorough—whatever you want, while a woman [just] sees mostly pictures.

"To Think with Feeling"

Despite these statements that pay tribute to logical thinking, Zohar also lashed out against thinking that lacks feeling, this time, too, within the feminine context:

And there are customs! See the custom at a funeral, a woman walking with her head covered, you are one of the funeral party, or you're related to someone— you walk with a head covering. But when I went down to the street after Rabin's assassination, and an Arab said to me *"mā-bitastahîsh"*—she is not embarrassed? His wife without a head covering. After all this is not an issue of faith; this is a custom. ["Are you talking about Leah Rabin?" I ask] That's the one. For this is not a matter of belief. Let's assume she does not want to observe commandments, but this is a custom. "From tip to toe," says the Arab, "she is all gold bracelets like they are selling in a store." It is customary during shivah to not wear jewelry. But this is a custom, no more [than that]. So they say to me, "She certainly didn't know." If she didn't know, mores the pity . . . I do not have to hear from an Arab how she is not embarrassed. So a woman must learn the customs of the country she is in, and she has to be a bit sensitive to things that hurt.

Zohar's criticism of Leah Rabin recalls Herzfeld's cultural intimacy paradigm, discussed in relation to bumper stickers. Zohar's disapproval of Rabin's lack of sensitivity to the manner in which her actions affect others invites consideration from the perspective of cultural intimacy. Zohar's language locates her as a member of the founding generation and thus upholding the "moral family leadership" (1997, 12).

The combination of masculine knowledge (perceived as linked to the Occidental-European) with feminine knowledge (associated with the Oriental-local-Arab) constitutes the unique Orientalist axis in the authoritative life story of Zohar Wilbush when she stressed the need, prevalent in Eretz Israel, for "thinking with feeling." She repeatedly attested about herself that "they always said about me that I think by palpation." The world of gender distinctions, the one of feeling and emotion in contrast to logical thinking, and the one of the local spatial-cultural versus the foreign, Arab versus European, intersect in various contexts. All along her life story, the "habitus" that Zohar created links routine experiences (and mainly folk arts, clothing, cooking, fauna, and flora) and broad political and historical categories. But serious scrutiny shows that her discourse transformed, in many ways, the "little" experiences—related to actions, to physical surroundings, and to immediate experiences—into universalist, political, and "great" historical categories.[16] We return to the map of the Ottoman Empire hanging proudly over the desk in the living room, and to the responses given by Zohar when asked about it:

Why this map? Because it is a hundred and something years old, and with it I know exactly where I am. In my first document [attesting] that I am in this world; it clearly states I am Ottoman. It is written in Turkish. Of course, Rabbi Kook signed it, but it is written in Turkish. The Turkish provided opportunities, until the World War they were very helpful to the Jews, much more than the Mandate government. They always tried to develop. They tried to decorate. Every one of their buildings is ornamented. The Turks, when they built, they immediately decorated, too. A Turk first of all decorates the city where he lives.

Her autobiographic narrative is a discourse woven between the individual, as expressing the "habitus," and the historical process. The "habitus" explains the historical process in which the Ottoman Empire map is a marker of the starting point to which Zohar wishes to return. Her life story sets up intersecting axes, and on them the English represent unemotional logic also connected to masculinity, while the Arabs represent a culture of knowledge that is not always based on logic. She sees the Ottoman Empire, into which she herself was born, as a model for the merging of "building with ornamentation," of logic with emotion. One may explain the name change of Zohara Wilbushewitz as along two axes: the one between the feminine and the masculine, and the other between the Jewish-European and the Orient. By changing her name from Wilbushewitz to Wilbush (that her father determined) and from Zohara to Zohar, she initiated a shift from the Jewish-European-feminine pole, to which she had belonged from birth, toward the masculine and Oriental pole (composed in this case of two portrayals presented, in other contexts in her narrative, precisely as contrasting), a pole that is not definitely acquired and that, therefore, cannot be the primary substitute. About her name change, she related:

> If you take my documents, the British passport and British identity cards, [you will see] it is written: Sarah Zohara, Sarah for my father's mother's name, but Mother did not want Sarah. 'Cause she didn't like the sound . . . so if you see pictures of the first [or] second class of the Gymnasia, they would go out for a trip wearing kafiyyas and ajals, Arab clothing. Then it was a kind of Oriental poesy. So, then they gave me the name Zuhura, they made it Zuhura instead of Zohara. Zuhura in Arabic is a flower, zuhoor. ["How did this turn into Zohar?" I asked] How did this turn into Zohar? When the Russian immigration came. Did you ever hear them talking with their accent? Every *h* is a *g*, isn't it? So then it was "Zogara" or "hara" or something like that. Avshalom, may he rest in peace [Avshalom Feinberg, her uncle], I have letters from him, used to call me Zuhoor. But Zuhoor was going too far. It is a bit too much. And so when I came to Jerusalem, I arrived two years before the state, I decided—Zohar.

In a similar way, the romantic attraction to men, who personify in their body the merging of the East and the West, which she described at various points in her narrative, is a fantasy for a different Orientalism, that which is personified by the Armenian men, whom she first meets during a visit to Alexandria as a teenager:

> I personally do not like the light blond who has no distinctiveness. Nor the eyes that are like water and as if they do not see; I much more like dark hair and dark eyes. At the time, when I was in Alexandria for the first time, I was fifteen when I took a trip there (since my uncle was in Alexandria, so I went there), so for the first time I encountered an Armenian orchestra. I said: "These are the men I want!" Their skin, too, is not black like the black man, but yet not completely white. And their eyes are not brown and not green. So I liked the Armenians.

And elsewhere we find:

But what, in Alexandria I decided that the most handsome men are the Armenians. From the entire Orient and from all of Europe the most handsome man is the Armenian. They are not black and they are not white. They are a kind of special caffe latte. In Alexandria I decided that the most handsome man is the Armenian! The Armenians have maintained their race. I don't know if you have met an Armenian orchestra or Armenian athletes, an Armenian is a man worthy of the name *man*!

The aspiration to merge opposites, for joining East with West, feminine and masculine, is a fantasy of complementary relations. Zohar binds her life story, her very clear memories that are transmitted with such great sincerity and candidness and interwoven with detailed descriptions regarding the many colors of the soil, the scents of the flowers during the different seasons, and with expressions in many languages, to the point of learning lessons based on the fantasy of merging emotion and logic that complement each other, which are expressed in the melding of the "rounding," "decorating" feminine and the "direct," "sharp," "graceless" masculine. These insights are "recruited" in her life story for the sphere of politics and leadership.

She explained:

See, it is impossible to be in this country and be an American like Golda Meir or Bibi Netanyahu. Both she and he are Americans. Do they know the country? Give them this [*points to a myrtle branch*]; will they know what it is? Here sat a girl from Beit Ḥinukh [school] and asked me, "Who did you vote for, Peres or Bibi?" I said, "Peres is a Pole, Bibi from eight to eighteen was in America, so he looks at the Arabs like the blacks or the Indians." "So for who?" she asks again, so I said "Yig'al Alon." "He's dead." So I said, "But he was the only one who understood the country, he was the only one who understood."

And on another occasion she said:

We miss Yig'al Alon more than anyone else, because he knew the country's inhabitants—both Jews and Arabs. He knew the surrounding countries. What I said about Golda Meir, I said that she was an alien plant among her people. Why? Because when the head of intelligence came to her and said—"The Arab countries want to attack us." Four countries attacked. More than a thousand people were killed. The head of intelligence came to her and told her they were preparing. So what did she answer? "He's a fantasizer. He's an Oriental Jew. . . ." For her, all the Oriental Jews were hallucinators. She, the American, she's practical! Why was he the head of intelligence? Because he knew Arabic, because he understood the mentality. But she held him in contempt, she summed him up as "he's a fantasizer." . . . Golda Meir did not know the country, she was not familiar with its customs, she didn't know anything. Bibi, I have nothing for or against him. But Bibi went to America when he was eight, stayed there until he was eighteen. He looks at the Arabs and doesn't understand the mentality, he does not understand what is going on around him. So they said to me, "Stop! He's begun to learn Arabic." Thank you! And if he learned Arabic, so what? You have to know the customs. You want coffee *'ahwe*, so I am ready to make *'ahwe*, but from me you'll get Bedouin *'ahwe*, not from powder and irradiated milk. Yig'al Alon knew how to talk to every Arab, and he was familiar with them down to the last detail.

The "Americanization" processes taking place in Israeli society and leadership symbolized for Zohar a unidirectional culture, masculinity without femininity, a separation between the "small," material, local, intimate experience, and the "grand" politique and history, or, in other words, the lack of the cultural "habitus." This lack is symbolized in her statements by the vacuum Yig'al Alon left behind him.[17] Yig'al Alon's image, which represents for her a combination between knowledge and feeling, between Occidental and Oriental, between the alien and the local, repeatedly appears in Zohar's life story: and in contrast looms a feminine figure, that of Golda Meir, with the traditional contrast between femininity and masculinity intersecting and turning about in her image, which portrays in Zohar's eyes, precisely in a female body, the keenness of the confrontation.

The construction of autobiographical memory is shaped as an interpretive and didactic process, in which the life story of the individual—especially impressive in this case—allots it place for scrutiny and analysis, linking the individual body and the other with historical experience.[18] So the "feminine orientalism," which becomes decoded through her life story, constitutes the individual voice of the one defining herself—from the very outset of her life story—as an "atypical woman" and as "unique," and a window to the broad cultural perceptions of the "Yishuv aristocracy" in Eretz Israel, and especially to the feminine voice that reverberates in it.

Zohar related the story of her life to Israeli women younger than herself in a way that reveals a complicated, unique Orientalist worldview, personified through the fashioning of symbols and meanings taken from the concept of "habitus," in which body and knowledge are interconnected; in it personal experience becomes a source of generative authority that explains the world. The status of knowledge that the narrator wishes to grant herself exposes a system of relations between pairs of contrasts, the basic one of which is the contrast between the female body and the male body. The rhetoric of the statements and the fashioning of the life story, characterized by authoritative setting up of pairs of contrasts that repeatedly disassemble each other in the course of the narrative, create disharmony between the private life story and the shaping of her life story through a dialogue between us, as a didactic story with a vision of acceptance and harmony. Here another, tragic level of connection is revealed: the personal life story creeps into the text against its will when it is recruited for the didactic, harmonious story.

This multidirectional system of relations between physical daily experiences that are formulated as traditional femininity or traditional masculinity and broad categories of politics and history are capable of drawing one's attention to theoretical directions that examine the concept of culture and folk epistemology as a process of constructing contrasts and the negating symbolic connection, replete with fantasies, between "small" and private worlds, and between those considered large and universal.

Notes

This chapter is based on an article, "A Woman's Life Story as a Foundation Legend of Local Identity," originally published in *Jewish Women in Pre-State Israel*, ed. Ruth Kark, Margalit Shilo, and Galit Hasan-Rokem, 141–65 (Lebanon, NH: Brandeis University Press, 2008).

1. The life story of Zohar Wilbush was related to the writer of this article and to another listener, Sharon Agur, who assisted in the fieldwork.

2. In this context, see Said (1990).

3. See particularly Bourdieu (1977, 1990, 52–79).

4. On Geertz's interpretation of culture as an exegetical system, see Geertz (1973). For the development of the idea of the habitus, see Bourdieu (1977, 52–65).

5. See Bourdieu (1977, 66–79).

6. See Said (1978).

7. On the connection between ethnography, Orientalism, and power, see, for example, Clifford (1988); on power, resistance, colonialism, and women, see, for example, Comaroff (1985).

8. On mutuality, see, for example, Bhabha (1994, 66–84); Spivak (1985); Scott (1992). On deconstruction, see Derrida (1984); Spivak (1987, 169–95); Young (1995). On Lacanian thinking, see J. Butler (1993).

9. See Said (1985); Radhakrishnan (1992); Butler (1993); Yeğenoğlu (1998).

10. In this context of interest is Young's (1995, 75–173) discussion, which addresses in a new manner the concept of hybridity in the colonialist context in Bhabha (1994); and also in Yeğenoğlu (1998, 35).

11. On the political aspect of Palestinian representation by means of embroidery and other feminine crafts, see, for example, Frank (1996). For a fresh perspective on the connection between personal biography and objects, see Hoskins (1998).

12. In this context Yoram Bilu writes:

> There are many ways, all of them partial, to analyze and understand life histories. The portrait of the Other crystallizes only through the process of its construction, during the course of the interaction between the researcher and the object of the study. The design of the portrait is guided, inter alia, by the researcher's prior knowledge (such as social conventions, cultural traditions, theoretical paradigms, and so on). This system is likely to be such a useful framework for sorting through, organizing, and processing the raw data that in some cases it might be possible to accept the blunt claim that ethnography and biography, more than they create a "narrative" are created by it." (1986, 350)

See also Bilu (2000). On the rhetoric of biography and the importance of the literary aspects through which the narrative is fashioned, see also Lieblich, Zilber, and Tuval-Mashiach (1995). For another discussion of these aspects, see, for example, Crapanzano (1992).

13. Here, and throughout this chapter, the term *authenticity* is used differently than in other chapters as it reflects Zohar's personal use and understanding of the concept.

14. This text is characterized by the repeated use of Arabic terms, undoubtedly intended to reinforce the local impression Zohar wants to present. To each term a "translation" is usually appended. I wish to thank Ruth Kark, who drew my attention to the Arabic name Buzaburah used by Zohar, which is Mikhmoret today.

15. For a discussion of the construction of Otherness and the concept of a different kind of temporality, see Fabian (1983).

16. This, too, recalls cultural intimacy and the way that Zohar is involved in "shaping the meaning of national identity" (Herzfeld 1997, 9).

17. Yig'al Alon was one of the legendary members of the Palmach; he was a founding member in 1941 and appointed the commander in chief in 1945.

18. For an important discussion of memory and its narrative, see Bahloul (1996), particularly chapter 5. Ethnographic and theoretical material that deals with life stories and their narrative design is a broad, expanding field in the research of culture that treats it only by allusion.

6 The Intimate Career of a Transitional Object

Needlepoint Embroideries

THIS CHAPTER GREW out of an intimate setting of women in discomfort. The decoding of this discomfort engendered interpretations in dialogue with thinkers like Julia Kristeva, Michelle Foucault, Violette Morin, and Donald Winnicott.

Several years ago I opened my house to an exhibition of textiles, including wall hangings in which the designer integrated old and sometimes worn-out pieces of ethnic weaving and embroidery into a contemporary oeuvre. Some of the wall hangings integrated needlework embroidery, known in Israel as *gobelins*, a designation of a once-popular female practice. *Gobelins* are industrial prints of well-known paintings, which were precision embroidered stitch by stitch, by women in Israel.[1] The *gobelins* in the current exhibition presented images of aristocratic women and were accompanied by texts from Jewish sources; their present context endowed them with a measure of reflexivity and even humor (see figures 6.1 and 6.2).[2]

All the works on exhibit were enthusiastically received by the public—mostly women admirers of textiles—with the exception of the few that included *gobelin* needlework. For most of the observers, those works became invisible. They hesitantly turned their gaze on the exhibit designer—as if no longer certain of her capabilities. The very reappearance of the *gobelin* on the wall triggered confusion, and the atmosphere became charged. The present chapter examines this tension borne by the *gobelin* needlepoint embroidery. Through a look at the complexity of the present attitude toward *gobelins* within the framework of the domestic developmental cycle, this chapter focuses on complex dynamics related to feminine and maternal creativity, suggesting new directions for observation. The strong feelings of discomfort, which I have identified and will formulate systematically, were based on in-depth interviews with the embroiderers and their family members.[3]

Gobelin embroidery is a highly simplified expression of the embroidery tradition to which they seek to belong. *Gobelin* embroidery was a common women's practice in Israel in the past, as it was in other places in the world.[4] Printed canvases were sold by the multitude, ready for the embroidering hands of women, who chose the picture they "filled" with a dense half-cross-stitch weave, one considered simple

Figure 6.1. '*Eshet ḥayil* (valiant woman), wall hanging, Miriam Salamon, 2002.

Figure 6.2. *Tsena Ur'ena* (a book for women on the weekly Torah portions), wall hanging, Miriam Salamon, 2002.

Figure 6.3. A pre-embroidered *gobelin* canvas.

to learn, based on precise color instructions printed on the border of the print (figure 6.3).[5] The typical *gobelin* pictures include scenes from the imagined lives of refined Western European nobility. Especially popular were noblewomen, who can be assumed to embroider *gobelins* in their free time, as well. The making of *gobelins* may express the desire for appropriation of the lives of the nobility through a Sisyphean effort to transport the distant and desired to the walls of the domestic space. At the end of the embroidery process—usually after many months of monotonous and painstaking labor—when the painting is "clothed" in embroidery threads, it must then be framed, and the residents and visitors of the household may be shown the immortalized handiwork of the embroiderer, usually the mother of the family. The framing of the *gobelin* is usually the sign to begin work on a new one.

The present ethnographic study examines the range of emotions of the *gobelin* tale.[6] To understand the expressions of discomfort linked to *gobelin* embroidery in the present, we begin where the discarded *gobelins* incorporated into the exhibit were obtained—in the flea market of Jaffa. An expert in the field of textiles, who was familiar with the changing supply of textiles in this market, informed me that after years in which they were rarely to be found, recently the market had become flooded with *gobelins*. The *gobelins*, with their luxurious frames, arrive

Figure 6.4. Jaffa flea market, 2010.

in the marketplace, in the state they were in when pulled off the walls. Even if a certain length of time may have passed between their removal from the wall and their arrival in the market, their ornate framed appearance hints that the needle-work may have been thrown out in disgust by a family member eager to get rid of the nuisance. They are often found in groups—hinting again that they are likely the work of a single anonymous hand (figures 6.4, 6.5, and 6.6). In addition, their ridic-ulously low price aggravates the insult: the seller will justify the few dozen shekels he asks for by emphasizing the value of the frame rather than that of the *gobelin* embroidery those frames were designed to display.

Let us now leave the flea market and go back to the beginning, to the embroi-derer and her family. The *gobelin* pictures, an industrial reproduction invested with the industriousness of the "good hands" of the embroiderer, were charged with a fine eye for small distinctions, precision in following instructions, and sometimes even desire. All these transformed them into valuable objects, far beyond their monetary worth. In Israel, the practice of *gobelin* embroidery flowered in the 1970s and 1980s.[7] However, in a process revealed by Pierre Bourdieu, the politics of taste gradually infiltrated the houses of the embroiderers and their familiars.[8] The embroiderers' families, and gradually, the makers themselves, came to con-sider the *gobelins* as icons of bad taste. In a process not devoid of tragic overtones, the *gobelins* became invisible and finally unworthy objects of disgrace. Thus, the

Figure 6.5. Jaffa flea market, 2010.

attempt of the embroidering women to transform themselves into modern women through a feminine means of expression (the use of needle and thread for non-functional, decorative, and perhaps artistic ends), had become a sign of lack of taste and "traditional" femininity.[9]

The axis of time, especially the axis of lived time and its link to objects is the central theme of Janet Hoskins's book *Biographical Objects* (1998), which demonstrates the vital force of objects in her subjects' life stories.[10] She draws on a 1969 article by Violette Morin, a French sociologist, who distinguished between two categories of objects—the "biographical object" and the "protocol object" (a trade object).[11] The relations of the individual with the biographical object endow the object with its local identity, particular and private; the relations with protocol objects are global, generalized, and produced mechanically. In these terms, the embroidered *gobelins* are a hybrid object—straddling the two categories. Industrial prints of works of art sold en masse are protocol objects, designed for the practice of industrious women, who attempt to transform them into biographical objects. The *gobelin* embroiderers seek to transform the printed pictures (protocol objects) diffused throughout the world, which mark them as modern and progressive women, into biographical objects through hours of devoted, loving effort. In this process, traditional women's practice is mobilized to create an object that will identify the embroiderers with modernity. The hybrid finished product was

Figure 6.6. Jaffa flea market, 2010.

an attempt to retain and exemplify the productive and empowering conjunction of the two opposing categories; in the course of time, however, the tensions that intersect in the finished *gobelin* product effaced the entire value of the production, as aspired to by its makers. The intersection of additional tensions inherent in the finished product, among them that between the aristocratic images and the daily life of the embroiderers, the luxury of the frame as opposed to the simple embroidery techniques, and the transformation of the unique nature of the original painting into its popular embroidered representations, contributed to this erasure.[12] The framed picture hung on the wall became a coordinate of intersecting tensions, tensions that may both produce and explain the further trajectory of the picture, as well as the discomfort surrounding it. This understanding, which became clearer as the research progressed, posed a challenge. in their current permutation, the *gobelins* erased themselves, but the strong feelings of confusion remained, testifying to the particularly charged nature of this popular expression.

The appearance of the *gobelins* on the floor of the flea market is the final scene in the drama of their passage from living room walls, removed by someone who no longer desired them. Thus, the time at which the research took place was one of disinheritance and exclusion. So, for example, one interviewee, when asked if he knew of women who embroidered *gobelins*, answered, "What do I care about *gobelins*? They're just bored housewives who sought some way of passing the time. . . . It's a waste of your time; why deal with this?" Or, alternatively, the reaction of a woman who specialized in textile techniques, said, "*Gobelins* are boring. I don't see anything in them—no creativity, nothing."[13]

These reactions reminded me of the words of a member of the group of "folk embroiderers" in Jerusalem, discussed in chapter 4. One of the participants spoke of the needlepoint of the women of the group, presenting it in opposition to *gobelin* embroiderers: "Our preoccupation," she explained, "is not that of printed gobelins or passing time by turning a needle round and round. . . . For us, this is research on a country, its culture, the materials and techniques they use there." For this group of embroiderers, *gobelins* were at the bottom of the scale of embroidery works.

Surprisingly, even among *gobelin* embroiderers, some doubted the value of their own work. Sarah, who had embroidered dozens of them, explained: "Everyone but just everyone did this. Like I told you, you don't need to invest thought here; you don't need to invest anything. Just one thought: choosing the picture. That's it. That's the only thought. . . . The *gobelin* didn't require anything. No thought. Just a little patience, that's all [*claps her hands*]. The colors are already there; you didn't need to choose them. You didn't need anything." The interviews I conducted with the embroiderers focused their reflexive capacity by means of the private act of embroidery done by the speaker; there, the memory of the "sacrifice of time" as well as the sacrifice of her "hands and eyes" took up the central place in the interview, as opposed to the reticence and even embarrassment that she displayed toward the *gobelins* now.

Another link between picture and practice was at the core of Nitza's response—she embroidered a large *gobelin*, which still hangs in her comfortable and well-kept living room amid many other pictures on the walls: "*Gobelins* are interesting, insofar as I remember that *gobelins* of things like flowers and scenery and ladies were embroidered by everyone! Because [you might think that] only bourgeois ladies embroidered. But everyone did it! . . . Because it was easy, and it has, like the tranquility of handiwork and an aristocratic air because of what was printed on them . . . whether it was educated women or uneducated ones, or whatever category . . . anyone could do it!"

The discourse presents this craft as popular and accessible to all women. Thus, the practice, including the European and aristocratic images that typified it, was seen as a supraethnic and interclass arena, women's handiwork that crossed and dismantled boundaries.[14] Most of all, in the interviews I heard that it marked a period—the 1970s and early 1980s—in which Israeli women were submerged by a wave of *gobelin* embroidery.[15]

When the women were asked to reflect on the *gobelins* that they had embroidered and framed nearly forty years ago, it brought to mind the passage of time, inviting reflection on women's creative work and on their lives as part of a feminine collective marked by the emergent fashion of *gobelins*. For the women I interviewed, that time was the past, a specific time in their lives in a world moving from tradition to modernity, and marked by transformations resulting from their immigration to Israel.

The complex reciprocal relations between the lives of the embroiderers and their family members and the life of the embroidery are central themes in the discourse of the *gobelin* embroiderers, whether they be explicitly stated or merely hinted at. The timeline and the marking of the perishable and the eternal proved to be central in the story told by the *gobelin* embroiderers. Let us now trace that line. We choose a canvas for the *gobelin*, embroider it patiently, accompany the maker to the framing gallery, choose a luxurious frame for it, hang it with pride on the wall, or give it as a present to her family. From the minute we hang the picture on the wall, the family members will look at it less and less, until, after a number of years, it will be removed and transferred to the storage room or thrown out of the house.[16]

Sites of Desire: Choosing the Canvas

"Mom embroidered one *gobelin* after another. She finished another one almost every month. She embroidered a *gobelin* of an amorous couple and one of a pair of horses and flowers and hunting trips. Most of them, she framed and hung on the walls of the living room. Some of them were given to my aunt and her friends" (Avituv 2001, 42).[17]

Judith, who embroidered many *gobelins* and who now has only three of them on the walls of her living room (figure 6.7), said:

> I went with my husband to choose them. Always together. My husband would really, really like it that I did them. He would leave me in peace and arrange a place with a lamp so that I could sit and work, because he liked that. Loved it. I made this woman and then we put it in the living room. Too bad that I never took a picture of her in her place in the living room of the old house.

Sarah explained:

> Autumn leaves in Europe—you see they are much prettier than here in Israel. I saw this in pictures. It's beautiful. Really, really . . . there's much more color there, much more! . . . You see all the snow-covered mountains, you see all the trees, the forests. . . . I wish I could have been there maybe to visit, to see. So she brought this home . . . it's attractive, it attracts people. What can I do with the dry hills here, with this desiccated earth, what could they do with it? . . . So, they brought the foreign countries here.

At another time, Sarah shared with me her thoughts on why the preferred canvases depicted women:

Figure 6.7. Yehudit Mizraḥi in her living room, next to her *gobelin* pictures.

A woman, no matter how much she worked outside, nevertheless maintained herself, took care of herself no matter what, cleaned the house . . . [but] the scenery gets first place. . . . A woman would do a thousand and one things. She would work and paint and maintain the house and pretty herself, and prepare, and so on and so on. And the husband wouldn't do a thing. Nothing. So she found what to do. She also found what to do [the *gobelins*].

Dina, who embroidered dozens of *gobelins*, of which only two still hang in her pleasant apartment in an assisted living complex, said:

I had a boss who would travel to France nearly twice a month. There were meetings there to bring in new immigrants. . . . So he would bring me some. There they had prettier ones, that were also cheaper, and more pictures so you could choose what you wanted. There are many of nature, and of forests; there's water and there are naked people and dancing people and beauties. You could have whatever *gobelin* you wanted!

On another occasion, Dina attempts to recall even a small number of the *gobelins* she embroidered:

That was the painting of scenery—the flour mill with its water, I loved that scene best of all. I also did many of beauties, I did one nude who was reclining, and also did that one who was reading. That's at my daughter's house; I also did the woman playing music, but whom did I give it to? Whom did I give it to?

Sarah explained:

> Then it was something new. It was the fashion. You do something new, an innovation. Look, take the *gobelin*, embroider, hang it on the walls. . . . I would do the dancing girl for my sister. That was the only picture on her wall. There were no [other] pictures. Exactly, there were no [other] pictures.

The embroiderers' choice of a specific picture to clothe with threads or to "bring to life"—in the words of one of the embroiderers—exemplifies the longing for an imaginary world, which the embroiderers sought to appropriate for themselves by passing the threaded needle through each and every one of the holes in the canvas grid.

The repertoire of prints included artworks of a variety of painters and periods, most of them from Western European classics. But when the embroiderers speak of the choice of printed canvases to embroider, they make no mention of the original artist; they obscure the particular painting by classifying the pictures in groups: flowers, autumn leaves, scenery, beauties, as well as "the naked one," "the dancing girl," or even other, more familiar titles like "the one who plays music" or "the one who reads."[18] Thus, the difference between original and repetition is blurred; what is central is the choice of picture, just like the one on the neighbors' walls, as well as the ease of the technique, which repeats tiny identical units. Thus, the domestic *gobelin* embroidery, which all recognize as something made with the simplest stitches, and which repeats itself monotonously, is a kind of "lowered" imitation of monumental textile works or a "degenerate" version of a famous painting, a pleasing illusion.[19] Another expression of the discomfiting hybridity contained in the pictures is that the layer of embroidered threads separates, distances, and perhaps erases the embroidered object, whose initial choice signified a touching distance between the embroiderer and the embroidered image.

Embroidering Desire

"'My eyes are being ruined,' sighed mother while leaning over the huge gobelin spread out on her lap. Her thick-lensed, black-framed eyeglasses were perched on the bridge of her nose, as she reconstructs, with amazing patience, with needle and thread, the models drawn on the cloth" (Avituv 2001, 42).

Rama told me that even though she embroidered her entire life, she only embroidered a single *gobelin*, and that only in order to experience this technique.[20] She said:

> Even today, it's not possible for me to sit without doing something. I sit in front of the television and do something. . . . I have a friend who makes *gobelins*. Her

entire house is filled up with *gobelins*. . . . She had a period like that, and she made them and framed them, and her entire house got filled up with *gobelins*. . . . But to do *gobelins* like that is the most boring thing.

Sarah recounted:

My son was born in '69. And then . . . I looked for something to do. And at the time it was very fashionable to do gobelins. So I did *gobelins*, and made them and made them and made them. Not just for myself . . . I made many *gobelins*. . . . How much can you cook and clean and do? . . . I looked for something to do, and then there were the *gobelins* . . . and I finished one, and another one, and another one. . . . Just to pass the time somehow.

Doris, Sarah's sister-in-law, explained:

They taught the girls, the women, to make them daughters of the household. A warm atmosphere . . . [it gave] a girl a good and positive character. You're not on the streets. . . . You're a member of the household. And a woman at home should learn such things. You and the handicrafts, it gives . . . the . . . you know, the tranquility, too . . . the beauty. . . . Look, the *gobelin* . . . you know, it's so beautiful, you only go over the [canvas] lines, you go over the lines, you go over them. . . . The picture is already there, you just have to paint it with the existing colors.

Alongside these perspectives, presenting them as a way of filling time or as an experience of traditional womanhood, many spoke with much more longing of *gobelin* embroidery as a deep experience. Thus Nitza:

With a *gobelin*, there isn't much. . . . It's the simplest, even young girls can do it . . . *Gobelin* is the easiest. You still have that tranquility, and you see how it takes shape, because the threads are shiny and it's prettier. You get something prettier than what you get from the print. . . . It becomes beautiful. . . . The very work is a pleasure! I say that it's fun to embroider—the hours I spend sitting in the light and embroidering, and *thinking of my own affairs* [emphasis in original], its hours of fun! I don't want to delve into the [private] story of the embroidery! . . . When you do this beautiful thing, you can speak to yourself better! It's something internal—including the colors and everything—I know this from personal experience . . . those were good hours . . . I know from my own experience that you're in a good place. Something good happens to you . . . I don't remember, I don't remember that I had sad thoughts, because I was doing something! . . . For us, it's difficult to sit with our hands folded, we have to do something. . . . For the kids, the hours that mother was working on the gobelin were hours of tranquility. . . . This related to something pleasant linked to mother. . . . The house was in good times when mom was embroidering. . . . Those were good hours.

On another occasion, she said, "When I embroidered, I really felt that I was giving life to the painting!"

Dina explained:

> I very, really love to do handiwork. I don't like to sit without anything . . . I really, really love handiwork. But really! . . . To be calm. And then you can do whatever you want. If someone doesn't like handiwork, he shouldn't start with it. Only if you love it. For me, it's something. I'm calm. And I look at it all the time! Wow, it'll be beautiful! Look how it's coming out. Look what colors! Honey, you should know that *gobelins* and small things like that ruin the eyes! Of course they do! I use drops for years already, because of the dryness in my eyes. I'm eighty-one years old now.

The views of the process of embroidering cover a wide range from "just passing time" and preventing idleness, through monotonous labor, to a manifestation of traditional women's housework to an appreciation of it as an emotional and even spiritual experience—a meditative practice that connects the embroiderer to herself. Through the archetypically female needlework linked with *gobelins*, this connection takes center stage and is exalted.

In addition, the hours of the past spent at embroidery were linked with their present-day bodies as well as with their modern lives in the present. Several women testified of themselves as no longer embroidering but of adopting activities that would mark them as modern women instead.[21]

Desiring Eternal Life: The Finished Embroidery

> Mom looked at it, and suddenly felt a thump in her heart, and she hurried outside and actually found Grandma Lilly on the terrace, hunched over the railing, half her body already in the World to Come. She wants to kill me slowly, and pulled her by her arm back into her bedchamber near the living room: now sit here, Momchu, it's not yet time for supper. Why are you looking at me like that, it's me, Hinda. What are you afraid of? As if we're going to slaughter you here? Raise your feet, sit up straight, don't cry now, you need to lie down, okay, go ahead and lie down, here, look how pretty that is on the wall, what beautiful colors, parrots and monkeys and trees, all this you did, mommy-chu, this is your gobelin, now look at it well and you just rest a while. And she covered Grandma Lilly up to her chin with the Scottish plaid blanket, and tucked the corners of the blanket deep under the mattress. (Grossman 1994, 10)

Rama, in speaking of the work of *gobelin* embroidery, said:

> Good work is when the picture is good, when the rows are precise. When the transition between the rows is precise. . . . When she finished a work, then her daughter and the people around her would say, "Oh, how beautiful!" In other words, we definitely have here the motivation of receiving appreciation. . . . The housewife is appreciated and that means that she does not just cook and clean, but that she also is creative in her own eyes. Although you can always say that there is no creativity involved, it gave them something in life. The moment they

see this hanging on the wall, they decorated their houses. They had difficulty giving them away, just as it is always difficult to give away things like that.

Yehudit:

We liked that very much. The work itself and to frame it, and place it on the wall. [Later, with some pain:] So all of them watched me when I was working, my husband was very proud of me, the kids too. Together, we decided where to hang them. But today, they don't do such things. How many can you do? How many can you hang up?

Rama:

This is a very difficult story, What do you do with the finished work? You don't see in it any commercial value, because of the number of hours you invest in it. . . . That's one of the things. . . . One of the problems of women's work. . . . Appreciation of the gobelins, for example, they got from other women, because that was part of women's culture.

Sarah:

[The husbands] would brag about this outside. Outside—yes. My wife embroidered . . . my wife made these things. Come and see what things my wife made. . . . Look, first of all, she sat at home and didn't go out in the streets. The woman in the house.

Yehudit:

I gave *gobelins* to my sister-in-law, to my husbands' sisters, I would give presents. Or sometimes there was a wedding or something, then they would bring more, but only to someone close, who could appreciate it. People who I knew valued this and liked it, and I knew that they couldn't make them on their own.[22]

Dina:

I made and made. I made some much bigger than this one. One I made very big [and it took] fifteen years. There were animals, and this one . . . I gave to my brother's son. They told me that it was not modern, and my daughter didn't want it. So my brother's son said: OK, give it to me. I want it! . . . My daughter came: why did you put the *gobelins* up? It's not the fashion anymore [*in a tone of anger and scorn*] . . . I did not sell the *gobelins*.

After many hours of punctilious work, the moment arrives when every millimeter of the print is covered with embroidered threads. At this moment of pleasure and satisfaction with handiwork, the creator is dispatched with the piece of embroidered cloth to the frame store, where, several days later, she will walk out with the embroidered piece framed in a luxurious frame, with the piece of cloth "preserved" behind glass.[23]

We now trace the path of the framed *gobelin* from this peak point onward. When it is framed and hanging on the walls of the house, the *gobelin* will invite more in the months and years that follow, made by family members who continue to embroider and frame their works. Within the rigid framework, the embroidery continues to embody, for family members and visitors of the home, the presence and dedication of "Mom."

Yet once they are hanging on the walls, the artistic character at the base of the embroiderer's choice is gradually erased, and the *gobelin*—in the family's consciousness—joins the Sisyphean traditional household tasks incumbent on the housewife. These tasks, in essence, are not designed to be permanent, and this enables—and sometimes even encourages—the family to develop a kind of blindness toward them. Moreover, insofar as the *gobelin* is a rag hung on the wall, it is further distanced from its painted original, advancing its decline into invisibility.[24] A tension is created between the *gobelin* pictures that cover the walls of the house and embody the mother's fantasy to be seen, and the tendency of the family to blur and even efface the mother's housework. Thus, when I asked the family members of the embroiderers and other visitors to the house about the pictures, in most cases, all they could tell me was, "There were all sorts of *gobelins* there." Thus, the pictures underwent a process of erasure, whose sources and realization we now examine.

The Fading of Desire: *Gobelins'* Latter Trajectory

The period in the lives of the *gobelins*, which lies at the core of this section, examines the steadily weakening tie between the *gobelin* oeuvres and the walls of the embroiderer. The weakening of the link—a process that affected each and every one of the embroiderers and their family members—is subject to a broad and varied process of interpretation on the part of the embroiderers, whose materials and ways of conceptualizing them is examined below.

Yehudit:

> After we moved house, I didn't mount the picture in the guest room for a long time, until I finally decided to put it there. In the previous house, it was in the living room, over the sofa. But now it wasn't important any more, not important. At one time someone also told me, "Sell it!" So I said: "I have no idea what price I could ask. . . . You won't even pay one hundred shekels for it, but for me, it's worth even ten thousand! It's so much work, I made it with so much love, that it's priceless."

Doris:

> That's it, I have some . . . two or three of flowers that must be in the storeroom downstairs. One picture of a windmill is hanging in the living room; all the *gobelins* were in the living room. . . . And when we moved here, at the beginning

I put them up . . . [and then] I took them down. . . . It . . . didn't find its proper place. It's not . . . I too saw that it didn't speak to me there. So I took it down.

Some displayed open scorn toward the *gobelins* they had made with much enthusiasm in times past. For many, moving house was a prominent signpost in the decline in the status of the *gobelin* pictures. This decline was expressed in the questions that the embroiderers and the members of their families asked themselves. Should they hang up them up in their new homes at all? And if so, all of them? Should they place them in a more out-of-the-way place in the new apartment, to be demoted to the storeroom, or even to be taken out of the house entirely? The move to a new house or the remodeling of an existing one is seen as a sign of progress and renewal. At this point, the *gobelins*, which had becoming steadily less visible, were returned to the field of vision for reevaluation. Frequently, this transition marked an additional stage in the process of their exclusion, or, alternatively, the proclamation and renewal of the long-term covenant between the embroiderer and the *gobelins*.

Rachel related:

Two years ago, I gave the *gobelins* away. After I renovated my house, my friends told me that it's not modern . . . *gobelins* are not modern . . . [*pointing to the large* gobelin *of an aristocratic couple*]—it would really be a pity to throw this out. . . . This is a very pretty picture; it's very big. The frame also cost a lot of money . . . I like them. . . . No one hangs up *gobelins* today. Maybe it will make a comeback at some point.

As to the question of where the *gobelins* would go in the future, many interviewees were anxious about the fate of their works and presumed that even their daughters might refuse to adopt them and throw them out of the house.[25]

Yehudit whispered:

"Look, imagine when we die. My daughter won't put this up in the house! . . . I will tell my daughter to remove them from their frames, and keep the *gobelins*. It's much easier to keep that way. My granddaughter, maybe someday it'll make a comeback, become fashionable again. Sometimes such things return.

Rama noted:

That's a difficult question. I too ask my daughters if they want me to give them something, but they don't want [anything]. For me, that's very painful—what will happen to this? . . . What to do with this?

Miriam, whose mother embroidered many *gobelins*, both in Morocco and after her immigration to Israel, provided an additional response to this refusal. Miriam mused:

Today, I don't know if I would bring *gobelins* into my home again; it makes the atmosphere in the home heavy, somber, kind of antiquated. . . . It's something of a previous time, since today you won't sit and waste time on *gobelin* handiwork. . . . It evokes a gloomy atmosphere, those old houses—an old, musty smell. A kind of gloominess. Their mother worked on this for months. Do you know what it's like to match threads with each other? It's a tremendous amount of work!

In this interview, the speaker sought to distance herself from the *gobelins*. The infinite time invested in the embroidery signified for her their belonging to a traditional women's world from which she wanted to extricate herself. A modern woman, who wanted her house to reflect her modernity, could not allow herself to bring *gobelins* into the house. This conception is not related to the aesthetic evaluation of the *gobelins*, but to the "traditional" investment in its fabrication.

Jacqueline reacts similarly toward the *gobelins* still hanging on the walls of her mother-in-law's apartment in the retirement home:

Now, my mother-in-law is eighty-seven years old, and she's quite sick now. . . . She's in a retirement home. So, briefly, the question arose, that if she has to go to a geriatric section, she'll have to liquidate the apartment. That's part of the [arrangements in the] retirement home. So I just thought, like, what am I going to do? Like, I saw some things you can contribute . . . but *gobelins* . . . I don't know what I'll do [with them]. But I don't think I'll hang them in my house.

In the following words, we see a process that begins with the death of the embroiderer, a process of gradual disintegration. At the first stage, even if it was proclaimed as being "without sentiments," it nevertheless preserved a link between the women who "adopted" the *gobelins* and were ready to take them to their homes and the embroiderer who passed away.

Sonia said of her neighbor:

In Rivka's house, there were *gobelins* that were embroidered by Monica and given to her as a present. When she died, she passed most of the *gobelins* on to Rachel. Rivka renovated her house, and then her sister Esther arrived and said that with the renovation, the pictures had to go, because they were no longer fashionable. Consequently, we received seven *gobelins*. Without any sentiments, they were all divided up, except for three that were miraculously saved and remained with Rivka.

The interview from which I just quoted took place in the house of Sonia, who "gathered into her house" her neighbor's and her aunt's *gobelins*. This interview presented an opportunity for her to proclaim her hopes with respect to the *gobelins* that were in her house, which she wished to see living an eternal life on the house walls. Turning to her daughter, she said:

I have no worry in my heart that you, my second daughter of the family, who is energetic like her mother, will inherit the *gobelins*. I hope that I'm not condemning her to a sentence. I doubt that my two other daughters will be interested in this . . . I want you to count; we have eleven *gobelins* in the bedroom . . . images from the Renaissance, as well as a pair of Gypsies, a pair of bears, and two *gobelins* with flowers. If I had more room, I would bring more from Rivka [her neighbor who gave her them]. The house will soon be renovated, and these pictures will accompany me in the bedroom after the renovation.

The spokeswoman makes a covenant with the *gobelins*. It seems that it is no accident that we find juxtaposed on the walls of her house in a matriarchate composition her mother's *gobelins* (which, according to her, accompanied her from the moment of her birth), others made by the aunt of her neighbor (Monica), which were "adopted" by her after a period of several years in the house of her neighbor Rivka, as well as *gobelins* she had embroidered herself. The spokeswoman, who was interviewed by her daughter, took advantage of her interest to incorporate her into the intergenerational covenant between the members of the family with respect to the *gobelin* works. The daughter, however, when asked if she would hang them in her house, responded with discomfort. The writing, so it appears, was on the wall.

Discussion

At the time when the *gobelin* was embroidered, the picture—that of aristocratic coquettish European women, portrayed against the background of their life worlds—was a colorful refuge from the gray quotidian lives of the embroiderers. Amid the exhausting drudgery of her life, the *gobelins*—gloriously framed and impressive under glass—were a promise of the enduring memory of her handiwork. However, in the extensive course of their fabrication and in their prominent appearance on the household walls, seeking to glorify the mother of the household, they would eventually become an aesthetic burden and an abject, embarrassing object. In most cases, the career of the *gobelin* ended with its removal and complete disinheritance. The precise and tedious work of embroidery and its luxurious framing were meant to materialize the fantasy of the embroiderer. In the end, however, that same classic picture, painstaking embroidery work, and magnificent frame embodied forces that erased each other, leaving their conjunction as a touching souvenir of the original fantasy of the embroiderer.

Most of the embroiderers I interviewed testified that the fantasy had dissipated. This dissipation was concretely expressed through the transfer of the framed *gobelins* from the living room to the dining room, from the dining room to the corridor or to the storeroom, and, often, with their disposal outside the home. The description of this process—often accelerated by the younger generation—was accompanied by the embarrassment I described above. How did it come to be that such a labor-intensive piece of work—which represented a classical and valued painting, properly executed and gloriously framed, made by the mother of the household for the glory of the home and its family members—became an embarrassing burden?

This embarrassment, which was echoed with varying intensity in the stories of all the *gobelin* embroiderers I interviewed, has remained unapproachable both in voice and in meaning. Its inapproachability is inextricably linked to the nature of the object that evoked such embarrassment: if the picture was once glorified as a work of art and a testimony to the embroiderer's competence, it was now seen as a mere source of past pleasure or an alternative to idleness. Its discourse gave rise to the discomfort of the women who wondered what *gobelin* embroidery was doing on the wall of a modern design exhibit. Could the designer have embroidered them by herself? If so, what did such an exhibit have to do with them? And, if not, where did they come from? What, they may ask, does this say about the *gobelins* still hanging in their own mothers' antiquated homes, those stowed in the storeroom, those already thrown away, or—woe unto us—those whose whereabouts have been lost or forgotten?

The confusion of those of the *gobelin* embroiderers who do not understand why their works have fallen into disfavor, and the confusion of others who embroidered uncountable *gobelins* in the past but now feel they wasted their time; the confusion of the daughters and daughters-in-law of the embroiderers who sense the oppression of traditional maternal investment in the *gobelins*, an oppression conflicting with their own desire to experience themselves as progressive women—all these create an additional discomfort surrounding the question of the future of those *gobelins* that still remain in their possession. Finally, there is also the question posed by the interviewees, who wonder why a researcher from the university might be interested in works like these.

All these expressions of discomfort testify to the multisynaptic links of attraction and repulsion that may serve as the emotional and cultural underpinning of the embarrassment linked to the *gobelins*. The artwork is a charged arena of struggle, based on a complex system of representations of peace and tranquility—both in theme and in praxis. I now try to link the analysis of this specific case with several intersecting hermeneutic tendencies.

In her book *Powers of Horror: An Essay on Abjection*, Julia Kristeva (1982) seeks to fathom the nature of abjection, which she links with femininity and, particularly, motherhood. In a breathtaking analysis, she returns frequently to the link between the conceptualization of abjection and the representation of the mother. The gaze turned toward the mother contains the tragic nature of existence. Her body is at the same time the fount of birth and the grave—the promise of life and the tragedy of finitude. In Kristeva's words, she "gives us life, but without infinity," gives us the now and takes away eternity.[26] As she contains both life and death together, the relation to the mother incurs a dynamic of separation, dominated by scorn and repulsion.

The *gobelin* picture represents these depth dynamics in their cultural garb: designed by a masculine-dominated culture industry, it presents to all the illusion of infinity that the embroiderer, innocently or through cunning, imposes on the members of her household. Thus, through the picture embroidered with her own hands, the perishable body of the mother is linked to eternity, while the magnificent and presumptuous frame embodies its opposite and thus invokes the mechanism of abjection. Guided by conflicting emotions, by what is present and what is absent, Kristeva's identification of the abjection linked to the mother leads us to reexamine the *gobelins* and the relations they engender as the concrete cultural and temporal expression of a universal mechanism of feeling.[27]

The current study is located at a specific time period in the continuum of the life of the embroiderer, as well as in the chronology of the *gobelin* they embroidered. This emplacement in time, both of the embroidery as well as the tales told about it, elicits the relations of the embroiderer and her surroundings to the *gobelin*'s time of origin, to the framed product, and to its future destiny. The choice of relating to women's folklore through the embroidery turns the gaze to practices of folk creativity, which contain well-defined aspects of erasure. These include the changes that took place in the embroiderers' lives and those of their entourages, the changing fantasies and the changing obligations of the women toward themselves, their family members, and the homes in which the *gobelins* were created and hung.

The pictures mark the space as heterotopic, one that returns the viewer from the scenery of illusion to reality. In the gap that opens between them, the abject takes root. The space in which we live, writes Foucault, is a space "thoroughly imbued with quantities and perhaps thoroughly fantasmatic as well: The space of our primary perception, the space of our dreams, the space of our first perception, of our dreams, and that of our passions hold within themselves qualities that seem intrinsic."[28] The heterotopic space is a counterspace to the utopian spaces portrayed in the *gobelin* pictures. With its aristocratic images, embroidered and enclosed in luxurious frames, the *gobelin* is an utopian paradise, which, hung in the apartment of the embroiderer, replicates over and over again its inherent contradictions, both the Garden of Eden and the Expulsion.[29] The walls are transformed from the signifiers of a counterplace to that imprisoned in the frame, which is essentially and principally unreal. In Foucault's words, they embody "a general relation of direct or inverted analogy with the real space of Society."[30] Once glass encloses the embroidered images, the picture becomes still more complicated: the hand of the embroiderer caressed the utopian spaces. Their framing and presentation on the walls of her home make them into a clearly heterotopic expression, which is magnified by the glass separating between the embroiderer and the framed picture, between the pliable and the rigid, between the rag and the picture, and between the body of the embroiderer and her home. These reflect, when inspected, the image of the observer against the background of the utopian space and exemplify how, in the consciousness of the observer, the place has become a "placeless place."[31]

The *gobelin* pictures are simultaneously industrial and hand-embroidered, protocol objects and biographical objects (to use Morin's terminology),[32] placed in a singular and prominent position on the scale between the traditional and the modern, and, in particular, between traditional women and modern ones. Here, traditional women are represented by their real or imagined mothers and grandmothers, by all those embroiderers who no longer embroider; whereas the modern women may be their daughters and daughters-in-law, or they themselves, years after the *gobelin* has been completed. The look from the modern, woefully, makes the traditional abject, and the aspiration of the traditional person to become modern even more abject. As the *gobelin* embroideries are, at each stage of their history, linked to hearth and home, this discourse is, first and foremost, a family discourse. It gazes at the transition stages between tradition and modernity in women's internal family understanding. In Israel this is also linked to processes of migration experienced by the embroiderers, who came from a wide variety of countries of origin.

The complexity surrounding the relation to *gobelin* pictures, which explicitly arose in the interviews, marks the domestic space as a vibrant space in which the transition between "tradition" and "modernity" is made by the daughters (and sometimes the sons) of the family, each woman in her own way. It raises the question of the place of the *gobelin* in this process. While the mother created them so that her dedication and her home dwelling—but also her link to modern aesthetics—would be immortalized on the wall, in the course of time, her creation became abject. This is true whether she accepted this position with respect to her work or opposed it ineffectually. Thus, the relation to the *gobelins* provides us with a key to understanding this wider dynamic of transition.

This interpretation leads me to suggest that we view the pictures as "transitional objects." This concept, borrowed from Winnicott's psychology of object relations, refers to the image of the mother and the child's link with this image through actual objects. Situated in the ambiguous space between the real and the imagined, it is simultaneously rooted in both external and internal realities. I seek to borrow the term from the realm of the frustrating and anguish-laden relations of the separation of the child from its mother and apply it to the realm of folk culture and the process of internal and external separation from the image of the traditional mother of the home, the mother who invests all her energy in the satisfaction of the needs of the members of her household.

Soft in tissue, rigid once framed, the *gobelin* picture embodies the aspiration for transition—from a corruptible female nature to a durable one, in a large number of parameters: feminine and masculine, practical and impractical, beautiful and ugly, museum-quality painting and simplistic embroidery, humble walls and luxurious frames, modest apartments and aristocratic luxury—the *gobelins* contain within themselves oppositions that hint at the desire for transition. In my classifying of them as "transitional objects," their destruction is foreseen; the completion of the transition requires their elimination, and the abjection that is linked to it is further strengthened.

The long and painful process leading to the inevitable separation is linked to the puzzling discomfort mentioned at the beginning of this chapter. This discomfort is generated by the renewed confrontation with the transitional object when it is suddenly returned to the wall, newly dressed in royal garments. The generalized discomfort that led to the research on the *gobelin* pictures has been clarified through the research ethnography, yielding additional insights related to "transitional objects" in collective cultural contexts. The proposed application of "transitional objects" to cultural production in Israel of the 1970s and early 1980s and their subsequent developments may yield new directions for analysis in other contexts, as well.

Notes

This chapter is adapted from Salamon (2013).

1. Originally, Gobelin was a Parisian factory for the production of pictorial wall carpets and upholstery fabrics using tapestry techniques, which is a complex weaving technique. This factory, founded by the Gobelin family, was located at 42 rue des Gobelins, and provided wall carpets made using this technique to the royal house and the French monarchy from the seventeenth century on. Although it was not the only factory specializing in the weaving of pictorial wall carpets, its name became a trademark for such hangings. Later on in Israel, the name "Gobelin" became the signifier of embroidery done with cross-stitch or half-cross stitches on printed canvases that often copied the themes, and sometimes the pictures themselves, that appeared on the woven tapestries. Gobelin embroidery, unlike the sophisticated and complicated technique of the original woven carpet, requires only a single embroiderer, a needle and thread, and a canvas with a grid of holes; it usually portrays scenery, aristocratic or hunting scenes, and characters dressed in all their finery. Thus, these themes became dominant in choice of the themes to be printed on the canvases when *gobelin* works became domesticated as a popular women's practice. For a comprehensive survey of wall carpets in Europe, see Campbell (2010, 188–99).

2. I thank Yair Garbuz, who, in our conversations, noted the place, and primarily the absence, of humor in relation to the *gobelins*. It seems that at the time that these works were presented, the humor that might have enabled the renewed display of the *gobelins* on the wall was not prevalent. The wall hangings that included *gobelin* embroidery (see figures 6.1 and 6.2) were created by Miriam Salamon, the author's mother.

3. The concept of domestic developmental cycles suggested by Meyer Fortes in 1958 is a dynamic concept, replacing a static notion of the household. In this chapter I show how folk cultural aspects are enmeshed in such developments.

4. The number of *gobelin* pictures embroidered in Israel cannot be estimated, but their popularity in houses and markets and the words of embroiderers and store owners testify to the centrality of this practice in the later 1970s and early 1980s in Israel. A comparison of the practice of *gobelin* embroidery as well as an examination of the life course of the pictures in other places of the world may prove to be a fruitful subject for research. It is, however, beyond the scope of the current research.

5. The embroiderer purchases an industrially produced printed grid that takes up the entire canvas. She then fills it with a dense texture. Although one may embroider the canvas with a variety of stitches, *gobelins* are made exclusively with a very simple cross-stitch (diagonal), which does not require special embroidery skills and relies on minute differences in the color of the thread to execute the picture successfully. *Gobelin* embroidery has various levels of difficulty. The complexity of the embroidery depends on the size and density of the holes in the canvas and the precision in changing tones in each section. More delicate work is based on a denser canvas and tiny holes, and the embroidery is done with thinner threads. This is called "petit point," a type of handiwork that some of the interviewees attributed to their mothers and grandmothers in Europe. Since the embroidered canvas is less flexible than other cloths, it was customary to integrate them into the living room of the house, where they served solely as decoration—mainly as wall hangings but also in pillows or as upholstery fabrics for furniture, where women had time to sit and embroider while the household help, nannies, and cooks were busy with housework that yielded no material product or a product that was consumed soon after. See photo of pre-embroidered canvas (figure 6.3).

6. The interviews for this chapter were conducted with sixteen embroiders and their family members, as well as with other interlocutors who were linked to the *gobelins* in different ways. Among the embroiderers and their family members, some saw the research as worthy and important, whereas others suggested I research more important projects, like Yemenite embroidery or Palestinian embroidery. Thus, the ambiguous feelings were evoked by *gobelin* embroidery even before the first interview question was posed. In an interview I conducted with Rama Yam, an expert in embroidery, she suggested: "Maybe it's the dream of another life, on another experience. But the problem is that you've chosen a kind of work done by women whom I am not sure are capable of giving you the answers."

7. Testimony of the embroiderers and interviews with owners of stores of raw materials and of frames. On the *gobelin* embroideries and their flourishing in Israel of the 1970s, see Neiman (2010), who writes of Israel of the 1970s, "Back in the Seventies, *gobelin* or tapestry needlework, was all the rage. There was far less television to watch and so an afternoon coffee could be quietly—or noisily—passed with good women friends, all of whom came equipped with a plastic bag filled with thick needles, French embroidery thread and canvas printed with the most horrifically sentimental romantic prints, also imported from France."

8. This concept, originating with Pierre Bourdieu, is frequently mentioned in his book *Distinction: A Social Critique of the Judgment of Taste* (1984).

9. In her book *The Subversive Stitch*, Roszika Parker (1984) identifies the inherent connection between the history of embroidery and changing conceptions of womanhood and "feminine" behavior, from the Middle Ages to the present.

10. For a discussion regarding objects within life stories, see Held (2009, 81–114).

11. This distinction was first formulated by Morin in her research on the changing meaning of objects in modern French. Her writing was translated into English and appears in Hoskins (1998, 7–11).

12. In this connection, we should mention the words of Ella Shohat, who attempts to link various decorative practices of "commercialized romantic nostalgia": "like plastic flowers, 'crystal' chandeliers, pseudo-velvet wallpaper, gilded pendulum clocks or posters of horses galloping against the background of the setting sun, and other markers of commercialized romantic nostalgia. In Israel of the 70s, the painted picture of the blue-eyed boy with tears flowing on is cheek, called the 'weeping child,' evoked the maternal and even paternal instinct of parents whose own children scarcely resembled the Dickensian child who acquired a warm home within the housing project" (2003, 92).

13. In a highly empathetic article, Ariel Hirschfeld opposes the definition of women's needlework as a sign of domestic boredom and notes the wakefulness that accompanies it, one that simultaneously enables "a comfortable state in which traditional women would pass time that was not tedious, but was definitely not boredom at all." This state enables work and listening simultaneously: "And I remember well my mother: Her listening to music or anything else while crocheting was wakeful and completely focused. It was not by-the-way. This work created a renewed focused alertness, from one direction, while the story or the music created it from another" (2010).

14. Thus, for example, Ella Shohat seeks to contrast the *gobelin* embroidery within the "Mizrahi" discourse she examines, including the set of rules it generates. She writes, "The gobelins too brought the scent of other places and times into the shabby dwellings . . . The illusion of space in the gobelin pictures was in dramatic opposition to the modest room in which the gobelin was hung, just as the royal style of the noblewomen did not resemble the world of the Mizrahi woman at all; through her embroidery work she introduced an unknown world into the fabric of her life" (2003, 92–93). Sarah Chinski (1997) also seeks to reveal the ethnic and gender-based division that took place in the Bezalel Art Academy during the period of Boris Schatz, one that directed the artists of Mizrahi origin to the workshops that created popular folkloric art, whereas those of Eastern European origin were directed to the more prestigious realm of creators of high art.

By contrast, an embroiderer said to me in an interview: "Mizrahim didn't make them. They like to cook Mizrahi food, to bake, but they didn't make *gobelins*." In the course of fieldwork, I found that in practice, the embroidery of *gobelins* in Israel crossed ethnic and social lines but not gender ones.

15. *Gobelin* designated the 1970s and early 1980s as "the years of the *gobelins*" in Israel. This clear demarcation appeared in all the interviews, usually as the introduction to the personal story linked to this embroidery. Their shared vocabulary marked their embroidery as one stitch in an embroidery project in which many participated: "the season of the *gobelins*," "everyone embroidered then," "this was the period in which there was a real mania for *gobelins*," or "then I made *gobelins* without end." Thus, the embroidery of *gobelins* was seen as a bounded phase in their life trajectory. In their stories, today no one embroiders *gobelins* anymore. This same consciousness of the passage of time also appears in Yaron Avituv's book, *A Note from Mother*: "We can divide up mother's life into periods: the period of crocheting, the period of sewing, the period of cooking, and so on. She would enter a period like that with energy and enthusiasm, specialize in the field, but lose interest after two or three years and turn to a new field" (2001, 42).

16. In this connection, we can say that the abjection that attaches itself to the *gobelin* pictures links the product itself, the means of its production, and the relation of the family—especially the sons and daughters—to their mother. According to Kristeva (1982), sentiments of abjection dominate the relation to the mother at the deepest levels.

17. Unless otherwise noted, all translations from the Hebrew texts are those of the author.

18. This also appears in most of the mentions of *gobelin* pictures in Hebrew literature, where they were mentioned mainly to create atmosphere and to present the aesthetics of a certain

time period. There are several examples, in which the images in the pictures are described, without mentioning the original artist whose painting served as the basis for the embroidered canvas. For example, Alona Kimchi (1996, 52): "Fat Jana is also from Russia, from the city of Vilnius, She's learning to play piano. She has a piano in her house. Really shiny, of brown wood, lacquered. All the furniture in her house is pretty, covered with the same lacquer. There are pictures on the walls, one of Jana's mother, Faina Filipovna, when she was young and considered beautiful, one of Jana's two parents—Faina Filipovna and Alik on their wedding day, and one, the largest of all, embroidered with all sorts of colored threads, and on it a shepherd and a shepherdess and all sorts of sheep and goats under the trees, This picture is called a 'gobelin.' The shepherd and shepherdess are dressed in festive clothes: she, with a dress like a party dress, and he with 'ballet' slacks." Or, as in Chaim Be'er (1979, 229): "On the wall was a gobelin in a heavy golden frame—the picture of a pair of lovers sailing in a boat on a lake in the light of the full moon—and underneath it, on the buffet, between a dish of oranges and a half-finished crocheted woolen vest, was a pink flower made of crepe paper, whose stem was like that of surveyors, held by a stylized green hand—the symbol of the exhibit 'Conquering the Wilderness,' which took place two years previous in Binyanei Ha'ooma."

19. The use of the term *gobelin* for the domestic embroidery may be seen as a hint that they are a cheap and simplified copy of the original weavings, which were considered sophisticated, demanding exacting planning and execution and even control of complicated weaving techniques.

20. See Yam (2002).

21. Thus, Sarah explained that in the past the *gobelins* served as a means for keeping herself occupied within the domestic walls: "to keep myself busy, to pass the time somehow . . . otherwise, what would I do with myself? Today I have an occupation. I'm finished with the gobelins, I started with artistic embroidery—I finished . . . We have an office here at home. I work in the office. And I go out of the house almost every day. On Sunday, I go to folk dancing for two hours. On Tuesday I go to exercise class. On Wednesday—house cleaning—and on Thursday, exercise class again, and then to listen to all sorts of lectures and stuff. On Friday—among the pots . . . to welcome the children and grandchildren."

22. Marcel Mauss (1967), in his famous essay on the gift, provides insights into the complexities and conflicts inherent in the giving of gifts. The various levels of meaning and importance attributed to the gift influence the ability to transfer it further. According to Mauss, we may claim that the *gobelin* picture is assigned great emotional weight because of the tedious work of embroidery invested in it; thus, it becomes an object that contains some of the soul of the embroiderer and therefore cannot be transferred as a commodity. Even as a present, it can be given only to family members or close friends of the embroiderer. In this connection, see also Silber (2005, 7–30). See also Appadurai (1986, 3–63); Weiner (1992); Kopytoff (1986).

23. My choice of the word *preserved* to describe the relations between the embroidered cloth and the frame with its glass follows from the attitude of most of the embroiderers to this transformation. We might choose other words in this context, such as *imprisoned, guarded, protected,* and perhaps even *fortified* or *rigidified.* The owners of the Jerusalem frame store recounted that during the 1970s, the framing of *gobelins* was his main preoccupation and included several dozens (!) of frames each week. This flow has ceased almost entirely in recent years.

24. Thus, in an interview conducted with the artist Yair Garbuz on this topic, he pointed out the powerlessness of the *gobelins*, to the extent that the exact same scene that might move the observer of the picture to tears passes through his consciousness unremarked when it is transferred to cloth. He explains this transformation as essentially linked with it being a rag: "it always reminds us of a rag—a wall carpet. It always reminds us of a rag that, true, is on the

wall so you don't step on it. But theoretically, you could step on it; so how emotional can you get about it?"

25. The complexity of feelings linked to the future of the *gobelin* pictures engulfs the family even when they, like Yaron Avituv, decide, in an uncommon move, to hang them on the walls of their houses: "After her death, I hung some of the *gobelins* on the living room wall. 'Who painted these pictures?' asked one guest. 'My mother,' I said. 'But they're not paintings, they're *gobelins*.' 'Oh, *gobelins*,' he dismissed them scornfully, as if it was another bit of kitsch" (Avituv 2001, 42).

26. Kristeva (1982, 159).

27. In a sentence particularly relevant to the present context, Kristeva (ibid., 10–11) writes: "We may call [abjection] a border; abjection is above all ambiguity. Because, while releasing a hold, it does not radically cut off the subject from what threatens it. On the contrary, abjection acknowledges it to be in perpetual danger. But also because abjection itself is a composite of judgment and affect, of emotion and yearning, of signs and drives."

28. See Foucault (1986, 23).

29. For a discussion of the double nature of the Garden of Eden as a nostalgic space, see Hasan-Rokem (2010, 156–65). For a study of the contexts of the Garden of Eden in various religious and cultural contexts from antiquity to the present, see Elior (2010).

30. Foucault (1986, 24).

31. In this context, Foucault's words on the mirror are particularly relevant: "In the mirror, I see myself there where I am not, in an unreal, virtual space that opens up behind the surface; I am over there, there where I am not, a sort of shadow that gives my own visibility to myself, that enables me to see myself there where I am absent: such is the utopia of the mirror" (ibid.).

32. Quoted in Hoskins (1998, 7–9).

Part II Recapitulation

Needle Texts—Knowledge, Passion, and Empowerment

CHAPTERS 4, 5, AND 6 manifest how embroidery is indeed stitched—or perhaps saturated—with a wealth of understandings and depth of feeling. A completed project becomes progeny, a sign of motherly toil, a marker of cultural capital, or a backwater of antiquated tradition. Embroidering is a foundational act of a community, a quasi-sacred study of a text, a link to a communal past, or a way of exploring the world. While their makers may consider them as evidence of their accomplishments and precious heirlooms to be passed on, their children often recoil from markers of a femininity and domesticity they construe as antiquated and confining.

The in-depth observations of embroidery and its makers reveal it to be an interactive process of praxis and discourse—an instance of embodied knowledge. The ways in which women engage in, speak about, display, or discard embroidery attests to the potential of the apparently banal, the humble, and the quotidian in representing femininity and Israeli identity. The story of the role model Zohar Wilbush demonstrates how embroidery—like cooking, local dialects, odors of flora and fauna, and folk arts—is integrated into a life story that links routine experiences to broad political and historical categories. Her story lionizes a woman who is the progeny of the aristocratic elite—the founding pioneers—as well as an individual teacher and intrepid traveler. The account reflects the ways that Orientalism and gender roles in Israeli society are exemplified and occasionally subverted.

Chapter 6 sounded a counterpuntal note to the stories of empowerment through embroidering. There, the humble *gobelin* became an arena of struggle between generations and worldviews. It took on cultural meanings and signified contested views as it passed from the embroiderer's hands, through a succession of rooms in the house, until its exile to a bazaar floor, dusty storeroom, or rubbish bin. The study of the Jerusalem women's embroidering group situates the women and the researchers, showing us how talk about embroidery is a way of dividing up the world into male and female, modern and traditional, bearers of taste and the vulgar. The ritual of the women's embroidery meetings consolidates the group and empowers its members through the appropriation of male techniques of study and hermeneutics. It also marks the boundaries of the group through shared symbols of women's solidarity and a discourse of authority, innovation, and authenticity. Embroidery is deciphered through a collective process, performed individually but evaluated and approved by the group members, who thus reinvest individual women's effort with more transcendent meanings. Women's embroidery is shown to be a potent women's ritual symbol. It comes to articulate group experience and feminine discourse while anchoring both in bodily practice.

In each of the studies, embroidery becomes a key to being in the world as a woman and as an Israeli, as well as a vehicle for transmitting cultural knowledge. In Zohar Wilbush's life story, this knowledge is valued in the academic and curatorial world and, no less important, by the groups of women disciples who look up to her as a role model. The *gobelins'* material history speaks volumes about changing Israeli attitudes to family, women's work, time, and modernity.

Far from being the banal objects of idle time, embroidered pieces are filled with passion and sometimes conflicting meanings. They can be symbols of modernity and bearers of tradition, cherished progeny and sacred text, private devotion and window on the world, prized art or despised "kitsch." The analysis moves from the sheltered alcove of the armchair and the repetitive rhythm of the moving needle to broader vistas: it casts a gaze at predecessors and offspring, East and West, tradition and modernity, among many others. All these meanings make it a privileged arena for investigating female identity and the dynamic processes of change in contemporary Israel.

Unquestionably, this is not the final episode in the story of the embroidered works dealt with in this section.[1] The pieces of folk embroidery of the Jerusalem group are applied hermeneutical studies of traditional crafts; at some future date, they may be redone as part of an entirely different enterprise. So, too, may the *gobelins* now cast into dusty cellars and bazaar floors be recollected and revived through incorporation into new composite works, where they may become bearers of new meanings. Then the embarrassment that now greets them may be transformed into a source of pride. Like many of the materials in this book, the career of the embroidered is, as of yet, unfinished.

Note

1. On "Second Life" of traditions, see Kirshenblatt-Gimblett (1998).

PART III

Between the Public and the Private—the Mirrors of Ambivalence

Part III Invitation

*Emplacing Israeliness—Shifting
Performances of Belonging and Otherness*

W<small>E STARTED OUR</small> presentation of Israeli folk culture with a performance occurring on a platform accessible to all: bumper stickers on Israel's roads. Although the participants each travel in their own trajectories, the voices of the stickers broadcast in a common language and created a single chorus, now joyous, now discordant. We then turned to the practices of needlework, exploring positions and commentaries rooted in intimate experiences and discourses projected in both domestic work and in expanding contexts.

In this part of the book, we introduce the notion of an "intermediate sphere" and turn our gaze to varied but vital arenas of Israeli folk expression. Their shared feature is the processing of change and transformation in sites not easily labeled as public or intimate. These intermediate spheres, which are perhaps the most visited in Israeli folklore research, are marked by the prominence of otherness, an otherness integral to the tension between the character of Israel as the state of the Jews and the diverse groups that comprise Israeli polity. The venues chosen for analysis are three examples of a vast and variegated field. All that occurs in intermediate or mediating spheres actually takes place within a specific group and yields a sense of togetherness, while processing the public, the private, and whatever straddles the border between them. The mechanisms and dynamics of the intermediate sphere create ties between people and empower them. Here, cultural transmission takes place in fragile, elusive, or unstable spaces. Such spaces forge participants into a group that responds to many social and personal needs while reflecting and refracting processes within broader Israeli society. A deeper look at these spaces reveals not only the travails of migration but the tragic tones of conformity and the price individuals and groups pay to belong.

The mediating sphere includes sites of bonding, refuges of comfort, venues for venting rage, and places to gather strength before setting out on paths that may lead to change. Folk cultural expressions in this realm assume common local knowledge or a shared cultural intimacy that give them meaning and potency. Yet those institutions and expressions do not enclose participants in an insular environment. They also express and confront the changing values of surrounding Israeli society.

They mediate between the national and the particular, channeling discomfort and tensions in ways that create interpersonal links, in situations as disparate as enjoying humorous stories together or participating in lotteries. Such leisure sites are meeting grounds characterized by similarity and difference, inclusion and exclusion, tradition and innovation. Places like these provide a venue for internalization and mediation of national ambivalences and vulnerabilities, for expressions of individual sentiments of temporal, spatial, linguistic, and corporal loss, as well as for the consolations of a shared fate.

Chapter 7 looks at the humorous stories of Beta Israel, the Ethiopian Jews, as they reflect now on the initial stages following their immigration to Israel from rural Ethiopia. Chapter 8 provides another look at the same community, leading the readers into the lives of its women. It focuses on an empowering local cultural enterprise, that of credit associations, which inherently ties together tradition and innovation. Chapter 9 returns to the topic of humor and analyzes David Levi jokes. These constitute a vital and especially fertile humorous cluster that was highly popular during a specific historical period in the evolution of Israeli politics and self-definition.

The voices in these chapters may arise from within the particular community, as in the case of the two studies of the Beta Israel, or may be heard in jokes told by the majority culture about David Levi, a powerful national politician portrayed as a Levantine upstart. In all three studies, the cultural expressions bind performers together in shared complicity, obligation, or affection.

The David Levi jokes, in particular, hold up a mirror to attitudes toward the other, as well as to the otherness within all Israelis. The cultural intimacy of these forms makes them a suitable arena for reflections, often below the level of consciousness. They reveal focal experiences of Israeliness: the pain of adjustment and the loss of one's native country, language, and culture, along with imagined expectations of the majority society. The lottery circle, too, does not merely express the insular culture of the participants. As a financial institution from below, it provides an implicit critique of the paternalism from above expressed through the banks and monetary arrangements that govern the majority society. Thus, probing a position on the margins amplifies the subtleties of dialogue with a majority discourse and practice that remains hidden from most Israelis' threshold of consciousness.

In these "ordinary," apparently peripheral cultural forms, the conceptions of self and other, in-group and "majority" Israeli culture, women and men, are often articulated in expressive forms, which are coded and indirect. In fact, as I gradually learned, the more the experience touches on core, embodied senses of being, the more these articulations seek an outlet in shared, nonpersonal, and even commonly produced forms of expressions. In the case of the Ethiopian Israelis, it portrays immigrants' encounters with life in Israel through comical staging, which encodes some of the more fundamental vulnerabilities of this group's dramatic passage. It is the light and entertaining nature of jokes that makes them an important vessel through which troubling and sensitive issues can be contained and processed. Participation in the joke-telling event fosters active engagement around topics in which uncertainty abounds, such as in the many tensions inherent in the fluid and rapid dynamics of modern multicultural societies. The exploration of jokes, understanding what makes them funny—and for whom—reveals themes that remained veiled from extra-community audiences. The voices from the margins invite us to reconsider the models of community that many of us take for granted (Pratt 1991a, 34).

By collecting humorous stories and following lottery/credit meetings over a stretch of time, we can chart a trajectory of the migrants' experience, and their changing personal and collective conceptions. The new meanings and inflections carried by the Ethiopian lottery/credit institution in its present Israeli context changes in group cultural, gender, and power relations.

All three cases in this intermediate sphere reflect and process the fluidity of Israeli society with its strong ethos of unity, yet often characterized by unspoken and silencing rifts. They constitute social spaces where, in Pratt's terms, cultures meet, clash, and grapple with one another. Each is an attempt to internalize and mediate national ambivalences and vulnerabilities and tensions between inner and outer identities. At the end of the day, each ultimately leaves the indecisive situation unresolved.

7 The Floor Falling Away

Dislocated Space and Body in the Humor of Ethiopian Immigrants in Israel

THIS CHAPTER FOCUSES on humorous stories that circulate among Ethiopian immigrants now living in Israel.[1] Highly popular in the community, these reflexive narratives address the unfathomable shock experienced by Ethiopian Jews when relocating. The stories articulate their traumatic encounter with life in Israel by targeting specific characters as the butt of Ethiopian humor—the elders, newcomers, or, as in many personal anecdotes and memorates, the newly arrived self. This corpus of humorous narrative is thus characterized by the embarrassing clash of the quintessential "traditional" Ethiopian, with a new landscape, time-scape, and body-scape.

Through these humorous stories—with their repetitive evocation of images and associations—the group's dramatic transformation from rural Ethiopia to modern, urban Israel is processed and mediated. The stories are typically told at gatherings that function as a kind of spontaneous "support group," where participants engage in cathartic laughter, marking their very beings as that which underwent a journey and a transformation, even if this passage is associated with vulnerability or shame. As a form of expression considered "entertaining," the humorous story is a particularly apt medium for the transmission of cryptic intragroup content. Exploration of this form, then, provides a window onto subterranean themes that, in other research venues and protocols, such as in explicit responses to direct questioning, generally remain veiled from the extra-community audience. At the same time, it invites us to interrogate this particular aesthetic form and to understand its mechanism better.

Collective Self-Humor among Ethiopian Immigrants in Israel

Studies on acculturation humor among immigrants distinguish between self-directed and other-directed humor.[2] Indeed, within the overall corpus of humor related to Ethiopian immigrants, almost no overlap can be found between these two distinct bodies of humor. The self-directed Ethiopian Israeli humorous corpus is profoundly different from jokes told about "the Ethiopians" in general Israeli humor circles. Jokes *about* the Ethiopian community told by non-Ethiopians focus on color and other distinguishing features, while the Ethiopians' own humorous tales deal with the traumatic experience of encountering modern Israel.[3] A staple of many humorous scenarios, in the latter corpus, is the depiction of the ignorance and "primitiveness" of the subject of the story; in these contexts, Ethiopian elderly people or newcomers, who represent the clash between past and present, are technologically and culturally incompetent.

In the course of our research on Ethiopian Israeli women's gatherings, which will be dealt with in chapter 8, a participant referred to the sharing of humorous stories as a central feature of these meetings. These fleeting and general mentions indicated that the humor touched on issues of acculturation, but that the informants were unable to reproduce the stories out of their original context. Acquiring the stories as told in their natural, immediate setting required an appropriate research strategy.

The humorous stories were all collected between 2008 and 2009, in face-to-face sessions with members of the Ethiopian community in Israel, in which the author of this chapter took part, assisted by a student of Ethiopian origin. Having immigrated to Israel as a child, such intimate humor-sharing sessions were familiar to him, even before engaging in the research project. As a member of the community, he was able to collect much of the material through routine participation in community gatherings.

Such small, intimate events as the aforementioned sessions are considered an appropriate setting for humor, and, in fact, one of their main attractions is the presence of laughter.[4] Typically family members and neighbors, all members of the gathering are sharers in the inside classification of "what is funny." These gatherings thus provide—apart from pure pleasure—support, a sense of equality, and a sense of common fate.

The stories we collected were told by members of the first waves of Ethiopian immigration, who have been residents of Israel for about twenty years. These humorous anecdotes are usually told as a part of an ongoing dialogue, in which the teller and listener take turns in their "roles"; a teller becomes a listener and vice versa in the course of the interaction. At the same time, younger-generation Ethiopian Israelis enjoy these events.[5] Often the stories told were already familiar to the participants, and their retelling, which resulted in explosive laughter, was indicative of their cathartic nature. Vividly expressive of the immigrants' encounter with Israel, the stories are endowed with a perspective on the tellers' own assimilation experiences and contribute to the crystallization of a unique humorous corpus. Our analysis examines the contents of this corpus against the background of the dramatic transformations that members of this Ethiopian Israeli community have undergone.

Immigration from Ethiopia to Israel

Originally, the Beta Israel (Falasha) lived in rural northwestern Ethiopia.[6] The community was dispersed among five hundred small villages composed of straw huts, constructed from local materials (branches of trees, straw, and mud), with the help of neighbors, in a matter of a few days. The homes and the villages had no access to modern technology. For the most part, no water system existed; rather, water was brought by women from a stream or a well in clay jars on a daily basis. Cooking was carried out by women over an open fire. The basic food staple was *injera*—a spongy batter made of teff (an indigenous Ethiopian grain) and prepared on a griddle. This was eaten with sauces made of pulses and greens during the week, and with meat such as beef, goat, lamb, or chicken on holidays. The *injera*, which is typically shared by several people, was torn into strips and used to soak up the sauce (*watt*). Ethiopian Jews earned their livelihood predominantly from labor-intensive traditional horticulture, as well as from handicrafts—they specialized mainly in weaving, blacksmithing, and pottery. The Beta Israel saw themselves as a distinct religious group, identifying strongly with the Torah (*Orit*, the Hebrew Bible written in Ge'ez), observing its laws meticulously, and dreaming of the coming of the Messiah and their return to the legendary Jerusalem.[7]

From 1977 onward thousands of Ethiopian Jews were airlifted to Israel, notably in two dramatic operations—Operation Moses in 1984 and Operation Solomon in 1991.[8] Today, following the arrival of additional Ethiopian immigrants, the Ethiopian Israeli community of immigrants and their offspring consists of more than 125,000 people.[9] This community experienced radical change in a short period of time.

The warm and affectionate reception that greeted the Ethiopian immigrants, at the level of media coverage, government slogans, and other popular expressions, far exceeded the welcome enjoyed by any other immigrant groups to Israel and was a facet of the smothering paternalism accompanying their arrival.[10] Their traditional background and biblical Judaism suggested an ancient image, which was interwoven with romantic notions that the Jews of Ethiopia came "straight out of the Bible into the twentieth century."[11]

Nevertheless, even after the onset of the immigration process in 1977, bitter disputes about their identity continued. Questions related to the Beta Israel's Jewish legitimacy, which were caught up in matters of origins and race—their visible racial otherness along with the arduous immigration process—are the bases for the many struggles that have challenged their assimilation into Israeli society.[12] Central to this, for example, is that throughout much of the twentieth century, and even after the founding of the state of Israel, the authenticity of the Beta Israel claim to Judaism was questioned by Jewish authorities. It was only in 1973 that the chief Sephardi rabbi, Ovadia Yosef, ruled that the Beta Israel were

Figure 7.1. A woman in front of her home, Ethiopia 1984. Courtesy of Galia Sabar.

descended from the lost tribe of Dan. This ruling paved the way for the Beta Israel's immigration into Jewish Israeli society under the Law of Return. Even after those rulings, however, their "Jewishness" remained the subject of dispute and controversy.

Despite the personal impact, often with adverse implications, of this situation, the matter became a collective issue and was dealt with through public forums. These were publicly acknowledged controversies that became milestones of the group's struggle for acceptance. The collective nature of this struggle to some extent sheltered the individual from the undermining effects of these difficulties. It should be noted, however, that while these salient issues dominated the public discussion of Ethiopian assimilation, they are entirely absent from their humor. They are literally "no joking matter." Rather, it is the day-to-day encounter with a totally new socio-technical orientation, cosmology, and universe that is realized and mediated.[13] This encounter is experienced as a private earth-shattering event, to which the individual now claims attention.

Mediation through Humor

Ethiopian immigrants—plucked out of their traditional, rural way of life—experienced severe shock on their arrival in Israel, where they were moved into modern absorption centers, hotels, apartment blocks, and mobile homes (see figures 7.1 and 7.2). This infrastructure provided an efficient solution for the

Figure 7.2. A newcomer from Ethiopia in front of her new home, Ma'ale Edumim, Israel, 1986. Photo: Doron Bacher. © Beit Hatfutsot Photo Archive, Tel Aviv.

immigrants' material needs, but it often left them isolated and dependent on the absorption authorities.[14] Many of the immigrants were housed in apartments—in hotels, or in temporary or permanent residences—with an identical inner form, in which the Ethiopian newcomers arranged their furniture in almost completely identical ways. When I arrived at these housing projects, I could anticipate with a surprising degree of certainty what their internal layout would be. This is one, obviously archetypal, dimension of foreignness, encountered by the immigrants in the encompassing environment. Other dimensions emerge as forming clear structuring and meaningful elements in the world of the humorous stories.

The group's humor dealt almost exclusively with issues imbedded in re-orientation, in the most intimate and personal sense. This point requires clarification. While it is often expected that the experience of immigration will produce cultural disorientation, a metaphorical sense of the "ground falling out from under one's feet," the humorous stories also bring to the surface a submerged experience of disorientation not otherwise registered or expressed in direct discourse. This sense of disorientation is concrete in temporal, spatial, and corporal terms. The intensity of the disorienting experience as portrayed in the stories brought an awareness of other accounts of the airlift from Ethiopia to Israel, an event that shattered every familiar dimension of time and space. The humor, therefore, processes a radical rupture of basic embodied knowledge and gives expression to "the ground falling away" in an utterly literal sense. It can be said, to use Pierre Bourdieu's (1990b) terminology, that the move from rural Ethiopia to Israel shook the very foundations of the immigrants' *habitus*. The experience of corporal disorientation is crystallized through the accumulation of stories and their reiteration of central themes to produce a tacitly shared, even if not explicitly acknowledged, insight.

A distinctive and unique system of coordinates marks this repertoire of stories. At its center is the fracturing of a basic spatial orientation, to the point of loss of control and loss of equilibrium, a spatial, temporal, and physical vertigo that accompanied the experience of immigrating to Israel, which the act of storytelling and laughter seeks to stabilize.

The presentation of the stories themselves is organized in thematically related clusters and accompanied by analytic remarks, pertaining to some of their most prominent features. This classification is to a great extent congruent with the intracultural classifications as they emerged in the context of collecting the stories, when one story gave rise associatively to another.

The Stories

Vertigo

"I Was Afraid the Floor Would Fall Away"

My cousin came to Israel three days before. He arrived on Tuesday, and I arrived on Thursday, and only a week later did I discover that he was one floor beneath me. We ran into each other in the stairwell. I didn't understand that you had to turn on the light [*laughs*]. I went out the door and treaded carefully because I was afraid the floor would fall away. I went into the stairwell; suddenly I heard someone ask me: "Who are you?" And I said: "Who are you," and so we discovered cousins living above one another! All because we didn't know how to turn on the light in the staircase. We didn't go out of the house all week. We were told that this was the toilet and the shower, and all week were shut indoors.[15]

"We Threw Out All the Keys"

Our whole family immigrated in 1990. After we arrived, we had no idea where the entrance was or where the exit was. We didn't know where the doors were. We didn't know the entrance and exit to and from the house, or the keys . . . or that when you open the door it opens up, and when you close it, it closes. We were so scared when we saw the keys in the door: when you close it, it closes, and when you open it, it opens. We then took all the keys and threw them out, so that we wouldn't be locked in. And so when we went out, the door stayed open.

"In Just One Room"

When we first came to Israel we were put together, the whole family, in some apartment. For a whole week we all sat together in just one room because we were sure that the other rooms had other families sitting in them.

In the chronicle of the humorous encounter, this group of stories hearkens back to the first days of living in Israel by marking with explicit chronological precision the beginning of the new epoch. The profound signaling of the primary rupture is embedded in the story itself, as in the first verse of Genesis (or other tales of mythical legendary origins): "In the beginning . . ." In the corpus of humorous stories, this becomes "during our first days in Israel." In the course of these first days, as the stories testify, the world turned outside in: bathing and eliminating, formerly associated with the river and the bushes, became part of the house in an embarrassing, even mortifying, way. The floor is no longer only on the ground, and day and night lose their distinctiveness. Outside the entrance to the home (in the hallway) it is constantly night, and inside, day can be created by flipping a switch. The external space of night can swallow up family members, preventing awareness of their close neighboring presence.

The door, and the key attached to it, are a focal point of the threat. This threshold between outside and inside is so foreign that the door is perceived as an arbitrary being that imposes a new definition of cosmos and chaos, and focuses the immigrants' sense of their loss of control of space. The keys, given to endow them with a sense of control over their homes, are described in the humorous stories as if they were malevolent agents, bent on instilling chaos into their lives. Mysterious partitions surround them, leaving the family enclosed in a small space, threatened by the unknown, in what will end up being their own home.

Spatial Dislocation

The next two stories underscore the helplessness felt by the immigrants by tying together body and space. Both take place in situations of hospitalization, where this association is particularly menacing. These relatively long and elaborate stories dwell on the hospitals, elevators, and relatives who lose their sense of proximity to others.

"All Day Long I Went Up and Down"

One Ethiopian immigrant, his child got sick, so he took him to the hospital with a *madrikh* [literally, a guide; in this case a Hebrew-speaking Ethiopian immigrant who served as an interpreter to assist the newcomers]. At the hospital, they told him: "Your child needs to stay here in bed. Look after him." At the very same time, an Ethiopian acquaintance of his, whose son also had become sick and had been hospitalized, was staying in the same hospital. The acquaintance came to visit the new immigrant's son, and now the immigrant wanted to repay the visit and sit at the bedside of his acquaintance's son. He said: "You came to visit my son; now I, too, will visit with your son. My own son will stay here alone." The immigrant followed the acquaintance out of the room, and went up with him in the elevator, and got out on another floor. After the visit he tried to go back to his son, who had stayed alone. He presses on the elevator button and goes up, goes down, down again and up, but doesn't know how to get back. All day long, up and down, up and down with the elevator, but he doesn't know how to go back to the room. Other Ethiopians came, and so he asked them: "My son is hospitalized here. I went to visit someone else, but I can't find my way back to the room. All day long I went up and down. And I don't know how to go back to the room." Those people laughed and laughed, and then took him to the room were his son was hospitalized. They laughed and laughed with him about the incident, and went and showed him his son's room.

Following this story, one of the listeners recalled a story, which is recounted as a personal memorate saturated with content concerning the birth of her first daughter to be born in Israel, a short time after her arrival.

"The Room Moves Away"

I, too, when I went to give birth to Yisraela in 1990, they took me and one other woman in labor in an ambulance. She was lying down; I was sitting. When I got to the hospital, I gave birth. When the doctors began to arrive, I became frightened. I gave birth quickly. I gave birth and didn't know if it was a daughter or a son. They showed me, but took the baby away. I thought that, the way it is with us, that after the birth they would put her next to me. I had meant for her to sleep with me, so that I could hug her, and I would sleep with her. I was in pain, I waited a bit and searched . . . but no child. My husband was with me, they gave him a chair to sit down. I said to him: "You . . . ," I said to him: "We gave birth to a newborn; where is she?" He answers: "One woman took him away." So I got mad: "How can you be silent? I'm ill; I'm in pain. You go look. Go after her, the same way she went."

So now he's going down the same path she went, and he sees that the room is moving away from him . . . the room in which I'm sleeping is moving away. When he sees how far it is, he comes back to me once more. He's afraid that I will become lost to him. And then he goes back again. I ask: "Did you find it?" "No." It was a large hospital. . . . And so he goes and goes and goes . . . and when he sees he's gone too far, and when he fears he's losing me, he comes back. That was at night. All night it was like this. Morning arrived . . . I said: "How could it be that a child is lost, and you are silent. If I had not been ill, it would not have happened. . . ." Later, at eight o'clock in the morning, the doctors brought a guide, an interpreter. I ask the guide: "Last night I gave birth to a newborn . . ." I could not say if it was a boy or a girl. "I don't know where it is . . . someone took it away. Search for me." In fact, the child was in the children's room. Later the guide said to me: "Don't worry, don't worry, the child was found. How do you feel? How is your health?" And then he says to me: "Go bathe and eat."

So I bathed, and after that I went to the dining hall that was filled with birth mothers. I met a friend there, and turned to her, and said: "I came here last night and gave birth to a newborn, and someone took it." The friend said to me: "Surely he is where my child is." And she says, "Don't worry, don't worry." I did not eat the food, because I could not eat, because the child had been lost. We stood up, and in fact that child was sleeping in the children's room, in a room that was ready. I and another Ethiopian went into the children's room, following the nurse's signal [*indicating the way the nurse had signaled*]. We go after her, reach the children's room, and see a lot of children there. At that time, many were giving birth. Perhaps one hundred babies. Then I ask the Ethiopian [woman]: "Do you think that my child is here, too?" "Yes, surely he is here. Mine is here, too." I could not believe it. I have an identification card on my arm, and the newborn has an identification card, and then they bring her to me on the bed. And then I look: She's white and cute [this sentence is spoken in Hebrew]: "Ah, for sure this is my daughter. From all of these, this one is mine? How did you take her out of all these here?" "This is your girl, this is your girl." She was diapered, for sure they told me whether it was a boy or a girl, but I did not understand them. I didn't know if it was a boy or a girl, so I took her into the room, and opened the diaper, to see if it was a boy or a girl. I was glad, I nursed her, we took her back to the infants' room . . . later I came to the hotel [which then served as an absorption center], I told them what happened, and we laughed so hard. [They ask her husband]: "Where did you go on your searches?" And then he says: "I got there and back, I got there and back."

The two hospital stories reflect on spatial dislocation and loss of control. They bespeak a very singular sense of being out of orbit, unmoored, and at the same time of being helplessly trapped, a wordless and terrifying experience, for which the metaphor of a "horror ride" occurs to me, as a listener. In both accounts, one of the parents feels that he or she is alone in experiencing the nightmare, and both refer to the disintegration of an intimate family relationship within the hospital setting. Instead of healing, assistance, and repair, the hospital imposes separation and loss. The first story, like the beginning of the second story, speaks explicitly of a loss of spatial orientation. In the second story, there is an additional loss, that of direct connection between the father, the mother, and their newborn child. The interpreter's soothing words after an entire night of loss are left hovering in the air and do not unite her with her newborn. Even after she reaches the infant ward, where she is shown her baby, the entire setting—the room, cribs, identification tags, the baby's color—appears to her inconceivable and almost perverse, and the reunion with her child remains uncertain. Within this chaotic scenario, where she is bereft of any embodied knowledge on which to rely, opening the baby's diaper is the only familiar anchor from which she can resume a certain degree of control.

Resonating throughout the story is the extreme experience of aloneness. Although the two parents talk to each other, they are not together in this nightmare, but rather separate and alone. The family unit has come apart at the joints, and no help is available.

Is This Food?

The following stories take us further along in the chronology of the immigrants' journey of acculturation, as the humorous gaze turns to food.

"Where Is the Chicken?"

When we were new immigrants at the absorption center, they brought us frozen chicken, and told us: this is chicken, and it's for eating. We open up and see that it's a rock. We try to hold on to the leg and move it, but it's all rock. We look: they told us there was chicken. [In wonderment and derision:] Where is it? We waited and waited, after some time we threw it out, because it's rock . . . [*pauses to reflect*]. Yes. These were the mistakes we made when we were new immigrants. It's not a mistake. It comes from stupidity and ignorance.

"We Thought It Was Cheese"

The dish [washing soap] paste in the plastic container—we thought it was *Qewe* [a type of soft cheese common in Ethiopia], we spread it on the *injera* and tried to eat. We made bets among people, it's *Qewe*, it's not *Qewe*, it's *Qewe*, it's not *Qewe*, and we laughed because of this.

"They Ate the Soap"

When the immigrants from Ethiopia arrived I was an absorption guide, and we greeted them at the hotels. At first we put them in the lobby, and then we went up to distribute soaps and shampoo, and diapers, in the room. What happened and made me laugh was that we put the soap in the showers, and the bars of soap were dark, so the children thought it was cake and ate it.

"They Would Put Flour in the Toilet"

Another story I remember was that the large families were given two mobile homes, and there was a toilet in each mobile home, and they thought that one was for kneading dough, and the other was a toilet. They would put flour in the toilet and flush the water down and couldn't understand where the flour went.

"He Washed His Hands in Toilet Water"

One guest came to my house. I told him to have some *injera*. He went to wash his hands. So we said to him, there's a faucet here, but he went to wash his hands in the toilet and said: "This is clean water. In Ethiopia we would drink water that horses had walked through in one direction, and monkeys from the others" [*mimics the visitor's swallowing motion and laughs*], and that's how he washed his hands in toilet water, and ate *injera*.

"Nothing Left!"

We were told that there was meat in this country . . . so we went, we brought the rolled meat [ground meat] and washed it in water [under the faucet]. Everything fell apart, and so nothing was left from it!

"How to Use Them?"

We were so ignorant; everything was new. We brought flour from Ethiopia, and special foods from Ethiopia. We carried them the whole way, but when we came to the absorption center we didn't know how to use them, and threw them out.

"The *Injera* We Grew Up On"

We didn't know how to turn on the gas, whether to turn the knob left or right. Never mind the gas stove . . . even the things that we knew, like how to cook the dishes, we didn't know. The *injera* we grew up on, we didn't know how to cook it. Never mind the things we had just encountered [in Israel]; the very things we grew up on, how to make the *injera*, suddenly [the knowledge] disappeared. Kneading dough in the toilet [*laughs*]!

Edible and inedible foods mix together unrecognizably, cleaning detergents are eaten while food is flushed down the toilet. This confusion in identifying primary bodily functions—feeding, cleaning, and evacuating—lies at the center of these stories' mechanism of humor. In the following stories, even the familiar becomes inexplicably unfamiliar.

Where Is My Home?

These take us a small step beyond the phase of initial perceptual shock, while preserving a great many of the original themes of destabilization. Here the sense of losing home continues to be a focal point of personal and communal vulnerabilities. These more advanced phases in the chronology of the absorption journey still merit mediation through their treatment in humorous tales.

"She Lost Her House"

One woman told me she had bought a house in a new place. Three days after moving into her new house she goes shopping in her new neighborhood, but when she wanted to go back home, she didn't know how to get back. She couldn't ask anyone where she lived, because no one knew her. So she walks around and around and then sees someone and asks him about the neighbors who had arrived a few months earlier. "Do you know the house of Abba Mulu?" So he asks her, "Where are you going?" So she says to him: "I'm going to Abba Mulu." So he says to her, "Okay, come, come, come after me." And then he asks her: "Where do you think I'm going?" And he realized she had lost her house. And so she followed him, and when they arrived there he said: "Here is your house."

"Where Is *agar Bet*?"

One man lost his way home. He didn't know how to ask about a specific place. So he asked the driver: "Where is *agar bet*?" [Do you understand?] He wanted to know where he lived but did not know how to say it.

[A participant in the event says:] Yes, it happened to me. It was night, I went up from Lod to Ekron, and I didn't know I had reached Ekron. I was dizzy. And then I asked the driver: "Where is *agar bet*?"

The words *bayit* and *bet* mean "house" in Hebrew and Amharic, respectively. *Gar* in Hebrew means "to live" or "reside," while the Amharic term *agar* is a central cultural concept in Ethiopia, meaning "homeland" or "home turf" (Levine 1965, 77). The boundaries of the *agar* are not precisely delimited, and the concept can be used to describe an area, a province, or a person's nation. However, the designation is an in-group one, and when a person says *agar bet* he or she means, precisely, homeland.[16]

Among Ethiopian Jews, just as among their neighbors in rural Ethiopia, it was customary to go from neighbor to neighbor to announce the annual memorial of a person's death, or to use a messenger to make the rounds instead of the mourners.

"He Came to His Own House and Invited Them"

A woman held a memorial ceremony and she told her husband to call the neighbors. So the husband went out and called all the neighbors. He went up floors and down floors. Finally he came to his own house and also invited them [*all the participants laugh*].

"I Found Out That I Was in a Different Apartment"

When I lived in the mobile home, Mesfen and I were neighbors. I made a mistake and walked inside his mobile home [thinking it was my own]. And I saw a broken bed. I thought that my son had broken it. I was sorry that he had broken the bed: "Oy, oy, how have you broken a government bed?" I looked suddenly, and found out that I was in a different apartment. And that is so funny!

"Come Open My House"

A woman who lived on the second floor [of the hotel that served as an absorption center], tries to open the door on the first floor with her key. She tries and tries, but cannot open it. The person in charge of opening all the doors, he comes. His name is Michael. "Michael, come open my house." He opens the door for her, [and] suddenly she sees, inside the house, a huge tape recorder. A week before they [the authorities] had distributed small transistors. And she begins to thank the government: "Yesterday, you gave us a small tape, and now a big tape, thank you very much!" All that time, she and her friends are sitting and watching. Suddenly she notices that in the house there is clothing and shoes of a man, and she was a divorcée living alone. After that she burst out laughing and went out.

These stories are situated at a slightly more advanced point in the chronology of adjustment to the new environment, a temporal position signaled by the internal elements of the narrative: an annual memorial ceremony is performed, people take taxis, and are already home owners. The protagonists of the stories have found their "land legs" in the new place, to some extent, yet they still search for the lost home (Ofer 2005; Doleve-Gandelman 1990). Nevertheless, by now they have developed the resourcefulness for "finding the way home" in the practical, and even the abstract, sense of the word.

OK? OK!

As in many of the humorous tales, the narrative requires a coda that will mark it as a story that makes one laugh. This narrative ploy, which turns the tragic reality of loss of control into an amusing story with a happy ending, leads us to another cluster of stories, in which this very compliant survival tactic itself becomes an object of humor. The disorientation implied in these situations is captured in the banality of the word *beseder* (OK), which the story exploits in various ways. *Beseder* may take on several meanings: it may be a straightforward affirmation that "things are OK," thus indicating agreement; in other words, there are no complaints and everything is fine. Literally, the word means "in order," that is, that everything is in order and in correct sequence. These meanings imply a type of conformity or compliance. Used appropriately, the word suggests that the speaker agrees with or is in compliance with the requirements of the situation. The humorous stories, however, point out the incongruous use of this pivotal word, one that plays up the comical aspect of the situation. By responding to various circumstances with the same word, *beseder*, the butt of the joke is portrayed as indiscriminately mouthing the only word he knows. The upshot of this is beyond his control; like a bullet in roulette, sometimes the word benefits him and sometimes it fails him. Unsurprisingly, the butt of the joke is not aware of the outcome.

"OK"

One woman was working as a cleaner together with an Israeli [non-Ethiopian] woman. And then the Israeli woman didn't come to work for a week. A week later she came back, and the Ethiopian, asked her, "Where were you?" "My husband died." She, the Ethiopian says to her: "OK." I told her that my husband died and you say "OK" to me. "OK." Only a few days later did she understand, and then she began to cry with her.[17]

"OK? OK!"

An Ethiopian in Israel hitched a ride; they picked him up. One guy was sitting in the back, and there was the driver. He sat near the driver. Suddenly the guy sitting in the back lifts his head and shouts upward. So the hitchhiker looks up, and while he's looking that one [sitting behind] reaches his hand into the front pocket of the hitchhiker and pulls out his money. Afterward the guy in the back yells again and looks down. The hitchhiker looks down, and the thief reaches his hand into the side pocket and pulls money out of it as well. After they took his money, they ask him [the hitchhiker]: "OK?" He says: "OK." And that's how they got three hundred shekels out of him. [When the punch line is uttered (OK? OK!), the teller bursts out in cathartic laughter.]

"*Abba* OK"

A group got onto a bus. Some older Ethiopian guy got in. And then the driver told him to pay. And he went to sit down. He told him to pay. He said to him:

"OK." The driver told him to pay a few times, and each time he told him "OK." And then they call him "Mr. OK" [*Abba beseder*] and they laugh about it. He doesn't pay. Whatever they say to him, he says, "OK."[18]

The elevator, like the bus and the taxi, are central icons in the humorous stories of Ethiopian immigrants. The newcomers first encountered elevators in the hotels where many were housed upon arrival in Israel. Riding in the "traveling box" was a source of a great deal of anxiety, as it involved, apart from learning a new technical mode of operation, movement along an entirely new plane. In the world the Ethiopians knew, one could move and orient oneself only horizontally. Here entirely new spatial dimensions presented themselves. The familiar, and only possible horizontal plane, seemed to flip vertically and allow movement along an unimagined axis.[19] Furthermore, their very own domestic spaces were now plotted along this unfathomable vertical plane.

The centrality of the elevator, taxi, bus, and other modes of movement in Ethiopian Israeli humor is indicated by their appearance under the rubric of "jokes" within internet forums of the Ethiopian community in Israel.[20] Examples include the following: An Ethiopian woman gets into a cab and tells the driver: "Driver, please take me to Watati!" [an Ethiopian female name], and an Ethiopian adult and his young son enter the central bus station [to go to Be'er Sheba]. In the station, they enter the elevator, and then the father says out loud "*tchakunhu* [take us] to Be'er Sheba."

This joke elicited the following response:

This story isn't a joke, it's an incident that happened in Ḥadera [a city with a large Ethiopian population]. An adult got into an elevator in Ḥadera and asked one of the riders in the elevator to press the button for Netanya [another city in Israel with a large Ethiopian community].

Another response:

Here's a real incident that happened to a friend of mine on the bus. She was on her way home, and two older Ethiopian women sat next to her . . . briefly, they had to get off, so one of them got up to press the stop button. In short, they started to get nervous when they saw that the driver wasn't stopping. In the end he stopped for them some five to six steps away from the stop, and then one of the women came to him and yelled: "Driver, I called you; why didn't you answer?" I don't know if this made you laugh, but it had me doubled over.

Reality as Virtual, Virtual as Reality

Another channel in the comic panorama of the "absorption journey," which the community returns to again and again, is the encounter with the images and sounds emerging from the television and radio sets. Because these stories deal "merely" with the virtual world, the "butts" of the humor are rendered less vulnerable, as they are baffled by illusory images rather than by material realities.

"There Was a Fire in This Film"

In Saddam's era [in reference to the first Gulf War, a short while after Operation Solomon, when the teller immigrated to Israel], we were told to turn on the television. So we turned the TV on and saw a movie. There was a fire in this film, and then they jumped up to turn off the TV, I remember that [*laughs*]. . . . We pressed [the button]; it turned off. All it was, was a movie, that had a fire in it [*laughs*].

"Water on the Screen"

An elderly Ethiopian woman sat in front of the television and watched. Suddenly she saw a fire. She was alarmed, ran quickly to bring water and poured it on the screen.

"The Television Doesn't Hear Him"

One man is watching television and he is viewing an "impolite" film. Very quietly, so that the television doesn't hear him, he whispers to the person sitting next to him: "Look at all the fuss they're making."

"I Felt Bad about Kicking Them Out"

An elderly Ethiopian woman sat all night in front of a turned-on TV set. In the morning the children in the home asked her why she stayed up that way? So she pointed to the TV, which was still on and said: "I felt bad about kicking them out of the house."

"Where Did the Guy from the Radio Go?"

There was another incident: An Ethiopian had a radio that played and talked. It broke down. So he says to his friend, "It looks like he went somewhere." "What, where did he go?" And then he began to beat it [the radio] up. What, didn't he come back yet? He must have gone somewhere, he's not here.

Another aspect of disorientation, arising from lack of discrimination between reality and its virtual representation, is embodied in the following stories:

"In the End He Discovers It's Only a Doll"

An adult walks down the street, where there are shop windows with mannequins. He turns to one of the mannequins and says, "Good morning." She doesn't respond, and he again says, "Good morning." When she doesn't respond he says to her: "Are you being disrespectful when you don't answer?" In the end he discovers it's only a doll and walks away.

"The Dolls Make Fun of Us, Too?"

An elderly person stood at the bus stop and saw a mannequin in a shop window with a man's clothes. He turns to him and asks where a certain bus line goes to, but the mannequin does not respond. After he understands that it's a mannequin he says, "Isn't it bad enough that people make fun of us, the dolls, too, make fun of us, and ignore us."

Discussion

The overt and covert contents of the self-directed humor of Ethiopian immigrants in Israel serve as a vehicle for processing the drama of dislocation, providing an expressive avenue of its traumatic implications. The spontaneous storytelling occurrence, in which people share stories they consider funny, provides a compelling reflexive outlet. Examination of this humor repertoire reveals a set of otherwise inaccessible contents, as well as the unique processing mechanisms and aesthetic forms involved in their expression.

The first step toward defining the particularity of this corpus is the delimiting of its outlines. I begin, therefore, with the absent. Had I been asked, before embarking on this particular research, what contents I expected to encounter in the humor of Ethiopian immigrants in Israel, I would probably have indicated those typically thought to signify the challenges to the group's assimilation in Israel. This discourse frequently revolves around familiar pitfalls and particular difficulties that reverberated in the Israeli public sphere, and even earned international attention at times: challenges to their legitimacy as Jews; their difficult odyssey to Israel, and the excruciating wait in transition camps; once in Israel, questions of religious belonging and racial difference; and the ordeals vis-à-vis the (state) apparatus.[21]

Surprisingly, however, although these contentious issues had personal reverberations, which I expected to shine through the stories, none of these issues appears in the in-group humor documented in this study.[22] Rather, the present humor corpus registers utterly different levels of trauma, intimately tied to the existential nightmare associated with the sense of loss of orientation, such as basic physical orientation to the environment. The ground fell out from under one's feet. The basic distinctions embedded in the body's perceptual field—between day and night, between inside and out, between up and down—disintegrated in a moment.

The raw impact of this "seismic event" is registered in the repertoire, as are the timid attempts to regain balance. Although the stories are couched in the language of cultural manifestations, they powerfully suggest a profound tie between an embodied experience and its cultural construction. To draw on a notion from the physiological world, one might even suggest that the humorous stories unwittingly interpret a physical shock to the body's *proprioceptive* faculties; in other words, to the very biological mechanics of processing inputs from within the body and from the visual field to determine its disposition in space.[23]

The humorous corpus reflects an attempt to organize the response to this upheaval and render it meaningful. The stories contain signs of temporal arrangement that plot them along the axis of acclimatization to life in Israel. They reflexively process a primary vertigo that did not have, and could not have, direct expression, and whose meaning and intensity only became apparent to me through the close scrutiny of a comparative set of common themes dispersed throughout the corpus. This tapestry of stories depicts a primordial experience in which chaos invades the world of private being. Exposing it involves shame and concealment.

The incarnation of the experience in harmless comic form suggests that time has passed and that transformation has been achieved. The power resides in the gap opened up between the innocent and the seemingly banal story, and the shattering dimensions of the meanings that are bridgeable by the relaxed mode of humor. The tellers of personal funny anecdotes mark themselves as having gone through a successful, if not completed, transition. Now they can laugh about their former selves.

Content, however, is only one element of the stories' mechanisms. The cumulative effect of composing, hearing, recalling, and, especially, repeating these stories enables internalization and mediation of common ambivalences and vulnerabilities to be effected. Thus, the close reading of this specific corpus may enlighten our understanding of how humor may channel and mediate transforming processes.[24]

The devastating experience, which at the time of its occurrence was utterly mute, finds its voice and manages to undergo reconstruction as a shared story. While the teller of the tale is structurally distanced from the story's characters by the storytelling conventions, the character itself simultaneously expands and becomes a generalized figure, preventing the individual from feeling alone. Moreover, it labels itself as a "funny story," through its enactment of a specific social setting, as well as a formal textual coda. Although the tales cast different characters in the role of protagonist, the stories retain their intimate autobiographical reference and, therefore, direct shame inward. This mechanism is potentially empowering. By acting as the makers of their own shame, the tellers maintain a certain degree of control over their lives.

Both in the plotting of contents and in the forgiving tone in which they are told, the humorous tales are reminiscent of family stories that are told about the mistakes children made when they were young. These stories are characterized by an easy spirit, the revelation of innocence met with forgiving and accepting laughter. The attenuation of vulnerability is achieved by expanding the circle of participants: on the one hand, the errors described in them authentically express the tellers' experience of vertigo, while at the same time mark them not as a personal loss of equilibrium but rather as reflective of the shared predicament of everyone present.[25] Thus, the remedial power of the story lies in the identification it creates, in the closeness of the "support group" that is formed at the very moment the tale is told.

I have observed a similar transformation, possibly even in more radical intracultural terms, in humorous narratives related to mislaid meat in which what was intended to fortify the individual's body gets lost as a result of disorientation later interpreted humorously. Unlike the stories that have been discussed here, the humorous tales of mislaid meat lack a harmonizing ending. In them the incomplete process of arrival is harrowingly concrete (Salamon 2010).

Among the tellers and listeners who take turns delivering stories, a sense of *communitas* emerges, which I should like to call a *delayed communitas*.[26] I use this term because, in contrast to Turner's definition of *communitas*, the Ethiopian immigrants to Israel, according to their own stories, did not experience a simultaneously shared sense of a common fate during the transition. Rather, during these particularly difficult periods, they felt isolated and did not share their vertigo with those around them.

Only later, and through the lens of humorous stories, are they able to share their confusion and vulnerability and experience this *delayed communitas* that unites them in retrospect with their fellow Ethiopian Israelis. Seen in this light, it is not surprising that so many of the stories cited above speak of thresholds, liminal places such as doorways, elevators, cars, buses, and bus stations, in which notions of location and place are challenged. Indeed, one repeatedly hears of the lone person unable to locate himself or herself in space; adrift in a strange world, detached from not only the surrounding people but also from the landscape or physical space itself.

This delayed response transforms aloneness into togetherness: the birthing mother, her husband, the one who threw away the chicken, the one who washed away the ground meat, the one who lost her house, and all those who entered other people's houses—each one of these characters alone was unable to express his or her distress. The story that binds them all together offers restoration. Moreover, the narrative context allows the tragic materials to undergo transformation by converting elements of vulnerability into elements of pleasure.

Notes

This chapter is based on an article entitled "The Floor Falling Away: Dislocated Space and Body in the Humour of Ethiopian Immigrants in Israel," originally published in *Folklore* 122, no. (2011): 16–34. Copyright © The Folklore Society, reprinted by permission of Taylor and Francis on behalf of the Folklore Society.

1. For additional themes articulated in the humor of Ethiopian Israelis—also appearing in five of the twenty-eight stories presented here, see Salamon (2010).

2. See, for example, Apte (1985); Boskin and Dorinson (1985); Lowe (1986).

3. For studies on humor and assimilation to life in Israel, and to Israeli society, see Oring (1981, 2003); Zilberg, Herzog, and Ben-Rafael (2001); Shifman and Katz (2005). See also chapter 2 in this book.

4. A participant in such a meeting recounted: "So we drink, we chat, we talk . . . all kinds [of talk]. Who was where, who did what, all kinds of things. . . . Those who work in a kindergarten tell about the children at the Ethiopian children's kindergarten, or about the new

immigrants . . . they talk, they laugh, about how they behave, that they don't know [how to behave], and then we also drink *bun* [coffee] . . . I take a shower, put on perfume, wear jewelry from here, not from Ethiopia. It gives a feeling of fun." For a study of these gatherings, see Salamon, Kaplan, and Goldberg (2009), or see chapter 8 in this book.

5. In the northern Ethiopian culture in which immigrants to Israel previously lived, with its emphasis on respect and honor, such self-deprecation is rather rare. Therefore, one might suggest that perhaps the form, and not only the content, is innovative in this corpus. I thank the anonymous reader for this remark. In addition, a new body of humorous stories, based on the well-known Ethiopian trickster Abba Gevrehana is now told among Ethiopian Israelis IDF soldiers. This emerging corpus of humor, which is still not fully established, seems to stand in opposition to the current body of humorous Ethiopian stories and deserves future study.

6. In most publications relating to the group while in Ethiopia, they were usually referred to as "Falasha." They themselves employ the name "Beta Israel" (the House of Israel) when referring to their Ethiopian past and when referring to their new position in Israel.

7. Ge'ez, the ancient Ethiopian language, now Ethiopia's Semitic liturgical tongue used by Jews and Christians alike. The Torah-centered religious observance of the Beta Israel is a function of their existence as a Jewish community, distinct from other Jewish communities.

8. Much has been written on these two operations. For a general description of their progress and outcome, see Kaplan and Rosen (1993). On the centrality of the Exodus story in the immigration of the Jews from Ethiopia to Israel, see Ben Ezer (2002).

9. These newcomers are considered to be different from the immigrants who had arrived in Israel up until Operation Solomon (1991). On these groups, and especially on the *Falashmura*, see, for example, Kaplan (1993); Salamon (1994); Shabtay (2006); and especially Seeman (2009).

10. For a summary description of the immigration to Israel ('*aliyya*), including references to many other publications, see, for example, Kaplan and Rosen (1993); Kaplan and Salamon (2003, 118–22). On basic aspects of their assimilation in Israel, see Westheimer and Kaplan (1992); Kaplan and Salamon (2003).

11. An attempt to obscure the impression of "otherness" was made by placing the Beta Israel's skin hue on a continuum with that of earlier Jewish immigrant groups, in particular, the Jews of Yemen and India. This corpus is characterized by jokes that are mainly "good-natured." In the first stages of the Ethiopian immigration to Israel, the dominant jokes focused on categorizing the Ethiopians in the spectrum of Jewish colors; see Salamon (2001, 2003). Jokes such as, "What's the difference between an Ethiopian and a Yemenite? Five minutes' baking," or "Why did they bring the Ethiopians to Israel? To become spare parts for the Yemenites," emphasized the resemblance of the Ethiopians to the other Jews, and attempted to avoid their categorization as racially other. At the time of writing, jokes about Ethiopians told by non-Ethiopian Israelis relate strongly to their color by comparing Ethiopians to different types of chocolates. This highly generative cycle fully accepts their blackness, as well as their "sweetness" and belonging to Israeli society. For a theoretical consideration of "storyability" (what gets told as a story) and tellability (who has the right to tell a story), see Shuman (1986, 54–76).

12. For these struggles, including especially the debate over their personal conversions, the blood scandal, see Seeman (2009). Regarding other race-oriented struggles, see Salamon (2003).

13. Their everyday assimilation was, and still is, of course, a multifaceted challenge consisting of issues concerning language, health, education, employment, and much more. The various ways in which humor participated in the assimilation of different ethnic groups to life in Israel is still to be studied. Relevant examples are Zilberg, Herzog, and Ben-Rafael (2001), who deal with humor as related to nostalgia, lost status, and longing for homeland and culture among newcomers to Israel from the former Soviet Union; a study by Shifman and Katz (2005),

on jokes told mainly by Eastern European Jews about the *Yekkes* (German Jews); Rosen on bitter humor (1999, 156–58). On the *chizbat* of the *Palmach*, see Oring (1981; 2003, 97–115).

14. And while Israel was prepared to absorb and accommodate its newcomers, the sheer number of Ethiopian immigrants inundated the state's absorbing capacity. For a study of the paternalistic attitudes of the absorption officials toward the Ethiopian newcomers, see Hertzog (1998). For a highly relevant comparison, see Schely-Newman (2010, 2011).

15. According to the immigrants, in rural Ethiopia all forms of sanitation took place in nature. No man-made products were used for sanitation purposes. On that topic, Reidolf Molvaer wrote, "Traditional sanitary practices survive over most of Ethiopia. Any reasonably hidden place in nature can be used as a 'toilet.' . . . This is a custom inherited from generations back, so few see any harm in it or feel any strong urge to change it, except in crowded towns where there are not enough open spaces" (2007, 97).

16. Mistakes, both lexical and semantic, deriving from phonetic similarities between the Ethiopian languages Amharic or Tigrinya and Hebrew, are a source of many humorous anecdotes told within the Ethiopian Israeli community. Language and space intermingle: the linguistic affinity between Hebrew and Amharic, which underlies the slippage between the words *bayit* and *bet*, *gar* and *agar*, contributes to the confusion.

17. Crying is a customary way to comfort a grieving person. On the term *beseder* ("OK," "all right," "in order") as a central humorous idiom of former Soviet Union immigrants in Israel, see Zilberg, Herzog, and Ben-Rafael (2001).

18. The title *Abba* denotes respectability and honor, usually connected with elders.

19. Most of the immigrants were airlifted to Israel, a fact that is, of course, a focus of meaning in this discourse. Nevertheless, it is not part of their explicit humor. This may be due to the secrecy of the entire operation, but possibly also to its being an isolated and extreme experience. The fact that this event remains outside the scope of the humor invites further study. In addition, although the immigrants' humor is far more concrete and physical, it is worth mentioning that the very concept of immigration to Israel is called *'aliyya*, literally ascent or advancement, understood as both physical and spiritual, or moral. On the concept of *absorption*—the term used for assimilation—there is the sense of losing one's own former features and becoming undifferentiated. For an enlightening discussion of these concepts in Israel, see Golden (2002, 9).

20. At the time of research, these were the only available examples of online jokes popular among young Ethiopian Israelis.

21. The Beta Israel journey and struggle for recognition is the focus of an extensive amount of literature. For some of the main issues, see Corinaldi (1998); Ben Ezer (2002); and Kaplan and Salamon (2003).

22. Lowe (1986, 439) observed that "although minorities have often entered into full citizenship through long and arduous struggle, this procedure has sometimes been both shortened and sweetened when they have made up their minds to enter laughing," the case of the Ethiopian Israelis' humor paints a much more complex picture. It shows that while they cathartically laugh in relation to certain issues, other issues—seemingly traumatic struggles, for example—are completely absent from their humor. Two opposing speculations emerge. One possibility is that what seems traumatic to non-Ethiopians is not in fact what is actually traumatic to them in reality; another possibility is that these struggles are so painful that they cannot be expressed in a humorous fashion at all. Yet another option is to look at this as part of a process: in the present stage of their assimilation journey, humor mediates mundane, intimate experiences. While they have surmounted these initial difficulties, the perspective required in order to be able to laugh about specific vulnerabilities, does not yet exist for the issues that are not yet fully resolved.

23. This is a new concept in the study of immigration. Research on proprioceptive faculties (popularly known as the "sixth sense") is occurring in the life sciences.

24. The unique capacity of humor in containing and processing both individual and collective vulnerabilities is highly apparent in the case of immigration and relocation. For a comparative study of humor among new settlers, including in Israel, see Oring (2003).

25. It must be stressed here that it is not my intention to claim these stories are told to create shared bonds, or to process the traumatic experiences of these early days in a new land. Rather, through their humorous narration, Ethiopian immigrants are able to tell their stories, entertain and amuse their audiences, and share simultaneously in the experience of the past. And in the bond that emerges from sharing a joke, they laugh together.

26. According to Turner (1969), *Communitas* is the communion of fellowship, which involves sentiments of close relations and structural likeness between individuals.

8 What Goes Around, Comes Around

Rotating Credit Associations among
Ethiopian Women in Israel

ONE OF THE characteristic sites for the performance of humoristic tales among Ethiopian women is their periodic gatherings in rotating credit associations. This chapter, which depicts the organization and the symbolic dimensions of these meetings, shifts our attention from the lack of orientation, vicissitudes of immigration, and powerlessness in the face of radical life changes to instances of ritual behavior that point to the establishment of agency and security among Ethiopian immigrants.

Once a month, on or around the twentieth, a group of Ethiopian Israeli women meet in their neighborhood in Israel. They are members of an *iqqub*, spending an evening during which, in their words, "they drink with money." The group's members all immigrated to Israel about twenty-five years ago and have young children for whom they receive National Insurance child benefit payments on the twentieth of every month. Another *iqqub* meets once a month, always after the twenty-eighth. It also has about ten members, mostly mothers of adult children. The women in this second group do not work, but rather subsist on their old-age pension, which they receive on the twenty-eighth of each month. In both these cases, the *iqqub* serves as a member-organized financial and social support group. While not limited to women by definition, these are clearly gender-based organizations. This chapter will focus on *iqqubewoch* of Ethiopian Israeli women.[1]

An *iqqub* (sometimes referred to as *quve*) is established when a small group of ten to twenty women come together to create a rotating financial circle, typically on a local or even neighborhood basis. The amount of money to be contributed by each member at the monthly meeting is determined in advance by the participants, and the entire fund collected is awarded at each meeting to one participant, who has been chosen by lottery. The amount paid by members per session varies widely among groups, ranging at the time of our research from three hundred to one thousand shekels. The length of an *iqqub* cycle is determined by the number of members, each of whom contributes a fixed sum at each meeting, and receives the entire pool once per cycle. A lottery held at the end of each meeting decides who among those who have not yet received the "jackpot" will receive it at the next meeting. In most *iqqubewoch*, this lucky recipient is also the hostess of her "jackpot" meeting. After a cycle is completed, members may choose either to dismantle the group or start a new cycle. These local organizations serve as group credit and savings mechanisms that are unique in their social and symbolic aspects. Each group formulates its own bylaws and holds its monthly ritual meeting, which adheres to binding rules (referred to by members as "laws"), which are recorded in an internal document specifically regulating the meetings' hosting, agenda, and content.

While the world of Ethiopian Israeli women has been addressed in the literature on the Ethiopian community's integration in Israel, the *iqqub* and the central role of women within it has not yet been the subject of intensive research. Numerous reports, articles, and dissertations have focused on domestic violence, divorce, single-parent families, menstrual purity, and the redrawing of gender relations, but the cultural aspects of finances and financial initiatives by Ethiopian Israelis, and women in particular, have been neglected.[2] The one exception is the conventional wisdom that the Israeli system of Bituaḥ Leumi (National Insurance, the Israeli social security system) has afforded these women a degree of economic independence they lacked in Ethiopia.

The study of the *iqqub* is of interest not merely because it can shed light on yet another feature of the lives of Ethiopian Israelis, but rather because of its nature as a complex mechanism of tradition and renewal: its existence challenges paternalistic assumptions regarding the status of Ethiopian immigrants vis-à-vis the state and its institutions and the experience of Ethiopian Israeli women specifically.[3] Our study examines a phenomenon that has gathered momentum over the years that encompasses a significant percentage of Ethiopian Israeli women.[4] In addition, this financial association serves as a generative focus for gender relations and the dramatic changes that have affected them. Ethnographic examination of the *iqqub* and its internal discourse allows us to focus on our ever-expanding understanding of the dynamics of change among the group's cultural, gender, and power relations.

As has been demonstrated in scholarship, the process of migration for African labor has led to a break with life and opportunities in their homelands, but it has also afforded working classes and, in our example, women new opportunities for cultural, personal, and material renewal and empowerment, as working-class Ethiopian women, including many who have been transformed from peasants and artisans to members of an urban working class, have sought empowerment and economic security through the establishment of independent credit and loan institutions.[5] Even those who have not formally entered the labor markets have benefited from stable incomes due to the social policies of the Israeli welfare state. Indeed, this case raises the interesting general question of whether one needs to actually work in a paying job in either the formal or informal sector to be part of the working class.

Moreover, the example of the *iqqub* correlates with the wider phenomenon of African working classes in an African diaspora who have established safety nets that employ cultural practices and symbols from homeland traditions (Ethiopia—real or imagined) and synthesize these with local cultural and material circumstances in the host society. The study of the *iqqub* contributes to our understanding of how working classes borrow cultural forms to enhance and ensure their economic security as well as a sense of social belonging. We also get a sense of how material practices are linked to cultural practices.

In terms of literature on working classes in the African diaspora, Ethiopian Israelis present a particularly interesting case because their identity can be seen to be divided between two competing conceptions of homeland and diaspora. Ethiopian Israelis are obviously part of the Ethiopian diaspora in the plain sense of the dispersion of Ethiopian nationals from their homeland. As such they are the second-largest Ethiopian diaspora community, exceeded in numbers only by the United States.

However, while there is little question that Ethiopian Israelis should be included in any discussion of Ethiopians abroad—as refugees, immigrants, migrant laborers, or even trans-nationals—their place in the Ethiopian diaspora is far more complex. Virtually all recent literature on diaspora is in agreement that "diaspora" is not a product of merely geography but also of worldview and cultural orientation; a "diaspora consciousness" (K. Butler 2001; Safran 1991, 1999, 2005; Gilroy 1994; Clifford 1994). In this respect, it must be noted that Ethiopian Israelis to a significant extent portray themselves and are depicted by other Israelis not as an Ethiopian diaspora but as a Jewish community that has returned "home" after centuries in the African diaspora (Salamon 2003; Kaplan 2005). Moreover, they are to an extent perhaps unequalled by any African migrant group in the world highly visible in their new surroundings. Prior to the immigration of the Ethiopians to Israel, the total number of residents in Israel of sub-Saharan African descent—including the Black Hebrews of Dimona (Markowitz, Helman, and Shir-Vertesh 2003) and Ethiopian Christians (Cerulli 1943; Pedersen 1983) probably did not exceed a thousand people. Even the influx of African guest workers from Ghana and Nigeria in the 1990s (Sabar 2004) only slightly altered this situation.

One consequence of this situation is that in Israel virtually all people of African descent are assumed to be Ethiopians by most other citizens of the country. Consequently, Ethiopian Israelis need to invest far less energy in the "performance" of their Ethiopian identity than do their countrymen in other diaspora communities, in which other populations of African descent are well established (Salamon 2003). Thus the flourishing of the *iqqub* in Israel is not an attempt to make a public display of their Ethiopian identity, but rather an internal sharing of an intimate inner group sensibility.

The *Iqqub* and Similar Financial Associations

Rotating financial associations have been documented in varied cultural contexts. Termed ROSCAs (rotating savings and credit associations), they have been the subject of longitudinal studies whose results have been published in detailed quantitative reports and social and economic research, particularly of the functionalist anthropological school.

In 1962 Clifford Geertz published an article on ROSCAs in Java in which he suggested that they represent an "intermediate stage" or the product of the transition from a traditionalist agrarian to a commercial society. Geertz viewed these associations as educational mechanisms by which traditional peasants learned to become traders in the broad cultural sense. In 1964 the British anthropologist Shirley Ardener, who conducted research in Cameroon and Nigeria, published a comprehensive article describing the phenomenon's prevalence and diversity. Ardener defined a ROSCA as "an association formed upon a core of participants who make regular contributions to a fund which is given, in whole or in part, to each contributor in rotation."[6]

Some forty years later, Ardener reexamined the phenomenon in the opening chapter of a volume which she coedited.[7] This collection of papers focused on contemporary, exclusively female groups. Its comparative perspective emphasized the need to understand the phenomenon of the different ROSCAs in each of their own particular cultural contexts.

Although *iqqub* associations are not documented in Ethiopia prior to the late nineteenth and early twentieth centuries, they are nonetheless customarily treated as a "traditional" Ethiopian institution. Based on evidence for the existence of similar associations in India, Southeast Asia, and Africa, it has been claimed that the institution was imported into Ethiopia via Indian traders. Others have asserted that the Ethiopian *iqqub* originated in the country itself and spread among the different ethnic groups, thus becoming a pan-Ethiopian cultural institution that includes Ethiopians regardless of religion, ethnicity, class, or gender.[8] Whatever its origin, the research literature is in agreement regarding the *iqqub*'s prevalence during the second half of the twentieth century in urban Ethiopia and the inroads made by similar rural Ethiopian associations. The flourishing of such associations in Ethiopia is typically explained by the proliferation of the use of money, financial instability, and the absence of a formal banking system.[9]

Iqqub associations are ubiquitous in present-day urban Ethiopia as well as in many rural areas where a money-based economy has been established. Moreover, similar associations have been documented among Ethiopian immigrants to the

West, as well as in the Ethiopian diaspora in a number of cities, including Boston, Los Angeles, Washington, and New York; Toronto, Canada; and Oxford, England. Previously, many of these Ethiopian émigrés were well-off city dwellers, primarily from Addis Ababa.[10]

Complex references to the Israeli banking system, welfare, and National Insurance authorities figure prominently in the discourse of Ethiopian Israeli *iqqub* associations. These references dismantle the dichotomy that positions formal against informal economic reasoning. Here we examine the way *iqqub* members perceive the phenomenon in its entirety as a system whose financial and symbolic threads are interwoven, forming a unified, flexible, and virtuosic cultural entity that invokes references to both Ethiopian and Israeli contexts.

Economic Considerations

In our interviews, particularly at the outset of each conversation on this topic, interviewees were often ill at ease. Apparently, this had to do with their concern that the *iqqub*—which is not familiar to non-Ethiopian Israelis—is viewed as improper, perhaps even forbidden and illegal. The fact that use is often made of "government-colored" money—National Insurance money, which is exchanged outside the formal banking system—seems to add to this feeling of unease.[11] The concealed, loaded, internal, perhaps even subversive nature of these associations is perhaps an explanation for their near-total neglect in the vast literature documenting Ethiopian attempts to cope with the dramatic changes experienced in Israel.[12] Their existence was revealed to us by chance during interviews with Ethiopian Israelis on entirely different topics. One interviewee told us explicitly, "In Israel the *iqqub* is considered illegal, is considered gambling. . . . Most Ethiopians do *iqqub* quietly, because they have heard maybe that here in Israel gambling is not allowed."

Nonetheless, once we began asking directly about these credit associations, referring to them using Ethiopian terms, we heard about them repeatedly. Discussions of the topic became relaxed and more specific as the interviews progressed. Interviewees' initial hesitancy to discuss the phenomenon melted away, and they became increasingly proud as they described its financial advantages and even proposed—in an almost missionary tone—that the female interviewer join them in "drinking with money." In most interviews, the *iqqub*'s social importance was explicitly stated. The interval between collecting and receiving the money is understood as an important component in sustaining the ongoing commitment between group members. In view of the shared financial arrangements, members are committed to maintaining stable relations between group members and to helping each other in times of celebration and mourning, thereby adding a moral dimension to the *iqqub*. Thus, alongside the financial explanation—generally immediately following it—the interviewees stressed the associations' importance in both supporting their lives outside the meetings and in the social enjoyment of the meetings themselves. Through the ritual and symbolic mechanisms that encourage and process the codes that lie at the foundation of each group, the mutual commitment is validated anew at each meeting. One participant told us:

> The *quve* is not only for money. If you are in a *quve*, if God forbid something happens in your family, there is more support, [members] come, help with money, too, and with expenses, and with hosting guests, and in celebrations— you feel a more personal connection, more responsibility toward each other. In general—it is customary to help each other, to come visit when someone is sick, visiting when [someone] dies, especially. You make sure you go. If you don't go, no matter the reason, you are not forgiven! And that is hard. In Ethiopia it was easier to go to one another's [home], here—it's harder.

In summing up the *quve*'s advantages she added, "It's good. When you want to buy something and there's no money—the *quve* helps—it gives hope."

As stated above, the characterization of the *iqqub* as a "traditional" association warrants careful consideration, all the more so as regards the Beta Israel in Ethiopia. While similar associations are found in many parts of Ethiopia, and some Ethiopian Israelis knew of and sometimes even participated in such groups, most of our interviewees stated that there was no *iqqub* in their villages in Ethiopia and that they had learned of its existence only after making 'aliyya to Israel. This was explained by the practical aspect of a traditional rural economy that lacked significant use of money.[13] The Jews of Ethiopia immigrated to Israel in several waves and by a number of routes, and many of the Beta Israel began to take part in financial groups while awaiting 'aliyya.[14]

Another point touches on terminology and the insights it reveals. While meetings are often conducted in a mixture of Hebrew, Amharic, and Tigrinya, Hebrew is the language in which the group's rules are written, as it is most of the immigrants' primary written language. Nevertheless, the association is perceived as uniquely Ethiopian and is always referred to by its Ethiopian name. Use of Ethiopian terms to conceptualize the association is shared throughout the Ethiopian diaspora around the world, connecting Ethiopians outside of Ethiopia with Ethiopian cultural heritage. Thus, the *iqqub*'s appearance in Israel can be largely viewed as yet another expression of the complexity embodied in the term *preserving tradition* as applied to Ethiopian and other ethnic manifestations in Israel.[15] Whether participants became familiar with the *iqqub* while still in their villages in Ethiopia, during their transition period via Addis Ababa or the Sudan, or only following 'aliyya to Israel, an ever-increasing number of Ethiopian-Israeli women appear to be utilizing the support offered by these kinds of "Ethiopian" associations in their new life in Israel.

This support, which relies on a mutual assistance mechanism that originated in Ethiopia, does not mean that participants are unfamiliar with the "new" Israeli banking system. Rather they maintain a symbiotic relationship with the banking establishment; it is split in members' consciousness between the poles of the empowering and the threatening. State money deposited in the bank becomes the primary source of the female *iqqub*'s funds, while the bank itself is described in the "male" terms of exploitation and hidden knowledge. Both these poles were repeatedly described as central to the foundations of *iqqub* associations in Israel.

Thus, for example, a female participant of about seventy, who depended on income supplements and her old-age pension, explained: "Look, today it is hard with the banks. They take service fees and they are not "OK" anymore. For every page you print out, they take a service fee. Even on savings there is a service fee of about three hundred shekels a year.... Maybe I if I lack something, or my son needs something ... he cannot get [a loan from a bank] because he is too young. This month it's my turn to receive [the *iqqub* fund] on the twenty-ninth."

In another interview, a young woman of about twenty explained, "The adults here can't save money in the bank—they don't work—so they can have something like 'savings' from the National Insurance."

Further, as a member of another *iqqub* indicated, it is intended to complement, not replace, the banking system. In contrast to the bank, which is portrayed as alienating, forbidding, and inaccessible, the *iqqub* is familiar, tailor-made to fit the participants' needs. The *iqqub* in Israel, whose timing is determined by the date on which National Insurance payments or employees' salaries are deposited in the bank, facilitates a connection between the two financial systems. Both practically and symbolically, it allows members to "own" the alienating system, while assimilating it into the traditional institution. One participant explained:

> The advantage of the *quve* is that there's no "minus" to close. When you take a loan from the bank, you pay back interest, as well. There is no interest in the *quve*. If you need the money urgently, you can ask to be first. If you need quick cash to pay back loans or to cover your overdraft at the bank, you can quickly use the *quve* so you will have [money]. There is no overdraft with the *quve*. What there is, you get *netto* [clear]. It helps you return money after you took a loan from the bank, you can cover it with the *quve*. And there is also the social aspect, which there isn't at the bank. They [the members] help with other things. They see that you have something urgent—talk to each other and decide how to help. The *quve* is not just money, but also help on a daily basis.

Another participant described:

> We put in six hundred shekels each time. When there were two of us, it was twelve hundred shekels. [Now] every month it's six hundred. I now receive one

thousand shekels a month from National Insurance. [I have] six children, so I receive one thousand shekels. I put six hundred in the *iqqub*. On the day of the party I have to bring the money. I receive money for the children on the twentieth of the month. If this falls on a Thursday, we don't have [a meeting]. There are weddings, there are parties, so we meet as close as we can after the twentieth, perhaps the twenty-first or twenty-second . . . as late as the twenty-fifth, but no later. We try not to be later, so there will still be money.

While the *iqqub* described above includes only mothers of children under eighteen, an older women's group holds its meetings according to the date of deposit of their income supplements: "We have an *iqqub*. Every month we hold it, girls only. They [the men] have one, too—did you think they'd give it up? [Our *iqqub*] is of girls we trust. We've had it for three years already. . . . We always hold it on the twenty-ninth of the month. Do you want to join us? We'll collect you [take you on]. . . . Whoever drops money on time, collects money on time."[16] Another participant compares the *quve* in Gondar with one held in Israel, where employed men and women participate. She reiterates the arrangement whereby the *iqqub*'s dates coincide exactly with receipt of salaries in the participants' bank accounts:

> In Israel, in my *quve*, everyone works. . . . Once a month in Israel we get a salary on the tenth of the month, so the *quve* is on the Friday evening. We have the *quve* before Shabbat. . . . In Ethiopia we would hold the *quve* at the home of a woman who sold *mashilla* [roasted corn kernels] and all kinds of things like that—a fixed place. We went to her place, and didn't know who would receive that evening. Here in Israel, wherever we hold it, the hosts receive the money that evening, unless someone asks to move up his turn—then we let him. . . . Now there are fourteen people in my *quve*—each person puts in one thousand shekels a month, and receives fourteen thousand at his turn. We set the amount at the beginning. If someone wants [to give] two thousand shekels, she'll put in her daughter and her name, too. If someone wants to pay double, he'll get double on his name.

Social Considerations

In the participants' discourse, the social support provided by the *iqqub* is fortified by the connection between the formal financial system and the informal social system. The close link between financial and social benefits, of which the *iqqub* constitutes a practical and ideological axis, has been identified in other cultural contexts, as well. For example, Taa (2003, 255) quotes an interviewee, an immigrant from Ethiopia to Toronto, as follows: "Indigenous organizations . . . are comfort zones that shelter immigrants from desperation. They support a positive start up in the new country. . . . These organizations are good places of comfort."

In contrast to the attitudes expressed by participants of the female *iqqub*, a male interviewee described the enjoyment he derived from his family *iqqub* in connection with the topics raised by the group's men and women of all ages. "People come to our *iqqub* from all over: from Netivot, from Jerusalem, from Haifa. It's a great pleasure. We tell stories; it connects us to Ethiopia. I was disconnected. For me it's been a history lesson. We talk about politics. Not personal, family matters."

This family *iqqub* always takes place on Saturday, and the money is transferred before Shabbat begins, corresponding with the group's historical and religious themes and its heterogeneous composition. But here, as well, an emphasis is placed on laughter as a central liberating component. He added:

> In my group, two older families live on National Insurance and all the rest work. The women and the men. We come on Friday, for the whole weekend [Friday and Saturday]. Each person brings some food. There is a kiddush, Shabbat songs; we sing a lot and exalt the creator. The person in charge writes down whose turn it is at the beginning, then each person takes out money, it is counted and collected. The person in charge writes down that each person has given the host money. In Ethiopia, I don't know if it was done . . . I recommend having an *iqqub*. It connects you to your roots. It's not the same as at the bank. You need the human touch, the laughter. The material aspect is not the important thing. Everyone talks with everyone. The young people tell jokes. One of the pleasures there is telling jokes about the day-to-day blunders. It's spontaneous. Lots of laughter. Everyone laughs with everyone. They tell how it was in the villages, everyone tells how it used to be [in Ethiopia]; we make comparisons.

Both the historical stories and the jokes about the blunders can be deciphered as a dismantling and reassembling of loaded themes in the lives of the Ethiopian community in Israel. The supportive group framework, along with the financial concretization enabled by its ongoing commitment, is shared by the different *iqqubewoch* in Israel. Examination of the female *iqqubewoch*, their unique characteristic praxis and discourse, reveals explicit female empowerment. This issue, for which we found no parallel in the literature on ROSCAs around the world, was striking in its clarity for Ethiopian Israeli women. Expressions of empowerment are used to describe the very existence of the *iqqub* in Israel, as well as the specific content raised during its monthly meetings. A participant in a young mothers' *iqqub* recounted:

> So we drink, we chat, we talk . . . all kinds [of talk]. Who was where, who did what, all kinds of things. Sometimes [*laughs*] about the husbands, too. Sometimes we tell about the [children's] kindergarten . . . some work for the Jewish Agency and they tell about what goes on at the agency, or those who work in a kindergarten tell about the children at the Ethiopian children's kindergarten,

or about the new immigrants, those from the agency tell, about the Falashmura they talk, they laugh, about how they behave, that they don't know [how to be-have], and then we also drink *bun* [coffee].[17] Sometimes maybe a little about clothes. We dress nicely with a little bit of gold. I wear nail polish, but not too much, not like for a wedding. I take a shower, put on perfume, wear jewelry from here, not from Ethiopia. It gives a feeling of fun.

The immigration theme is processed at the young mothers' group meetings: fixed topics are discussed, accompanied by liberating laughter. Other subjects ex-clusive to the female *iqqub* include references to family life and intimate relations between men and women, as well as couples' financial arrangements and use of their money. The marking of the *iqqub* money as "female" is central to the inter-pretation of the issues processed within its framework.[18] A clearly empowering connection is created between the state and the women by means of the desig-nated funds that are transferred on fixed dates from the state to the women and from the women to the *iqqub*, using the funds in a way that corresponds with the state's original intent. Another participant spoke explicitly of female empower-ment: "There's *quve* for women only. There's also *quve* for men only. In every aspect, when it is mixed, the women are not free. They won't feel free. So usually there are men separately and women separately. . . . The *quve* betters her status. First of all, she gets self-confidence. She can buy things for herself, and she can buy for the house and the children."

Indeed, in the present study, the *iqqub*'s image as an institution of women's empowerment clearly emerges from the words of many participants. For example, a female participant in a mixed *iqqub* recounted:

Most important are the meetings. The money is worthwhile, too. Now, here, we want to be with each other. The women love to be together and stay after the [financial part of] the *quve* and talk to each other. The men leave right after the *quve*. When the men are present [we] are guarded, like your religious people, even with eyes open, we don't look [at members of the opposite sex]. Even me, and I was born in a city . . . when the men leave, the women speak, talk about their husbands, "He doesn't give me money; he doesn't act nicely." There is no embarrassment, everything is on the table. Anger between husbands and wives—we tell each other about that, too.

The *iqqub* offers Ethiopian Israeli women both support and enjoyment. The women extol the liberating framework of the association in general and of each meeting. If, however, the ROSCA is by its very nature a supportive, empowering counterinstitutional framework, then the ethnographic study enables us to deci-pher particular manifestations of this empowerment. The remainder of the discus-sion, then, provides an in-depth examination of the *iqqub*'s meetings, symbolic and ritual aspects, and discourse.

Founding and Rules

The founding of an *iqqub* group typically comes out of an initial conversation between two or more women. They propose additional participants, usually from among their neighbors or relatives who live nearby. One participant recounted: "Those who have means build a group for others with means, money follows money. Those who have go to those who have. . . . Anyone can set up a *quve*. It doesn't have to be family; it can be acquaintances or neighbors. But from the same region. But it's kind of a problem to stop—if I received a sum of money, I have to continue the round until everyone has received, and only when it's my turn to receive, I'm allowed to leave."

In the Israeli *iqqub*, the founders choose women similar to them financially, that is, with the same funding sources. At the founding meeting, they set a rigid framework of binding rules that are formulated in writing in a detailed contract and are not to be revoked. While typically women (and men) in rural Ethiopia did not know how to read or write, most of the younger women in Israel have acquired a degree of literacy. However, this important resource is still not taken for granted among the community. The group's dynamic components are set carefully at the outset, as well. A female member discussed evasion, social sanctions, and discontinuation of membership:

> Whoever wants to join, the most important thing is to bring money. She has to pay; there is no such thing [as not paying]. So far this has not happened. You know what they would do to her? They'd finish her until she paid. They'd send the "big ones" [respected members of the community] to her, to tell her that she owes money and if she doesn't pay . . . or else, she can say she has no money so she can't continue—that's different. If she can't, we'll return her money as long as she hasn't taken [from the fund] yet.

Another member lent a tough, obligatory aspect to participation in the *iqqub*, "Whoever wants to stop, can't! If he returns what he received—then he can leave, but there's no chance, because it's a lot of money."

In another interview a female member added:

> Everyone has [an *iqqub*]; there are a lot of them. I'm in one, for instance, but there are some who drink at several. There's one woman who has a six-hundred-shekel *iqqub* with us, and another of seven hundred shekels, so every month she puts in thirteen hundred shekels for both her *iqqubewoch*. Over there [at the second *iqqub*] there are sixteen people, so whenever it's hers [her turn to receive the fund] it's a lot of money! . . . But there are some who talk; there are a lot of them. There are girls who bad-mouth, or just come and talk, so you understand? We don't want them. Look, we've been drinking now for, how long? Five years. So five years we've been. There was just one who participated and left, and she's already come back. She came back again. Because [when she

left], she didn't have enough money. She was drinking for two, so she didn't have enough money. So she said she didn't have enough. Now she's back. Because she was with us on the first list, we let her come back, but if she hadn't been with us, we wouldn't have let her back. Got it?

This description indicates the group commitment established at the group's founding meeting, exemplified in the participant's interpretation of the term *iqqub* as fixed, a binding obligation.[19] While this obligation is a moral one, it also finds expression in the group's bylaws. Members can be added to the circle only if all members agree. Often the newest member will be marked separately and will participate in the group's financial aspects only, not its social aspects. Conversely, a participant who was herself present at the founding of the group is allowed to return after leaving.

Another expression of this attitude is found in the words of a male participant, who described members' strong commitment to each other:

The original group has continued from 1998 until today, nine years without interruption. We have become a family already. It has happened that people met and even got married. Connections have been made. During mourning or celebration, the *iqqub*'s people come and help. I, for example, was abroad, and I intend to return to the same *iqqub*. A special place is reserved for me. They will be offended. If I go to another *iqqub*, they'll be offended. That's because a good connection was made between everyone. . . . Whoever is late pays a fine. It is set ahead of time. At our *iqqub* it was one hundred shekels. If you didn't notify twenty-four hours before the meeting that you'll be late or that you cannot come, you're fined. If you don't come, depending on the reason, if it is justified. That evening we'd call him and maybe forgo his fine. If someone was ill, couldn't make it, we'd understand; in general we believe them.

The *iqqub* is indeed characterized by a binding set of rules and regulations, which may be classified by the formality of their formulation. Interviewees have described the recording of rules in bylaws or a contract of sorts, typically at the group's founding meeting. This document is usually kept by the founding members.[20] The documented rules exist alongside those set verbally at the same meeting and rules of conventional behavior that do not need to be put in writing. One participant talked about the rules:

We also have a letter; we wrote everything down. We wrote down what needs to be brought, that whoever is late has to bring ten shekels. . . . The money [for being late] goes into the fund. We already have three hundred shekels in late fees [*laughs*]. I actually pay a lot for being late. Yes, I've already paid about sixty shekels, over the five years I have had to pay. You're late, so you pay. Because it's not good to be late. Let's say we start at six thirty, then if you arrive at seven thirty . . . then it's good to come on time, not be late. Because let's say we want to eat, some let's say came straight from work and haven't eaten. So we want to start and wait until she comes. So if she pays, she'll come on time. Everyone comes on time. They come in panting [*demonstrates*]. Running, kind of. Everyone really looks at their watches. Five minutes late, they already pay ten shekels. So we know that if we are five minutes late, we pay. Then you may even come earlier. You need to come at 6:30, so you'll come at 6:25, maybe 6:00. Doesn't matter. The important thing is not to come after 6:30. That's how it's done, that's how we wrote it. We also wrote in the beginning about the food, what to make. We wrote that there needs to be chicken, *injera* (a pan-fried Ethiopian bread), and eggs to put inside, hard-boiled eggs. And fruit and drink. About food and lateness we wrote.

The commitment is intensified by setting the rules alongside the sanctions that follow in the event of their violation.[21] Using a somewhat functional approach, the "late fees" may be interpreted as a form of "practicing" punctuality, among other modern skills needed for a bureaucratized, legalized world, within a supportive framework. This component of adapting to Israeli society may be linked with participants' description of adherence to the rules that they have created for themselves, and the empowerment created by the very ability to shape for themselves rules that are typically imposed on them from above. Here the narrator described the meeting's liberating elements. In another conversation we held on the topic, she explained that it was important not to be offended by the teasing that goes on in meetings, which was well known among participants: "We already know that we don't have to be offended."

Below we present two descriptions of what constitutes proper, customary participants' behavior, from two male participants in mixed-gender family *iqqubewoch*:

> Each person comes with groceries for Friday and Shabbat: seeds, beverages, cookies. My offering was simple. I was a soldier, and I wasn't ashamed. Each according to his ability. There are no fixed things—not necessarily. When I was a soldier, I prepared chicken—all parts. If there are the funds, someone makes mutton—it's recommended. I was a soldier then, and I couldn't afford it. Some made meat instead of chicken. *Tella* [beer]—a very, very strong drink, like champagne. Only Ethiopians have it. Some women drink it, but mostly men. *Tella, injera, buna*, coffee. On Saturday night we drink *buna, kulu* [roasted seeds], popcorn. Hummus if someone brings it. When we come to someone's house, we sit, whoever wants asks for water, drinks, and later refreshments are brought, and only afterward chicken. We eat. We eat after collecting money, after, only after.

In another example, which demonstrates the range of rule making, another male participant recounted:

> When we had the *iqqub* we had a lottery, but what did we do? We would give like this: one hundred shekels. Now twenty shekels to help out the person who

invited us, to make the food, to buy food and drink, to cover the expenses for food. He brings *injera*, *wat* [general term for Ethiopian spicy sauce], he buys beer, and things like that [*laughs*]. So now we said we would add another twenty shekels. The same day we give [the money] to whoever prepares. Oh, I remember now! Then it was one hundred shekels that we distributed like that. What did we do? Out of the one hundred shekels, twenty went for food and I think fifty shekels went to the person [who hosted us] and with another thirty shekels we opened a bank account and kept it there. . . . We also said that if someone's, say, father or mother dies, we'd give them three hundred shekels. If a brother or someone dies, we'd give them two hundred shekels. We made a kind of ranking of how much to give. . . . I myself sat and wrote it [*laughs*]! It was the first time I received a list in Amharic, I think I still have the list of rules. I still have that list. . . . I need to look for it. . . . Yes, we made rules and, by the way, we also got certification that so-and-so's father died, so everything is documented [*laughs*].

The second description illustrates a creative merging of *iqqub* and *iddir* (an Ethiopian burial society providing financial support in the case of death). Money intended to assist in death ceremonies has been linked to the transfer of funds for savings and credit. The detail and meticulousness of examination and documentation "emulate" the relationship between the individual and the authorities. For this interviewee, himself a researcher of Ethiopian culture, an expression of the uniqueness of this merging was revealed from and within itself in his embarrassed laughter that exploded following mention of the kinds of food to be served according to the binding list; the explicit documentation of the sum to be given when a relative dies, quantifying grief according to familial relationship; and the presentation of an official death certificate to the members of the family group.

Ritualistic and Symbolic Aspects

A participant in a young mothers' *iqqub* explained:

When there is an *iqqub*, you'll see how neat the house is. The girls come. They tidy up the house, prepare food. They prepare chicken, sauce, *injera*, spicy sauce; they prepare one vegetable salad; and beverages—they buy beverages. Except for beer. We need only black [malt] beer. We need a regular cola—Coca-Cola—and we need all flavors of Prigat [fruit drink]: mango, orange, and melon. We need them all. There are eight of us. Only eight of us drink. There are others who participate in the money so they send it with them [the "drinking" participants]. Let's say, she takes her husband's [money], too, so she'll host [the *iqqub*] twice. What can we do? She'll hold it twice a year. So that's how it goes. . . . Mom was in, but I took her out. There's not enough money. But she wouldn't come [to the meeting itself], she only put in the money, and later I took her out. . . . We who drink the money [all of us] are my age, no older. It's kind of like, free, nice, without getting so offended. We try, we say what we want, but you can't get offended. But if someone insults you, you'll retaliate, but don't get hurt.[22] There are some who really talk nonsense. There are a lot who want to joi,n but we don't let them in. We talk about the man, what he does, what he doesn't do. We drink *bun*, drinks, and everything. We speak in Hebrew.

This thick description touches on issues central to the female *iqqub* in Israel. The list of food to be served is conveyed with an almost magical meticulousness, accompanied by terms such as *we need, we need only black beer, we need them all*. Thus a transformation occurs from the social and economic obligations of the *iqqub* to its food, whose substance as an offering for the guests contains two stakes of obligation: social and financial.

The meeting is of women of similar age and family status. Not random, this uniformity is embodied in ritual rather than money. Others, such as female relatives who do not fit the group profile or male relatives, may take part in the group only if another member serves as agent on their behalf. They may thereby enjoy the group's financial benefits, but not its social and ritualistic aspects. In the changing world of Ethiopian Israeli women, *iqqub* associations and their specific cultural manifestations constitute a highly meaningful experience, whose building blocks incorporate the financial, the social, the ritualistic, and the symbolic. In the attempt to understand the depth of meaning of their experience, we wish to refer to the lottery held at the closing part of each meeting. This component encapsulates complex, at times contradictory, themes that sometimes stand in contrast to the phenomenon as a whole. In addition to its above-mentioned features, the lottery determines the order of the financial and ritualistic rotation. And while all members are included, only the *iqqub*'s social core takes part in the ritual. Thus, the lottery creates a split between the financial and the social.

In a few cases, the order of rotation is set ahead of time, sometimes even at the group's founding meeting. However, most *iqqubewoch* choose to determine the order by monthly lottery, in a procedure that is a central pivot of meetings. The lottery is conducted as follows: The names of all members, even those who do not attend meetings, are written on small pieces of paper, which are then carefully folded into tiny uniform paper squares and placed in a bowl. A representative is sent out of the room (this could be a member who has already won the fund or the hostess's child, for example) and then called back in to pull out a square. The winner's name is revealed: she will receive next month's fund and, usually, if she is a full "drinking" member, host the group at her home. At the next meeting, only members who have not yet won the jackpot will participate in the lottery. All interviewees noted the option of negotiating the order of rotation in the case of a member who urgently needed the funds.

Close scrutiny of the lottery procedure reveals perceptions that are connected with the *iqqub* and cultural understandings enfolded therein that warrant viewing the lottery as a substantial key to the entire *iqqub*. In this manner, we assert, the juncture of the lottery is particularly loaded with symbolic meaning as regards the world, its existing order, and the illusive, arbitrary nature of fate. As social order is determined by chance, it contains a tense, loaded, constant pivot at the intersection of certainty and randomness. The lottery and its unique characteristics are connected by way of encoding with the remainder of the *iqqub*'s components. One member described the lottery as the most pleasurable part of an entirely pleasurable meeting. Despite the concrete financial expectations the lottery evokes, it is described in terms of sisterhood, corresponding with the relative satiety experienced by the women in Israel.[23] The discourse of the lottery reveals oral references to the *iqqub*, attaching relaxed, "satiated" terms to it, as well. One participant recounted:

> Let's say that today I did the *iqqub*. So after we eat, everyone puts in the money and we have a lottery. Now I, let's say that I have already eaten [received the fund], then I'm out. Whoever has already eaten, has taken the money, [is] not in the lottery. We call the lottery *ija* . . . *ija* means "lottery." OK, so if I go out [to act as the drawer of the lottery], my name is not in the lottery. So we take little pieces of paper, and write on each one the names of those who haven't yet eaten in this round. We put them on a plate and someone chooses. This is how, each time, we choose the hostess for the next time.

She went on to explain:

> We have a lottery for those who haven't eaten yet . . . whoever did not see, pulls out. Opens up whatever she draws. The name is written of whoever's turn it is next month. We pull out just one for next month. Next time, [we do it] again, from those who have not been in this round. In the next round, everyone again, again from the beginning, there's everyone, until it ends. The last one doesn't need a lottery.

Closing Words

The paternalistic view, which dominates most of the literature, portrays the arrival of the Beta Israel from Ethiopia as a manifestation of sponsorship by the state of Israel and world Jewry, which has left them little control over their lives. All financial aspects of the immigrants' lives appear to be dictated "from above." Through varied support and welfare mechanisms, the state views itself as the primary factor exercising control over the funding sources of passive, needy groups. Thus, without detracting from the importance of this support, and in practical and symbolic reciprocity with it, the phenomenon of Ethiopian financial associations presents an important alternative that has emerged "from below." Alongside the symbolic processing of broad cultural themes, these associations also embody empowerment and change.

Although rooted in a particular Ethiopian experience, the flourishing of the *iqqub* and its framing as an Ethiopian institution—both in structure and terminology—should not lead us to invoke simplistic notions of continuity or preservation. As the material above shows, these cultural practices emerge from a far more complex matrix of creativity in which elements of "tradition" mobilized in a new setting, not to preserve the past, but to confront the challenges of a new future. For many of the participants their only firsthand experience of the *iqqub* takes place after their arrival in Israel.

Conceptualization of the financial circle by means of oral terms can be deciphered as a moderate double bind of feeding and eating, between satiating the other and satiating one's self. As the *iqqubewoch* we have chosen to examine are mainly women's groups, the symbols of nourishing are colored by themes that are connected with relationships between women and the financial establishment, relationships among women, relationships between women and men, and relationships between women and children. Multidirectional encoding is also found in the conceptual system connecting the lottery with eating, while concepts of eating and drinking ("drinking with money") transform the winner/eater into a "feeder," by virtue of the very act of her winning. In addition, the *iqqub* and the lottery at its heart are a game, a show of the potential for change. The very drawing of the lots exhibits ambiguity. It is not excessively dangerous, as the gamble does not pose a risk of real uncertainty. There is only uncertainty regarding the order in which the "jackpot" is received; there is no risk of not receiving at all. Thus, the ritualized lottery with its precise rules moderately processes themes that lie between certainty and uncertainty, between the individual and society, between suspicion and trust, between control and loss of control, and above all between the individual and his or her fate. In the world of the *iqqub*, these contrastive pairs coexist, representing for participants the intertwining of past and present, the ensuing potential for change, and the social accompaniment that enables this change, as well as its limitations.

Notes

This chapter is based on Hagar Salamon, Steven Kaplan, and Harvey Goldberg, "What Goes Around, Comes Around: Rotating Credit Associations among Ethiopian Women in Israel," *African Identities* 7, no. 3 (2009): 399–415, www.tandfonline.com/.

1. The plural of *iqqub*. Our interviewees usually use the singular form even when speaking of multiple groups.

2. For reports on the Ethiopian community in Israel, see, for example, Weil (1991, 2004); Shabtay and Kacen (2005); Leitman (1993); Leitman and Weinbaum (1998); Phillips-Davids (1998, 1999). The cultural research is heavily loaded with exoticism. We would like to suggest that issues on which Ethiopian Israelis' rationality and agency are so central may tend to be ignored.

3. For research on the state's paternalistic attitudes, see especially Hertzog (1998).

4. While similar frameworks exist, comparisons between the various *iqqub/quve* in Israel show that they differ from one another in their composition and rules. In some cases, a number of participants share a single membership; in others, one participant may wish to double her share in the circle, or to deposit and receive money for a "covert member," typically a female relative who is unable to be an active participant at meetings. In such cases, the active representative is also the host of the covert member's *iqqub* meeting. The amounts of money deposited also vary among groups, as do group size and makeup. Sometimes, a participant wishes to exchange her turn to receive the fund with that of another member. In one interviewee's words, "There is a list, there is a lottery, but even more we take into account who has asked for the money today." Another interviewee said, "Usually, even if there is a lottery, if there is a person who gave a little, if there is a person who needs the money . . . I give him my turn. He says, he asks for his turn [to receive the money] so [we] put him now."

5. We are grateful to Chaim Rosen for pointing out the dramatic rise in the percentage of Ethiopian women participating in the workforce over the past decade. According to the Israeli Central Bureau of Statistics 52 percent of Ethiopian women between ages twenty-two and sixty-four in 2007 are in the workforce as opposed to only 22.8 percent in 1995–96.

6. See Ardener (1964, 201).

7. See Ardener and Burman (1995); Peer (1998).

8. For a broader discussion of these institutions, see Schaefer and Amsalu (2005); Tubiana, Pankhurst, and Eshete (1958); Dejene (1993).

9. See also Dejene (1993); D. Levine (1965, 278–79). For essays published primarily for their linguistic content, but concerned with the topic, see Leslau (1968, 209–15; 1982); Leslau and Kane (2001). Varying types of ROSCAs are prevalent in Ethiopia and are based on religion, locality, occupation, and gender. Apparently, their fundamental similarities enable flexibility and facilitate transition between types of associations. In most of Beta Israel's villages, where money was used only minimally, there were no such savings and credit associations without immediate, defined objectives. Mutual assistance organizations, however, did exist and were even commonplace in these rural areas. These organizations assisted with agricultural manpower, food preparation, or payment for events such as weddings or burials (*iddir*), when one-time fund-raising of a relatively large sum was required. These customs were an integral part of the lives of Beta Israel in Ethiopia. The practice of helping pay for weddings or burials still exists among Ethiopian Israelis, retaining clear elements of reciprocity and group commitment. Carefully documented amounts of money are involved, serving, in fact, as some community members who are invited again and again to celebrations have helplessly remarked, to reimburse the host's contributions to previous celebrators.

10. See, for example, Ornguze (1997); Taa (2003); Almedom (1995).

11. Interviewees often revealed that many Ethiopian Israelis avoid depositing money in the bank or taking out bank loans, owing to their difficulties in managing a relationship with a bank and their mistrust of the banking system, as well as their objection to paying interest. This phenomenon is particularly prevalent among the older generation and is connected with Ethiopian Jews' "everyday resistance" as presented by Kaplan (1997). See also Sabar (2008, especially 96–173) on African migrant workers in Israel.

12. In the entire and rather broad body of published research on Ethiopian Israelis, we found a marginal reference to the phenomenon in Schwarz (2001, 56–58). It is also discussed in Chaim Rosen's unpublished essay on economic life in the town of Kiryat Malachi.

13. An *iqqub* participant who came to Israel in 1983 from Walqayt through Sudan, recounted: "There, in Ethiopia, we didn't have such a thing [*iqqub*]. No one had it. Maybe in the city they had it, but in the village they didn't have it. We didn't have it. Also, there was no money; we didn't use money. Everyone did for himself. Everyone had cows. They would milk them, maybe only *bun* [coffee] they would go and buy, but otherwise they didn't buy anything."

14. For example, as Anbesa explained, "*Iqqub* is a custom that comes from there, so you don't change the name. Now even people who come from Ethiopia today, they come after seven, eight years in the big cities, so they're not like those who came during Operation Moshe or straight from the villages. So new things have come into the community this way, too."

15. See Kaplan and Rosen (1993).

16. At the time of our research, National Insurance benefits were paid as follows: children's benefits on the twentieth of the month, old age and dependents' pensions on the twenty-eighth.

17. The Falashmura are a group of people related to Beta Israel, who were converted to Christianity in the past, while living in Ethiopia. Many of them have returned to Judaism and have subsequently been brought to Israel. The relations between the Falashmura and Beta Israel are highly complex. On the complexity of these relations, see Salamon (1999, 56–73).

18. For Israeli immigrant women narrating their lives, see Schely-Newman (2002).

19. Linguistic references were made only when participants were explicitly questioned on the topic. Most did not respond to the challenge, explaining that this was the name of the association in Ethiopia. We received varied responses containing popular linguistic interpretations that in some cases relied even on Hebrew. For example, while one participant used Leslau's dictionary for his linguistic interpretation: "Where does the word *iqqub* come from? It comes from *aqabba*, which is to guard, that has to do with guarding," a Tigrinya-speaking participant proposed her own explanation, connected with the Hebrew root *k.b.ʻa.* "to set" or "set" (fixed) and corresponding in her consciousness with her group's binding nature, regularity, and carefully followed rules. Differentiating between *mehaber* and *iqqub*, she said, "*Iqqub* is like *mehaber*. It means to drink without money, that's the meaning of the word *mehaber*. It's just [taking] turns. But *iqqub* is always with money. *Iqqub* is fixed, [a determination]."

20. This is an essentially symbolic, rather than legal, document. Cognizant of the rules, members do not typically go back and refer to the document.

21. In Ethiopia, certain functionaries were appointed at the time of the group's founding. This has not been the case at any *iqqub* we have encountered in Israel. In Ethiopia, the functions were judge or chairman (*musa*), elected by all members, to be responsible for supervising the group's smooth management and adherence to the rules; secretary, in the event that the judge is illiterate, whose role is to record all monies and prepare the lottery; treasurer, mentioned in two interviews; and alternating guarantors, filled by members who have not yet received the fund and are therefore not yet debtors. The rationale for the absence of functionaries in the *iqqub* in Israel is that the risk of nonpayment is mitigated by several factors: selection of participants according to the means of payment available to them, the infeasibility of evasion following the drawing of the lottery and winning the jackpot, and participants' shared literacy skills.

22. This is a particularly apt description of the "joking" relationships illustrated in Radcliffe-Brown's classic comparative research. On joking relationships as a characteristic of states of structured tension, see Radcliffe-Brown (1940).

23. While the *iqqub* in Ethiopia usually occurred on market days, whose revenue was by no means guaranteed, the connection in Israel with reliable, fixed state funds contributes to the sense of satiety.

9 "David Levi" Jokes

The Ambivalence over the Levantinization of Israel

CHAPTERS 7 AND 8 emphasized how recent immigrants have creatively expressed uncertainty and vulnerability in the face of their new lives in Israel. The present chapter, following an insight formulated at an earlier period of immigration, shifts perspective and presents an instance of "reciprocal change" (Weingrod 1962), where vulnerability and uncertainty are articulated in the folklore of "established" Israelis. We have identified such processing in what Israelis have come to call "David Levi jokes." The following leads us into this humorous cycle. "During one of (then Israeli foreign minister) David Levi's visits to the White House, the guards are surprised to discover him climbing onto the roof of the building. They ask him to descend immediately, so he says: 'But I heard them say that the drinks are "on the house."'"

The above joke may seem enigmatic to most readers: superficial, and hardly funny, it is an unexpected "opener" for a book chapter. In fact, in Israel, this and related jokes, part of a joke cycle known as "David Levi jokes," are regarded as extremely funny, among a wide cross section of the population. Focusing on the intricate relationship between these jokes and evolving Israeli identity, I attempt to unearth the semiotics of this joke cycle, to shed some light on its unique nature and unlikely popularity.

Dynamic and vital, the joke is a form of creative expression that occupies a unique place in social and cultural discourse. Characterized by collectivity and anonymity, appearing to be light and entertaining, jokes constitute an important vessel through which troubling and sensitive issues can be contained and processed. As a discursive medium, jokes enable a reflexive mechanism to unfold and develop. Participation in the joke-telling event fosters active engagement around topics in which uncertainty abounds, such as in the many tensions inherent in the fluid and rapid dynamics of modern, multicultural societies.[1] In the present work, this phenomenon is examined by considering the David Levi joke cycle as a medium through which Israeli national identity with its concomitant tensions and vulnerabilities is channeled and mediated.

In recent years, much academic attention has been devoted to conceptualization of the mediating role of jokes, particularly their interpretive potential. However, while in the international study of humor, and ethnic humor in particular, comparative studies such as by Apte (1985) and Davies (1990, 1991, 1998) predominate, the present study concentrates on a specific joke cycle, within a particular cultural context. The study focuses on this humoristic corpus as a catalyzing agent in the evolution of Israeli identity.[2] Humor, as I hope to demonstrate, is a unique prism for exploring the cultural matrix within which the construction of identity is carried out. While this chapter focuses on a culturally specific example, I believe that it has wider applications to the study of the unique relationship between joke cycles and dynamics of ethnic and national identity in other cultural contexts.

The joke cycle that is the focus of the present chapter, known in Hebrew as *Bedihot David Levi* (David Levi jokes), is representative of a pivotal phase in Israeli humor, emerging at a key transitional period in the evolution of Israeli identity. Its popularity was documented in diverse and heterogeneous social and ethnic contexts, proving itself to be a pan-Israeli phenomenon that transcends gender, and even age differences. The ethnographic material is based on fieldwork conducted from 1995 through 2002, in which David Levi jokes were recorded in personal interviews and joke-telling events were observed. In addition, complementary materials were collected from joke archives and the internet.[3]

Analyzing some of the most popular jokes in this cycle reveals them as multifaceted cultural manifestations that enable internalization of an aspect of Israeli identity toward which there is great ambivalence: the Levant within and the Levantine "other."[4]

Through these jokes, with their repetitive laundering of images and associations, an Israeli Levantine identity is mediated. The salient feature of this mediation is thus not limited to form or content but is rather the phenomenon of the joke cycle in its entirety, including the transformative effect of self-humor. Integral to this process is the meeting of the national and the particular, such that in the telling/listening event, participants are personally confronted with and forced into enactments in which Levantine identity is momentarily adopted whether by active mimicry or passive participation.

Between East and West

The David Levi joke cycle features as its protagonist a caricature of the Israeli politician David Levi.[5] Levi emigrated from Morocco to Israel and, within just a few years, rose from a run-of-the-mill construction worker to the uppermost echelon of Israeli politics, peaking in his appointments to the posts of deputy prime minister and foreign minister.[6]

The significance of this particular rise to power is illuminated by its historical context. Historically, modern Zionism and Israeli state institutions were
dominated by European Zionist movements. The mass migration of Jews from
Moslem countries in the 1950s shifted the demographic and ethnic balance in
Israel's Jewish society, posing a challenge to the Ashkenazic hegemony, and
sparking conflicts regarding the location of Israeli national identity on an East-
West axis.

David Levi emphasized his ethnic origin throughout his political career, and
as such came to represent the influence and political potential of Israelis of *Mizraḥi*
(Eastern) Jewish origin.[7] The development of the DL joke protagonist can be
attributed to a combination of factors that identify him with the constructed image
of the Moroccan Jew. Prominent among them are certain biographical details: he
makes his home in the geographic and social periphery of Israel in the "development town" of Beit Shean and is the patriarch of a large family.[8]

David Levi's appearance as the butt of a joke cycle can be understood on a
number of levels, but foremost among them is that as an Oriental or "Mizrahi" Jew,
he has symbolized the growing legitimacy of the "Levant" in Israel.[9] His entrance
into the Israeli political core, to become the official representative of the State
abroad, magnified the relevance of the topic.[10] The DL jokes inflate the Levantine
stereotype through the DL character and insert him in situations, whether domestic or professional—including meetings with foreign dignitaries, an example
of what Oring (2003) refers to as "appropriate incongruity"—in which DL, and by
implication all of Israel, are exposed as extremely uncouth, and yet at the same
time, "one of us." The identification between the Levantine DL and the Jewish
Israeli collective are the key mechanism in the process of internalizing Israeli
Levantinization. These jokes, then, play a role in the internalization and processing
of incongruities inherent in the blurring of boundaries, and particularly, the
Levantinization of identity.

Language and Vulnerable Identities

The convention that Israel is an "island of Western culture within the Levant" with
its concomitant colonialist overtones has been eroded over the years by many
factors.[11] Chief among them are the demographic shift and the revival of the Hebrew language. The latter, a key achievement of the Zionist enterprise, linguistically united Jews of diverse ethnic origins and transformed the fossilized, religious
language of sacred texts into the official and primary spoken language of modern Israeli society. One of the many ramifications of this revival was to linguistically return the Jews to their Semitic, Levantine origins.[12] The linguistic aspect
of Levantinization has further been intensified over time by the incorporation of
Arabic expressions into colloquial Hebrew. This phenomenon surfaced already in

the period of early settlement (the Yishuv), and took expression in comic genres of the period, as Oring demonstrates in his pioneering research on Israeli humor.[13] In the DL joke cycle the relationship between language, humor, and identity assumes new dimensions, in which the "other" is not uniquely external, but rather mingles with the Levant within the individual and within Israeliness.

The ambivalence and anxiety toward Levantinization conveyed mainly through language in the joke cycle must be viewed in the context of a number of interrelated phenomena. First, ambivalence and anxiety toward Levantinization are exacerbated as political conflict with Arab neighbors and the resulting need for differentiation continue to be a main trope running through many aspects of Israel's national agenda. It is not incidental, then, that most native-born Israelis do not have a command of Arabic, even though it is one of Israel's three official languages.[14] A related notion is that the insistence on retaining the primacy of Hebrew exacts a double price and leaves Israelis on shaky ground on the East-West axis. The problematic attitude toward Arabic and the loss of linguistic mastery enjoyed by previous generations living in the Diaspora all contribute to an experience of increasing isolation.[15]

The fact that the most popular, vital, and rich cluster within the DL joke corpus is the metalinguistic jokes reflects the powerful symbolism of language as vessel for identity.[16] The jokes in this cluster deal with ignorance of English, and the inability to distinguish between Hebrew and English, including many jokes that reflect even an incomplete command of Hebrew.[17] In the DL joke repertoire, the metalinguistic device exploits the theme—whether in bold strokes or sophisticated nuance—of an isolation resulting from gross ignorance and lack of sophistication usually vis-à-vis symbols of Western "sophistication" and power.

Working in tandem with the metalinguistic device are other expressions of ignorance. These are conveyed in childish phrases and behaviors that emphasize the gap between chronological and mental age, lack of basic technical understanding, and jokes predicated on the contrast between an impressive and elegant external appearance and the embarrassing social, intellectual, and linguistic limits attributed to the DL character.[18] Combined with the metalinguistic mechanism, these themes provide mutual reinforcement within a semiotic matrix, in which Israeli identity is negotiated and mediated.

The themes prominent in these jokes relate to vulnerabilities particular to Levantinization in Israel. One theme uses caricaturized images to play on the embarrassment associated with the growing visibility of cultural expressions by Oriental or Mizraḥi Jewish groups, of which the "Moroccans" were the largest and most visible.[19]

Another theme is that of isolation. In contrast to the prevalent conceptualization of Israel as a "Western island" in the Middle East, these jokes belie a self-image of provincialism relative to the West, yet at the same time, sentiments of belonging to the Orient.

The jokes provide an outlet for dealing with this process not only by channeling perceptions and tensions reflecting discomfort, but also through laughter in which both teller and listener take part.

David Levi Constructed by Humor

The name David Levi is a generic, nonethnically specific, and popular Jewish name, which could be described as the Jewish equivalent of the American John Doe, or the Jewish American Joe Shmo, as is elaborated below. However, within the context of Israeli humor, it is clear to all that these specific jokes relate to a known political figure with a salient ethnic identity.

At the explicit level, the jokes are about David Levi "the Moroccan," whose professional and educational achievements "do not justify" his ascension to the uppermost political echelons of Israeli political power. Their manifest content is personal, insulting, at times crude, a fact that locates them in the context of ethnic tensions in Israel. Typical to their telling is an apologetic tone both regarding the content and their base humoristic level, a fact that does not detract from their popularity and their ability to bring about great laughter among teller and audience alike, in a wide range of social and socioeconomic milieus, including among Mizrahi Jews. The nuances that distinguish a DL joke-telling event in a purely Mizrahi context versus an Ashkenazic context notwithstanding, the fact that the joke is told in mixed forums suggests a pan-Israeli phenomenon that affects Israelis of many ethnic backgrounds.[20]

Given that David Levi is a high-ranking politician, it is significant to our argument that the main preoccupation of the DL jokes is not politics. The world of the jokes' content is that of daily routine, sometimes to an extreme: elementary school, the house in Beit Shean, and the mundane routines of life: changing a lightbulb, preparation of a family meal, driving in his car, making a purchase at the corner store, and so on. Even in encounters with the great leaders of the world, the image does not change, a fact that contributes an additional humoristic component to the joke.

Depiction of the ignorance and "primitiveness" attributed to the butt of the joke is a staple of many joke scenarios in which DL is shown to be technologically incompetent or, in the symbolic language of the joke, incompetent vis-à-vis the Western world.

One element that lends DL jokes their pan-Israeli flavor, as mentioned, is the name David Levi itself. David is perhaps the most popular of traditional Hebrew names, originating with the biblical King David, and as such appears in numerous versions: the formal pronunciation, (Dávid), popular East European Diaspora nicknames (Dúvid, Dúvidl), and popular Israeli nicknames (Dúdu, Dúdi). Of these, Dávid, like certain other names accented only popularly on the penultimate (Hebrew: *mil'el*), (e.g., Móshe and Ráchel, the name of Levi's wife) is associated with colloquial, nonelite speech. Even the term *Dávid Lévi joke* triggers this association because of the popular pronunciation of both the first name and the surname with the accent on the penultimate: Dávid Lévi. The colloquial nature of this pronunciation is further emphasized by the contrast to the way the name is pronounced in official forums, including the media, with the stress on the ultimate (Hebrew: *Milra'*), namely, Davíd Leví. The notation Dávid Lévi diacritical notation is used in the jokes presented in an attempt to convey this layer of their effect.

DL jokes are rarely told one at a time, such that at a single joke-telling event much "information" about the DL character may be conveyed. The composite effect of the interplay between the jokes in identity mediation suggests that the jokes' order of appearance in the field, which is impossible to trace accurately, is less important than the breadth of their context, through which the DL joke character and concomitant stereotypes take shape through the telling and hearing of a critical mass of DL jokes.[21]

Thus stated, the chronology of the jokes does support the claim that the jokes in the DL cycle are a dynamic expression of ethnic change in Israeli society and its power structure. The burgeoning of DL humor began following the real David Levi's first major appointment as minister of housing and construction, with a second peak following his appointment as foreign minister. The cycle thus developed in parallel to the change in the distribution of ethnic political power, symbolized by the political advancement of David Levi, and significantly, subsided when this change solidified.

In presenting and interpreting these jokes, both the manifest humoristic level, conveyed mainly through the punch line, and the more hidden messages revealed through careful examination of the joke's construction, must be considered. Most revealing is the joke context, which conveys the subtle, symbolic message hidden in the dimensions of the joke's form and content.[22] The present semiotic analysis of these jokes takes into consideration the complex interplay and overlap between content and form.

The challenge of conveying these jokes to an "outside" audience includes overcoming the obstacle of cultural fluency and linguistic skills required to convey essential information necessary for interpreting them. A second, no less formidable, task relates to the necessarily interpretive act of fixing such a fluid and dynamic cultural expression, which by nature changes in every telling, within an academic text. The following representative sample of the corpus was selected to exhibit the most prominent elements of the cycle. The order of presentation is intended to convey, in a cumulative manner, the particular cultural understandings necessary for appreciating the deeper significance of the entire cycle.

#1 ("The Hairdo")
Stick a pin in Dávid Lévi, and all that's left is the hairdo.

This joke targets a physical characteristic of the real Levi—his puffy hairdo—and caricaturizes it, generating a powerful image of a foppish character, a blowup doll. The doll pops at the mere prick of a pin, leaving behind only his hairdo.

The tension in the discrepancy between outward respectfulness and inner lack of content appears in a generative continuum throughout many of the jokes in this corpus. This trope appears in many of the jokes, even when it is not the main theme. The trope is amplified in other jokes in which the DL character's ignorance is exposed to the outer world in international settings, culminating in the White House.

Inflated confidence in combination with basic lack of orientation taken to an extreme is highlighted in the following joke:

#2 ("Driving against Traffic")
One day, Dávid Lévi's secretary [or, in a different version, his wife, Ráchel] hears on the radio that a lunatic is driving against the traffic on the Jerusalem–Tel Aviv highway. Knowing that this is Dávid's route, she immediately phones his car to warn him. "Just one lunatic?" Dávid screams back at her. "Here they're *all* driving against the traffic!"

In this joke DL drives dangerously, confident that all the others are in error. The image arouses a latent worry that the Israeli foreign minister is self-confidently leading them on a collision course. In the context of the DL joke cycle, this joke is associated by the audience to other jokes in the cycle in which the protagonist displays an astounding lack of awareness of his situation, a trope of general, on-going Israeli anxiety. This interpretive direction is supported by many jokes in the cycle. A striking example is the DL jokes that exploit the theme of exposure:

#3 ("Polgat")
Dávid Lévi becomes foreign minister and goes to meet the president of the United States. In preparation for the meeting, his aides give him a little note to remind him of some basic greetings and niceties in English, which he is to place in his suit pocket and consult when necessary. As soon as he arrives at the meeting, he "goes blank" but remembers the note. In a panic, he reaches into his jacket pocket, and, upon examining the very small and crumpled note, which seems somehow to have become stuck to his suit, he declares with great pomp and festivity: "Polgat." [He has unwittingly just read the manufacturer's name from the label.]

In this joke, DL opens his suit pocket, exposing his innards before a distinguished forum representing the pinnacle of world power. What is revealed is the label of a local Israeli textile factory apparently attached to his suit. Moreover, as in all other jokes in this cycle, the DL character carries out his blunder with great pomp and circumstance. The joke audience gains a privileged view of the symbolic DL, who is exposed through the narrative, while the setting suggests an even larger-scale exposure of the nation vis-à-vis the world. A reflexive process in the joke-telling event is thus set in motion, by which Israeli identity is brought to the fore, exposed in public, and subjected to common reflexive negotiation.

Throughout the joke cycle, exposure occurs on many levels—one locus under the humoristic spotlight is the protagonist's home:

#4 ("Careful, R-A-C-H-E-L")

In the house in Beit Shean, a lightbulb burns out. Without hesitating Dávid jumps on the table, dressed in shorts, to change the lightbulb. Handing him a spare bulb, Ráchel says, "Dávid, be careful, your B–A–L–L–S [spelling it out] are showing." Sometime later, another bulb burns out. This time, Ráchel jumps onto the table and the whole family gathers round. Dávid hands her the spare bulb, not forgetting to add: "Careful, R-A-C-H-E-L [spelling out the wrong element in the sentence], your panties are showing."

Aside from bringing the theme of exposure to a graphic extreme while the protagonist exhibits an Edenic lack of awareness, these jokes usher the audience into the innermost chamber of the character's home. Images from one joke mingle with another, creating a composite character, exposed from his innermost chamber through his most public role. DL's exposure of a secret and encoding of the wrong message leaves the realm of the private and enters the national as DL, foreign minister and presumably keeper of state secrets, encounters world leaders in other jokes. The expanded associative range in which jokes set in the home are linked with those set in elite international forums, re-creates for the audience the tension between the inner and very personal versus outer and national identities.

DL jokes in the domestic setting also introduce stereotypes of the Mizraḥi man at home. The character's hometown is emphasized. Beit Shean, an Israeli "development town" located in the "periphery," is typical of the towns in which many new immigrants to Israel, particularly Mizraḥi Jews, were encouraged to settle. The protagonist is portrayed as the grand patriarch coveting his wife's modesty, caricaturized even further by the incongruity between his exposure ("balls") and hers ("underpants").[23] The stereotypical patriarchal role surfaces also in the following joke, when DL shuns his wife's attempt to help him accomplish a male task:

#5 ("Reaching the Bulb")

In the living room of the house in Beit Shean, a lightbulb burns out again. Dávid, with his usual diligence, gets on the table to change it. Ráchel, seeing him standing on the table, brings him a newspaper and says: "Dávid, stand on the newspaper." "Not necessary," he replies. "I can reach the bulb just fine like this."

From the intimate setting in Beit Shean, exemplified in jokes 4 and 5, the joke cycle spans outward to other realms. The following jokes exploit a theme common to many jokes in the cycle—the protagonist's inability to manipulate basic technology and again, in the wider sense, a reflexive national self-questioning and insecurity. This is accentuated when the protagonist is cast as minister of construction and housing, a post held by the real David Levi.

#6 ("Working—Not Working")

One winter when Dávid Lévi was minister of construction and housing, his driver turned to him and said, "Mr. Minister, we have to check the car's systems. Please, sir, could you help me check if the wipers are working? I'll turn them on, and you look and tell me." Dávid sticks his head out the window. When the driver says "Well?" Dávid, after taking a good look, replies, "It's working—not working—working—not working."

The following joke again combines the elements of technological and linguistic incompetence:

#7 ("Rise")

When Dávid Lévi becomes minister of housing, he receives a new office and a new car. But unfortunately, he needs to take the car to the garage every week for repairs. So the people at the office ask him: "Say, Dávid, what's wrong with the car?" "It's fine," he says. "I get into the car, turn on the ignition . . . put it into first gear—no problem . . . into second—no problem . . . I shift into third—no problem . . . it's only when I shift from fourth into Rise"

This joke, at the straightforward level of the text, portrays a DL who is unaware that *R* stands for "Reverse"; in fact, he is certain that it is the gear that follows fourth and stands for "rise," Hebrew slang from the Yiddish/German *reissen*, meaning to tear, that is, to tear up the road, reminiscent also of the sound and connotations of the word *race*. He describes to the garage mechanic how he advances toward his desired speed, to the ultimate speed of "tearing up the road." This evokes the stereotype of the Mizrahi man as an aggressive driver. Reading further between the lines, the (self-)mocking narrator implies that for DL, the "backward" Mizrahi, the gear for progress is Reverse.[24]

In addition to the metalinguistic aspect is the recurring theme of the mismatch between DL's external facade (new office and shiny new car) and his behavior. The theme of technological shortcomings is woven throughout the cycle, and returns with DL to the domestic and personal settings in the following two jokes:

#8 ("The Off Setting")

Dávid Lévi and his wife receive a new oven. In honor of the event, Dávid decides to pamper his wife by preparing a chicken dinner. After the chicken has sat for two hours in the oven, he calls to his wife, "We have to return this oven.

The dinner's been on for two hours and nothing's happened." "What did you do?" she asks. "Well," he says, "I put it in the oven and turned it to the right setting." "What setting is that?" she asks. "What do you mean, what setting? "Off," [*of* in Hebrew means "fowl," usually referring to chicken] of course!"

#9 ('The Chicken Is Off')

Dávid Lévi goes on a vacation to London with his wife, Ráchel. They enter a fancy restaurant and are handed the menu. Dávid wants to flaunt his savvy, but the only word he knows is *chicken*, so that's what he orders. A short time later the waiter returns and says [this sentence is quoted in English, even when the joke is told in Hebrew]: "I'm sorry sir, but the chicken is off." Dávid turns to his wife, chuckling, and says [in Hebrew], "He's telling *me* that chicken is *of*?" [i.e., that the word *chicken* means *of*.]

Fleshing out the fictional biography of DL is the following branch of the DL joke cycle, featuring jokes that "support" the adult DL character's lack of sophistication by "demonstrating" his "ineptitude" even in childhood. As in other jokes in this corpus, the protagonist is represented as exceedingly self-confident and unaware of his limitations. This branch achieves its ultimate effect within the context of the larger cycle, as the listener, following cumulative exposure to a variety of DL jokes, associates the DL who "embarrasses" his compatriots by his blunders as Knesset member and minister, with DL, beaming child living in a fool's paradise.

Most jokes in this branch are relatively short, many of them constructed in the question-and-answer format, posing an ostensibly simple question. The tense moment between the telling of the question and the revelation of the answer sets the tone for a secondary moment of tense expectation: Will the listener "get" the joke? This hierarchical dynamic, possibly understood by association as a paternalistic attitude toward the DL character, momentarily thrusts the listener into the company of DL, strengthening the potential identification between DL and the audience. The listener is momentarily left standing on shaky ground, while the anticipation of laughter, a sign that he or she "got" the joke, is forthcoming; thus is the listener's "competence"—alongside that of DL—put to the test, a unique dynamic enacted in the DL joke-telling event to which I return in the final section of the chapter.

#10 ("Beautiful Years")

What were the eight most beautiful years of Dávid Lévi's life?
A. From first to second grade!

#11 ("High School Diploma")

Why did the word *ḥag* [holiday] appear on Dávid Lévi's high school diploma?
A. Eight years, three grades.

The numeric value of the two letters making up this word in Hebrew, have the values 8 and 3, respectively.

#12 ("Completing a Puzzle")

Dávid Lévi shuts himself in his room and asks that no one dare disturb him. Everyone walks around on tiptoes. Four days later he emerges, beaming. Holding the completed puzzle in one hand, he points to the box and says: "See, it says two to six years, and I did it in only four days!

#13 ("I Already Have a Book")

When Dávid Lévi was appointed minister [or on his fiftieth birthday, according to another version] his friends came to him and said: "Dávid, we wanted to buy you a present. After much deliberation, we decided on a book." "Thanks," says Dávid, "but you really shouldn't have. I already have a book."

The boundary between the jokes and reality is porous, enabling the impression of the DL character constructed through the jokes to seep into reality and setting off a dynamic dialogue between (assumed) reality and folklore. This encounter between reality and joke-lore became especially dramatic when David Levi assumed the post of foreign minister. A deluge of jokes relating to David Levi's new position ensued, and interviewees testify to a sense that the real politician's progress was in fact the "best joke of all." Reality was thus appropriated by humor, blurring the boundary between the two.

The sampling of jokes presented to this point, selected for their panoramic presentation of essential elements of the DL joke corpus, provide the background necessary for a deeper appreciation of the most common and central jokes in the cycle. In this group of jokes, DL encounters the symbols of Western power: multinational technological corporations, the White House and its dignitaries, the streets and huge department stores of New York, and even the United Nations. National identity, I suggest, continues to be explored in these arenas through the themes discussed above—brazen self-confidence with chauvinistic overtones that relate closely to extreme insecurity and incompetence—with an emphasis on national isolation.

The metalinguistic device is one of the main strategies used in these DL jokes to highlight internal Israeli ethnic tensions and touch on themes pertinent to identity. While it appears in many versions of DL jokes, as in jokes 8 and 9 above, it is most powerfully exploited in the "international" arena, which hyperbolizes the protagonist's ignorance by a distinguished setting (i.e., the White House, UN) and powerful characters (i.e., the president of the United States). These jokes, comprising the core cluster of the cycle, are presented in jokes 14–23.

Consider the following joke, a terse concentration of elements that relate to the tension inherent in the East-West dialectic:

#14 ("*To'em* IBM")

When Dávid Lévi became minister of housing and construction he was given a brand-new office. The next morning the secretary came in and saw him on all fours, licking the new computer. Horrified, she asked, "Dávid, what are you doing?" "I was told," he said, "that it's *to'em* IBM." [This joke relies on the homophones in Hebrew: *toem* meaning "compatible," as in *to'em IBM*—"IBM compatible," but also meaning "to taste." The DL character misinterprets the context and tries "tasting" the computer, since it is *to'em IBM*.]

DL, as a government minister, has access to the most advanced technology available, but does not know how to use it. This gap becomes absurd when he confuses the phonetic similarity between the word *to'em* (compatible) with its homophone *to'em* (to taste), and crawls up to the computer to "'taste" it. The East is symbolized in the joke by the sensual and animalistic while the West, by the technological and the rational, with its implied hierarchy.

#15 ("General Electric")

Ráchel and Dávid order a new refrigerator for their kitchen in Beit Shean. Ráchel comes home and sees Dávid standing at attention in front of the newly arrived refrigerator giving a salute. Seeing her surprised look, he says: "Ráchel, please meet General Electric."

This absurd image—verging on the iconic—in which the name General Electric elicits a programmed response by DL, mixes realms: public-private, masculine-feminine, inanimate-human, primitive–high-tech. The blind salute triggered by an inanimate object and symbol of American technology undermines his attempt to enter the space as man-in-command, contributing vivid images that relate to the East-West dynamic, the organizing axis of the DL joke cycle.

The jokes discussed thus far take place in Israel (except for the London restaurant in joke 9, a version of the locally situated joke 8). Another group of jokes very typical to this cycle deals with DL's excursions outside Israel, in which he is representing the state of Israel abroad. These jokes are set sometimes in Africa, but mainly in Washington and New York, exploiting constructed global dichotomies to emphasize the joke's message.

#16 ("What's the *Meter?*")

When Dávid Lévi was minister of housing and construction, he headed a delegation to Africa, as a guest of the African ministers of housing. To impress their distinguished Israeli guests, all dressed in formal attire, the African hosts take them to a building site. Scaffolding and construction pits are everywhere. Suddenly, Dávid falls into a pit. The hosts, terribly concerned, gather around the pit and call down, "Dávid Levi, what's the matter?" "*Meter?*" replies Dávid. "It's at least two, maybe two and a half meters!"

This joke, along with its many variations, plays on the phonetic similarity between two words, one in a Hebrew and one in English.[25] The protagonist does not understand the question, and to compensate, latches on to the word *matter*, which he mistakes for *meter*. His indignation that the worried onlookers do not properly appreciate the depth of his fall exacerbates the element of embarrassment. Once again the gap between the respectable, elegantly dressed "Western" delegation to Africa, on the one hand, and the clumsiness of the fall and ensuing display of linguistic ineptitude, on the other, reinforce the disparity between the advanced and the primitive, between knowledge and ignorance. Falling into the pit, DL is literally brought down.

#17 ("Martini")
During a fancy reception at the White House, a waiter approaches Dávid Lévi and offers him a drink. "Martini?" "No," says Dávid, "Mar [Mr.] Dávid Lévi."

Provinciality in this joke is conveyed doubly. Apparently, the protagonist is not familiar with this well-known drink. Moreover, he assumes he is being addressed in Hebrew as *Mar* ("Mr.") Tini, and boldly corrects his interlocutor. Similar to this joke is the following permutation, which combines the chauvinist element and the East-West encounter held together by another metalinguistic inspiration:

#18 ("*Yesaydu*")
Dávid and Ráchel Levi are invited to the presidential inauguration ceremony at the White House. The two are sitting on the lawn when Ráchel says to Dávid; "Is this the White House? It's not even white." Dávid looks at the building and then hears the president say, "Yes, I do." Grinning he says to Ráchel: "Don't worry, the president says it will be whitewashed" [*yesaydu*—"they will whitewash"].[26]

The translation, which is intended to comfort DL's wife, potentially arouses the opposite feeling among the Israeli audience hearing the joke. This joke recalls in its combination of elements the joke "On the House." In joke 18, DL's confusion between an English phrase and a phonetically similar Hebrew verb betrays the character's absurd assumption that the president of the United States, during his inauguration ceremony, is taking the opportunity to earnestly reassure his guests, in Hebrew, of all languages, of the government's intention to paint the White House in the near future.

The following joke, yet another example in this series, sets up a hilarious situation in which the protagonist, sent to represent Israel in the UN for the first time, is nervous about his English. While in the previous joke he was entirely unaware of his limitations, in this joke, his very awareness is the joke's basis. As in the Polgat joke (joke 3) his fear is stated explicitly. Intent on taking seriously the advice to speak very slowly, he does not even notice that he is speaking Hebrew, not English. His realization is delayed by the fact that by chance, he is picked up at the airport by an Israeli cab driver:

#19 ("Getting to the UN")

Dávid Lévi is sent to represent Israel in the UN for the first time. As he is nervous about his English, his assistant advises that he speaks very slowly. Entering a cab, he approaches the driver:

"*A-ni tsa-rikh le-ha-gi-aʿ la-ʾum*" [I need to go to the UN] (he says in Hebrew), taking pains to pronounce every syllable.

They arrive at the UN, where Dávid says: "*A-ni tsa-rikh le-ha-gi-aʿ la-sha-ʿar ha-dro-mi*" [I need to get to the south gate].

They drive a while longer, when the cabbie, kindly joining Dávid by speaking slow Hebrew, asks:

"*Me-ʾey-fo ʾa-ta?*" [Where are you from?]

"*Mi-Bet-Shean*" [From Beit Shean], answers Dávid.

The cabby is amazed: "*Wa-lla, gam ʾa-ni mi-Bet-Shean!*" [No kidding! I'm also from Beit Shean!]

Dávid, completely taken aback, looks at him, and says, still speaking slowly: "*Az la-ma ʾa-naḥ-nu me-dab-brim ʾan-glit?*" [So then why are we speaking English?]

In this joke, provinciality is again drawn to its absurd extreme, sketching brilliantly, in a few short strokes, a very complex situation. The protagonist is utterly oblivious even to the fact that both he and the driver are native Hebrew speakers. Moreover, he does not recognize that his driver is one of the many Israeli cabbies in New York. It does not occur to him that his "American" driver might not be familiar with the Israeli border town of Beit Shean, which he mentions with no explanation. The significance of this multiple ignorance is magnified by the fact that his destination is the UN, where he is headed to represent the state of Israel.

#20 ("The River and the *Visher*")

Dávid Lévi is invited to speak with the president of the United States. The president courteously inquires as to Dávid's many children, particularly the two who serve in the army. Beaming with pride, he seizes the opportunity to answer, without hesitation: "One is in the river and the other is in the *visher*."

DL has literally translated the acronyms NAḤAL (acronym for an elite IDF military brigade *Noʿar Ḥalutsi Loḥem*), but phonetically the same as the word *naḥal* [river]), and MAGAV (acronym for the border police, *Mishmar Gvul*, but phonetically the same as the word *maggav* [windshield wiper]. Although *maggav* is the official word for windshield wiper, the Germanic/Yiddish *visher* is the term commonly used). The error is so unlikely and the transitions so complicated, that its comprehension is quite a challenge even for the native speaker. Indeed, DL's complete lack of understanding regarding commonplace acronyms appears to be the point of the joke.[27]

#21 ("Aftershave")
On his first visit to New York, Dávid Lévi and his aide go to Macy's to buy presents. Suddenly he begins pacing nervously. A few minutes later, he turns to his aide and asks, "Tell me, how do you say *aftershev* in English?"

This joke, in addition to utilizing the recurring element of linguistic incompetence, is relevant at another level to the issue of national identity. The scene of reveling in the consumer fleshpots of the Western world in order to bring precious luxuries back home is familiar to every Israeli, particularly from the days when import goodies were virtually nonexistent in Israel, and so it plays on a latent sense of provincialism still lurking. In the joke scene, the "provincial" Israeli consumer abroad is taken over by a shopping frenzy to obtain products not available back home. An additional recurring DL-cycle element alluded to in the joke's context is the reference, via the prop of the aftershave (with its Hebrew-English confusion), to DL's careful attention to external appearance, which resonates with jokes focused on the contrast between the character's outer form and inner content, a theme exploited in joke 1, above.

As we have already seen, most of the metalinguistic jokes are contextualized in New York and Washington, DC, the symbolic locations of Western hegemony and power.[28] The following joke, in addition to the metalinguistic punch line, describes a state of disorientation in this majestic landscape. "Getting" the joke requires of the listener privileged knowledge—familiarity with the basic elements of a typical New York City street corner:

#22 ("Walk, Don't Walk")
On his second visit to the United States, Dávid Lévi decides to walk around New York City. He takes the phone number of the Israeli Embassy with him, just to be on the safe side. Half an hour later, he calls from a pay phone: "I'm lost. Could you send a car to pick me up and take me to the hotel?" "OK," says the security officer. "Where are you?" "Well," he says, "I'm at the corner of 'walk' and 'don't walk.'" [DL pronounces these *wallak* and *don't wallak*, contributing an additional humoristic element explained below.]

At the joke's most basic level, the protagonist is mocked for failing to recognize basic traffic signals, certain that they display the street name. The joke's role in identity negotiation, however, lies at the deeper layers of meaning. DL assumes that *walk* stands for *wallak*, a slang word in Hebrew adopted from the Arabic, used in a context of camaraderie and familiarity. This usage of Hebrew/Arabic slang draws attention to the key theme of Levantinization that these jokes manipulate. The inability to distinguish the slang *wallak* from the ubiquitous *walk* and *don't walk* forms the metalinguistic core of the joke, accentuated by the elementary nature of these terms, both linguistically and as urban survival skills. The combination of the English *don't* with *wallak* is particularly amusing, as it illustrates to an extreme the mingling between East and West characteristic to Jewish Israel. Interestingly, Oring (2003) points out that this expression, which is Arabic for "by God," appears in printed collections of early Israeli humor, during a period when within the humoristic discourse, it was clear that this term was Arabic.[29] In the present joke, we see a new layer in the evolution of Israeli humor. There is a blurring of boundaries between English, Hebrew, and Arabic, which forms its humoristic core.

At the level of the joke-telling event, the teller must pronounce *wallak* properly, as if she were an "insider" familiar with this slang. Both teller and audience thus become momentarily Mizraḥi or perhaps Arab, transforming the participants into a living demonstration of Levantinization.

The trilingual play is brought to a crescendo in the international diplomatic setting, where DL makes an overinvested effort to speak eloquently, refraining from using Arabic slang in favor of a standard Hebrew word, which he translates into English. Predictably, and in absolute disproportion to the effort invested, the protagonist bungles the translation, resulting in a humoristic effect that might be called linguistic slapstick:

#23 ("Let's Talk Postcards")

Dávid Lévi becomes foreign minister and sets out to meet the president of the United States for the first time. Needless to say, he is very nervous, and asks for advice as to how he should behave. His advisers tell him: "Don't worry, just be *dugri* [direct, face-to-face, honest] with him; you know, be frank. That's always the best policy." The big day arrives, and he meets the president. They shake hands, pose for photos, and sit down together. Dávid Lévi opens the conversation and says: "Mr. President, let's talk postcards."

The adviser's instruction to speak to the president *dugri* derives from the Arabic *dughri* (straight), here meaning "openly."[30] DL, understanding that such slang is inappropriate to such a dignified setting, makes a point to use the standard Hebrew synonym, *gluyot*. The catch is that *gluyot* in Hebrew has two meanings and, characteristically, DL chooses the wrong one (postcards) in his translation. The effect created by DL's ignorant use of sophisticated commutative logic instead of the obviously correct translation of the word resembles the effect of his caricaturized hairdo—inflated and empty.

Further, the phrase "let's talk *dugri*," a common segue into an intimate conversation, indicates parity between the speakers, rendering the failed and absurd

translation into a hyperbole of the inequity between the two leaders and, on another level, of the power relations between the two nations.

The ever-present reflexive quality of these jokes takes on a most overt expression in
the following joke, rendering it a suitable "last word" for this representative sample of the corpus. Resounding through this joke, in which DL is the listener to the
joke about himself, are the parallelisms and overlap between the butt of the joke,
the listener, and the national self: "A man approaches Dávid Lévi and says, 'Have
you heard the latest Dávid Lévi joke?' 'Excuse me,' Dávid Lévi responds, 'I'm Dávid
Lévi.' 'That's OK,' says the man. 'I'll tell it slowly.'"[31]

Negotiating Israeli Identity

Denial, ambivalence, and inner conflict have always been present in the ways
Israelis, including Mizrahi Jews, regard social and cultural manifestations of Arab
culture within mainstream Israeli Jewish culture. The conflict these expressions
arouse is closely bound to the fact that Israel is in a state of chronic, violent conflict
with the Palestinians and much of the Arab world. A number of historical circumstances, including the predominance of European Zionism and the relationship of sustenance and dependence with the Western world and particularly with
the United States, have also contributed to Israel's cultural tendencies toward the
West, denying and suppressing Levantine aesthetics.

The ambivalence toward Arab culture does not clearly distinguish between
expressions that originate in the surrounding predominantly Moslem Arab culture
and those emanating from the Semitic roots of Judaism. Throughout the history
of the state, ambivalence prevailed regarding Judeo-Arab cultural expressions,
and they took root only gradually, in a variety of social and cultural expressions.
The most dramatic of these was the entrance of Mizrahi Jews into the political
mainstream. It thus comes as no surprise that DL jokes are not political in the
usual sense, since it is not David Levi himself or his views that pose a threat but
rather what his political success represents—the entrance of the Levant into the
Israeli *Politik*.[32]

Notably many of the jokes recounted among Israelis about David Levi circulate in other cultural contexts about other figures and groups, where their relative
relationship with their environment shares some but not all the characteristics of
the presently discussed corpus. Thus, in other countries where fluency in English
may not always have characterized the political leaders the same linguistic mechanisms as the DL jokes may appear. Likewise a number of these jokes may be
found in the more or less internationally distributed repertoire of numbskull
tales (Jason 1972). The nonindigenous character of these narrative traditions creates
yet another reflexive layer for cultural interpretation of the jokes. While ridiculing

DL for his failing proficiencies, the narrators of the jokes recruit borrowed cultural products, adapting them to local needs, in ways parallel to the toilsome processes of adaptation that they have DL undergoing. It is thus as performers who are better equipped in turning the foreign into "our" culture, rather than as representatives of some kind of imagined authenticity, that these narrators of jokes celebrate their superiority vis-à-vis the object of their amusement. It is possibly moments in their own imperfectly adapted pasts that they are able to reiterate and symbolically conquer by targeting an official figure connected with—perhaps paternal—authority. Joking about DL the Levantine, the joking community reinstates its own Levantine identity by creating an internal ranking of levels of adaptation.

The jokes themselves operate on a number of levels. At the level of content, ethnic images are transmitted through nuances of language and inflection and through elements of the Israeli cluster of stereotypes associated with Mizrahi culture, among them illiteracy and lack of sophistication, male chauvinism, a large, warm family, life in a development town, superficiality, and "hot-bloodedness." These themes are repeated both in the punch line of the joke and at the level of the less direct message, through construction of the background, the tone, and the joke's setting.

Content, however, is only one element of the joke mechanism. Interviews and observations of the joke-telling event—how these jokes are told and heard—reveal a number of key elements in the dialogic dimension of joke telling through which socioethnic processes in present-day Israel are expressed and mediated. The teller of the joke "mimics" the stereotype of the Mizrahi Jew using gestures, associations, and terminology associated with this identity, as if "trying on" the trappings of a Levantine identity that is gradually becoming internalized. The power of these jokes to penetrate the very identity of the individual as she or he enacts the dynamic related in the joke is subtly enhanced by the generic name of the famous politician. In effect, David Levi could be any Israeli Jew, implying that we share many qualities with the protagonist, no matter what "side of the joke" we are on. Dávid Lévi jokes are thus an outlet for Israelis to expose national and personal vulnerabilities as they "try on" aspects of the Levantine national self, through language, gesticulations, and, above all, self-mockery.[33]

Distinct from the phenomenon observed by Mintz (1999, 237), in which jokes "dress" cultural tensions to make them appear "less threatening, more acceptable," at the level of the joke-telling event, DL jokes in fact tend to thrust participants into a highly charged topic that arouses not-always-comforting sentiments.[34] This is due in part to their participatory style and is most salient in metalinguistic jokes, in which the subject is being mocked publicly for his or her linguistic ignorance.

In the case of DL jokes set on the international stage, the joke-telling event also re-creates the public tensions and embarrassment narrated in the joke. This joke-telling encounter, a parallel process in which the power relations between teller and listener are isomorphic with the power relations between the audience and David Levi, is in effect a mimetic model of the interaction between the linguistic and the social, which enact certain relationships pertaining to belonging and identity.[35] The cumulative effect of composing, hearing, recalling, and especially repeating these jokes enables internalization and mediation of national ambivalences and vulnerabilities.

These jokes, once so vital and popular, have lost their potency in the world of Israeli humor in the past few years, which relates to continually changing dynamics of national identity with its East-West preoccupation. Just as the *chizbat* was once central to this aspect of Israeli identity, later making way to further phases of humoristic expression, the vista remains open for the development of new dialogic devices to mediate the next round of challenging identity issues, in new, entertaining ways.

Notes

This chapter is based on the article "The Ambivalence over the Levantinization of Israel: 'David Levi' Jokes," *Humor: International Journal for Humor Research* 20, no. 4 (2007): 415–42.

1. For a similar view, see also Mintz (1976; 1999, 237); Davies (1990, 8).

2. See, for example, Mikes (1950); Ben Amos (1973); Nevo (1985, 1986); Nevo and Levine (1994); Nilsen (1993, 200–207); Ziv (1986a; 1986b; 1988, 113–31; 1991); Oring (1973, 1981, 1983); Alexander-Frizer (2008, 427–65).

3. I wish to thank Edna Hechal from the Israel Folklore Archive (named in honor of Dov Noy) for her assistance.

4. The encounter between Ashkenazic Jewry and the Levantine space of Eretz Israel was not lacking in Orientalist exotic charm and fascination, but this was directed at representations of the "otherness" of the Oriental. This phenomenon corresponds with Said's Orientalism as a discourse in which the West presents the Orient and the Oriental as an object for research and domination, imagination, and romanization. Fascination with the "exotic" Orient was highly complex in the Israeli case. Other cultural expressions of Israeli dialogue with the Levant appeared in a 1998 exhibit at the Israel Museum entitled *Kadima*.

5. To preserve the distinction between the real David Levi and the character in the jokes, the latter shall henceforth be referred to as DL.

6. Born in Morocco in 1937, David Levi immigrated as a young man in the mass North African immigration to Israel in 1957. Prior to his rise in politics, he was a construction worker, a biographical fact significant to his political persona. He first became a *Knesset* member in 1969, and his political star has risen steadily ever since. In 1979, following the rise of the Likud party, he was appointed consecutively to two key ministerial positions in Israeli government: minister of housing and construction (a post he maintained in the tenth, eleventh, and twelfth Knesset terms) and subsequently minister of absorption. Overlapping with this period, between 1990 and 1992 he also served as deputy prime minister, a post to which he would return several

times. Later in his political career, Levi formed an independent political power base in founding the *Gesher* party. This breakthrough peaked with his appointment as foreign minister in 1996, a post to which he returned twice, including under the left-wing Barak government.

7. The distinction in Judaism between Ashkenazic and Sephardic was to some degree superseded in Israel by the distinction between Ashkenazic and Mizrahi, that is, those Sephardic Jews from Arab and non-Arab Moslem countries. The North African immigration, particularly immigrants from Morocco, was perhaps the most prominent numerically and culturally.

8. Development towns are small towns constructed by the government during the years following establishment of the state, and settled, at government initiative, by Mizrahi immigrants. These towns constitute the geographical and social periphery of Israel, and most of them face high unemployment and concomitant social difficulties. For a study on the "Sabra myth" and Jewish past, see also Zerubavel (2002). For study of folklore in Beit Shean, see Bar-Itzhak and Shenhar (1993). See also Noy (1965).

9. The very reference to DL jokes evokes, for most Israelis, a nonspecific association to the Levant, due to DL's biographical specifications, and to the Levant's presence both in the national collective consciousness and in the individual experience. The term *Levant*, it should be noted, is employed widely in this chapter, preferred for its broad connotations. Related terms (*Oriental, Mizrahi, Arab, East-West*) are used when a more specific connotation is intended. The term *Levant* embodies a spectrum of associations as varied as the diversity of Israeli society itself. Among the themes to which it relates are national ones of identification along an East-West axis, internal power relations, historical isolation and insecurity, and subnational and personal themes of ethnic pride, feelings of belonging, and vulnerability as Israelis.

10. While the significance of this joke cycle is often pondered—whether in the press or in personal conversations—no scientific study has been published on the topic. Informal analyses of the jokes tend to attribute the infatuation with the subject either to the personal qualities attributed to him (outward appearance, manner of speaking, political comport), or to stereotypes associated with his ethnic origin. See for example, the humor supplement by Anonymous (1998, 16).

11. Often associated with the image of Israel as "the only democracy in the Middle East."

12. On the revival of the Hebrew language, see, for example, Morag (2003, 330–52).

13. I refer here to Oring's (1981, 122–30) discussion on the *chizbat* of the Palmah, and recently, the chapter "Colonizing Humor," in *Engaging Humor* (Oring 2003, 97–115), comparing the colonial humor of Australia, the United States, and Israel. In his discussion of the *chizbat*, Oring points out that identity conflicts were celebrated rather than mediated. In contemporary Israel, however, the historical setting for DL jokes, Israeli folklore has become the vessel for the containment of the Levantinization of Israeli society.

14. Language is, of course, connected to power relations and hierarchies. Although exhaustive treatment of this matter is beyond the scope of this chapter, it is indicative that most communication between Israeli Jews and Palestinians transpires in Hebrew. While many Jewish schoolchildren study spoken or literary Arabic in the public schools, there are astoundingly few native-born Israelis who have mastered the language.

15. Although considered one of the miraculous achievements of Zionism, the ascendancy of the Hebrew language exacts a high price that has not begun to be properly acknowledged. Multilinguistic skill, an advantage once associated with Diaspora Jews, has been replaced by the linguistic isolation of the young generation, ironically impeding the links between Israel and the "West" at the level of the most personal experience.

16. For studies on metalinguistic jokes and humor in Middle Eastern, Arabic-speaking societies, see Shehata (1992); Muhawi (1994); and Al-Khatib (1999). The metalinguistic mecha-

nism and, in fact, a number of the humoristic elements found in the cycle, exist in other cultures, as well, especially in the category of international numbskull jokes. This, however, does not negate their particularist significance as a medium for Israeli identity mediation with original combinations of ethno-linguistic elements. Another interesting example of an original Israeli humoristic corpus with unique linguistic characteristics combining Hebrew, Arabic, and Yiddish is the *chizbat*, from the period of the Palmaḥ (prior to the founding of the state), elaborated by Oring (1981).

17. Levi's knowledge of French gains no expression in these jokes. The complex relationship between French and East-West identity in Israeli society is a matter for future study. Also of note is that while French is listed as one of Levi's languages on the official government Knesset website, his knowledge of Moroccan Arabic is not.

18. The jokes that are the focus of the present chapter could be considered politically incorrect on many counts, and I direct the reader to Saper (1994), and to the fascinating, unresolved debate on political correctness that was the focus of a special issue of *Humor* (Anon. 1997, 453–513).

19. For a discussion of images of specific Mizraḥi groups in Israeli society, see Goldberg (1984).

20. Comparative research on how these jokes are told in different Israeli ethnic contexts is a topic unto itself and worthy of further investigation, although such a study would be a complex undertaking given the radical desegregation in recent years and the large extent of ethnic mixing and mixed identities. This is not to claim that when the joke is told by Ashkenazic supporters of the labor party, for example, that the joke-telling experience is devoid of antipathy for the Mizraḥi population, and disappointment at the latter's overwhelming support for the Likud party. While this is insufficient to account for the entire phenomenon of the DL joke cycle, it is an inherent tension. I thank an anonymous reviewer for pointing out the need to make this point explicitly.

21. An intriguing example of the uniqueness of the ethnographic aspect of the telling of these jokes relates to the observation that in many cases, the joke-telling event takes on the narrative quality of a "life story." In such cases, the series begins with childhood, continues with the house in Beit Shean, and culminates in DL's visits abroad as a Knesset member and minister, organized as a kind of running order by addition of the words, "first visit," "second visit," and so on. An in-depth understanding of this phenomenon calls for further study and methodological innovation.

22. On communication and context, see Briggs (1988, 1–22).

23. I am grateful to an anonymous reviewer for drawing my attention to this lack of parallel, leading me to consider its significance.

24. I thank an anonymous reviewer for this insightful interpretation.

25. For a similar joke in Arab culture, see Muhawi (1994).

26. According to another version, after his third visit to the United States, David Levi returns to Israel and excitedly tells his friends that the marines guarding the White House recognized him and spoke Hebrew with him. "How so?" they inquire. "When I was walking around Washington I noticed that the White House isn't even white. So I went up to one of the guards and said, "You know, White House is not white," and he reassured me, "Yesaydu."

27. This would be equivalent to referring in French to a member of the SALT negotiating team as a *sel* member.

28. In an article dealing with Jordanian jokes, Al-Khatib (1999, 274), presents a metalinguistic joke similar in the protagonist's lack of basic linguistic understanding: "a villager, who did not speak English well," set in New York City. Al-Khatib cites the importance of education as

one of the joke's messages, conveyed through mockery of the uneducated villager. As the present chapter demonstrates, in the DL metalinguistic jokes, a variation of this trope, the social tensions are siphoned through signifiers of the constructed Ashkenazic- Mizrahi/West-East dichotomies, so fundamental to the Israeli sociocultural landscape.

29. See also Oring (1981), regarding the *chizbat* of the Palmaḥ.

30. On *dugri* as a key term in Israeli culture, see Katriel (1986).

31. I thank Professor Steve Kaplan, who in reading this chapter contributed this joke.

32. David Levi has himself observed that the jokes about "him" express the threat posed by the political successes of immigrants from North Africa (Anon. 2002, 23).

33. It is interesting to consider these points in relation to Oring's (2003, 114–15) observation regarding the connection between national pride and self-humor prominent in the formation of modern national identities in the nineteenth century.

34. For a discussion of other highly emotional forms of cultural articulation in Israeli society, see Salamon (2001).

35. On other models linking language and reality, see Hymes's (1967) characterization.

Part III Recapitulation

Between Longing and Belonging—the Folkloric Expressions of Ambivalence

WE HAVE SEEN the vital cultural charge borne by everyday and seemingly insignificant metaphors and objects, such as elevators, lottery monies, and hairdos. In the context of the jokes, stories, and credit institutions discussed, these items mediate ambivalences between tradition and Israeli modernity, East and West, the individual and the wider society. They become vehicles of negotiation, reflexivity, and empowerment. The discussions in the preceding part reiterate the strong ties between folkloric genres, daily life, and the alleged common ground of Israeliness.

In each of the cases discussed, the expressive forms tell us much about the in-group and the Israeli surroundings, perhaps more than the participants themselves are aware of or care to reveal. Humorous Ethiopian-Israeli stories provoke riotous laughter among tellers and listeners; but behind the laughter, we come to discern the pain of migration and the difficulties of adjustment to a paternalistic society.

In the case of the *iqqub*, we see how an Ethiopian institution that had little place in the nonmonetarized village life in Jewish areas of Ethiopia becomes a social support mechanism, an expression of female empowerment, and, in the eyes of its practitioners, an embodiment of tradition. The new voluntary network mitigates the disorientation and dependence on the state generated by money, and migration's perpetual wrenching of personal values from things, by endowing the practice with the aura of intimacy and the pride of exclusive possession. The *iqqub*, practiced by urban Ethiopians elsewhere, obtains moral status as an act of resistance to the impersonal Israeli banking system, and provides the potential to mediate marginality.

Through each of these cases, Israeli identity is brought to the fore, exposed in public, and subjected to common reflexive negotiation.

The participation in the joke-telling event draws the teller and listener together in their shared mockery of provincialism and primitiveness. Yet the sharing of the joke fosters active engagement in which uncertainty abounds—the tensions of multicultural societies, Israelis' insecurity in the world, and Israelis' conflicted sense of provincialism with respect to the West. The jokes displayed sentiments of belonging to an Orient Israelis have taken great pains to reject but that is now being increasingly reclaimed. The joke has its teller and listener momentarily adopt the position of the Levantine through active mimicry or passive participation. It reminds all that the Levantine is not merely the other of the Israeli collectivity, but the Levantine within all Israelis.

The DL joke cycle's popularity has gradually waned, and presently no heir for the protagonist has emerged in the all-Israeli joking repertoire. The processes of immigration and adaptation, however, continue to be productive in the realm of humor created in Israel, demonstrated by the proliferation of the Ethiopian humorous stories.

Another issue to be considered is that although humor is a subversive form of expression, associated with it are boundaries between what is and is not a "joking matter." These shift to reflect the changing sensitivities and concerns of a society. In this matter, jokes and bumper stickers share this sense of decorum vis-à-vis what can and cannot be discussed. The boundaries of acceptability are a subtext of varied folk genres. In the case of humor, this boundary is often delineated according to an associated feeling of embarrassment. As vividly demonstrated by the Ethiopian immigrants' loss of equilibrium, humor is an emotionally complex vehicle, as its associated sense of embarrassment is related to sentiments of vulnerability and ambivalences.

Each folk cultural form studied represents the intertwining of past and present, the ensuing potential for change, the social accompaniment that enables this change, and its limitations. To appreciate the interplay of traditions and modernity, in-group commonalities, and broader societal structures, we situated each case at a particular period in the migrant group's life course as well as in the evolving Israeli society (as we did in the other parts of this book). Certain "traditional" idioms must retain the force of their cultural origins to speak to the participants employing them. In accordance with the nature of the entire sphere, the moment reflected in chapters 7, 8, and 9 is an intermediate one. The objects and symbols—bouffant hairdos and mangled English, lost ways and objects, social security payments and Ethiopian rituals—carry the resonances of diverse and sometimes conflicting places of origin. The symbols, like those who perform them, are liminal or hybrid ones, capturing a moment neither here nor there, or both here and there.

It will be interesting to see what kind of jokes are told about the first Ethiopian minister. What jokes will Ethiopians come to tell about Israeli leaders and other sectors of Israeli society if they move further toward integration or if power structures shift? Their idiom of meat may become foreign to their children who ate *luf* in the army and *shawarma* from the corner food stand. If more Ethiopians become entrepreneurs, will the role of the *iqqub* change or take on new significance? Will it serve as a site of female solidarity if women become primary breadwinners?

The current analysis lays the groundwork for tracking these changes in folkloric expressions, holding them up as a mirror to the evolving Israeli society and power structure, its adaptability, deficiencies, and uncertainties.

Beyond its portrayal of Israeli realities, the analysis demonstrates how potently folkloric forms demonstrate the dynamics of social ties as well as the negotiation of power relations between minority cultures and state institutions. These arenas of the mediating sphere process themes that lie between certainty and uncertainty, between control and loss of control. They reflect changes in group cultural, gender, and power relations; the longings of migrants for a previous homeland; their accommodation to their new homes; the group's consciousness of a shared fate; and their strategies of coping with loss and marginality. Jokes about others are incisive self-portraits, while the inclusion of what is new under the embrace of tradition shows how dynamic and fluid the processes of ethnic and national identity really are.

Closing Words

The Birth of Public Enunciation from the Spirit of Everyday Life

COMPLETING THE PRESENT book marks the end of a research chapter, which obviously is not concluded nor ever will be. This kind of research journey cannot have a uniform sequence or a prescheduled destination. What guided its itinerary was a deep and powerful intuition regarding the significance of the creativity bubbling in front of my very eyes. With time I discovered that this folk energy is a perpetual spring of inspiration and strength in the lives of many Israelis, who attempt to cope and make sense of life in a country full of complexities and paradoxes, an immigrant country in which events develop with such speed and intensity that citizens are often left breathless.

The ideas we have touched on mediate between intimate and public spheres; older and younger generations; traditional preferences and changing aesthetic and cultural values; religious and political beliefs and the open road.

The synthetic scholarly view of these and other folkloric sites discussed in the different chapters enables us to witness the interactive construction of "Israeli folk mind." The theoretical insights brought to bear on these arenas acknowledge and demonstrate the interconnectedness of the various spheres and discourses in Israeli society and culture. Thus, multiple voices are united in a matrix of collective creativity—constantly reworking "tradition" in new contexts.

The folk expressions studied in this book demonstrate, through the magnetic connection between users and producers, the powerful sense of unity at the base of Israeli culture. This communal foundation promotes the feeling that Israel is a safe shore, a home, for diverse groups of people.

Because of the nature of this study, a strong sense of unity and solidarity remains the backdrop for these expressions. While this was evident in much of the folk materials I came across, some of the encounters that produced the ethnographic bases of my work have brought me into close contact with sorrow, injustice, abjection, and humiliation, all spiced with more than a pinch of humor. The many different pains, communal and private, create a reality of separation and isolation, which is all the more tragic in light of the publicly promoted restorative ethos of the state of Israel: healing the traumatic wounds of exile and gathering its fragments into a unified whole. The sites visited in the course of the book are thus powerful not in their measured harmony but in the discord they express. They are places of transformation of such vulnerabilities and pains into cultural materials.

The journey I set out on in this book was not always an elegant or pleasurable one. The destination was, and still is, not clear. Israel, as witnessed by its rich folk creativity, is still very much in the making. Although the separate sites display much uncertainty, the totality of the ethnographic encounters, both as social phenomena and private experience, displays a measure of strength. The rough edges of life and the contradictory and conflicted richness of human interactions are often transmitted through humble items. These mundane materials expand people's capacity for acceptance of themselves and of others. They broaden the world of my interlocutors, through their performance and interaction with them, and they enrich my own, through the synthesizing and sometimes ironic spectrum of ethnographic distance. Hopefully, they have by now affected the reader, who has accompanied me on this journey. It is the matter-of-fact and unauthored nature of such cultural materials and their seemingly spontaneous coming into being that makes them receptacles for the wealth of human feeling and creativity.

In the opening words of this book, I encouraged the reader to join me on a journey with the promise to witness the alchemy that can turn common everyday creations into profoundly expressive materials that manifest the many ways in which people try to process and understand complex emotions and events. While these materials are around us all the time, the real magic occurs when they insist that we carefully listen to them and appreciate the profundities of their message.

I hope that the reader, who feels that I have fulfilled the promise, will adopt this perspective and look at the folklore creations that exist all around us with eyes full of surprise, curiosity, and enthusiasm.

Bibliography

Abrahams, Roger D. 1993. "After New Perspectives: Folklore Study in the Late Twentieth Century." *Western Folklore* 52 (2/4): 379–400.

Abu-Lughod, Lila, and Catherina A. Lutz. 1990. "Introduction: Emotion, Discourse, and the Politics of Everyday Life." In *Language and the Politics of Emotions*, edited by Catherine A. Lutz and Lila Abu-Lughod, 1–23. Cambridge: Cambridge University Press.

Agassi, Judith Buber. 1977. "The Unequal Occupational Distribution of Women in Israel." *Signs* 2 (4): 888–94.

Aguirre, Adalberto Jr. 1990. "Social Communication and Self-Identification: Participatory Behavior on the Freeway." *Journal of Popular Culture* 24 (2): 91–101.

Alexander, Tamar, and Galit Hasan-Rokem. 1989. "Spatial Elements in the Proverbs of the Jews of Turkey: The World and the Home." *Pe'amim* 41:112–33. [In Hebrew.]

Alexander-Frizer, Tamar. 2008. *The Heart Is a Mirror: The Sephardic Folktale*. Detroit, MI: Wayne State University Press.

Al-Khatib, Mahmoud A. 1999. "Joke-Telling in Jordanian Society: A Sociolinguistic Perspective." *Humor* 12 (3): 261–88.

Allison, Anne. 1994. *Nightwork: Sexuality, Pleasure and Corporate Masculinity in a Tokyo Hostess Club*. Chicago: University of Chicago Press.

Almedom, Astier M. 1995. "A Note on ROSCAS among Ethiopian Women in Addis Ababa and Eritrean Women in Oxford." In *Money-Go-Rounds*, edited by Shirley Ardener and Sandra Burman, 71–76. Oxford: Berg.

Anderson, Benedict. 1983. *Imagined Communities: Reflections on the Origin and Spread of Nationalism*. London: Verso.

Anonymous. 1997. "Debate: Humor and Political Correctness." *Humor: International Journal of Humor Research* 4–10:453–513.

———. 1998. "Humor Supplement." *Ha'Ir*, July. [In Hebrew.]

———. 2002. "Marocco Sakin." *Yediot Aharonot 7 Yamim Weekend Supplement*, November 8. [In Hebrew.]

Appadurai, Arjun, ed. 1986. *The Social Life of Things: Commodities in Cultural Perspective*. Cambridge: Cambridge University Press.

———. 1988. "How to Make a National Cuisine: Cookbooks in Contemporary India." *Comparative Studies in Society and History* 30 (1): 3–24.

Appadurai, Arjun, Frank J. Korom, and Margaret A. Mills, eds. 1991. *Gender, Genre, and Power in South Asian Expressive Traditions*. Philadelphia: University of Pennsylvania Press.

Apte, Mahadev L. 1985. *Humor and Laughter: An Anthropological Approach*. Ithaca, NY: Cornell University Press.

Ardener, Shirley G. 1964. "The Comparative Study of Rotating Credit Associations." *Journal of the Anthropological Institute* 94 (2): 201–28.

Ardener, Shirley G., and Sandra Burman. 1995. "Women Making Money Go Round: ROSCAs Revisited." In *Money-Go-Rounds: The Importance of Rotating Savings and Credit Associations for Women*, edited by S. Ardener and S. Burman, 1–20. Oxford: Berg.

Austin, J. Langshaw. 1962. *How to Do Things with Words*. Cambridge, MA: Harvard University Press.

Avituv, Yaron. 2001. *A Note from Mom*. Tel Aviv: Am Oved. [In Hebrew.]

Azmon, Yael, and Dafna N. Izraeli. 1993. "Introduction: Israel—a Sociological Overview." In *Women in Israel: Studies of Israeli Society*, edited by Yael Azmon and Dafna N. Izraeli, 1–21. New-Brunswick, NJ: Transaction.

Babcock, Barbara A. 1986. "Molded Selves: Helen Cordero's 'Little People.'" In *The Anthropology of Experience*, edited by Edward Bruner and Victor Turner, 316–43. Urbana: University of Illinois Press.

———. 1993a. "At Home, No Women Are Storytellers: Ceramic Creativity and the Politics of Discourse in Cochiti Pueblo." In *Creativity in Anthropology*, edited by Smadar Lavie, Kirin Narayan, and Renato Rosaldo, 70–99. Ithaca, NY: Cornell University Press.

———. 1993b. "Feminisms/Pretexts: Fragments, Questions, and Reflections." *Anthropological Quarterly* 66 (2): 59–66.

Bahloul, Joelle. 1996. *The Architecture of Memory*. Cambridge: Cambridge University Press.

Bakhtin, Mikhail. 1981. *The Dialogic Imagination*. Edited by M. Holquist. Translated by. C. Emerson and M. Holquist. Austin: University of Texas Press.

Bar-Itzhak, Haya. 2005. *Israeli Folk Narratives: Settlement, Immigration, Ethnicity*. Detroit, MI: Wayne State University Press.

Bar-Itzhak, Haya, and Aliza Shenhar. 1993. *Jewish Moroccan Folk Narratives from Israel*. Detroit, MI: Wayne State University Press.

Bar-On, Mordechai. 1985. *Peace Now: Portrait of a Movement*. Tel Aviv: Hakkibutz Hameuchad. [In Hebrew.]

Bauman, Richard. 1975. "Verbal Art as Performance." *American Anthropologist* 77 (2): 290–311.

———. 1992. Introduction. *Folklore, Cultural Performances, and Popular Entertainments*. New York: Oxford University Press.

Bauman, Richard, and Charles L. Briggs. 1990. "Poetics and Performance as Critical Perspectives on Language and Social Life." *Annual Review of Anthropology* 19:59–88.

Be'er, Chaim. 1979. *Notzot*. Tel Aviv: Am Oved. [In Hebrew.]

Ben-Amos, Dan. 1969. "Analytic Categories and Ethnic Genres." *Genre* 2 (3): 275–301.

———. 1971. "Toward a Definition of Folklore in Context." *Journal of American Folklore* 84 (331): 3–15.

———. 1973. "The 'Myth' of Jewish Humor." *Western Folklore* 32 (2): 112–31.

———. 1981. "Nationalism and Nihilism: The Attitude of Two Hebrew Authors toward Folklore." *International Folklore Review* 1:5–15.

———. 1998. "The Name Is the Thing." *Journal of American Folklore* 111 (441): 257–80.

Ben Ari, Eyal, and Yoram Bilu, eds. 1997. *Grasping Land: Space and Place in Israeli Discourse and Experience*. Albany: State University of New York Press.

Bendix, Regina. 1998. "Of Names, Professional Identities, and Disciplinary Futures." *Journal of American Folklore* 111 (441): 235–46.

Bendix, Regina, and Galit Hasan-Rokem. 2012. "Introduction." In *A Companion to Folklore*, edited by Regina Bendix and Galit Hasan-Rokem, 1–6. Malden, MA: Wiley-Blackwell.

Bendix, Regina F., Aditya Eggert, and Arnika Peselmann. 2012. "Introduction: Heritage Regimes and the State." In *Heritage Regimes and the State*, edited by R. F. Bendix, A. Eggert, and A. Peselmann, 11–20. Göttingen Studies in Cultural Property, Volume 6. Göttingen: Universitätsverlag Göttingen.

Ben Ezer, Gad. 2002. *The Ethiopian Jewish Exodus: Narratives of the Migration Journey to Israel 1977–1985*. London: Routledge.

Ben-Porat, Ziva. 1985. "Intertextuality." *HaSifrut* 34:170–78. [In Hebrew.]

Bhabha, Homi K. 1994. *The Location of Culture*. London: Routledge.

Bilu, Yoram. 1986. "Historyat ḥayyim KeTekst." *Megamot: Behavioral Sciences Quarterly* 29 (4): 349–71. [In Hebrew.]

———. 2000. *Without Bounds: The Life and Death of Rabbi Yaaqov Wazana*. Detroit, MI: Wayne State University Press.

———. 2009. "'With Us More Than Ever': Making The Late Rabbi Present in Messianic Chabad." In *Leadership and Authority in the Ultra-Orthodox Community: New Perspectives*, edited by K. Caplan and N. Stadler, 186–209. Tel Aviv: Hakkibutz Hameuchad. [In Hebrew.]

Bloch, Linda-Renee. 2000a. "Mobile Discourse: Political Bumper Stickers as a Communication Event in Israel." *Journal of Communication* 50 (2): 48–76.

———. 2000b. "Rhetoric on the Roads of Israel: The Assassination and Political Bumpers." In *The Assassination of Yitzhak Rabin*, edited by Y. Peri, 257–79. London: Macmillan.

Blumberg, Rae Lesser. 1976. "Kibbutz Women: From the Fields of Revolution to the Laundries of Discontent." In *Women of the World: A Comparative Study*, edited by Lynne B. Iglitzin and Ruth Ross, 319–44. Santa Barbara, CA: ABC—Clio.

Boskin, Joseph, and Joseph Dorinson. 1985. "Ethnic Humor: Subversion and Survival." *American Quarterly* 37 (1): 81–97.

Bourdieu, Pierre. 1977. *Outline of a Theory of Practice*. Cambridge: Cambridge University Press.

———. 1979. *Algeria 1960*. Cambridge: Cambridge University Press.

———. 1984. *Distinction: A Social Critique of the Judgment of Taste*. Trans. Richard Nice. Cambridge, MA: Harvard University Press.

———. 1990. *The Logic of Practice*. Stanford, CA: Stanford University Press.

Boyarin, Daniel. 1990. *Intertextuality and the Reading of Midrash*. Bloomington: Indiana University Press.

Briggs, Charles. 1988. *Competence in Performance: The Creativity of Tradition in Mexicano Verbal Art*. Philadelphia: University of Pennsylvania Press.

Briggs, Charles, and Amy Shuman. 1993. "Theorizing Folklore: Toward New Perspectives on the Politics of Culture." *Western Folklore* 52 (2/4): 109–34.

Bruner, Edward M. 1984. "Dialogic Narration and the Paradoxes of Masada." In *Text, Play, and Story: The Construction and Re- Construction of Self and Society*, edited by E. Bruner, 56–75. Washington, DC: American Ethnological Society.

———. 1993. "Epilogue: Creative Persona and the Problem of Authenticity." In *Creativity in Anthropology*, edited by Smadar Lavie, Kirin Narayan, and Renato Rosaldo, 321–34. Ithaca, NY: Cornell University Press.

Butler, Judith. 1993. *Bodies That Matter: On the Discursive Limits of "Sex."* New York: Routledge.

Butler, Kim D. 2001. "Defining Diaspora, Refining a Discourse." *Diaspora: A Journal of Transitional Studies* 10 (2): 189–219.

Campbell, Thomas. 2010. "Tapestry." In *5,000 Years of Textiles*, edited by J. Harris, 188–99. London: British Museum Press.

Case, Charles E. 1992. "Bumper Stickers and Car Signs Ideology and Identity." *Journal of Popular Culture* 26 (3): 107–18.

Cerulli, E. 1943. *Etiopi in Palestine Storia Della Communita Di Gerusalemme.* 2 vols. Rome: Liberia dello Stato.

Chen, Sarina. 2001. "Temot Merkaziyyot BaRetorika UvaPraksis Shel Shoḥarey HaMikdash." PhD diss., the Hebrew University of Jerusalem. [In Hebrew.]

Chinski, Sara. 1997. "The Lace-Weavers from Bezalel." *Teoria UVikkoret* 11:177–205. [In Hebrew.]

Clifford, James. 1988. *"On Orientalism." The Predicament of Culture: Twentieth-Century Ethnography, Literature and Art.* Cambridge, MA: Harvard University Press.

———. 1994. "Diasporas." *Cultural Anthropology* 9 (3): 302–38.

Comaroff, Jean. 1985. *Body of Power, Spirits of Resistance: The Culture and History of a South-African People.* Chicago: University of Chicago Press.

Corinaldi, Michael. 1998. *Jewish Identity: The Case of Ethiopian Jewry.* Jerusalem: Magnes.

Crapanzano, Vincent. 1992. *Hermes' Dilemma and Hamlet's Desire.* Cambridge, MA: Harvard University Press.

Csikszentmihalyi, Mihaly, and Eugene Rochberg-Halton. 1981. *The Meaning of Things: Domestic Symbols and the Self.* Cambridge: Cambridge University Press.

Dasenbrock, Reed Way. 1993. "A Rhetoric of Bumper Stickers." In *Defining the New Rhetorics*, edited by T. Enos and S. Brown, 191–206. Newbury Park, CA: Sage.

David Grossman. 1994. *The Book of Intimate Grammar.* Trans. Betsy Rosenberg. New York: Farrar, Straus, and Giroux.

Davies, Christie. 1990. *Ethnic Humor around the World: A Comparative Analysis.* Bloomington: Indiana University Press.

———. 1991. "Exploring the Thesis of the Self-Deprecating Jewish Sense of Humor." *Humor: International Journal of Humor Research* 4 (2): 189–210.

———. 1998. *Jokes and Their Relation to Society.* Berlin: Mouton de Gruyter.

De Cesari, Chiara. 2012. "Thinking through Heritage Regime." In *Heritage Regimes and the State*, edited by R. F. Bendix, A. Eggert, and A. Peselmann, 399–413. Göttingen Studies in Cultural Property, Volume 6. Göttingen: Universitätsverlag Göttingen.

Degh, Linda. 1994. *American Folklore and the Mass Media.* Bloomington: Indiana University Press.

Dejene, Areda. 1993. *The Informal and Semi-Formal Sectors in Ethiopia: A Study of the Iqqub, Iddir and Credit Co-Operatives.* Nairobi: Africa Research Consortium Research Paper 21.

Derrida, Jacques. 1984. "Deconstruction and the Other: An Interview with Richard Kearney." In *Dialogues with Contemporary Continental Thinkers*, edited by R. Kearney, 107–26. Manchester: Manchester University Press.

Doleve-Gandelman, Tsili. 1990. "Ethiopia as a Lost Imaginary Space: The Role of Ethiopian Jewish Women in Producing the Ethnic Identity of Their Immigrant Group in Israel." In *The Other Perspective in Gender and Culture: Rewriting Women and the Symbolic*, edited by Juliet Flower MacCannell, 242–57. New York: Columbia University Press.

Dorst, John. 1983. "Neck Riddle as a Dialogue of Genres." *Journal of American Folklore* 96 (382): 413–33.

———. 1990. "Tags and Burners, Cycles and Networks: Folklore in the Telectronic Age." *Journal of Folklore Research* 27 (3): 179–90.

Dotan, Eyal. 2000. "HaKets LaTrauma: Sterelizatsia VeTishtush Beyitsug HaZikkaron [An End to the Trauma: Sterilization and Obliteration in Memory Representation]." *Teorya UVikkoret* 17:27–34. [In Hebrew.]

Dow, James R. 1991. "Forward: Folklore, Politics and Nationalism. Special Issue." *Asian Folklore Studies* 50 (1): 1–3.

Dow, James R., and Hannjost Lixfeld, eds. 1994. *The Nazification of an Academic Discipline: Folklore in the Third Reich*. Bloomington: Indiana University Press.

Dundes, Alan. 1966. "Metafolklore and Oral Literary Criticism." *Monist* 50 (4): 505–16.

———. 1987. *When You're Up to Your Ass in Alligator: More Urban Folklore from the Paperwork Empire*. Detroit, MI: Wayne State University Press.

———. 1991. *Never Try to Teach a Pig to Sing: Still More Urban Folklore from the Paperwork Empire*. Detroit, MI: Wayne State University Press.

Dundes, Alan, and Carl R. Pagter. 1978. *Work Hard and You Shall Be Rewarded: Urban Folklore from the Paperwork Empire*. Bloomington: Indiana University Press.

Elbogen, Ismar. 1993. *Jewish Liturgy: A Comprehensive History*. Trans. Raymond P. Scheindlin. Philadelphia, PA: Jewish Publication Society.

Elior, Rachel, ed. 2010. *The Garden of Eden in the Past/East: The Traditions of the Garden of Eden in Israel and among the Nations*. Jerusalem: Magnes. [In Hebrew.]

Endersby, James W., and Jay Mechling Towle. 1996. "Tailgate Partisanship: Political and Social Expression through Bumper Stickers." *Social Science Journal* 33 (3): 307–17.

Fabian, Johannes. 1983. *Time and the Other: How Anthropology Makes Its Objects*. New York: Columbia University Press.

Farrer, Claire R. 1986. "Introduction." In *Women and Folklore: Images and Genres*, edited by Claire R. Farrer, 11–21. Prospect Heights, IL: Waveland Press.

Feige, Michael. 2002. *One Space, Two Places: Gush Emunim, Peace Now and the Construction of Israeli Space*. Jerusalem: Magnes. [In Hebrew.]

Fleischer, Ezra. 2012. *Statutory Jewish Prayers: Their Emergence and Development*. Jerusalem: Magnes. [In Hebrew.]

Fortes, Meyer. 1958. "Introduction." In *The Developmental Cycle in Domestic Groups*, edited by Jack Goody, 1–14. Cambridge Papers in Social Anthropology 1. New York: Cambridge University Press.

Foucault, Michel. 1986. "On Other Spaces." *Diacritics* 16 (1): 11–12, 22–27.

Frank, Gelya. 1996. "Crafts Production and Resistance to Domination in the Late 20th Century." *Journal of Occupational Science* 3 (2): 56–64.

Freeman, June. 1987. "Sewing as a Women's Art." In *Women and Craft*, edited by Elinor Gillian, Su Richardson, Sue Scott, Angharad Thomas and Kate Walker, 55–63. London: Virago.

Gal, Susan. 1991. "Between Speech and Silence: The Problematics of Research on Language and Gender." In *Gender at the Crossroads of Knowledge: Feminist Anthropology in the Postmodern Era*, edited by Micaela di Leonardo, 175–203. Berkeley: University of California Press.

Geertz, Clifford. 1962. "The Rotating Credit Association: A 'Middle Rung' in Development." *Economic Development and Cultural Change* 10 (3): 241–63.

———. 1973. *The Interpretation of Cultures*. New York: Basic Books.

Georges, Robert A., ed. 1991. "Taking Stock: Current Problems and Future Prospects in American Folklore Studies. Special Issue." *Western Folklore* 50 (1): 1–126.

Gilroy, Paul. 1994. "Diaspora." *Paragraph* 3 (17): 207–12.

Ginsburg, Faye, and Anna Lowenhaupt Tsing. 1992. *Uncertain Terms: Negotiating Gender in American Culture*. Boston: Beacon.

Goldberg, Harvey. 1984. "Meymadim Historiim VeTarbutiim shel Tofa'ot 'Adatiyot [Historical and Cultural Dimensions of Ethnic Phenomena]." *Megamot* 28 (2–3): 233–49. [In Hebrew.]

———. 1987. *Judaism Viewed from Within and from Without: Anthropological Studies*. New York: State University of New York Press.

———. 2001. "Ethnic and Religious Dilemmas of a Jewish State: A Cultural and Historical Perspective." In *State Formation and Ethnic Relations in the Middle East*, edited by Usuki Akira, 47–64. Osaka: Japan Center for Area Studies, National Museum of Ethnology.

Golden, Deborah. 2002. "Storytelling the Future: Israelis, Immigrants and the Imagining of Community." *Anthropological Quarterly* 75 (1): 7–35.

Goshen-Gottstein, Alon. 1987. "God and Israel as Father and Son in Tannaitic Literature." PhD diss., Hebrew University of Jerusalem. [In Hebrew.]

Gumperz, John. 1982. *Discourse Strategies*. Cambridge: Cambridge University Press.

Habermas, Jürgen. 2002. *Religion and Rationality: Essays on Reason, God, and Modernity*. Ed. Eduardo Mendieta. Cambridge, MA: MIT Press.

———. 2008. *Between Naturalism and Religion: Philosophical Essays*. Cambridge: Polity.

———. 2011. "'The Political': The Rational Meaning of a Questionable Inheritance of Political Theology." In *The Power of Religion in the Public Sphere*, edited by Eduardo Mendieta and Jonathan Vanantwerpen, 15–33. New York: Columbia University Press.

Hanson, Paul W. 1993. "Reconceiving the Shape of Culture: Folklore and Public Culture." *Western Folklore* 52 (2/4): 327–44.

Harari, Yuval. 1997. "How to Do Things with Words: Philosophical Theory and Magical Deeds." *Jerusalem Studies in Jewish Folklore* 19–20:365–92. [In Hebrew.]

———. 2010. *Early Jewish Magic: Research, Method, Sources*. Jerusalem: Mosad Bialik and Ben-Zvi Institute. [In Hebrew.]

Hasan-Rokem, Galit. 1978. "Cognition in Folktales: Aesthetic Judgments and Symbolic Structures." *Scripta Hierosolymitana* [Studies in Hebrew Narrative Art] 27:192–204.

———. 1982. *Proverbs in Israeli Folk Narratives: A Structural Semantic Analysis.* Folklore Fellows Communications, no. 232. Helsinki: Academia Scientiarum Fennica.

———. 1997. "Studying Folk Culture and Popular Culture." *Theory and Criticism: An Israeli Forum* 10:5–13. [In Hebrew.]

———. 2007. "Dialogue as Ethical Conduct: The Folk Festival That Was Not." In *Research Ethics in Studies of Culture and Social Life. Folklore Fellows Communications,* edited by Bente G. Alver, Tove I. Fjell, and Ørjar Øyen, 149–61. Helsinki: Academia Scientiarum Fennica.

———. 2010. "Erotic Eden: A Rabbinic Nostalgia for Paradise." In *Paradise in Antiquity: Jewish and Christian Views,* edited by Marcus Bockmuehl and Guy G. Stroumsa, 156–65. Cambridge: Cambridge University Press.

———.2012. "Material Mobility vs. Concentric Cosmology in the Sukkah: The House of the Wandering Jew or a Ubiquitous Temple." In *The Future of the Religious Past III: Things,* edited by Birgit Mayer and Dick Boumann. New York: Fordham University Press.

Haskell, Guy. 1994. *From Sofia to Jaffa: The Jews of Bulgaria and Israel.* Raphael Patai Series in Jewish Folklore and Anthropology. Detroit, MI: Wayne State University Press.

Hazan, Haim. 1998. "The Time of Place: An Anthropological View of Rabin's Grave." In *Rav Tarbutiyut Behevra Demokratit VeYehudit,* edited by A. Sagi and R. Shamir, 731–53. Tel Aviv: Ramot. [In Hebrew.]

Hazan, Haim, and Esther Hertzog, eds. 2012. *Serendipity in Anthropological Research: The Nomadic Turn.* London: Ashgate.

Held, Michal. 2009. *Let Me Tell You a Story / Ven, te kontare: The Personal Narratives of Judeo-Spanish Speaking Storytelling Women, An Interdisciplinary Research.* Jerusalem: Ben-Zvi Institute for the Study of Jewish Communities in the East. [In Hebrew.]

Hertzog, Esther. 1998. *Bureaucrats and Immigrants in an Absorption Center.* Tel Aviv: Tcherikover. [In Hebrew.]

Herzfeld, Michael. 1997. *Cultural Intimacy: Social Poetics in the Nation State.* New York: Routledge.

Hirschfeld, Ariel. 2010. "The Peak of Spiritual Relaxation." *Ha'aretz Supplement,* January 1. [In Hebrew.]

Hoskins, Janet. 1998. *Biographical Objects: How Things Tell the Stories of People's Lives.* New York: Routledge.

Hymes, Dell. 1967. "Models of the Interaction of Language and Social Setting." *Journal of Social Issues* 23 (2): 8–28.

Izraeli, Dafna N. 1981. "The Zionist Women's Movement in Palestine 1911–1927: A Sociological Analysis." *Signs* 7 (1): 87–114.

Jakobson, Roman. 1970. "Linguistics and Poetics." *HaSifrut* 2 (2): 274–85. [In Hebrew.]

———. 1990. "The Speech Event and the Functions of Language." In *Roman Jakobson. On Language,* edited by Linda R. Waugh and Monique Monville-Burston, 69–79. Cambridge, MA: Harvard University Press.

Jason, Heda. 1972. "Jewish-Near Eastern Numbskull Tales: An Attempt at Interpretation." *Asian Folklore Studies* 31 (1): 1–39.

Juhasz, Esther. 2004. "The Shiviti-Menorah: A Representation of the Sacred- Between Spirit and Matter." PhD diss., the Hebrew University of Jerusalem. [In Hebrew.]

Kaplan, Steven. 1993. "Falasha Christians: A Brief History." *Midstream* 39 (1): 20–21.

———. 1997. "Everyday Resistance and the Study of Ethiopian Jews." *Theory and Criticism: An Israeli Forum* 10:163–73. [In Hebrew.]

———. 2005. "Tama Galut Etiopia [The Ethiopian Exile Is Over]." *Diaspora* 14 (2–3): 381–96.

Kaplan, Steven, and Chaim Rosen. 1993. "Ethiopian Immigrants in Israel: Between Preservation of Culture and Invention of Tradition." *Jewish Journal of Sociology* 35 (1): 35–48.

Kaplan, Steven, and Hagar Salamon. 2003. "Ethiopian Jews in Israel: A Part of the People or Apart from the People?" In *Jews in Israel: Contemporary Social and Cultural Patterns*, edited by Uzi Rebhun and Chaim I. Waxman, 118–48. Waltham, MA: Brandeis University Press.

Katriel, Tamar. 1986. *Talking Straight: "Dugri" Speech in Israeli Sabra Culture*. Cambridge: Cambridge University Press.

———. 1988. "Haxlàfot: Rules and Strategies in Children's Swapping Exchanges." *Research on Language and Social Interaction* 22 (1–4): 157–78.

———. 1999. *Keywords: Patterns of Culture and Communication in Israel*. Haifa: University of Haifa and Zmora-Bitan. [In Hebrew.]

Kimchi, Alona. 1996. *I Am Anastasia*. Jerusalem: Keter. [In Hebrew.]

Kirshenblatt-Gimblett, Barbara. 1978. "Culture Shock and Narrative Creativity." In *Folklore in the Modern World*, edited by Richard M. Dorson, 109–21. The Hague: Mouton.

———. 1983. "Studying Immigrant and Ethnic Folklore." In *Handbook of American Folklore*, edited by Richard M. Dorson, 39–47. Bloomington: Indiana University Press.

———. 1988. "Mistaken Dichotomies." *Journal of American Folklore* 101 (400): 140–55.

———. 1996. "Topic Drift: Negotiating the Gap between the Field and Our Name." *Journal of Folklore Research* 33 (3): 245–54.

———. 1998. "Folklore's Crisis." *Journal of American Folklore* 111 (441): 319–21.

Kodish, Debora. 2012. "Imagining Public Folklore." In *A Companion to Folklore*, edited by Galit Hasan-Rokem and Regina Bendix, 579–97. Malden, MA: Wiley-Blackwell.

Kondo, Dorine K. 1990. *Crafting Selves: Power, Gender and Discourse of Identity in a Japanese Workplace*. Chicago: University of Chicago Press.

Kopytoff, Igor. 1986. "The Cultural Biography of Things: Commoditization as Process." In *The Social Life of Things: Commodities in Cultural Perspective*, edited by A. Appadurai, 64–91. Cambridge: Cambridge University Press.

Kravel, Michal., and Yoram Bilu. 2008. "The Work of the Present: Constructing Messianic Temporality in the Wake of Failed Prophecy among Chabad Hasidim." *American Ethnologist* 35 (1): 1–17.

Kristeva, Julia. 1967. "Bakhtine, le mot, le dialogue et le roman." *Critique* 23 (239): 438–65.

———. 1982. *Powers of Horror: An Essay on Abjection*. New York: Columbia University Press.

Lakoff, George, and Mark Johnson. 2003. *Metaphors We Live By*. Chicago: University of Chicago Press.

Lanser, Susan S., and Joan N. Radner. 1987. "The Feminist Voice: Strategies of Coding in Folklore and Literature." *Journal of American Folklore* 100 (398): 412–25.

Leitman, Eva M. 1993. "Ethiopian Immigrant Women: Transition to a New Israeli Identity." PhD diss., Ohio State University.

Leitman, Eva M., and E. Weinbaum. 1998. "Israeli Women of Ethiopian Descent." In *Ethiopian Jews in Ethiopia and Israel*, edited by T. Parfitt and E. Trevisan Semi, 128–36. London: Curzon.

Leslau, Wolf. 1968. *Ethiopians Speak: Studies in Cultural Background. Part 3: Soddo.* Berkeley: University of California Press.

———. 1982. *Gurage Folklore: Ethiopian Folktales, Proverbs, Beliefs, and Riddles.* Studien Zur Kulturkunde, no. 63. Wiesbaden: F. Steiner.

Leslau, Wolf, and Thomas Kane. 2001. *Amharic Cultural Reader.* Wiesbaden: Harrassowitz.

Levine, Donald. 1965. *Wax and Gold: Tradition and Innovation in Ethiopian Culture.* Chicago: University of Chicago Press.

Levine, Lawrence W. 1992. "The Folklore of Industrial Society: Popular Culture and Its Audience." *American Historical Review* 97 (5): 1369–99.

Levinson, A., and Y. Ze'evi. 1995. "Sticker Now." *Kol Ha'ir*, December 8, 2. [In Hebrew.]

Lieblich, Amia, Tamar Zilber, and Rivka Tuval-Mashiach. 1995. "Meḥappsim UMots'im: Hakhlala Ve'Avhana BeSippurey Ḥayyim [Seeking and Finding: Generalization and Distinction in Life Stories]." *Psykhologia* 5:84–95. [In Hebrew.]

Limón, José E. 1983. "Legendry, Metafolklore, and Performance: A Mexican-American Example." *Western Folklore* 42 (3): 191–208.

Lowe, John. 1986. "Theories of Ethnic Humor: How to Enter, Laughing." *American Quarterly* 38 (3): 439–60.

March, Kathryn S. 1983. "Weaving, Writing, and Gender." *Man* 18 (4): 729–44.

Markowitz, Fran, ed. 2013. *Ethnographic Encounters in Israel: Poetics and Ethics of Fieldwork.* Bloomington: Indiana University Press.

Markowitz, Fran, Sara Helman, and Dafna Shir-Vertish. 2003. "Soul Citizenship: Black Hebrews and the State of Israel." *American Anthropologist* 105 (2): 302–12.

Mauss, Marcel. 1967. *The Gift: Forms and Functions of Exchange in Archaic Societies.* New York: Norton Library.

Mechling, Jay. 1993. "On Sharing Folklore and American Identity in a Multicultural Society." *Western Folklore* 52 (2/4): 271–89.

Messick, Brinkley. 1987. "Subordinate Discourse: Women, Weaving, and Gender Relations in North Africa." *American Ethnologist* 14 (2): 210–25.

Mieder, Wolfgang, ed. 1997. *The Politics of Proverbs: From Traditional Wisdom to Proverbial Stereotypes.* Madison: University of Wisconsin Press.

Mikes, George. 1950. *Milk and Honey.* London: Andre Deutsch.

Mintz, Lawrence E. 1976. "Ethnic Humour: Discussion." In *It's a Funny Thing, Humour*, edited by A. J. Chapman and H. C. Foot, 287–89. New York: Pergamon.

———. 1999. "American Humor as Unifying and Divisive." *Humor: International Journal of Humor Research* 12 (3): 237–52.

Molvaer, Reidulf. 2007. "What Good Is Technical Assistance? A Problem Illustrated with an Example from Ethiopia." *International Journal of Ethiopian Studies* 3 (1): 91–113.

Morag, Shlomo. 2003. *Studies in Hebrew.* Ed. Moshe Bar Asher, Yochanan Breuer, and Aharon Maman. Jerusalem: Magnes. [In Hebrew.]

Morgan, David. 1998. *Visual Piety: A History and Theory of Popular Religious Images.* Berkeley: University of California Press.

———. 2005. *The Sacred Gaze: Religious Visual Culture in Theory and Practice.* Berkeley: University of California Press.

———. 2010. *Religion and Material Culture: The Matter of Belief.* London: Routledge.

Morin, Violette. 1969. "L'objet biographique." *Communications* 13 (1): 131–39.

Muhawi, Ibrahim. 1994. "The Metalinguistic Joke: Sociolinguistic Dimensions of an Arabic Folk Genre." In *Arabic Sociolinguistics: Issues and Perspectives*, edited by Yasir Suleiman, 155–76. Richmond, UK: Curzon.

Neiman, Rachel. 2010. "Nostalgia Sunday—Stitching in the Seventies." *Israelity* (blog), February 7. Available at https://web.archive.org/web/20100213181145/http://israelity .com/2010/02/07/nostalgia-sunday-stitching-in-the-seventies/.

Nevo, Ofra. 1985. "Does One Ever Really Laugh at One's Own Expense? The Case of Jews and Arabs in Israel." *Journal of Personality and Social Psychology* 49 (3): 799–807.

———. 1986. "Humor Diaries of Israeli Jews and Arabs." *Journal of Social Psychology* 126 (3): 411–13.

Nevo, Ofra, and Jacob Levine. 1994. "Jewish Humor Strikes Again: The Outburst of Humor in Israel during the Gulf War." *Western Folklore* 53 (2): 125–46.

Nilsen, Don L. F. 1993. *Humor Scholarship: A Research Bibliography.* Westport, CT: Greenwood.

Noy, Chaim. 2011. "The Semiotics of (Im)mobilities: Two Discursive Case Studies of the System of Automobility." In *The Politics of Proximity: Mobility and Immobility in Practice*, edited by Giuseppina Pellegrino, 61–81. Farnham, UK: Ashgate.

Noy, Dov. 1965. *Jewish Folktales from Morocco: Narrated and Collected in Israel.* Jerusalem Post Press.

———. 1971. "Folklore." *Encylopaedia Judaica* 6:1374–1410, Jerusalem: Keter.

Ofer, Nivi. 2005. "Sippur, U'Vayit: Mifgash 'im Nashim Mi'Etyopya BeYisrael [Space, Story, and Home: Encounter with Ethiopian Women in Israel]." PhD diss., the Hebrew University of Jerusalem. [In Hebrew.]

Oring, Elliott. 1973. "Hey, You've Got No Character: Chizbat Humor and the Boundaries of Israeli Identity." *Journal of American Folklore* 86 (342): 358–66.

———. 1981. *Israeli Humor: The Content and Structure of the Chizbat of the Palmach.* Albany: State University of New York Press.

———. 1983. "People of the Joke: On the Conceptualization of a Jewish Humor." *Western Folklore* 42 (4): 261–71.

———. 2003. *Engaging Humor.* Urbana: University of Illinois Press.

Ornguze, Emmanuel Daniel. 1997. "The Adaptation of Ethiopian Political Refugees in New York City (1985–1995)." PhD diss., New School for Social Research.

Palgi, Michal, Joseph R. Blasi, Menachem Rosner, and Marilyn Safir, eds. 1983. *Sexual Equality: The Israeli Kibbutz Tests the Theories.* Norwood, PA: Norwood Editions.

Parker, Rozsika. 1984. *The Subversive Stitch: Embroidery and the Making of the Feminine.* London: Women's Press.

Pedersen, Kirsten. 1983. *The History of Ethiopian Community in the Holy Land from the Time of Tewodros II till 1974.* Jerusalem: Tantur.

Peer, Smets. 1998. "Money-Go-Rounds for Women: Finance as Instrument or as Ultimate Goal in Lottery ROSCAss." *Anthropos* 93 (1/3): 209–15.

Perry, Yoram. 1988. "Stikerim, tsvaʻim, smalim." *Davar*, October 21. [In Hebrew.]

Phillips-Davids, Jennifer. 1999. "Fertility Decline and Changes in the Life Course Among Ethiopian Jewish Women." In *The Beta Israel in Ethiopia and Israel: Studies on the Ethiopian Jews*, edited by Tudor Parfitt and Emanuela Trevisan Semi, 137–59. London: Curzon.

———. 1999. "Migration and Fertility Transition and Changes in the Life Cycle among Ethiopian Jewish Women in Israel." PhD diss., Emory University, Atlanta, GA.

Pratt, Marie Louise. 1991a. "Arts of the Contact Zone." *Profession* 91:33–40.

———. 1991b. *Imperial Eyes: Travel Writing and Transculturation*. London: Routledge.

Raday, Frances. 1991. "The Concept of Gender Equality in a Jewish State." In *Calling the Equality Bluff*, edited by Barbara Swirski and Marilyn P. Safir, 18–28. New York: Pergamon.

Radcliffe-Brown, Alfred R. 1940. "On Joking Relationships." *Journal of the International African Institute* 13 (3): 195–210.

Radhakrishnan, Rajagopalan. 1992. "Nationalism, Gender, and the Narrative of Identity." In *Nationalism and Sexualities*, edited by Andrew Parker, Mary Russo, Doris Sommer and Patricia Yaeger, 77–95. New York: Routledge.

Ramanujan, Attipat Krishnaswami. 1991. "Toward a Counter-System: Women's Tales." In *Gender, Genre, and Power in South Asian Expressive Traditions*, edited by Arjun Appadurai, Frank J. Korom, and Margaret Mills, 33–55. Philadelphia: University of Pennsylvania Press.

Reif, Stefan C. 2006. *Problems with Prayers: Studies in the Textual History of Early Rabbinic Liturgy*. Studia Judaica 37. Berlin: Walter de Gruyter.

Rosen, Ilana. 1995. "German Folkloristic Research in the Service of Nazi Ideology." *Jerusalem Studies in Jewish Folklore* 17:119–27. [In Hebrew.]

———. 1999. *There Once Was . . . : The Oral Tradition of the Jews of Carpatho-Russia*. Tel Aviv: Diaspora Research Institute Tel Aviv University. [In Hebrew.]

Sabar, Galia. 2004. "African Christianity in the Jewish State: Adaptation, Accommodation and Legitimization of Migrant Workers 1990–2003." *Journal of Religion in Africa* 34 (4): 407–37.

———. 2008. *We're Not Here to Stay: African Migrant Workers in Israel and Back in Africa*. Tel Aviv: Haim Rubin Tel Aviv University Press. [In Hebrew.]

Safran, William. 1991. "Diasporas in Modern Societies: Myths of Homeland and Return." *Diaspora* 1 (1): 83–99.

———. 1999. "Comparing Diasporas: A Review Essay." *Diaspora* 8 (3): 255–91.

———. 2005. "The Jewish Diaspora in a Comparative and Theoretical Perspective." *Israel Studies* 10 (1): 36–60.

Said, Edward W. 1978. *Orientalism*. New York: Vintage Books.

———. 1985. "Orientalism Reconsidered." *Cultural Critique* 1:89–107.

———. 1990. "Zionism from the Standpoint of Its Victims." In *Anatomy of Racism*, edited by D. T. Goldberg, 210–46. Minneapolis: University of Minnesota Press.

Salamon, Hagar. 1993. "Blood between the Beta Israel and Their Christian Neighbors in Ethiopia: Key Symbols in an Inter-Group Context." *Jerusalem Studies in Jewish Folklore* 15:117–34. [In Hebrew.]

———. 1994. "Between Ethnicity and Religiosity: Internal Group Aspects of Conversion among the Beta Israel in Ethiopia." *Pe'amim* 58:104–19. [In Hebrew.]

———. 1999. *The Hyena People: Ethiopian Jews in Christian Ethiopia.* Los Angeles: University of California Press.

———. 2001. "In Search of Self and Other: A Few Remarks on Ethnicity, Race, and Ethiopian Jews." In *Jewish Locations: Traversing Racialized Landscapes,* edited by Lisa Tessman and Bat-Ami Bar On, 75–88. Lanham, MD: Rowman and Littlefield.

———. 2003. "Blackness in Transition: Decoding Racial Constructs through Stories of Ethiopian Jews." *Journal of Folklore Research* 40 (1): 3–32.

———. 2005. "Ha'Am in the Turbulent Discursive Sphere of Israeli Bumper Stickers." *Hebrew Studies* 47:197–234.

———. 2008. "A Woman's Life Story as a Foundation Legend of Local Identity." In *Jewish Women in Pre-State Israel: Life History, Politics, and Culture,* edited by Ruth Kark, Margalit Shilo, and Galit Hasan-Rokem, 141–65. Waltham, MA: Brandeis University Press.

———. 2010. "Misplaced Home and Mislaid Meat: Stories Circulating Among Ethiopian Immigrants in Israel." *Callaloo* 33 (1): 165–76.

———. 2013. "'Gobelin' Needlepoint: Introducing the concept of 'Transitional Object' to the Study of Material Culture." In *Textures: Culture-Literature-Folklore, for Galit Hasan-Rokem.* Edited by Hagar Salamon and Shinan, Avigdor, 691–714. Jerusalem: Jerusalem Studies in Jewish Folklore, 28. [In Hebrew.]

Salamon, Hagar, and Galit Hasan-Rokem. 1997. "Rokemot Et Atzman: Rikmah VeNashi-yyut BiKvutsa Yerushalmit [Embroidering Themselves: Embroidery and Feminin-ity in a Jerusalem Group]." *Teoria UVikkoret* 10:55–68. [In Hebrew.]

Salamon, Hagar, Steven Kaplan, and Harvey Goldberg. 2009. "What Goes Around, Comes Around: Rotating Credit Associations among Ethiopian Women in Israel." *African Identities* 7 (3): 399–415.

Saper, Bernard. 1994. "Joking in the Context of Political Correctness." *Humor: International Journal of Humor Research* 8 (1): 65–76.

Schaefer, Charles G., and Aklilu Amsalu. 2005. "Eqqub." In *Encylopaedia Aethiopica,* Vol. 2, edited by Uhlig Siegbert. Wiesbaden: Harrassowitz Verlag.

Scheindlin, Raymond P. 2001. "Communal Prayer and Liturgical Poetry." In *Judaism in Practice: From the Middle Ages through the Early Modern Period,* edited by Lawrence Fine, 39–51. Princeton, NJ: Princeton University Press.

Schely-Newman, Esther. 2002. *Our Lives Are but Stories: Narratives of Tunisian-Israeli Women.* Detroit, MI: Wayne State University Press.

———. 2010. "Constructing Literate Israelis: A Critical Analysis of Adult Literacy Texts." *Israel Studies* 15 (2): 196–214.

———. 2011. "Discourse of (Il)literacy: Recollections of Israeli Literacy Teachers." *Pragmatics* 21 (3): 431–52.

Schneider, Jane, and Annette B. Weiner. 1989. "Introduction." In *Cloth and Human Experience,* edited by Jane Schneider and Annette B. Weiner, 1–29. Washington, DC: Smithsonian Institution.

Schrire, Dani, and Galit Hasan-Rokem. 2012. "Folklore Studies in Israel." In *A Companion to Folklore,* edited by Galit Hasan-Rokem and Regina Bendix, 325–48. Malden, MA: Wiley-Blackwell.

Schwarz, Tanya. 2001. *Ethiopian Jewish Immigrants: The Homeland Postponed.* Richmond, UK: Curzon.

Scott, James. C. 1992. *Domination and the Arts of Resistance: Hidden Transcripts.* New Haven, CT: Yale University Press.

Searle, John. 1969. *Speech Acts: An Essay in the Philosophy of Language.* Cambridge: Cambridge University Press.

———. 1975. "A Taxonomy of Illocutionary Acts." In *Language, Mind, and Knowledge,* edited by K. Günderson, 59–82. Minneapolis: University of Minnesota Press.

———. 1979. *Expression and Meaning: Studies in the Theory of Speech Acts.* Cambridge: Cambridge University Press.

———. 1991. "Indirect Speech Acts." In *Pragmatics: A Reader,* edited by Steven Davis, 265–77. New York: Oxford University Press.

Seeman, Don. 2009. *One People, One Blood: Ethiopian-Israelis and the Return to Judaism.* New Brunswick, NJ: Rutgers University Press.

Sered, Susan Starr. 1987. "Ritual, Mortality, and Gender: The Religious Lives of Oriental Jewish Women in Jerusalem." *Israel Social Science Research* 5 (1–2): 87–96.

Shabtay, Malka. 2006. *Yehudey Etyopya Mizera' Beta Israel: Masa'am Mi"Beta Israel" LiVney ha "Falashmura" UleYehudey Etiopia.* Tel Aviv: Lashon Tseḥa. [In Hebrew.]

Shabtay, Malka, and L. Kacen. 2005. *Ethiopian Women and Girls in Spaces, Worlds and Journeys between Cultures.* Tel Aviv: Lashon Tseḥa. [In Hebrew.]

Shehata, Samer S. 1992. "The Politics of Laughter: Nasser, Sadat and Mubarek in Egyptian Political Jokes." *Folklore* 103 (1): 75–91.

Shifman, Limor, and Elihu Katz. 2005. " 'Just Call Me Adonai': A Case Study of Ethnic Humor and Immigrant Assimilation." *American Sociological Review* 70 (5): 843–59.

Shiloah, Amnon, and Erik Cohen. 1982. "The Dynamics of Transformation in the Music of Oriental Jewish Communities in Israel." *Pe'amim* 12:3–25. [In Hebrew.]

Shlain, Megina. 2003. *HaSuzani Va'Ani.* Jerusalem: Zohar Larikma. [In Hebrew.]

———. 2007. *Ethnic Embroidery.* Jerusalem: Zohar Larikma. [In Hebrew.]

———. 2009. *Tales of the Thread.* Jerusalem: Zohar Larikma. [In Hebrew.]

Shlezinger, Yizhak, and Zohar Livnat. 2001. "The Language of Bumper Stickers in Israel: Lexical, Syntactic, and Stylistic Aspects." In *Studies in Hebrew and Language Teaching in Honor of Ben-Zion Fischler,* edited by Raphael Nir and Ora Schwarzwald, 277–93. Even Yehuda: Reches. [In Hebrew.]

Shohat, Ella. 2003. "On Imitation and the Art of Kidnapping: On the Work of Yigal Nizri, 'Tiger.' " *Pe'amim* 94–95:89–94. [In Hebrew.]

Shuman, Amy. 1986. *Storytelling Rights: The Uses of Oral and Written Texts by Urban Adolescents.* Cambridge: Cambridge University Press.

Silber, Ilana. 2005. "On Marcel Mauss and the Paradoxical Charms of the Gift." In *The Gift,* 7–30. Tel Aviv: Resling. [In Hebrew.]

Smith, Herbert. 1988. "Badges, Buttons, T-Shirts, and Bumper Stickers: The Semiotics of Some Recursive Systems." *Journal of Popular Culture* 21 (4): 141–48.

Spiro, Melford. 1979. *Gender and Culture: Kibbutz Women Revisited.* Durham, NC: Duke University Press.

Spivak, Gayatri Ch. 1987. "Displacement and the Discourse of Woman." In *Displacement: Derrida and After,* edited by M. Krupnick, 169–95. Bloomington: Indiana University Press.

Spivak, Gayatri Ch. 1985. "Three Women's Texts and a Critique of Imperialism." In *Critical Inquiry* 12 (1), "Race," Writing, and Difference: 243–61.

Stolow, Jeremy. 2006. "Communicating Authority, Consuming Tradition: Jewish Orthodox Outreach Literature and Its Reading Public." In *Religion, Media and the Public Sphere*, edited by Birgit Meyer and Annelies Moors, 73–91. Bloomington: Indiana University Press.

———. 2007. "Holy Pleather: Materializing Authority in Contemporary Orthodox Jewish Publishing." *Material Religion: The Journal of Objects, Art, and Belief* 3 (3): 314–35.

———. 2010. *Orthodox by Design: Judaism, Print Politics, and the ArtScroll Revolution.* Berkeley: University of California Press.

Swirski, Barbara, and Safir Marilyn P., eds. 1991. *Calling the Equality Bluff: Women in Israel.* London: Pergamon Press.

Taa, Busha J. 2003. "The Role of Knowledge in the Integration Experience of Ethiopian Immigrants in Toronto." PhD diss., University of Toronto.

Tedlock, Barbara, and Dennis Tedlock. 1985. "Text and Textile: Language and Technology in the Art of the Quiche Maya." *Journal of Anthropological Research* 41 (2): 121–47.

Tubiana, Joseph, Richard Pankhurst, and Eleme Eshete. 1958. "Self-Help in Ethiopia." *Ethiopian Observer* 2 (1): 354–64.

Turner, Victor W. 1969. *The Ritual Process: Structure and Anti-Structure.* Chicago: Aldine.

Walzer, Michael et al. 2000. *The Jewish Political Tradition.* New Haven, CT: Yale University Press.

Weigle, Marta. 1992. *Spiders and Spinsters: Women and Mythology.* Albuquerque: University of New Mexico Press.

Weil, Aryeh. 1988. "The Wayfarer's Prayer," *Tradition* 24 (1): 38–49.

Weil, Shalva. 1991. *One-Parent Families among Ethiopian Immigrants in Israel.* Jerusalem: NCJW Research Institute for Innovation in Education.

———. 2004. "Ethiopian Jewish Women: Trends and Transformations in the Context of Transnational Change." *Nashim: A Journal of Jewish Women's Studies & Gender Issues* 8:73–86.

Weiner, Annette B. 1992. *Inalienable Possessions: The Paradox of Keeping—While Giving.* Berkeley: University of California Press.

———. 1994. "Cultural Difference and the Density of Objects." *American Ethnologist* 21 (1): 391–403.

Weingrod, Alex. 1962. "Reciprocal Change: A Case Study of a Moroccan Immigrant Village in Israel." *American Anthropologist* 64 (1): 115–31.

Westheimer, Ruth, and Steven Kaplan. 1992. *Surviving Salvation: The Ethiopian Jewish Family in Transition.* New York: New York University Press.

Wider, Rabbi Shaul. 2009. "Yahadut." *YNET.* Available at www.ynet.co.il/home/0,7340,L-4403,00.html.

Yam, Rama. 2002. *The Secret Charm of Needlework: On Women, Therapy, Crafts and Art and Their Contexts.* Tel Aviv: Tcherikover. [In Hebrew.]

Yassif, Eli. 1998. "The 'Other' Israel: The Reporter as Ethnographer and Cultural Critic." In *Israel: A Local Anthropology: Studies in the Anthropology of Israel*, edited by

Orit Abuhav, Esther Hertzog, Harvey Goldberg, and Emanuel Marx. Tel Aviv: Tcherikover. [In Hebrew.]

———. 1999. *The Hebrew Folktale: History, Genre, Meaning.* Bloomington: Indiana University Press.

Yeğenoğlu, Meyda. 1998. *Colonial Fantasies: Towards a Feminist Reading of Orientalism.* Cambridge: Cambridge University Press.

Young, Robert J. C. 1995. *Colonial Desire: Hybridity in Theory, Culture and Race.* London: Routledge.

Zerubavel, Yael. 1995. *Recovered Roots: Collective Memory and the Making of Israeli National Tradition.* Chicago: University of Chicago Press.

———. 2002. "The 'Mythological Sabra' and Jewish Past: Trauma, Memory, and Contested Identities." *Israel Studies* 7 (2): 115–44.

Zilberg, Narspy, Hanna Herzog, and Eliezer Ben-Rafael. 2001. "In-Group Humor of Immigrants from the Former Soviet Union to Israel." In *Language and Communication in Israel,* edited by Hanna Herzog and Eliezer Ben-Rafael, 129–50. New Brunswick, NJ: Transaction Publication.

Ziv, Avner. 1986a. *Jewish Humor.* Tel Aviv: Papyrus/Tel-Aviv University. [In Hebrew.]

———. 1986b. "Psycho-Social Aspects of Jewish Humor in Israel and in the Diaspora." In *Jewish Humor,* edited by Avner Ziv, 47–71. Tel Aviv: Papyrus/Tel-Aviv University. [In Hebrew.]

———. 1988. *National Styles of Humor.* New York: Greenwood.

———. 1991. "Introduction." *Humor: International Journal of Humor Research* 4 (2): 145–48.

Zoran, Gabriel. 2002. *Rhetoric.* Tel Aviv: Sifriat Poalim. [In Hebrew.]

Zuckerman, Moshe. 2001. *Ḥaroshet HaYisraeliyyut* [On the Fabrication of Israelism]. Tel Aviv: Resling. [In Hebrew.]

Index

Page numbers in italics refer to figures and tables.

HAGAR SALAMON is Max and Margarethe Grunwald Chair in Folklore at the Hebrew University of Jerusalem. She is head of the Institute for the Arts as well as the graduate program for folklore and folk culture studies and a research fellow at the Harry S. Truman Research Institute for the Advancement of Peace. Her long-standing interest in the cultural modes and practices in which issues of identity are negotiated and renegotiated has inspired a wide range of studies pertaining to Ethiopian Jews, women's folk creativity, and present-day Israeli folklore in both public and private spheres.